500
UNDER
500

From 100-Calorie Snacks to 500-Calorie
Entrées — 500 Balanced and Healthy Recipes
the Whole Family Will Love!

Lynette Rohrer Shirk
with Nicole Cormier, RD, LDN

A adams media
Avon, Massachusetts

Published by
Adams Media, a division of F+W Media, Inc.
57 Littlefield Street, Avon, MA 02322. U.S.A.
www.adamsmedia.com

ISBN 10: 1-4405-2973-6
ISBN 13: 978-1-4405-2973-3
eISBN 10: 1-4405-3015-7
eISBN 13: 978-1-4405-3015-9

Printed in the United States of America.

10 9 8 7 6 5 4 3 2 1

Library of Congress Cataloging-in-Publication Data
is available from the publisher.

Contains material adapted and abridged from *The Everything® Low Cholesterol Book, 2nd Edition* by Murdoc Khaleghi, copyright © 2010 by F+W Media, Inc., ISBN 10: 1-4405-0551-9, ISBN 13: 978-1-4405-0551-5; *The Everything® Low-Fat, High-Flavor Cookbook*, 2nd Edition by Linda Larsen, copyright © 2008 by F+W Media, Inc., ISBN 10: 1-59869-604-1, ISBN 13: 978-1-59869-604-2; *The Everything® Whole-Grain, High-Fiber Cookbook* by Lynette Rohrer Shirk, copyright © 2008 by F+W Media, Inc., ISBN 10: 1-59869-507-X, ISBN 13: 978-1-59869-507-6; *The Everything® Glycemic Index Cookbook, 2nd Edition* by LeeAnn Smith Weintraub, copyright © 2010 by F+W Media, Inc., ISBN 10: 1-4405-0584-5, ISBN 13: 978-1-4405-0584-3; *The Everything® Calorie Counting Cookbook* by Paula Conway, copyright © 2008 by F+W Media, Inc., ISBN 10: 1-59869-416-2, ISBN 13: 978-1-59869-416-1; *The Everything® Low-Salt Cookbook* by Pamela Rice Hahn, copyright © 2004 by F+W Media, Inc., ISBN 10: 1-59337-044-X, ISBN 13: 978-1-59337-044-2.

Readers are urged to take all appropriate precautions before undertaking any how-to task. Always read and follow instructions and safety warnings for all tools and materials, and call in a professional if the task stretches your abilities too far. Although every effort has been made to provide the best possible information in this book, neither the publisher nor the author are responsible for accidents, injuries, or damage incurred as a result of tasks undertaken by readers. This book is not a substitute for professional services.

The information in this book should not be used for diagnosing or treating any health problem. Not all diet and exercise plans suit everyone. You should always consult a trained medical professional before starting a diet, taking any form of medication, or embarking on any fitness or weight-training program. The author and publisher disclaim any liability arising directly or indirectly from the use of this book.

Many of the designations used by manufacturers and sellers to distinguish their product are claimed as trademarks. Where those designations appear in this book and Adams Media was aware of a trademark claim, the designations have been printed with initial capital letters.

This book is available at quantity discounts for bulk purchases.
For information, please call 1-800-289-0963.

CONTENTS

INTRODUCTION

Let's face it, what we all really want is simplicity—fast and easy dishes that taste great and keep the weight off. *500 Under 500* delivers just that in an easy-to-follow format.

With hundreds of recipes all under 500 calories, this cookbook allows you to eat just about anything while maintaining a 1,200- to 1,500-calorie-a-day regimen. From mouth-watering breakfast treats like Sunday Morning French Toast and Raspberry–Almond Milk Frappe to filling dinners like Sirloin Meatballs in Sauce and Sesame-Crusted Chicken, you'll never have to give up your favorite meals or sacrifice taste to achieve your weight-loss goals. Simply put, you can have your cake and eat it too!

In each chapter, you will also find ways to reduce calories and fat content in your foods and recipes by cooking with seasonings to add flavor instead of fat. Best of all, *500 Under 500* will show you that healthy meals don't have to be bland or boring, and that preparing satisfying and low-calorie recipes is easier than you think.

So what are you waiting for? Get closer to reaching your weight-loss goals with these healthy and delicious meals!

Happy eating!

CHAPTER 1

Breakfast

OATMEAL RAISIN SCONES

CALORIES: 375
SERVES 6

- 1 ½ CUPS ROLLED OATS
- ½ CUP ALL-PURPOSE FLOUR
- 2 TABLESPOONS WHEAT GERM
- 3 TABLESPOONS SUGAR
- ½ TEASPOON SALT
- 1 ½ TEASPOONS BAKING POWDER
- 6 TABLESPOONS COLD, UNSALTED BUTTER, CUT IN PIECES
- 2 EGGS
- ½ CUP BUTTERMILK
- ½ TEASPOON VANILLA
- 1 CUP RAISINS
- 1 EGG WHITE
- 2 TABLESPOONS RAW SUGAR

1. Preheat oven to 400°F. Line a baking pan with parchment paper or spray lightly with oil. Grind half of the oatmeal into flour in a food processor.

2. Combine remaining oats, oat flour, all-purpose flour, wheat germ, sugar, salt, baking powder, and butter in a food processor with a metal blade. Process until mixture resembles cornmeal.

3. In a large bowl whisk together eggs, buttermilk, and vanilla. Stir in raisins with a spatula or wooden spoon.

4. Add dry ingredients and fold in with spatula. Drop scones into rounds onto prepared baking sheet.

5. Brush scones with egg white and sprinkle with raw sugar. Bake for 15 minutes.

PER SERVING: Fat: 2 g **Protein:** 8 g **Carbohydrates:** 44 g **Sugar:** 37 g

---

BLACKBERRY-MANGO SMOOTHIE

CALORIES: 235
SERVES 2

- ½ BANANA
- 1 CUP FROZEN MANGO CUBES
- 1 CUP BLACKBERRIES
- ½ CUP VANILLA FROZEN YOGURT
- ¼ CUP ORANGE JUICE
- 1 TEASPOON HONEY

1. Place all ingredients in a blender and blend until smooth.

2. Pour into two glasses and serve as a quick breakfast.

PER SERVING: Fat: 3 g **Protein:** 4 g **Carbohydrates:** 53 g **Sugar:** 39 g

BLUEBERRY-LEMON SMOOTHIE

CALORIES: 261
SERVES 2

½ BANANA
1 CUP FROZEN BLUEBERRIES
1 CUP LEMON YOGURT
¼ CUP GRAPE JUICE
1 TEASPOON HONEY

1. Place all ingredients in a blender and blend until smooth.

2. Pour into two glasses and serve as a quick breakfast.

PER SERVING: Fat: 2.5 g **Protein:** 6 g **Carbohydrates:** 57 g
Sugar: 46 g

Blueberry Heaven

The United States produces 95 percent of the world's supply of blueberries. Maine produces the bulk of U.S. blueberries, followed by other northeastern states and Oregon. Many farms in these regions allow you to pick your own berries when they're in season.

STRAWBERRY-BANANA SMOOTHIE

CALORIES: 248
SERVES 2

1 BANANA
1 CUP FROZEN STRAWBERRIES,
   CUT UP
1 CUP VANILLA FROZEN YOGURT
¼ CUP ORANGE JUICE
1 TEASPOON HONEY

1. Place all ingredients in a blender and blend until smooth.

2. Pour into two glasses and serve as a quick breakfast.

PER SERVING: Fat: 4 g **Protein:** 4 g **Carbohydrates:** 50 g
Sugar: 37 g

SMOOTHIE WITH CHOCOLATE AND COFFEE

CALORIES: 200
SERVES 2

- 2 TABLESPOONS INSTANT ESPRESSO, DISSOLVED IN 2 TABLESPOONS HOT WATER
- 2 TABLESPOONS DUTCH PROCESS COCOA, DISSOLVED IN COLD WATER
- 1 PACKAGE SUGAR SUBSTITUTE, OR TO TASTE
- ½ CUP OAT BRAN
- 1½ CUPS PLAIN, LOW-FAT YOGURT
- 1 TABLESPOON ANISETTE LIQUEUR (OPTIONAL)
- 6 ICE CUBES

1. When the espresso and cocoa are dissolved, blend all ingredients in the blender and serve.

PER SERVING: Fat: 3 g **Protein:** 16 g **Carbohydrates:** 36 g
Sugar: 19 g

BANANA-KIWI SMOOTHIE

CALORIES: 237
SERVES 2

- 1 BANANA, PEELED, CUT IN 2" SEGMENTS
- 4 KIWI FRUIT, PEELED, CUT IN HALVES
- JUICE OF 1 LIME
- 1½ CUPS ORANGE JUICE
- 2 TABLESPOONS OAT BRAN OR KASHI
- 4 ICE CUBES
- 4 DROPS HOT SAUCE (OPTIONAL)

1. Place the banana, kiwi, lime juice, and orange juice in the blender and purée. Add the rest of the ingredients and blend until smooth. Serve chilled.

PER SERVING: Fat: 1 g **Protein:** 10 g **Carbohydrates:** 65 g
Sugar: 22 g

RASPBERRY–ALMOND MILK FRAPPE

CALORIES: 149
SERVES 2

1 CUP FROZEN RASPBERRIES
½ CUP ALMOND MILK
⅛ TEASPOON ALMOND EXTRACT
1 TEASPOON HONEY
¾ CUP VANILLA FROZEN YOGURT

1. Place all ingredients in a blender and blend until smooth.

2. Pour into two glasses and serve as a quick breakfast.

PER SERVING: Fat: 3.5 g **Protein:** 4.5 g **Carbohydrates:** 28 g
Sugar: 22 g

CORNMEAL GRITS

CALORIES: 176
SERVES 4

4 CUPS WATER
1 TEASPOON SALT
1 CUP POLENTA MEAL
2 TABLESPOONS BUTTER

1. Put water and salt in a saucepan and bring to a boil.

2. Gradually add polenta and stir constantly over medium-low heat until it has thickened, about 15 minutes. Stir in butter.

3. Serve immediately for soft grits or pour into a greased loaf pan and let cool. When cool, grits can be sliced and fried or grilled.

PER SERVING: Fat: 6.5 g **Protein:** 3 g **Carbohydrates:** 27 g
Sugar: 0.5 g

BLACKBERRY BUCKWHEAT FLAPJACKS

CALORIES: 352
SERVES 4

1 CUP ALL-PURPOSE FLOUR
½ CUP BUCKWHEAT FLOUR
3 TABLESPOONS SUGAR
1½ TEASPOONS BAKING POWDER
½ TEASPOON BAKING SODA
½ TEASPOON SALT
2 EGGS
3 TABLESPOONS MELTED BUTTER
1½ CUPS BUTTERMILK
OIL FOR GRIDDLE OR PAN
1 CUP BLACKBERRIES

1. Whisk together all-purpose flour, buckwheat flour, sugar, baking powder, baking soda, and salt in a large bowl.

2. Whisk together eggs, melted butter, and buttermilk in another bowl.

3. Stir egg mixture into the flour mixture until combined. There will be lumps; be careful not to overmix.

4. Pour about ⅓ cup batter for each pancake onto a hot oiled griddle or pan. Scatter several blackberries on top of batter. Flip pancake when bubbles have formed and started to pop through the batter. Cook on other side for a minute.

5. Serve hot with maple syrup.

PER SERVING: Fat: 11 g **Protein:** 13 g **Carbohydrates:** 56 g
Sugar: 12 g

BANANA CHOCOLATE PECAN PANCAKES

CALORIES: 245
SERVES 4

2 (1-OUNCE) SQUARES SEMISWEET BAKER'S CHOCOLATE
2 TABLESPOONS WATER
1 CUP PECANS
1 CUP WHOLE-WHEAT FLOUR
2 TEASPOONS BAKING POWDER
3 EGGS, WELL BEATEN
¾ CUP 2% MILK
6 TABLESPOONS HONEY, OR TO TASTE
1 TEASPOON PURE VANILLA EXTRACT
½ TEASPOON SALT
NONSTICK SPRAY
2 BANANAS, PEELED AND SLICED ¼"THICK

IN THIS RECIPE YOU CAN SUBSTITUTE NONFAT MILK FOR 2% MILK.

1. Melt chocolate with 2 tablespoons water and set aside to cool slightly. Lightly toast the pecans and grind in a food processor or chop by hand.

2. In a large bowl, mix whole-wheat flour and baking powder. Slowly beat in the eggs, milk, honey, vanilla, and salt and then chocolate mixture.

3. Spray a griddle or frying pan with nonstick spray. Heat to medium-high. Drop the pancake batter, about 2 tablespoons per pancake, on the hot griddle. Cover with banana slices. Turn when bubbles form at the top of the cakes.

4. Serve hot with butter, marmalade, or chocolate syrup.

PER SERVING (PLAIN): Fat: 7 g **Protein:** 11 g
Carbohydrates: 38 g **Sugar:** 12 g

SUNDAY MORNING FRENCH TOAST

CALORIES: 410
SERVES 1

- **1 TABLESPOON BUTTER, SALTED**
- **2 EGGS**
- **1 TABLESPOON VANILLA EXTRACT**
- **1 TABLESPOON CINNAMON**
- **2 SLICES WHOLE-WHEAT BREAD, CUT INTO TRIANGLES**

1. Heat a large griddle and brush with butter.

2. Crack eggs into a shallow bowl and beat well with vanilla extract and cinnamon.

3. Dip triangles of whole-wheat bread in the egg mixture, turning once to coat well.

4. Place the bread slices in the pan and cook for 2 minutes on each side, until crisp and golden brown.

PER SERVING: Fat: 24 g **Protein:** 17 g **Carbohydrates:** 31 g **Sugar:** 2 g

Low-Cholesterol French Toast
To make this recipe more heart-healthy, decrease the fat and cholesterol by forgetting the egg yolks. Try using ½ cup of egg substitute instead of 2 whole eggs. You can find egg substitute near the eggs in the dairy section in the grocery store.

BLUEBERRY CORNMEAL PANCAKES

CALORIES: 384
SERVES 4

- **1 CUP FLOUR**
- **½ CUP YELLOW CORNMEAL**
- **3 TABLESPOONS SUGAR**
- **1½ TEASPOONS BAKING POWDER**
- **½ TEASPOON BAKING SODA**
- **½ TEASPOON SALT**
- **2 EGGS**
- **3 TABLESPOONS MELTED BUTTER**
- **1½ CUPS BUTTERMILK**
- **OIL TO HEAT IN GRIDDLE OR PAN**
- **1 CUP BLUEBERRIES**

1. Whisk together flour, cornmeal, sugar, baking powder, baking soda, and salt in a large bowl.

2. Whisk together eggs, melted butter, and buttermilk in another bowl.

3. Stir egg mixture into the flour mixture until combined. There will be lumps; be careful not to overmix.

4. Pour about ⅓ cup batter for each pancake onto hot oiled griddle or pan. Scatter several blueberries over batter. Flip pancakes when bubbles have formed and started to pop through the batter on top.

5. Cook on other side for about a minute. Serve hot with maple syrup.

PER SERVING: Fat: 13 g **Protein:** 11 g **Carbohydrates:** 60 g **Sugar:** 13 g

DOUBLE CORN WAFFLES

CALORIES: 434
SERVES 6

3 EGGS
4 OUNCES CANOLA OIL
1½ CUPS PLAIN YOGURT
1¾ CUPS YELLOW CORNBREAD MIX
½ CUP CORN KERNELS
OIL FOR WAFFLE IRON

1. Whisk together eggs, canola oil, and yogurt.

2. Stir egg mixture into the cornbread mix to combine. There will be lumps; be careful not to overmix.

3. Fold the corn kernels into the batter.

4. Pour or ladle about ½ cup waffle batter onto preheated and oiled waffle iron and cook according to manufacturer's instructions.

PER SERVING: Fat: 25 g **Protein:** 11 g **Carbohydrates:** 34 g **Sugar:** 5 g

TOMATO AND FETA FRITTATA

CALORIES: 126
SERVES 1

2 EGG WHITES
1 EGG WITH YOLK
2 TABLESPOONS CRUMBLED FETA CHEESE
½ CUP TOMATOES, CHOPPED
NONSTICK COOKING SPRAY
SALT AND PEPPER TO TASTE

1. Separate two egg whites from the yolks and place in a medium-size bowl. Add one whole egg with yolk to the bowl with egg whites.

2. Whisk eggs, feta, and tomatoes together.

3. Cook the egg mixture over medium heat in a small skillet coated with cooking spray for 4 minutes or until eggs are firm. Do not stir.

4. Flip and cook the other side for 2 more minutes.

5. Salt and pepper to taste.

PER SERVING: Fat: 11 g **Protein:** 15 g **Carbohydrates:** 6 g **Sugar:** 2.5 g

Healthy Egg Dish
Quiches taste great, but are loaded with fat, cholesterol, and calories. Frittatas are a lighter option for a delicious and easy egg dish.

OATMEAL

CALORIES: 195
SERVES 4

2 CUPS WATER
1 CUP ROLLED OATS
¼ TEASPOON SALT
½ CUP DRIED CURRANTS
1 TEASPOON GROUND CINNAMON
4 TEASPOONS HONEY
2 TABLESPOONS CREAM
1 CUP ALMOND MILK, CHILLED

1. Bring water to a boil. Add the oats and salt and stir. Turn the heat to low and simmer 5 minutes.

2. Stir in the currants and simmer for 10 minutes, stirring occasionally.

3. Remove from heat and spoon cooked oatmeal into four bowls.

4. Sprinkle ¼ teaspoon cinnamon and drizzle 1 teaspoon honey on each bowl.

5. Mix the cream with the cold almond milk and serve it on the side in a small pitcher.

PER SERVING: Fat: 5 g **Protein:** 5 g **Carbohydrates:** 35 g **Sugar:** 15 g

---

CHICKEN BREAKFAST BURRITO

CALORIES: 467
SERVES 1

1 TABLESPOON OLIVE OIL
½ CUP GREEN BELL PEPPER, CHOPPED
¼ CUP ONION, CHOPPED
4 OUNCES CHICKEN BREASTS, DICED
1 WHOLE-WHEAT TORTILLA
¼ CUP SALSA
1 TABLESPOON SOUR CREAM
4 OUNCES CHICKEN BREAST, DICED

1. Place pan on medium-high heat and add olive oil. Combine chopped green pepper and onion and sauté in pan for approximately 5 minutes.

2. Add diced chicken to pan and cook until done, about 7 minutes.

3. Take whole-wheat tortilla and top with chicken and vegetable mixture.

4. Add salsa and sour cream, and then fold tortilla.

PER SERVING: Fat: 21 g **Protein:** 33 g **Carbohydrates:** 37 g **Sugar:** 1.5 g

Egg-Cellent
For extra protein without all the fat, try adding a scrambled egg white to the chicken burrito. High-protein breakfasts are a healthy start to the day and can help keep you satisfied until the next mealtime.

COTTAGE CHEESE PANCAKES

CALORIES: 354
SERVES 4

½ CUP WHOLE-WHEAT FLOUR
¼ TEASPOON SALT
¼ CUP OLIVE OIL
1 CUP LOW-FAT MILK
½ TEASPOON VANILLA EXTRACT
6 LARGE EGGS
1 CUP LOW-FAT COTTAGE CHEESE

1. Blend all ingredients in a blender until smooth. Use as batter for pancakes or waffles.

PER SERVING: Fat: 23 g **Protein:** 21 g **Carbohydrates:** 16 g **Sugar:** 3 g

Blueberry Pancakes

Try adding a few handfuls of blueberries to your pancake batter. Blueberries are an excellent source of antioxidant phytonutrients called anthocyanidins, which are responsible for the blue-red pigment seen in blueberries. Anthocyanidins help to protect the body from harm from free-radicals.

SAUSAGE AND SPICY EGGS

CALORIES: 383
SERVES 4

1 POUND ITALIAN SWEET SAUSAGE
¼ CUP WATER
1 TABLESPOON OLIVE OIL
2 SWEET RED PEPPERS, ROASTED AND CHOPPED
1 JALAPEÑO PEPPER, SEEDED AND MINCED
8 EGGS
¾ CUP 2% MILK
2 TABLESPOONS FRESH PARSLEY FOR GARNISH

IN THIS RECIPE YOU CAN SUBSTITUTE VEGETARIAN SAUSAGE FOR ITALIAN SWEET SAUSAGE AND NONFAT MILK FOR 2% MILK.

1. Cut the sausage in ¼" coins. Place in a heavy frying pan with the water and olive oil. Bring to a boil; then turn down the heat to simmer.

2. When the sausages are brown, remove them to a paper towel. Add the sweet red peppers and jalapeño pepper to the pan and sauté over medium heat for 5 minutes.

3. While the peppers sauté, beat the eggs and milk together vigorously. Add to the pan and gently fold over until puffed and moist.

4. Mix in the reserved sausage, garnish with parsley, and serve hot.

PER SERVING: Fat: 23 g **Protein:** 35 g **Carbohydrates:** 8 g **Sugar:** 5 g

YOGURT AND FRUIT PARFAIT

CALORIES: 303
SERVES 1

1 CUP NONFAT YOGURT
¼ CUP BLUEBERRIES
¼ CUP STRAWBERRIES, SLICED
4 TABLESPOONS ALMONDS, SLICED

1. Add ½ cup of yogurt to tall glass.

2. Layer ¼ of berries and 2 tablespoons of almond slices on top of the yogurt.

3. Place the remaining yogurt on top of the berry and almond layer.

4. Add the remaining ¼ cup of berries and 2 tablespoons almonds to the top of the second yogurt layer.

PER SERVING: Fat: 4 g **Protein:** 19 g **Carbohydrates:** 32 g **Sugar:** 18 g

Greek Yogurt

Try using Greek yogurt, preferably nonfat or low-fat, for a thicker, richer, and slightly tart parfait. Greek yogurt tastes great with sweet berries. For a simple snack, try adding a teaspoon of honey to plain Greek yogurt. What a treat!

BANANA NUT BREAD

CALORIES: 241
SERVES 8

1½ CUP WHOLE-WHEAT FLOUR
1 TEASPOON BAKING POWDER
1 TEASPOON BAKING SODA
1 TABLESPOON GROUND CINNAMON
1 TABLESPOON UNSALTED BUTTER, MELTED
4 BANANAS
1 LARGE EGG
1 TEASPOON VANILLA EXTRACT
⅓ CUP SPLENDA
1 CUP WALNUTS, CHOPPED

1. Combine flour, baking powder, baking soda, and cinnamon in a large mixing bowl.

2. Mix butter, mashed bananas, egg, vanilla, and Splenda in a medium-size mixing bowl.

3. Add banana mixture to flour mixture, stirring to moisten dry ingredients. Mix in walnuts.

4. Pour batter into a greased loaf pan. Bake at 350°F for 50–55 minutes.

PER SERVING: Fat: 12 g **Protein:** 6 g **Carbohydrates:** 32 g **Sugar:** 5 g

SMOKED FISH AND EGGS WITH GRILLED TOMATOES

CALORIES: 326
SERVES 4

NONSTICK BUTTER-FLAVORED
  SPRAY
4 SCALLIONS, CHOPPED
8 EGGS
½ CUP 2% MILK
½ POUND SMOKED SALMON OR
  HERRING, CHOPPED
4 OUNCES CREAM CHEESE,
  SOFTENED
GRILLED OR BROILED RED
  TOMATOES

*IN THIS RECIPE YOU CAN SUBSTITUTE
NONFAT MILK FOR 2% MILK AND
LOW-FAT CREAM CHEESE INSTEAD OF
REGULAR CREAM CHEESE.*

1. Spray a large frying pan with nonstick spray and add scallions. Sauté the scallions over medium heat until soft, about 3 minutes.

2. Beat the eggs and milk together and stir them into the pan with the scallions. Set the heat on low.

3. Sprinkle the top with salmon or herring and dot with cream cheese. When just set, cut in wedges and serve with grilled red tomatoes.

PER SERVING: Fat: 23 g **Protein:** 26 g **Carbohydrates:** 3 g **Sugar:** 0 g

Tomatoes for Breakfast

It seems that all over the British Isles, Spain, and the Mediterranean, you get grilled or broiled tomatoes with meals, from breakfast to dinner. They are perfectly delicious and very nutritious. Americans should have them more often!

BAKED GRAPEFRUIT WITH HONEY AND CHAMBORD

CALORIES: 76
SERVES 2

1 LARGE JUICY GRAPEFRUIT
2 TEASPOONS HONEY
2 TEASPOONS CHAMBORD
  (RASPBERRY LIQUEUR)

1. Preheat broiler to 400°F.

2. Cut the grapefruit in half. Loosen the sections with a grapefruit spoon or short paring knife.

3. Spread the honey over the grapefruit halves. Sprinkle with Chambord. Broil for 10 minutes, but be careful not to burn.

PER SERVING: Fat: 0 g **Protein:** 1.5 g **Carbohydrates:** 19 g **Sugar:** 18 g

SPINACH AND GORGONZOLA EGG WHITE OMELET

CALORIES: 463
SERVES 2

NONSTICK BUTTER-FLAVORED SPRAY

1 FROZEN SPINACH SOUFFLÉ, DEFROSTED

8 EGG WHITES, WELL BEATEN

⅛ TEASPOON GROUND NUTMEG

1 TEASPOON LEMON ZEST, FINELY GRATED

½ CUP GORGONZOLA CHEESE, CRUMBLED

SALT AND PEPPER

1. Prepare a nonstick pan with butter-flavored cooking spray. Make sure the spinach soufflé is thoroughly defrosted.

2. Place the pan over medium-high heat. Pour in the beaten egg whites and sprinkle with nutmeg, lemon zest, and cheese. Spoon 1 cup of the spinach soufflé down the middle of the omelet. Reserve the rest for another use.

3. When the omelet starts to set, fold the outsides over the center. Cook until it reaches your desired level of firmness.

4. Add salt and pepper to taste.

PER SERVING: Fat: 28 g **Protein:** 37 g **Carbohydrates:** 16 g **Sugar:** 3 g

---

BAKED APPLE PANCAKES

CALORIES: 334
SERVES 4

1 TABLESPOON BUTTER

4 MEDIUM TART APPLES, PEELED AND SLICED

3 TABLESPOONS BROWN SUGAR

½ TEASPOON CINNAMON

1 CUP FLOUR

3 TABLESPOONS SUGAR

1 CUP 1% MILK

2 EGG WHITES

2 EGGS

2 TEASPOONS VANILLA

3 TABLESPOONS POWDERED SUGAR

1. Preheat oven to 425°F. In a large ovenproof skillet, melt butter over medium heat. Add apples to the pan and sprinkle with brown sugar. Cook, stirring frequently, until apples are soft, about 12 to 15 minutes. Sprinkle apples with cinnamon and remove from heat.

2. Meanwhile, in medium-size bowl combine flour and sugar. Add milk, egg whites, eggs, and vanilla and beat just until smooth. Pour over apples in skillet.

3. Place pan in oven and bake for 20 minutes. Reduce heat to 350°F and bake for 12 to 18 minutes longer or until pancake is golden brown. Sprinkle with powdered sugar and serve immediately.

PER SERVING: Fat: 8 g **Protein:** 7.5 g **Carbohydrates:** 56 g **Sugar:** 30 g

SIMPLE AND SKINNY CHEESE OMELET

CALORIES: 129
SERVES 2

1 TEASPOON OLIVE OIL
½ CUP FAT-FREE EGG BEATERS
½ CUP LOW-FAT SHREDDED CHEESE

1. Heat the olive oil in a small skillet on low heat, then pour the Egg Beaters in to coat the surface and cook until edges show firmness.

2. Sprinkle the cheese evenly over the egg mixture and fold one side over the other.

3. Flip the half-moon omelet so both sides are evenly cooked.

PER SERVING: Fat: 7 g **Protein:** 14 g **Carbohydrates:** 2 g **Sugar:** 1 g

BARELY THERE EGG WHITE BRUSCHETTA

CALORIES: 395
SERVES 2

7 EGG WHITES
4 WHOLE EGGS
4 SLICES WHOLE GRAIN BREAD
1 CHOPPED TOMATO
½ CUP CHOPPED MUSHROOMS
1 SMALL ONION
¼ CUP FRESH BASIL
½ TEASPOON SALT
½ TEASPOON PEPPER

1. Beat egg whites and eggs together.

2. Heat chopped tomato, mushrooms, and onion in a large skillet. Add egg mixture and scramble. Add basil, salt, and pepper as you scramble.

3. Toast bread and top with the egg mixture.

PER SERVING: Fat: 13 g **Protein:** 35 g **Carbohydrates:** 44 g **Sugar:** 9 g

---

BLUEBERRY MUFFINS

CALORIES: 195
SERVES 12

LIGHT COOKING SPRAY
2 CUPS FLOUR
½ CUP SUGAR
1 TEASPOON BAKING POWDER
½ TEASPOON BAKING SODA
½ TEASPOON SALT
1 CUP LOW-FAT BUTTERMILK
1 EGG
½ CUP BUTTER, SOFTENED
1 CUP BLUEBERRIES

1. Preheat oven to 400°F. Prepare a muffin tin with light cooking spray.

2. Mix the flour, sugar, baking powder, baking soda, and salt in medium-size bowl.

3. Whisk buttermilk and egg together. Then add the butter and beat well. Add to flour mixture. Fold in the blueberries.

4. Spoon batter into 12 muffin cups and bake for 20 minutes or until the muffins spring back when touched.

PER SERVING: Fat: 5 g **Protein:** 4 g **Carbohydrates:** 36 g **Sugar:** 19 g

EGGS BENEDICT

CALORIES: 337
SERVES 4

- **3 TABLESPOONS SKIM MILK**
- **½ CUP LOW-FAT MAYONNAISE**
- **4 EGGS**
- **4 SLICES BACON**
- **4 SLICES WHOLE-WHEAT BREAD OR 2 WHOLE-WHEAT ENGLISH MUFFINS**

1. Mix the skim milk with the mayonnaise and heat in the microwave for about 40 seconds to warm.

2. Crack each egg into individual microwaveable bowls, being careful not to break the yolks.

3. Cover each bowl with plastic wrap and microware on high until the whites are cooked and yolks firm, about 2 minutes.

4. In a skillet, cook the bacon.

5. Place the bacon on the whole-wheat bread slices.

6. Add the eggs on the bacon and top each egg with 2 tablespoons of mayonnaise mixture.

PER SERVING: Fat: 18 g **Protein:** 15 g **Carbohydrates:** 27 g **Sugar:** 3.5 g

EGG AND CHEESE BREAKFAST PIZZA

CALORIES: 189
SERVES 8

- **1 TABLESPOON ALL-PURPOSE FLOUR**
- **1 (16-OUNCE) FROZEN PIZZA DOUGH**
- **NONSTICK COOKING SPRAY**
- **1½ CUPS EGG BEATERS**
- **½ CUP FAT-FREE MILK**
- **½ CUP LOW-FAT CHEESE, ANY FLAVOR**

1. Preheat oven to 375°F.

2. Sprinkle flour on a flat surface and roll out the pizza dough to a 12" circle, building up the edges so they're thick and high. Place the dough on a nonstick baking sheet and then prick the dough thoroughly with a fork.

3. Bake until light brown, about 15 minutes.

4. While the crust is baking, coat a skillet with cooking spray and beat the Egg Beaters and milk in a large bowl.

5. Scramble the mixture over medium heat, then place scrambled eggs on pizza crust and sprinkle with cheese.

6. Bake 7 minutes to melt the cheese, then slice with knife or pizza roller.

PER SERVING: Fat: 3 g **Protein:** 9 g **Carbohydrates:** 30 g **Sugar:** 1 g

BAKED SCRAMBLED EGGS

CALORIES: 213
SERVES 12

- ½ **CUP BUTTER**
- 20 **EGGS**
- 2 **TEASPOONS SALT**
- 1¾ **CUPS FAT-FREE MILK**
- ½ **CUP SHREDDED LOW-FAT CHEESE (OPTIONAL)**

1. Preheat oven to 350°F.

2. In a glass measuring cup, heat the butter in the microwave until melted.

3. In a separate bowl, whisk the eggs, salt, and milk.

4. Pour the melted butter and then the eggs into a 9" x 13" baking dish.

5. Bake uncovered for 8 minutes, then stir and add cheese if desired. Bake for 10 to 15 more minutes or until eggs are set.

PER SERVING: Fat: 16 g **Protein:** 13 g **Carbohydrates:** 3 g **Sugar:** 1 g

Incredible Edible Eggs

Eggs provide a tremendous amount of protein and very little carbohydrates, and they make you feel full. You should have one egg a day, but remember that so many things we consume daily already contain eggs. Before you have your daily dose of egg, make sure your other meals and snacks do not contain eggs or you could overdo it.

EGGS FLORENTINE

CALORIES: 288
SERVES 2

- 2 **ENGLISH MUFFINS**
- 2 **EGGS**
- 5 **OUNCES CHOPPED FROZEN SPINACH**
- 1 **TABLESPOON LOW-FAT MAYONNAISE**
- 1 **TEASPOON SALT**
- 1 **TEASPOON PEPPER**
- 2 **TEASPOONS SHREDDED LOW-FAT CHEESE**

1. Preheat oven to 350°F. Place muffins on a baking sheet.

2. Crack an egg onto each muffin. Bake for 10 minutes.

3. Meanwhile, heat the spinach in the microwave until soft and warm, about two minutes.

4. Add low-fat mayonnaise, salt, and pepper to spinach. Blend together.

5. Remove muffins and top with the spinach mixture. Add a teaspoon of shredded cheese and serve.

PER SERVING: Fat: 10 g **Protein:** 16 g **Carbohydrates:** 36 g **Sugar:** 1.5 g

MAPLE TURKEY SAUSAGE

CALORIES: 143
SERVES 4

- 1 POUND LEAN GROUND TURKEY
- 1 TABLESPOON MAPLE SYRUP
- ¼ TEASPOON FRESHLY GROUND BLACK PEPPER
- ⅛ TEASPOON MUSTARD POWDER
- ⅛ TEASPOON GROUND CLOVES
- ⅛ TEASPOON GROUND SAGE
- PINCH OF GROUND CINNAMON
- PINCH OF GROUND ALLSPICE
- PINCH OF GROUND MACE
- ¼ TEASPOON NATURAL MAPLE FLAVORING (OPTIONAL)

1. Mix together all the ingredients in a bowl. Cover and refrigerate overnight.

2. Shape the mixture into 4 flat patties. Cook over medium heat in a nonstick skillet or grill pan for 3 minutes on each side or until cooked through.

PER SERVING: Fat: 4 g **Protein:** 26 g **Carbohydrates:** 3.5 g **Sugar:** 3 g

OLALLIEBERRY POLENTA SCONES

CALORIES: 345
SERVES 6

- 1½ CUPS FLOUR
- ¼ CUP POLENTA MEAL
- 3 TABLESPOONS SUGAR
- ½ TEASPOON SALT
- 1¼ TEASPOONS BAKING POWDER
- 6 TABLESPOONS COLD, UNSALTED BUTTER, CUT IN PIECES
- 2 EGGS
- ⅔ CUP PLAIN YOGURT
- ½ TEASPOON VANILLA
- 1 CUP OLALLIEBERRIES
- 1 EGG WHITE
- 2 TABLESPOONS RAW SUGAR

1. Preheat oven to 400°F. Line a baking pan with parchment paper or spray lightly with oil.

2. Combine flour, polenta meal, sugar, salt, baking powder, and butter in a food processor with a metal blade. Process until mixture resembles cornmeal.

3. In a large bowl whisk together eggs, yogurt, and vanilla. Stir in olallieberries with a spatula or wooden spoon.

4. Add dry ingredients and fold in with spatula. Drop scones into rounds onto prepared baking sheet. Brush scones with egg white and sprinkle with raw sugar. Bake for 15 minutes.

PER SERVING: Fat: 14 g **Protein:** 8 g **Carbohydrates:** 45 g **Sugar:** 19 g

BLUEBERRY OAT BRAN MUFFINS

CALORIES: 258
SERVES 8

- 2 CUPS OAT BRAN
- ½ CUP SOY FLOUR
- 2 TEASPOONS BAKING POWDER
- ¼ TEASPOON BAKING SODA
- ½ CUP ALMOND FLOUR
- ½ TABLESPOON GROUND NUTMEG
- ¼ TEASPOON SALT
- 4 TABLESPOONS CINNAMON
- 2 TABLESPOONS FLAXSEEDS
- 1 TABLESPOON UNSWEETENED COCOA POWDER
- 1 TABLESPOON ORANGE ZEST
- 2 TABLESPOONS VANILLA EXTRACT
- ¼ CUP FRUCTOSE
- 2 TABLESPOONS VEGETABLE OIL
- ½ CUP PLAIN LOW-FAT YOGURT
- ½ CUP ORANGE JUICE
- 1 CUP BLUEBERRIES

1. Preheat oven to 350°F.

2. Combine dry ingredients and stir to mix well.

3. In a separate bowl, combine wet ingredients, except blueberries, and mix well.

4. Combine wet and dry ingredients, stirring until all ingredients are moist, fold in blueberries.

5. Spoon into a greased muffin pan or use muffin cups. Spoon equal amounts into each muffin cup. For 12 muffins, bake 20 to 25 minutes, or until muffin tops are golden brown. For 6 large muffins, increase the cooking time to 40 minutes.

PER SERVING: Fat: 11 g **Protein:** 10 g **Carbohydrates:** 40 g **Sugar:** 19 g

Orange-Cranberry-Oat Bran Muffins

Try trading out the blueberries in this recipe for tart fresh or frozen cranberries. Adding an additional teaspoon of orange zest will balance out the flavors nicely. You can use mini-muffin pans and a shorter cook time for fun bite-sized muffins.

HERBED OMELET WITH VEGETABLES

CALORIES: 164
SERVES 2

NONSTICK COOKING SPRAY

2 CUPS WHITE MUSHROOMS, SLICED

3 TABLESPOONS LOW-FAT MILK

2 TABLESPOONS SOUR CREAM

SALT AND PEPPER TO TASTE

2 TABLESPOONS GREEN ONIONS, CHOPPED

1 TABLESPOON CHIVES, CHOPPED

¼ TEASPOON DRIED TARRAGON

4 EGG WHITES

2 EGGS

1. Heat a large skillet over medium-high heat and coat with cooking spray. Add mushrooms until soft and liquid evaporates.

2. In a bowl, mix together 1 tablespoon of milk, sour cream, salt, and pepper. Whisk well and set aside.

3. In a separate bowl, mix 2 tablespoons of milk, green onion, chives, tarragon, egg whites, and eggs in a bowl. Stir well.

4. Pour egg mixture into greased pan over medium-high heat and spread evenly over pan. Once center is cooked, cover egg with mushrooms. Loosen omelet with spatula and fold over.

5. Pour sour cream mixture over omelet.

ER SERVING: **Fat:** 9 g **Protein:** 17 g **Carbohydrates:** 5 g
Sugar: 3 g

Low-Fat Alternative

Fresh herbs and mushrooms give this omelet tons of earthy flavor. In the summer, use fresh herbs from your own garden. To cut back on saturated fat, try using 6 egg whites and passing on the yolks.

APPLE DATE BREAD

CALORIES: 297
SERVES 12

NONSTICK BAKING SPRAY CONTAINING FLOUR
¾ CUP BROWN SUGAR
¾ CUP CHOPPED WALNUTS
2 TABLESPOONS BUTTER, SOFTENED
¼ CUP FLOUR
½ TEASPOON CINNAMON
1½ CUPS FLOUR
1¼ CUPS WHOLE-WHEAT FLOUR
½ CUP SUGAR
½ CUP BROWN SUGAR
2 TEASPOONS BAKING POWDER
1 TEASPOON BAKING SODA
½ TEASPOON SALT
1 EGG
1 EGG WHITE
1 CUP BUTTERMILK
¼ CUP ORANGE JUICE
1 CUP CHOPPED DATES
1 CUP FINELY CHOPPED, PEELED APPLES

1. Preheat oven to 350°F. Spray a 9" × 5" loaf pan with non-stick baking spray containing flour and set aside. In a small bowl, combine ¾ cup brown sugar, walnuts, 2 tablespoons butter, ¼ cup flour, and cinnamon and mix until crumbly; set aside.

2. In a large bowl, combine 1½ cups flour, whole-wheat flour, sugar, ½ cup brown sugar, baking powder, baking soda, and salt and mix well.

3. In a small bowl, combine egg, egg white, buttermilk, and orange juice and beat until combined. Stir into flour mixture until combined, then add dates and apples.

4. Turn into prepared loaf pan and sprinkle with the walnut mixture. Bake until loaf is golden brown and firm, about 60 to 70 minutes. Cool on wire rack.

PER SERVING: Fat: 8 g **Protein:** 4 g **Carbohydrates:** 50 g **Sugar:** 35 g

PEAR TEA BREAD

CALORIES: 267
SERVES 12

NONSTICK BAKING SPRAY CONTAINING FLOUR
1 (16-OUNCE) CAN PEAR HALVES
2½ CUPS FLOUR
½ CUP SUGAR
¼ CUP BROWN SUGAR
2 TEASPOONS BAKING POWDER
1 TEASPOON BAKING SODA
½ TEASPOON SALT
⅛ TEASPOON CARDAMOM
⅓ CUP VEGETABLE OIL
1 EGG
1 TEASPOON GRATED LEMON ZEST
2 TABLESPOONS LEMON JUICE
½ CUP POWDERED SUGAR

1. Preheat oven to 350°F. Spray a 9" × 5" loaf pan with nonstick baking spray containing flour and set aside.

2. Drain pears, discarding liquid. In blender or food processor, blend or process pears until smooth. Measure out 1 cup of purée. Reserve remaining purée for another use.

3. In a large bowl, combine flour, sugar, brown sugar, baking powder, baking soda, salt, and cardamom. In a small bowl, combine puréed pear mixture, oil, egg, and lemon zest.

4. Combine the two mixtures, stirring until just mixed. Pour into prepared loaf pan. Bake for 50 to 60 minutes or until loaf is golden brown and firm.

5. While the bread is baking, combine lemon juice and powdered sugar in small bowl. Remove bread from pan and cool completely on wire rack. Spoon lemon juice/powdered sugar mixture over hot bread.

PER SERVING: Fat: 7 g **Protein:** 3 g **Carbohydrates:** 30 g **Sugar:** 15 g

Fat Substitutes

Puréed fruit has long been used as a fat substitute. Puréed pears or applesauce are used in light breads and baked goods, while puréed prunes or raisins are a good choice in chocolate products. They add moisture and bolster the structure of the product, as well as preventing drying of the finished baked good.

RHUBARB MUFFINS

CALORIES: 216
SERVES 12

NONSTICK BAKING SPRAY CONTAINING FLOUR

2 CUPS FINELY CHOPPED RHUBARB

¾ CUP SUGAR, DIVIDED

1 TEASPOON GRATED ORANGE ZEST

¼ CUP BROWN SUGAR

2 CUPS ALL-PURPOSE FLOUR

½ CUP WHOLE-WHEAT FLOUR

1 TEASPOON BAKING SODA

½ TEASPOON BAKING POWDER

½ TEASPOON SALT

2 EGGS, BEATEN

½ CUP LOW-FAT BUTTERMILK

¼ CUP ORANGE JUICE

1 TEASPOON VANILLA

3 TABLESPOONS BUTTER, MELTED

½ TEASPOON CINNAMON

1. Preheat oven to 375°F. Spray a 12-cup muffin tin with non-stick baking spray containing flour and set aside. In a small bowl, combine rhubarb, ¼ cup sugar, and orange zest; let stand for 5 minutes.

2. In a large bowl, combine 6 tablespoons sugar, brown sugar, all-purpose flour, whole-wheat flour, baking soda, baking powder, and salt and mix well. Make a well in the center of the dry ingredients and add rhubarb mixture, eggs, buttermilk, orange juice, vanilla, and melted butter. Mix just until combined.

3. Spoon batter into prepared muffin tin, filling each cup two-thirds full. In a small bowl, combine remaining 2 tablespoons sugar and ½ teaspoon cinnamon; sprinkle over each muffin. Bake for 20 to 25 minutes or until muffins are golden brown and firm. Remove from muffin tin and cool on wire rack for 15 minutes before serving.

PER SERVING: Fat: 4 g **Protein:** 7 g **Carbohydrates:** 48 g **Sugar:** 26 g

Muffins

All muffin batter should be mixed just until the dry ingredients are moistened, but you have to be even more careful with these muffins. There will be some lumps in the batter; that's okay. They will disappear during baking time. Be sure to remove the muffins from the tins as soon as they are baked or they will steam and become sticky.

SAUSAGE AND EGG CASSEROLE

CALORIES: 220
SERVES 8

- 1 (16-OUNCE) BAG COUNTRY-STYLE POTATOES
- NONSTICK COOKING OIL
- 8 EGGS
- 4 TEASPOONS MAYONNAISE
- ¼ TEASPOON GARLIC POWDER
- ¼ TEASPOON ONION POWDER
- ¼ TEASPOON FRESHLY GROUND BLACK PEPPER
- ¼ TEASPOON MUSTARD POWDER
- 1 CUP SKIM MILK
- 8 (1-OUNCE) SLICES POTATO, SOURDOUGH, OR OAT BRAN BREAD
- ¼ POUND TURKEY SAUSAGE, COOKED AND CRUMBLED
- ½ CUP SHREDDED SWISS CHEESE
- 4 TABLESPOONS GRATED PARMESAN CHEESE

1. Preheat oven to 350°. Spray an 11" × 7" × 1½" oven-safe casserole dish with the nonstick cooking oil.

2. Add the frozen potatoes to a microwave-safe bowl; cover and microwave at 50 percent power for 3 to 5 minutes, until thawed and warm.

3. In a large mixing bowl, beat the eggs with the mayonnaise, garlic powder, onion powder, pepper, mustard powder, and milk. Tear the bread into bite-size pieces and stir them into the egg mixture. Fold the thawed potato mixture, the sausage, and shredded Swiss cheese into the egg mixture. Pour into the prepared casserole dish. Sprinkle the grated Parmesan cheese evenly over the top of the casserole.

4. Bake for approximately 35 to 45 minutes, until the eggs are set, the cheese is bubbling, and the top of the casserole is golden brown. Let sit for 5 minutes, then slice and serve.

PER SERVING: Fat: 13 g **Protein:** 17 g **Carbohydrates:** 25 g
Sugar: 5 g

Zapping Sausage

You can prepare the sausage for the Sausage and Egg Casserole by precooking it in the microwave. Put the sausage in a microwave-safe dish; cover, and microwave at 70 percent power for 3 to 5 minutes, turning the bowl halfway through the cooking time. Drain off the fat. Break the sausage apart with a fork. (The sausage doesn't have to be completely done because it'll finish cooking while you bake the casserole.)

VEGGIE PANCAKES

CALORIES: 86
SERVES 8

- **4 LARGE CARROTS, PEELED AND GRATED**
- **1 CUP SEEDED AND GRATED ZUCCHINI**
- **1 LARGE SWEET ONION, FINELY CHOPPED**
- **1 STALK CELERY, FINELY CHOPPED**
- **½ CUP UNBLEACHED ALL-PURPOSE FLOUR**
- **½ TEASPOON LOW-SALT BAKING POWDER**
- **⅛ TEASPOON MUSTARD POWDER**
- **PINCH OF SALT**
- **¼ TEASPOON PEPPER**
- **1 EGG**
- **¼ CUP SKIM MILK**
- **2 TEASPOONS CANOLA OIL**
- **NONSTICK COOKING SPRAY**

1. Add the carrots, zucchini, onion, and celery to a microwave-safe bowl. Cover and microwave on high for 4 minutes or until the vegetables are tender and the onion is transparent. Set aside to cool.

2. In a small bowl, thoroughly combine the flour, baking powder, mustard powder, salt, and pepper. In a larger bowl, beat together the egg, milk, and oil. Add the dry ingredients and stir until combined. Fold in the carrots, zucchini, and onions.

3. Bring a large nonstick skillet or griddle treated with nonstick spray to temperature over medium heat. Make a few pancakes at a time by ladling about ¼ cup of batter per pancake onto the heated pan surface. Cook for about 2 minutes on each side. Serve immediately.

PER SERVING: Fat: 3 g **Protein:** 4 g **Carbohydrates:** 12 g **Sugar:** 3 g

Keeping Pancakes Warm

Cooked pancakes can be transferred to a baking sheet and placed in a warm oven (150° to 200°F) to be kept warm while you prepare the rest of the pancakes and remaining meal entrées.

CHAPTER 2

Appetizers

LEMON BRUSCHETTA WITH CHOPPED OLIVES

CALORIES: 191
SERVES 12

- **6 TABLESPOONS OLIVE OIL**
- **3 TABLESPOONS LEMON JUICE, DIVIDED**
- **12 SLICES THREE-GRAIN FRENCH BREAD**
- **1 PASTEURIZED EGG WHITE**
- **2 TABLESPOONS DIJON MUSTARD**
- **10 LARGE BLACK OLIVES, CHOPPED**
- **10 LARGE CRACKED GREEN OLIVES, CHOPPED**
- **½ CUP CHOPPED FLAT-LEAF PARSLEY**
- **1 TABLESPOON FRESH OREGANO LEAVES**
- **¼ TEASPOON CRUSHED RED PEPPER FLAKES**
- **½ CUP CHOPPED TOASTED WALNUTS**

1. Preheat oven to 375°F. In small bowl, combine 2 tablespoons of the olive oil and 1 tablespoon lemon juice, and brush this mixture on both sides of the bread. Place on a cookie sheet and bake for 10 minutes, then turn and bake for another 10–15 minutes or until bread is toasted. Remove from oven and cool on wire rack.

2. Meanwhile, in blender or food processor, combine remaining 4 tablespoons olive oil, remaining 2 tablespoons lemon juice, the egg white, and mustard, and blend or process until blended and thick.

3. Stir in the remaining ingredients, cover, and refrigerate for 1 hour. Serve the olive spread with the toasted bread.

PER SERVING: Fat: 10 g **Protein:** 3 g **Carbohydrates:** 15 g **Sugar:** 2 g

---

CUCUMBER DILL CANAPÉS

CALORIES: 30
SERVES 6

- **1 ENGLISH CUCUMBER**
- **1 (3-OUNCE) PACKAGE LOW-FAT CREAM CHEESE, SOFTENED**
- **1 TABLESPOON LEMON JUICE**
- **¼ CUP NONFAT WHIPPED SALAD DRESSING**
- **1 TABLESPOON MINCED FRESH DILL WEED**
- **PINCH OF WHITE PEPPER**

1. Wash cucumber and slice into ¼" slices. Arrange on a serving platter. In a small bowl, combine cream cheese with lemon juice and beat well. Add salad dressing, dill, and pepper and beat until smooth.

2. Spoon or pipe cream cheese mixture on cucumber slices. Serve immediately or cover and chill up to 4 hours before serving.

PER SERVING: Fat: 2 g **Protein:** 1 g **Carbohydrates:** 1 g **Sugar:** 0.5 g

English Cucumbers

Cucumbers are very high in water content and vitamin C. The skins of regular cucumbers are usually waxed, so they must be peeled before serving. English cucumbers are not waxed, so you can serve them with the peel, which increases the fiber content, a component of cucumbers that may help lower blood pressure.

STUFFED JALAPEÑO PEPPERS

CALORIES: 41
SERVES 6

12 SMALL JALAPEÑOS

1 (3-OUNCE) PACKAGE LOW-FAT CREAM CHEESE, SOFTENED

1 TABLESPOON LEMON JUICE

¼ CUP SPICY SALSA

1 TEASPOON CHOPPED FRESH OREGANO

1. Cut jalapeños in half lengthwise. For a milder taste, remove membranes and seeds. Set aside.

2. In a small bowl, combine cream cheese with lemon juice; beat until fluffy. Add salsa and oregano and mix well.

3. Using a small spoon, fill each jalapeño half with the cream cheese mixture. Serve immediately or cover and chill for up to 8 hours before serving.

PER SERVING: Fat: 2.5 g **Protein:** 2 g **Carbohydrates:** 3 g **Sugar:** 1 g

Working with Hot Peppers

You must use caution when working with hot peppers such as jalapeños, Scotch bonnet, and habañeros. Capsaicin is the ingredient that gives peppers their heat; it's also an ingredient in pepper spray! Use gloves when working with peppers and never, ever touch your face, especially your eyes, until you have removed the gloves and thoroughly washed your hands.

GRILLED CHERRY TOMATOES WITH PARMESAN CHEESE

CALORIES: 49
SERVES 6

24 CHERRY TOMATOES

1 TABLESPOON EXTRA-VIRGIN OLIVE OIL

1 TABLESPOON RED-WINE VINEGAR

⅛ TEASPOON SALT

PINCH OF WHITE PEPPER

1 TABLESPOON CHOPPED FRESH MINT

2 TABLESPOONS SHAVED PARMESAN CHEESE

1. Tear off an 18" × 12" sheet of heavy-duty aluminum foil. Poke cherry tomatoes with the tip of a knife (to prevent splitting) and arrange on foil. In small bowl, combine oil, vinegar, salt, and pepper and mix well. Spoon over tomatoes.

2. Bring together foil edges and fold over several times, sealing the package. Leave some room for expansion during cooking.

3. Prepare and preheat grill. Grill the foil packet over medium coals for 4–6 minutes or until tomatoes are hot. Remove from grill, open package, and sprinkle with mint and shaved Parmesan. Serve immediately.

PER SERVING: Fat: 3 g **Protein:** 2 g **Carbohydrates:** 5 g **Sugar:** 3.5 g

PEAR, ROQUEFORT, AND WALNUTS ON ENDIVE

CALORIES: 112
SERVES 6

- 2 HEADS BELGIAN ENDIVE
- 2 RIPE PEARS
- 2 OUNCES ROQUEFORT CHEESE
- ¼ CUP CHOPPED WALNUTS

1. Separate the leaves of the endive and trim the stem ends. Lay the leaves out on a tray.

2. Core and slice the pears and lay a slice on each endive leaf.

3. Crumble a little Roquefort cheese onto the pear slices and sprinkle them with walnuts. Serve immediately.

PER SERVING: Fat: 6 g **Protein:** 4 g **Carbohydrates:** 16 g **Sugar:** 3 g

---

EGGPLANT CROSTINI

CALORIES: 398
SERVES 4

- 1 BAGUETTE LOAF OF BREAD
- ½ CUP OLIVE OIL, DIVIDED
- 6 CLOVES GARLIC, PEELED
- 2 JAPANESE EGGPLANTS
- 1 TEASPOON SALT
- ½ CUP GRATED PECORINO ROMANO CHEESE
- ¼ CUP DICED ROASTED RED BELL PEPPER

1. Preheat the oven to 350°F. Slice the baguette into ¼"-thick rounds and lay them out on a cookie sheet. Brush both sides with olive oil, then toast them in the oven for about 5 minutes. Turn them over and toast the other side.

2. Remove from oven, rub one side of each toast with garlic clove, and set aside.

3. Slice the eggplants into ¼"-thick slices, brush them with olive oil, and sprinkle them with salt.

4. Grill the eggplant rounds on both sides for about 10 minutes total.

5. Top each toast with a grilled eggplant round, sprinkle the Pecorino Romano cheese over the eggplant, and garnish each with roasted red bell pepper.

PER SERVING: Fat: 23 g **Protein:** 7 g **Carbohydrates:** 22 g **Sugar:** 1 g

YOGURT CHEESE BALLS

CALORIES: 94
SERVES 8

- ¼ CUP MINCED FLAT-LEAF PARSLEY
- ¼ CUP MINCED CHIVES
- 3 TABLESPOONS EXTRA-VIRGIN OLIVE OIL
- 1 TABLESPOON AGED BALSAMIC VINEGAR
- 2 CUPS PLAIN LOW-FAT YOGURT

1. To make the yogurt cheese, the day before, line a strainer with cheesecloth or a coffee filter. Place the strainer in a large bowl and add the yogurt. Cover and refrigerate overnight. The next day, place the thickened yogurt in a medium-size bowl. Discard the liquid, or whey, or reserve for use in soups and gravies.

2. Roll the yogurt cheese into 1" balls. On shallow plate, combine parsley and chives. Roll yogurt balls in herbs to coat. Place on serving plate and drizzle with olive oil and vinegar. Serve immediately.

PER SERVING: Fat: 7 g **Protein:** 5 g **Carbohydrates:** 8 g **Sugar:** 6.5 g

CAPONATA BAKED WITH BRIE

CALORIES: 232
SERVES 8

- 1 GREEN PEPPER, CORED, CHOPPED
- 1 ZUCCHINI, CHOPPED
- 1 SMALL EGGPLANT, CHOPPED
- 1 SWEET RED ONION, CHOPPED
- 2 TABLESPOONS CAPERS
- 10 GREEN OLIVES, SEEDED, CHOPPED
- ½ CUP OLIVE OIL
- 2 CLOVES GARLIC, CHOPPED
- 1 TABLESPOON SWEET BASIL, DRIED
- 1 TEASPOON OREGANO, DRIED
- SALT AND PEPPER TO TASTE
- 2 TABLESPOONS RED-WINE VINEGAR
- 1 SHEET FROZEN PUFF PASTRY, THAWED
- 6" ROUND OF BRIE

1. Sauté the vegetables and garlic in the olive oil over medium heat for 10 minutes. Add the herbs, salt, and pepper, and stir in red-wine vinegar. Cook for another 5 minutes.

2. Preheat the oven to 350°F. Roll out the pastry. Spread Brie on the pastry and spoon vegetables over all.

3. Bake for 25 to 35 minutes, or until pastry is nice and brown. Cut into manageable, appetizer-sized wedges and serve warm or at room temperature.

PER SERVING: Fat: 21 g **Protein:** 5 g **Carbohydrates:** 9 g **Sugar:** 5 g

BAKED CHICKEN WINGS

CALORIES: 211
SERVES 4

- 12 CHICKEN WINGS
- 3 TABLESPOONS SOY SAUCE
- ½ TABLESPOONS GARLIC POWDER
- 1 TEASPOON PAPRIKA
- 1 TEASPOON CAYENNE PEPPER
- 2 TEASPOONS AGAVE NECTAR
- SALT AND PEPPER TO TASTE
- 1 TABLESPOON OLIVE OIL

1. Wash the chicken wings and pat dry.

2. Combine all other ingredients except olive oil in a bowl. Add wings and coat with mixture. Cover and refrigerate for 1 to 2 hours or overnight.

3. Preheat oven to 425°F. Cover a baking dish with aluminum foil. Drizzle foil with olive oil. Place wings in one layer in baking dish.

4. Bake for 40 minutes or until golden brown. Turn the wings over after 20 minutes to allow for even cooking.

PER SERVING: Fat: 14 g **Protein:** 18 g **Carbohydrates:** 3 g **Sugar:** 1 g

LOLLIPOP LAMB CHOPS

CALORIES: 268
SERVES 14

- 4 CLOVES GARLIC
- 4 TABLESPOONS PARSLEY, MINCED
- 3 TABLESPOONS ROSEMARY
- RIND OF ½ LEMON, GRATED
- 3 TABLESPOONS DIJON-STYLE MUSTARD
- 2 TABLESPOONS OLIVE OIL
- SALT AND PEPPER TO TASTE
- 14 BABY RIB LAMB CHOPS (HAVE BUTCHER LEAVE LONG BONES ON AND TRIM THEM)

1. Blend everything but the chops in a mini–food processor or blender.

2. Pour into a large dish and add lamb chops, turning to coat both sides.

3. Broil or grill lamb chops for 3 minutes per side.

PER SERVING: Fat: 13 g **Protein:** 34 g **Carbohydrates:** 0 g **Sugar:** 1 g

Crowd Pleaser

Baby lamb chops are the star of the show at parties and special occasion. Your guests will love these delicious finger foods. They are fun to eat like chicken wings, but less messy and classier.

BAKED STUFFED CLAMS

CALORIES: 195
SERVES 4

4 FRESH CHERRYSTONE CLAMS, WELL-SCRUBBED AND OPENED, MEAT REMOVED

1 TABLESPOON LEMON JUICE

2 SLICES WHOLE GRAIN WHEAT BREAD, TOASTED AND CRUMBLED

1 EGG

1 TABLESPOON MAYONNAISE

½ TEASPOON DRIED DILL

2 TABLESPOONS BUTTER, MELTED

SALT AND PEPPER TO TASTE

2 TABLESPOONS PARMESAN CHEESE

IN THIS RECIPE YOU CAN SUBSTITUTE 2 TABLESPOONS OLIVE OIL OR HEART-HEALTHY MARGARINE FOR BUTTER AND LOW-FAT MAYONNAISE FOR REGULAR MAYONNAISE.

1. Preheat the oven to 350°F. Place the clam shells on a baking sheet.

2. Place the clam meat and the rest of the ingredients in the food processor or blender and pulse until mixed, but not puréed.

3. Spoon the stuffing into the clam shells and bake for about 20 minutes. Serve at once.

PER SERVING: Fat: 11 g **Protein:** 13 g **Carbohydrates:** 11 g **Sugar:** 3 g

Follow Your Nose and Your Ears!

When buying any kind of seafood, ask to smell it first. A fresh, salty aroma is fine; anything else is suspect—don't buy it! When selecting clams, make sure that they are tightly closed and make a sharp click when you tap them together.

PROSCIUTTO-WRAPPED ASPARAGUS

CALORIES: 185
SERVES 4

1 BUNCH FRESH ASPARAGUS

2 TABLESPOONS OLIVE OIL

1 TEASPOON KOSHER SALT

½ TEASPOON PEPPER

8 THIN SLICES PROSCIUTTO HAM

1. Bend one asparagus stalk near the cut end until it snaps. This will find the natural breaking point of the asparagus. You can discard the fibrous ends or use them for soup.

2. Using the snapped asparagus as a guide, measure and cut the other stalks at the same place and discard the woody ends. Toss asparagus with oil, salt, and pepper. Grill for about 5 minutes, until tender and tips are crispy. Set aside to cool.

3. Wrap a slice of prosciutto around three asparagus into a bundle. Repeat with remaining asparagus and prosciutto and serve warm.

PER SERVING: Fat: 14 g **Protein:** 9 g **Carbohydrates:** 5 g **Sugar:** 1 g

HONEY-SPICED ALMONDS

CALORIES: 101
SERVES 12

- 2 TABLESPOONS UNSALTED BUTTER
- ½ TEASPOON CINNAMON
- ⅛ TEASPOON GROUND CLOVES
- ⅛ TEASPOON GROUND GINGER
- ½ CUP HONEY
- ½ TEASPOON ORANGE ZEST
- 3 CUPS RAW ALMONDS

1. Put the butter, spices, honey, and orange zest in a large microwave-safe bowl. Microwave on high for 1 minute or until the butter is melted. Stir well to combine.

2. Add the almonds to the honey mixture and stir well to combine. Microwave on high for 3 minutes; stir well. Microwave on high for another 3 minutes; stir. Spread the nuts on a nonstick foil-lined baking sheet to cool. Be careful—the mixture will be very hot!

PER SERVING: Fat: 7 g **Protein:** 3 g **Carbohydrates:** 8 g **Sugar:** 6 g

---

STUFFED CELERY

CALORIES: 66
MAKES 12 PIECES

- WIDE ENDS OF 6 CELERY STALKS, CUT IN HALVES
- 5 OUNCES BRIE CHEESE, SOFTENED
- 2 TABLESPOONS CAPERS
- 3 TABLESPOONS CHOPPED WALNUTS, TOASTED

1. Lay the celery pieces on a cool serving plate. Remove the skin from the Brie and mash it with a fork. Mix in the capers.

2. Stuff each piece of celery and garnish with toasted walnuts.

PER SERVING: Fat: 6 g **Protein:** 3 g **Carbohydrates:** 1 g **Sugar:** 0 g

DEVILED EGGS WITH CAPERS

CALORIES: 69
SERVES 12

- 6 HARD-BOILED EGGS, SHELLED AND CUT IN HALF
- ½ CUP LOW-FAT MAYONNAISE
- 1 TEASPOON RED HOT PEPPER SAUCE, SUCH AS TABASCO
- 1 TEASPOON CELERY SALT
- 1 TEASPOON ONION
- 1 TEASPOON GARLIC POWDER
- 1 CHILI PEPPER, FINELY MINCED, OR TO TASTE
- 2 TABLESPOONS CAPERS, EXTRA-SMALL
- GARNISH OF PAPRIKA OR CHOPPED CHIVES

1. Scoop out egg yolks and place in a food processor along with mayonnaise, seasonings, pepper, and capers. Blend until smooth and spoon into the hollows in the eggs.

2. Add the garnish of paprika or chives and chill, covered with aluminum foil tented above the egg yolk mixture.

PER SERVING: Fat: 6 g **Protein:** 3 g **Carbohydrates:** 0 g **Sugar:** 0 g

Brine-Packed Capers
Capers are actually berries that have been pickled. You can get them packed in salt, but they are better when packed in brine. You can get larger ones or very, very small ones—the tiny ones are tastier.

WALNUT CHEESE BITES

CALORIES: 122
SERVES 4

- 4 OUNCES GORGONZOLA CHEESE
- 12 WALNUT HALVES
- 1 TABLESPOON HONEY TO DRIZZLE

1. Preheat oven to 350°F.

2. Sandwich 1 teaspoon cheese between 2 walnut halves. Place walnuts on a baking sheet.

3. Toast in the oven until cheese starts to melt, about 10 minutes.

4. Drizzle honey over walnuts and serve.

PER SERVING: Fat: 10 g **Protein:** 5 g **Carbohydrates:** 6 g **Sugar:** 5 g

Walnut Preparation
The walnuts in this recipe can be prepared as is, but are best if they are blanched. Boil them in water for about 1 minute and they will be softer and lighter in color. This mellows the walnuts' flavor.

STUFFED CUCUMBERS

CALORIES: 75
SERVES 4

- **2 LARGE CUCUMBERS**
- **3 OUNCES LOW-FAT CREAM CHEESE**
- **1 TABLESPOON LOW-FAT BLEU CHEESE**
- **1 TEASPOON DILL**
- **1 TEASPOON PARSLEY**
- **1 TEASPOON MINCED ONION**

1. Using a vegetable peeler, create stripes in the cucumber by peeling strips about ¼" apart, lengthwise. Cut ends off each cucumber. Scoop the seeds and pulp out of the cucumber with a melon baller.

2. Mix the cream cheese, bleu cheese, dill, parsley, and minced onion in a small bowl.

3. Place mixture inside the hollowed cucumbers using a pastry bag with a star tip.

4. Cover cucumbers with plastic wrap and refrigerate at least 1 hour.

5. Cut cucumbers into 1" circles and serve.

PER SERVING: Fat: 5 g **Protein:** 4 g **Carbohydrates:** 5 g **Sugar:** 2 g

MARYLAND CRAB CAKES

CALORIES: 494
SERVES 4

- **1 POUND LUMP CRABMEAT**
- **¼ CUP MAYONNAISE**
- **¼ CUP SOFT WHITE BREAD CRUMBS**
- **JUICE OF ½ LEMON**
- **1 EGG**
- **SALT AND PEPPER TO TASTE**
- **2 TABLESPOONS FRESH PARSLEY, CHOPPED**
- **½ CUP CANOLA OIL FOR FRYING**
- **TARTAR SAUCE**

IN THIS RECIPE, YOU CAN SUBSTITUTE LOW-FAT MAYONNAISE FOR REGULAR MAYONNAISE AND USE COOKING SPRAY INSTEAD OF CANOLA OIL.

1. Mix together all ingredients but the oil and tartar sauce and form into cakes.

2. Heat the oil in the frying pan to 275°F. Fry the cakes until well-browned on both sides. Serve with tartar sauce.

PER SERVING: Fat: 43 g **Protein:** 25 g **Carbohydrates:** 4 g **Sugar:** 1 g

Crab Cake Tips
The trick to making the best crab cakes is not skimping on the crab meat. Using fresh lump crabmeat will show through in the final result. Lemon juice and pepper serve to perk up the overall seafood flavor.

BROILED HERB-CRUSTED CHICKEN TENDERS

CALORIES: 170
SERVES 4

1 POUND CHICKEN TENDERS
¼ CUP OLIVE OIL
2 TEASPOONS DRIED THYME
2 TEASPOONS DRIED SAGE
SALT AND PEPPER TO TASTE
8 SKEWERS (IF WOODEN, SOAK SKEWERS)

1. Preheat broiler to 400°F. Rinse the chicken tenders and pat dry. Mix the olive oil, herbs, salt, and pepper. Dip the chicken tenders in this mixture.

2. Skewer each piece of herbed chicken tender and broil on a baking sheet for 3 minutes per side. Serve with any of the dipping sauces in this chapter.

PER SERVING: Fat: 17 g **Protein:** 4 g **Carbohydrates:** 2 g **Sugar:** 0 g

PITA TOAST WITH HERBS AND CHEESE

CALORIES: 77
SERVES 4

1 WHOLE-WHEAT PITA
2 TABLESPOONS CREAM CHEESE, AT ROOM TEMPERATURE
2 TEASPOONS GORGONZOLA CHEESE, AT ROOM TEMPERATURE
2 SPRIGS FRESH PARSLEY, MINCED
2 TABLESPOONS CHIVES, MINCED
SALT AND PEPPER TO TASTE

1. Toast the pitas and cut in fourths. Using a fork, mix the rest of the ingredients together in a small bowl. Spread on pitas and serve.

PER SERVING: Fat: 5 g **Protein:** 4 g **Carbohydrates:** 9 g **Sugar:** 1 g

RICE CAKES

CALORIES: 194
SERVES 4

- 1 CUP COOKED RICE, BASMATI OR ARBORIO
- 1 EGG
- 1 TEASPOON SUGAR
- CINNAMON TO TASTE (START WITH ¼ TEASPOON)
- ¼ TEASPOON SALT, OR TO TASTE
- ¼ CUP CANOLA OIL

1. Cool the cooked rice. Beat the egg, sugar, cinnamon, and salt together. Mix into the rice.

2. In a frying pan, heat the oil to 350°F and fry cakes until golden. Serve hot or cold.

PER SERVING: Fat: 15 g **Protein:** 2 g **Carbohydrates:** 12 g
Sugar: 2 g

How to Serve Rice Cakes

Rice cakes are so versatile. Since rice takes on the flavor of the foods around it, the options for serving these cakes are endless. Try pairing them with a baked white fish with lemon and pepper sauce or sautéed vegetables with soy sauce. Enjoy!

PARMESAN TUILLES

CALORIES: 36
SERVES 6

- 6 TABLESPOONS FRESH PARMESAN CHEESE
- 2 TEASPOONS CANOLA OIL
- SPRINKLE OF PAPRIKA

1. Grate the cheese, using a box grate on its coarsest side.

2. Heat the oil in a well-seasoned frying pan or a nonstick pan and drop small mounds of the cheese onto the pan, flattening with the back of a spoon. Fry for 2 minutes per side. Serve hot or cold, garnished with paprika.

PER SERVING: Fat: 4 g **Protein:** 2 g **Carbohydrates:** 0 g
Sugar: 0 g

WHITE BEAN BRUSCHETTA

CALORIES: 355
SERVES 6

1 (15-OUNCE) CAN CANNELLONI BEANS, RINSED AND DRAINED

⅓ TEASPOON THYME

¼ TEASPOON SEASONED SALT

GROUND PEPPER TO TASTE

2 TABLESPOONS CHOPPED VIDALIA ONION

1 SMALL CLOVE GARLIC, CRUSHED

⅓ CUP LOW-CHOLESTEROL MARGARINE, MELTED

1 LOAF ITALIAN BREAD, CUT INTO 12 1" SLICES

1. Put beans, thyme, salt, pepper, onions, and garlic in a blender or food processor. Purée until smooth.

2. Lightly spread margarine on bread.

3. Spread bean paste on each slice of bread.

4. Place slices of bread under broiler for 1 minute or serve cold.

PER SERVING: Fat: 6 g **Protein:** 6 g **Carbohydrates:** 25 g **Sugar:** 5 g

HONEY AND CHEESE STUFFED FIGS

CALORIES: 183
SERVES 4

8 MEDIUM RIPE FIGS

⅓ CUP CRUMBLED GORGONZOLA CHEESE

1 TEASPOON OLIVE OIL

¼ CUP HONEY

1. Preheat oven to 300°F.

2. Wash and dry figs. Make a slit in each one from top to bottom.

3. Stuff each fig with the cheese.

4. Roll each fig in olive oil and shake excess off.

5. Bake figs, watching them until they plump up, about 30 minutes.

6. Drizzle honey on baked figs when ready to serve.

PER SERVING: Fat: 4 g **Protein:** 3 g **Carbohydrates:** 37 g **Sugar:** 30 g

GRILLED VEGETABLE FOCCACIA

CALORIES: 425
SERVES 4

¼ POUND MARINATED KALAMATA OLIVES

½ CUP MARINATED SICILIAN CRACKED GREEN OLIVES

½ CUP ROASTED RED PEPPERS

1 (7-OUNCE) CAN DICED TOMATOES

2 TABLESPOONS OLIVE OIL

KOSHER SALT AND GROUND PEPPER TO TASTE

½ TEASPOON ITALIAN SEASONING

4 PIECES SOURDOUGH FOCCACIA BREAD

1. Mix all ingredients except bread together in a large bowl.

2. Spread mixture on foccacia bread.

PER SERVING: Fat: 24 g **Protein:** 8 g **Carbohydrates:** 44 g **Sugar:** 6 g

CHEESE STRAWS

CALORIES: 350
SERVES 6

1 (15-OUNCE) PACKAGE PIECRUST MIX

½ CUP SHREDDED LOW-FAT CHEDDAR CHEESE

½ TEASPOON CAYENNE PEPPER

LIGHT COOKING SPRAY

1. Preheat oven to 350°F.

2. Prepare piecrust mix according to directions.

3. Sprinkle shredded cheese over piecrust dough, then work it into the dough with your hands.

4. Roll dough into a circle, about 8" around, ⅓" thick.

5. Cut long strips about 1" wide.

6. Sprinkle both sides of each strip with cayenne pepper.

7. Place strips on baking sheet, lightly sprayed with cooking spray.

8. Bake until slightly brown.

PER SERVING: Fat: 23 g **Protein:** 6 g **Carbohydrates:** 30 g **Sugar:** 9 g

RAW OYSTERS ON THE HALF SHELL WITH MIGNONETTE SAUCE

CALORIES: 155
SERVES 2

- **2 SHALLOTS, MINCED**
- **1 TABLESPOON LEMON JUICE**
- **1 TABLESPOON ITALIAN PARSLEY, CHOPPED**
- **SALT AND PEPPER TO TASTE**
- **½ CUP EXTRA-VIRGIN OLIVE OIL**
- **12 RAW OYSTERS, ON THE HALF SHELL, RESTING ON A BED OF ICE**

1. Place the shallots, lemon juice, parsley, salt, and pepper in the blender. On low speed, slowly add the olive oil. Spoon over the oysters.

PER SERVING: Fat: 11 g **Protein:** 7 g **Carbohydrates:** 7 g **Sugar:** 1 g

Oysters

This is a wonderful holiday appetizer. You can make the mignonette sauce in advance. Oysters should be served the day they are opened. Tell your fishmonger not to rinse off the liquor (natural juice). The oyster liquor is full of great flavor!

CHEESE, OLIVE, AND CHERRY TOMATO KABOBS

CALORIES: 232
SERVES 4

- **6 BAMBOO SKEWERS SOAKED IN WATER**
- **LIGHT COOKING SPRAY**
- **6 CHERRY TOMATOES**
- **6 LARGE GREEN MARINATED OLIVES**
- **½ POUND JACK CHEESE, CUT INTO 1" CUBES**

1. Spray each skewer with the light cooking spray.

2. Arrange 1 tomato, 1 olive, and 1 cheese cube on each skewer.

3. Grill skewers for just a few moments until cheese starts to melt, then turn to grill all sides.

PER SERVING: Fat: 19 g **Protein:** 14 g **Carbohydrates:** 2 g **Sugar:** 1 g

CHICKEN AND PINEAPPLE FINGER SANDWICHES

CALORIES: 273
SERVES 4

1 SKINLESS CHICKEN BREAST

¼ CUP NONFAT PLAIN YOGURT

¼ CUP LOW-FAT MAYONNAISE

1 TABLESPOON LIME JUICE

1 TEASPOON CURRY POWDER

4 TEASPOONS FLAT-LEAF PARSLEY, CHOPPED

3 TABLESPOONS SLICED ALMONDS

1¼ CUP DICED PINEAPPLE

8 PIECES THIN WHITE OR WHEAT BREAD

½ CUP WATERCRESS WITHOUT STEMS

1. Cook chicken breast in boiling water about five minutes or until done.

2. While chicken is cooling, mix yogurt, mayonnaise, lime juice, curry powder, parsley, and almonds together.

3. Cut the chicken into bite-size pieces, then add chicken pieces and pineapple to the mixture.

4. Spread the mixture over slices of bread and sprinkle with watercress to serve sandwiches.

PER SERVING: Fat: 10 g **Protein:** 14 g **Carbohydrates:** 34 g **Sugar:** 26 g

Make Your Chicken Juicier

If you boil the chicken breast that still has a bone in it, the chicken will be juicier. Simply remove the bone after boiling.

CEVICHE—FRESH SEAFOOD IN CITRUS

CALORIES: 159
SERVES 4

½ POUND FRESH RAW SHRIMP, PEELED AND DEVEINED

½ POUND RAW TINY BAY SCALLOPS

2 SCALLIONS, MINCED

1 GREEN CHILI, SEEDED AND MINCED

JUICE OF 1 FRESH LIME

2 TABLESPOONS ORANGE JUICE

1 TABLESPOON CHILI SAUCE

2 TABLESPOONS PARSLEY OR CILANTRO

SALT AND PEPPER TO TASTE

2 TABLESPOONS OLIVE OIL

1. Rinse scallops and pat dry in a paper towel.

2. Mix all ingredients except the olive oil in a nonreactive bowl. Cover and refrigerate for 8 hours or overnight.

3. Just before serving, sprinkle with olive oil. Serve in large cocktail glasses.

PER SERVING: Fat: 11 g **Protein:** 18 g **Carbohydrates:** 4 g **Sugar:** 1 g

More About Ceviche

Ceviche is made by using the acid from citrus juice instead of heat to cook fresh seafood. It has been enjoyed in South America for centuries. Ceviche is made differently all over the world, but typically always contains fish and shellfish. Other common ingredients include thinly sliced onion, hot pepper, orange juice, lemon, garlic, corn, lettuce, and sweet potato.

CRUNCHY PARTY MIX

CALORIES: 247
SERVES 10

- 2 TABLESPOONS PEANUT OIL
- 1 TABLESPOON MINCED GARLIC
- 1 CUP UNSALTED WALNUTS
- 1 CUP UNSALTED ALMONDS
- ½ CUP UNSALTED PRETZEL STICKS, BROKEN INTO SMALL PIECES
- 1 TEASPOON CHILI POWDER
- 1½ TABLESPOONS LOW-SODIUM SOY SAUCE
- 1 TEASPOON CAYENNE PEPPER
- 2 TEASPOONS SPLENDA
- SEA SALT TO TASTE
- ½ CUP SEEDLESS RAISINS

1. Warm peanut oil and garlic in a heavy skillet.
2. Add all other ingredients except raisins, stirring constantly.
3. When thoroughly warmed and mixed, stir in raisins.
4. Remove from heat. Put into a serving bowl.
5. Chill and serve.

PER SERVING: Fat: 17 g **Protein:** 6 g **Carbohydrates:** 20 g **Sugar:** 10 g

Healthy Nuts

Buy nuts in small quantities, because they can become rancid fairly quickly. You can store nuts in the freezer, but be sure to thaw them completely before chopping or they will become oily.

STUFFED ZUCCHINI BOATS

CALORIES: 272
SERVES 2

- 2 LARGE ZUCCHINI SQUASHES
- 1 TEASPOON OLIVE OIL
- SALT AND PEPPER TO TASTE
- 4 OUNCES GROUND TURKEY
- ¼ CUP MARINARA SAUCE
- 2 OUNCES PART-SKIM RICOTTA CHEESE
- 1 TABLESPOON PARMESAN CHEESE, SHREDDED

1. Set oven rack at upper-middle position and turn broiler to high.
2. Slice each zucchini in half lengthwise. Using a spoon, remove seeds from zucchini halves, creating a hollowed center.
3. Rub zucchini with oil and season with salt and pepper to taste. Place on a baking sheet with open side facing up. Broil 8 minutes or until zucchini are fork tender. Meanwhile, brown ground turkey in a medium pan over medium heat.
4. Heat marinara sauce in a small saucepan.
5. Remove zucchini from oven and transfer to platter.
6. Combine ground turkey and marinara sauce. Spread a thin layer of ricotta cheese across zucchini; top with meat sauce. Sprinkle with Parmesan cheese.

PER SERVING: Fat: 11 g **Protein:** 20 g **Carbohydrates:** 27 g **Sugar:** 1 g

HAWAIIAN CHICKEN SKEWERS

CALORIES: 220
SERVES 8

- ¼ CUP COCONUT MILK
- 1 TABLESPOON TOASTED SESAME OIL
- ½ TEASPOON TABASCO SAUCE
- ¼ CUP PINEAPPLE JUICE
- 1 POUND CHICKEN TENDERS
- ½ FRESH PINEAPPLE, CUT INTO CHUNKS
- 2 TABLESPOONS LIME JUICE

1. In medium-size bowl, combine coconut milk, sesame oil, Tabasco sauce, and pineapple juice. Cut chicken tenders crosswise and add to coconut milk mixture. Cover and refrigerate for 8 hours.

2. Alternate chicken pieces and pineapple chunks on skewers, using 2 chicken pieces and 1 pineapple chunk per skewer.

3. Prepare and preheat grill. Grill skewers 6" from medium coals for 8–12 minutes, turning frequently, until chicken is thoroughly cooked. Sprinkle with lime juice and serve immediately.

PER SERVING: Fat: 5 g **Protein:** 18 g **Carbohydrates:** 17 g **Sugar:** 8 g

Skewers

Creating skewers with meats and fruits or vegetables is a great way to reduce your total meat intake. To make skewers, you can use wooden picks or metal skewers. If you choose wooden picks, soak them in cold water for at least 30 minutes before using. They will soak up some of the water and won't burn on the high heat of the grill.

BAKED COCONUT SHRIMP

CALORIES: 173
SERVES 8

NONSTICK COOKING SPRAY

⅓ CUP ALMOND FLOUR

½ TEASPOON GROUND RED PEPPER

SALT TO TASTE

JUICE OF ½ LIME

1 TABLESPOON AGAVE NECTAR

⅓ CUP EGG WHITES

¾ CUP COCONUT

1½ POUNDS EXTRA-LARGE SHRIMP, SHELLED AND CLEANED WITH TAILS REMAINING

1. Preheat oven to 425°F and lightly spray a baking sheet with nonstick cooking spray.

2. In a small bowl, combine almond flour, pepper, and salt.

3. In a separate bowl, mix lime juice and agave nectar and stir. Continuously stirring, add egg whites to lime-agave mixture.

4. Place coconut in a thin layer on a flat dish. Dip each shrimp first into the almond flour mixture, then in the egg white mixture, and then roll in coconut.

5. Place on baking sheet. Bake 10 to 15 minutes or until coconut appears lightly toasted.

PER SERVING: Fat: 9 g **Protein:** 20 g **Carbohydrates:** 10 g **Sugar:** 3 g

How to Pair Coconut

Coconut is a fun ingredient to work with because it is a delicious island treat. Coconut has the power to sweep the mind away to thoughts of a warm, sandy beach. However, it must be paired with the right ingredients to work well in a dish. Some flavors that coconut goes well with include lime, chocolate, pineapple, banana, orange, and shellfish.

GREEK QUESADILLAS

CALORIES: 289
SERVES 8

- 1 CUCUMBER
- 1 CUP PLAIN YOGURT
- ½ TEASPOON DRIED OREGANO LEAVES
- 1 TABLESPOON LEMON JUICE
- ½ CUP CRUMBLED FETA CHEESE
- 4 GREEN ONIONS, CHOPPED
- 3 PLUM TOMATOES, CHOPPED
- 1 CUP FRESH BABY SPINACH LEAVES
- 1 CUP SHREDDED PART-SKIM MOZZARELLA CHEESE
- 12 6" NO-SALT CORN TORTILLAS

1. Peel cucumber, remove seeds, and chop. In small bowl, combine cucumber with yogurt, oregano, and lemon juice and set aside.

2. In medium-size bowl, combine feta cheese, green onions, tomatoes, baby spinach, and mozzarella cheese and mix well.

3. Preheat griddle or skillet. Place six tortillas on work surface. Divide tomato mixture among them. Top with remaining tortillas and press down gently.

4. Cook quesadillas, pressing down occasionally with spatula, until tortillas are lightly browned. Flip quesadillas and cook on second side until tortillas are crisp and cheese is melted. Cut quesadillas in quarters and serve with yogurt mixture.

ER SERVING: **Fat:** 6 g **Protein:** 11 g **Carbohydrates:** 32 g **Sugar:** 2 g

Tortillas

Tortillas are made with flour or with corn. They may have no fat, but the typical 10" flour tortilla made with salt has about 400 mg of sodium! Read labels carefully to find no-salt tortillas. Flour tortillas are flavored with everything from spinach to red peppers to tomatoes. The corn tortillas have more nutrition and more fiber.

ARTICHOKES WITH AIOLI

CALORIES: 331
SERVES 4

4 WHOLE ARTICHOKES
1 LEMON, CUT IN HALF
1½ CUPS WATER
½ CUP DRY WHITE WINE
1 CLOVE GARLIC, MINCED
1 TABLESPOON OLIVE OIL
1 TEASPOON FRESH LEMON JUICE
¾ CUP MAYONNAISE

1. Prepare the artichokes by cutting the stems off the bottoms first. Rub the cut lemon on all the places of the artichokes you will cut to prevent browning. Next cut the top inch off each artichoke with a serrated knife and discard. Rub the lemon on the cut. Snip the thorny tips off the remaining leaves with kitchen scissors and rub the cut surface with the lemon.

2. Pull out the center leaves to expose the fuzzy choke in the center, and then scoop out the choke with a melon baller. Squeeze lemon juice into the center of each artichoke.

3. Pour the water and white wine into the bottom of a large pot. Place a steamer rack in the bottom of the pot and put the artichokes upside-down on the rack. Cover the pot with a tight-fitting lid and simmer for 50 minutes or until a leaf can be pulled easily from an artichoke. Remove the artichokes and let them drain and cool upside-down. Turn them over and chill them in the refrigerator.

4. Combine the garlic, olive oil, lemon juice, and mayonnaise in a food processor while the artichokes chill. Chill this quick aioli until ready to serve.

5. Put each chilled artichoke on an appetizer plate, spoon the aioli into the middle of each artichoke, and serve.

PER SERVING: Fat: 27 g **Protein:** 6 g **Carbohydrates:** 16 g **Sugar:** 3 g

STUFFED SNOW PEAS

CALORIES: 155
SERVES 6

- **8 OUNCES CREAM CHEESE**
- **1 TABLESPOON FRESH LEMON JUICE**
- **1 TEASPOON GRATED LEMON ZEST**
- **¼ CUP CHOPPED SMOKED SALMON**
- **2 CUPS SNOW PEA PODS**
- **½ CUP CHOPPED PARSLEY**
- **¼ CUP CHOPPED CHIVES**

1. Purée the cream cheese in a food processor. Add the lemon juice, lemon zest, and smoked salmon, and purée until smooth again. Scrape down the sides when necessary.

2. Put this cream cheese mousse into a large freezer bag and refrigerate.

3. Snap the stems and zip the strings off the snow pea pods and blanch them in boiling water for 3 minutes. Plunge them into ice water to cool, then drain completely on paper towels. Split the pods open on one side. Combine the chopped parsley and chives and set aside.

4. Remove the cream cheese mousse from the refrigerator and press the contents down into one corner of the bag. Snip the tip off the bag and pipe a row of the cream cheese mousse into each snow pea pod.

5. Squeeze the filling into each pea pod, so it sticks out of the side like a ruffle, and dip the tip of the ruffle in the chopped parsley and chives. Place the stuffed pea pods on a serving tray. Serve or wrap and refrigerate.

PER SERVING: Fat: 13 g **Protein:** 5 g **Carbohydrates:** 3 g **Sugar:** 1 g

Stuffed Vegetables

Stuffed vegetables can combine many different ingredients and turn your next cocktail party into a roaring success that's also full of nutrition! Think about making a cup of shrimp or crabmeat salad and stuffing it into halved Italian or jalapeño peppers.

CLAMS CASINO

CALORIES: 238
SERVES 4

16 LITTLENECK CLAMS, OPENED, JUICES RETAINED

4 TABLESPOONS BUTTER

1 SMALL ONION, FINELY MINCED

JUICE OF ½ FRESH LEMON

2 TEASPOONS FRESH PARSLEY, CHOPPED

½ TEASPOON DRIED OREGANO

½ CUP ROASTED SWEET RED PEPPER, CHOPPED FINELY

3 TABLESPOONS FINE WHITE BREAD CRUMBS

FRESHLY GROUND BLACK PEPPER TO TASTE

3 SLICES BACON, CUT IN 1" PIECES

1. Preheat oven to 400°F. Place the open clams on a baking pan.

2. In a saucepan over medium heat, add the butter, onion, lemon, herbs, and red pepper. Mix well when butter melts and sauté for about 4 minutes. Mix in bread crumbs and sprinkle with pepper. Moisten with reserved clam juice.

3. Divide the bread crumb mixture among the clams.

4. Put a piece of bacon on top of each stuffed clam. Bake for 12 minutes, or until the bacon is crisp and the clams are bubbling.

PER SERVING: Fat: 17 g **Protein:** 11 g **Carbohydrates:** 11 g **Sugar:** 3 g

Bacon
To reduce the amount of saturated fat and salt, Canadian bacon or vegetarian bacon can be used instead of regular bacon. The recipe will still be very flavorful with this healthier substitution.

BAKED STUFFED ARTICHOKES

CALORIES: 403
SERVES 4

2 LARGE ARTICHOKES

2 TABLESPOONS OLIVE OIL

2 CLOVES GARLIC, CHOPPED

½ SWEET ONION, CHOPPED

1 CUP WHOLE GRAIN CRACKER CRUMBS, MADE IN THE FOOD PROCESSOR OR BLENDER

1 TABLESPOON LEMON PEEL, MINCED

8 MEDIUM SHRIMP, PEELED AND DEVEINED

4 TABLESPOONS FRESH PARSLEY

½ TEASPOON FRESHLY GROUND BLACK PEPPER, OR TO TASTE

4 QUARTS BOILING WATER

JUICE AND RIND OF ½ LEMON

½ TEASPOON GROUND CORIANDER SEED

1 TABLESPOON PARMESAN CHEESE

1. Remove any tough or brown outside leaves from the artichokes. Using a sharp knife, cut off artichoke tops, about ½" down. Slam the artichokes against a countertop to loosen leaves. Cut in half, from top to stem, and set aside.

2. Heat the olive oil in a large frying pan over medium heat. Add the garlic and onion and sauté for 5 minutes, stirring. Add the cracker crumbs, lemon peel, shrimp, parsley, and pepper. Pulse entire mixture in food processor or blender.

3. Boil the artichokes with lemon and coriander for 18 minutes. Place the artichokes in a baking dish with ½ cup of water on the bottom. Pile with shrimp filling. Drizzle with a bit of the cooking water, sprinkle with Parmesan cheese, and bake for 25 minutes.

PER SERVING: Fat: 16 g **Protein:** 15 g **Carbohydrates:** 54 g **Sugar:** 3 g

SPINACH PUFFS

¾ CUP CHOPPED MUSHROOMS, INCLUDING STEMS

¼ CUP CANOLA OIL

1 (5-OUNCE) PACKAGE FROZEN CHOPPED SPINACH, THAWED, WATER SQUEEZED OUT

¾ CUP SHREDDED GRUYÈRE CHEESE

2 THAWED PUFF PASTRY SHEETS

¼ CUP LOW-CHOLESTEROL MARGARINE

1. Sauté mushrooms in canola oil.

2. Stir mushrooms with spinach and cheese.

3. Brush one pastry sheet with margarine.

4. Spread half of spinach mixture on one pastry sheet.

5. Cover with the remaining pastry sheet.

6. Top with remaining spinach mixture.

7. Cover and refrigerate for at least an hour.

8. Cut into four 1" wheels, like a pizza slice.

9. Bake on cookie sheet for 15 minutes or until brown.

PER SERVING: Fat: 36 g **Protein:** 9 g **Carbohydrates:** 8 g **Sugar:** 3 g

Appetizer Etymology

The word *appetizer* comes from the Italian word *mezzano*, which means an introductory course of foods. *Mezzano* was introduced in the fourteenth century to refer to certain foods eaten before a full meal.

OPEN-FACE WILD MUSHROOM WONTONS

CALORIES: 54
SERVES 24

- 1 TABLESPOON OLIVE OR CANOLA OIL
- 1 TABLESPOON UNSALTED BUTTER
- ½ CUP SLICED SHALLOTS
- ½ TEASPOON FRESHLY GROUND BLACK PEPPER
- ¾ POUND ASSORTED WILD MUSHROOMS (SUCH AS CHANTERELLE, WOOD EAR, SHIITAKE, MOREL), CLEANED, STEMMED, AND THINLY SLICED
- ¾ CUP WATER
- ¾ TEASPOON LOW-SODIUM CHICKEN BASE
- ¼ CUP INSTANT NONFAT DRY MILK
- ½ CUP RICOTTA CHEESE
- ½ TEASPOON HERBAL SEASONING BLEND OF YOUR CHOICE
- 24 WONTON WRAPPERS
- NONSTICK COOKING OIL
- 2 TABLESPOONS GRATED PARMESAN CHEESE

1. Preheat oven to 375°.

2. In a large, heavy nonstick skillet, heat the oil and melt the butter over medium-high heat. Add the shallots and cook, stirring, for 1 minute. Add the pepper and mushrooms; sauté until the mushrooms become soft and most of the mushroom liquid is evaporated, about 8 minutes.

3. Add the water and heat until it begins to boil. Dissolve the chicken base in the water. Reduce heat and add the nonfat dry milk, whisking to combine with the mushroom mixture. Add the ricotta cheese and herbal seasoning, and mix to combine; cook until heated through. Remove from heat.

4. Line a baking sheet with nonstick aluminum foil. Prepare the wonton wrappers by lightly spraying one side of each with the nonstick cooking oil. Place sprayed-side down on the foil. Evenly divide the mushroom mixture, placing a spoonful on each wonton wrapper. Top the mushroom mixture with the grated cheese.

5. Bake for 8 to 10 minutes or until the wontons are brown and crunchy and the cheese is melted and bubbly.

PER SERVING: Fat: 3 g **Protein:** 3 g **Carbohydrates:** 6 g **Sugar:** 3 g

Go Natural!

Most processed foods have high sodium levels that results from the combination of salt added to the food and the high sodium content of the preservatives. Deciding to do all you can to keep the foods you eat as close to natural as possible is a healthy goal.

CHAPTER 3

Sauces, Spreads, Dips, and Dressings

SEVEN-LAYER MEXICAN DIP

CALORIES: 78
SERVES 12

1 CUP LOW-FAT SOUR CREAM

1 TABLESPOON REDUCED-SODIUM TACO SEASONING

9 OUNCES FAT-FREE BEAN DIP

¾ CUP GUACAMOLE

½ CUP LOW-FAT SHREDDED CHEDDAR CHEESE

5 SCALLIONS, CHOPPED

1 TOMATO, CHOPPED

10 BLACK OLIVES, SLICED

1. Combine the sour cream and taco seasoning.

2. Spread bean dip on the bottom of a round serving bowl or edged platter.

3. Layer the guacamole next, spreading evenly over the bean dip. Layer the sour cream mixture, also spreading evenly.

4. Sprinkle the shredded cheese evenly over the guacamole and top with the scallions, tomatoes, and olives.

PER SERVING: Fat: 4 g **Protein:** 3 g **Carbohydrates:** 8 g **Sugar:** 4 g

BEAN SALSA

CALORIES: 84
SERVES 8

4 CUPS TOMATOES, CHOPPED

2 CUPS BLACK BEANS, COOKED

1 CUP ONION, DICED

1 JALAPEÑO, SEEDED AND DICED

½ CUP FRESH CILANTRO, CHOPPED

JUICE OF 2 LIMES

SALT AND PEPPER TO TASTE

1. Mix tomatoes, beans, onion, jalapeño, cilantro, and lime juice in a medium-size bowl.

2. Add salt and pepper as desired.

PER SERVING: Fat: 0 g **Protein:** 5 g **Carbohydrates:** 17 g **Sugar:** 5 g

FRUIT SKEWERS WITH DIP

CALORIES: 159
SERVES 4

- 4 KIWI FRUIT, SLICED IN ½" PIECES
- 8 LARGE STRAWBERRIES, SLICED IN HALF
- 2 MEDIUM PEARS, CUT INTO ½" PIECES
- 1 LARGE ORANGE, SLICED INTO ½" PIECES
- 1 CUP PLAIN, LOW-FAT YOGURT
- JUICE OF 1 LIME
- 2 TEASPOONS FRESH MINT LEAVES, FINELY CHOPPED

1. Arrange cut fruit pieces on 8 wooden skewers, alternating fruit types.

2. In a small bowl, mix yogurt, lime juice, and mint.

3. Serve fruit skewers with yogurt dip.

PER SERVING: Fat: 2 g **Protein:** 5 g **Carbohydrates:** 35 g **Sugar:** 20 g

Fresh Herbed Yogurt

Herbs and citrus make yogurt taste great. For a different flavor yogurt, try using fresh basil leaves and the juice of half a lemon. You may also use fresh fruits like bananas and apples.

CREAMY-CRUNCHY AVOCADO DIP WITH RED ONIONS AND MACADAMIA NUTS

CALORIES: 229
SERVES 2

- 1 LARGE RIPE AVOCADO, PEELED, PIT REMOVED
- JUICE OF ½ FRESH LIME
- 2 TABLESPOONS RED ONION, MINCED
- 2 TABLESPOONS MACADAMIA NUTS, CHOPPED
- 1 TEASPOON TABASCO OR OTHER HOT RED PEPPER SAUCE
- SALT TO TASTE

1. Using a small bowl, mash the avocado and mix in the rest of the ingredients. Serve chilled.

PER SERVING: Fat: 22 g **Protein:** 3 g **Carbohydrates:** 10 g **Sugar:** 3 g

BLACK BEAN DIP

CALORIES: 283
MAKES 2 CUPS

- 1½ CUPS BLACK BEANS, CANNED AND DRAINED
- ½ CUP VIDALIA ONION, FINELY MINCED
- 4 CLOVES GARLIC, MINCED
- 2 TEASPOONS RED HOT PEPPER SAUCE, OR TO TASTE
- JUICE OF 1 LIME
- ½ CUP SOUR CREAM
- ½ CUP CHOPPED CILANTRO OR PARSLEY
- SALT AND PEPPER TO TASTE

1. Pulse all ingredients in the food processor or blender. Serve chilled or at room temperature.

PER SERVING (1-OUNCE): Fat: 13 g **Protein:** 12 g **Carbohydrates:** 39 g **Sugar:** 12 g

Low-Fat Alternative

Try substituting nonfat or low-fat sour cream for regular to decrease the saturated fat content. The cilantro, onion, lime, and hot pepper sauce increases the flavor intensity of the black beans, so nobody will notice that you used a healthier sour cream.

SPICY CILANTRO DIP

CALORIES: 135
SERVES 6

- 2 CUPS EDAMAME BEANS
- 1 CUP LOW-FAT SOUR CREAM
- 3 TABLESPOONS RED-WINE VINEGAR
- 1 TABLESPOON OLIVE OIL
- ¼ CUP LIME JUICE
- 1 JALAPEÑO, DICED
- 1 BUNCH FRESH CILANTRO LEAVES, CHOPPED
- 1 RED BELL PEPPER, CHOPPED
- 2 SHALLOTS, DICED
- ¼ TEASPOON SALT
- ¼ TEASPOON BLACK PEPPER

1. Shell edamame beans.

2. Combine sour cream, vinegar, olive oil, and lime juice and purée in a blender or food processor until smooth.

3. Add edamame, jalapeño, cilantro, red bell pepper, shallots, salt, and pepper to the sour cream mixture and blend to a chunky texture.

4. Serve dip chilled.

PER SERVING: Fat: 9 g **Protein:** 6 g **Carbohydrates:** 9 g **Sugar:** 3 g

Time-Saving Tip

Edamame, or soy beans, are rich in iron, fiber, omega-3 fats, and many other nutrients. Buy edamame that have already been removed from the shell to save time during preparation. Shelled edamame can often be found in the freezer section at the supermarket.

MUSHROOM SPREAD

CALORIES: 158
SERVES 4

- 2 TABLESPOONS OLIVE OIL
- 1 SMALL SHALLOT, CHOPPED
- 3 CUPS WHITE MUSHROOMS, SLICED
- ¼ CUP CREAM CHEESE
- ¼ CUP DRY SHERRY
- 2 CUPS FLAT-LEAF PARSLEY
- SALT AND PEPPER TO TASTE
- 1 ZUCCHINI, SLICED
- 1 YELLOW SQUASH, SLICED
- 1 CARROT, SLICED

1. Heat oil in a pan and cook shallots until soft. Add mushrooms and cook until water is removed.

2. Blend mushrooms and shallots with cream cheese and sherry in a food processor until smooth. Add parsley, salt, and pepper to food processor and blend well.

3. Serve with grilled or raw vegetable slices.

PER SERVING: Fat: 10 g **Protein:** 5 g **Carbohydrates:** 11 g **Sugar:** 4 g

Dry Sherry Substitute

Sherry is a fortified wine that comes from southern Spain. It is considered an aperitif and is often served chilled. If you do not have dry sherry on hand, orange juice, pineapple juice, and nonalcoholic vanilla extract are considered good substitutes in correct proportions.

SUPER SPICY SALSA

CALORIES: 21
MAKES 3 CUPS

- 2 JALAPEÑO PEPPERS, MINCED
- 1 HABAÑERO PEPPER, MINCED
- 1 GREEN BELL PEPPER, MINCED
- 4 CLOVES GARLIC, MINCED
- 1 RED ONION, CHOPPED
- 5 RIPE TOMATOES, CHOPPED
- 3 TABLESPOONS LEMON JUICE
- ¼ TEASPOON SALT
- ⅛ TEASPOON WHITE PEPPER
- ¼ CUP CHOPPED FRESH CILANTRO

1. In large bowl, combine jalapeños, habañero pepper, bell pepper, garlic, red onion, and tomatoes. In small bowl, combine lemon juice, salt, and pepper; stir to dissolve salt. Add to tomato mixture along with cilantro.

2. Cover and refrigerate for 3–4 hours before serving.

PER SERVING (¼ CUP): Fat: 0 g **Protein:** 1 g **Carbohydrates:** 5 g **Sugar:** 1 g

Pepper Heat

The heat in a pepper is concentrated in its seeds and inner membranes. If you prefer a milder taste, just remove and discard the seeds and membranes before mincing. Remember, the smaller the pepper, the hotter. Habañeros and Scotch bonnet peppers are the hottest, while pepperoncini and Poblano peppers are milder.

FRESH BAJA GUACAMOLE

CALORIES: 133
SERVES 4

2 RIPE AVOCADOS
½ RED ONION, MINCED (ABOUT ½ CUP)
2 TABLESPOONS CILANTRO LEAVES, FINELY CHOPPED
JUICE OF 1 LIME
SALT AND FRESHLY GRATED BLACK PEPPER
1 SERRANO CHILI, MINCED
½ TOMATO, CHOPPED

1. Cut avocados in half. Remove the seed. Scoop avocado away from the peel and place in a mixing bowl.

2. Use a fork to mash avocado. Add the minced onion, cilantro, lime juice, salt, and pepper. Mix ingredients together.

3. Take chili pepper, cut open, and scrape out stems, seeds, and veins with the tip of a knife. Add to the guacamole to your desired degree of hotness.

4. Add chopped tomatoes just before serving.

PER SERVING: Fat: 11 g **Protein:** 2 g **Carbohydrates:** 10 g
Sugar: 0 g

Working with Hot Chilies
Put on rubber gloves when handling hot chili peppers. They can sting, burn, and irritate the skin. Avoid touching your eyes during or after working with chilies. Be sure to wash your hands with soap and warm water right afterward.

HOMEMADE HUMMUS

CALORIES: 128
SERVES 12

1 (15-OUNCE) CAN CHICKPEAS, DRAINED
2 CLOVES GARLIC, CHOPPED, OR TO TASTE,
½ SMALL WHITE ONION, CHOPPED
1 TEASPOON TABASCO OR OTHER HOT SAUCE
½ CUP FRESH FLAT-LEAF PARSLEY, OR CILANTRO, TIGHTLY PACKED
SALT AND BLACK PEPPER TO TASTE
½ CUP OLIVE OIL

1. Blend all ingredients in the food processor or blender. Do not purée—you want a coarse consistency. Serve with bagel chips or warm pita bread.

PER SERVING: Fat: 9 g **Protein:** 2 g **Carbohydrates:** 9 g
Sugar: 2 g

All-Natural Olive Oil Spray
To make your own olive oil spray, you can buy a clean spray bottle at a hardware store and fill it with olive oil. If using a spray bottle from your house, make sure it has never contained anything that could leave a harmful residue. Use this spray as an alternative to nonstick sprays that don't taste like olive oil.

WHITE BEAN DIP

CALORIES: 281
SERVES 4

2 CLOVES GARLIC, PEELED
½ TEASPOON SALT
1½ CUPS COOKED WHITE BEANS
⅓ CUP TAHINI
2 TABLESPOONS LEMON JUICE
2 TABLESPOONS OLIVE OIL
1 TEASPOON THYME

1. Purée the garlic and salt in a food processor. Drain and add the white beans and purée to a paste.

2. Add the remaining ingredients and process until smooth, scraping down the sides of the bowl.

3. Transfer the finished purée to a bowl and serve with crackers or pita bread and carrot sticks.

PER SERVING: Fat: 18 g **Protein:** 9 g **Carbohydrates:** 22 g
Sugar: 3 g

CRUDITÉS WITH RADISH DIP

CALORIES: 76
SERVES 8

¾ CUP COTTAGE CHEESE
¼ CUP PLAIN YOGURT
1 TABLESPOON GRATED PARSNIP
4 TABLESPOONS GRATED RADISH
1 TABLESPOON CHOPPED
   PARSLEY
1 TABLESPOON CHOPPED DILL
PINCH OF TURMERIC
PINCH OF CAYENNE PEPPER
½ TEASPOON SALT
RAW VEGETABLES FOR DIPPING

1. Combine cottage cheese and yogurt in a blender or food processor.

2. Add parsnip, radish, parsley, dill, turmeric, cayenne, and salt and purée until smooth.

3. Put the dip in a bowl on a platter and surround it with assorted raw vegetables for dipping.

PER SERVING: Fat: 2 g **Protein:** 3 g **Carbohydrates:** 15 g
Sugar: 1 g

GREEN SALSA

CALORIES: 332
MAKES 1 CUP

6 TOMATILLOS, CHOPPED, HUSKS DISCARDED

4 CLOVES GARLIC, MINCED

2 JALAPEÑO PEPPERS, CORED AND CHOPPED, SEEDS INCLUDED

½ CUP SOUR CREAM

½ CUP CILANTRO

SALT TO TASTE

1. Place all ingredients in the blender and pulse until coarsely chopped. Rest in refrigerator for 2 hours. Serve chilled.

PER SERVING: Fat: 24 g **Protein:** 1 g **Carbohydrates:** 24 g **Sugar:** 2 g

Tomatillo Tutorial

Tomatillos are husked tomatoes that look like green tomatoes when their papery husk is removed. You can find them in most major supermarkets. Choose unblemished tomatillos that fully fill out their husks.

SOUR CREAM AND GORGONZOLA DIP FOR CRUDITÉS

CALORIES: 268
MAKES 1½ CUPS

¾ CUP LOW-FAT SOUR CREAM

¼ CUP GORGONZOLA CHEESE, CRUMBLED

½ TEASPOON CELERY SALT

1 TEASPOON TABASCO OR OTHER HOT SAUCE

2 TABLESPOONS LEMON JUICE

1. Pulse all ingredients in the food processor or blender; serve chilled with a selection of raw vegetables.

PER SERVING (¼ CUP): Fat: 24 g **Protein:** 8 g **Carbohydrates:** 6 g **Sugar:** 1 g

MANGO SALSA

CALORIES: 209
MAKES 1 CUP

1 MANGO, PEELED AND DICED
¼ CUP SWEET ONION, MINCED
2 TEASPOONS CIDER VINEGAR
2 JALAPEÑO PEPPERS, CORED, SEEDED, AND MINCED
JUICE OF ½ LIME
2 TABLESPOONS CILANTRO OR PARSLEY, FINELY CHOPPED
SALT TO TASTE

1. Pulse all ingredients in the food processor or blender. Turn into a bowl, chill, and serve.

PER SERVING (¼ CUP): Fat: 0 g **Protein:** 2 g **Carbohydrates:** 24 g **Sugar:** 3 g

Mango Facts

Did you know mangos are the most popular fruit in the world? They are grown in tropical climates so are available to be enjoyed year-round. In many countries mango is eaten both ripe and unripe. The unripe mango is often pickled, seasoned, or made into a sauce and served with a savory meal. Sweet, ripe mangos can be made into juice, smoothies, and fruit salads.

ITALIAN DRESSING

CALORIES: 63
MAKES 1 CUP

⅓ CUP BALSAMIC VINEGAR
½ TEASPOON DRY MUSTARD
1 TEASPOON LEMON JUICE
2 CLOVES GARLIC, CHOPPED
1 TEASPOON OREGANO, DRIED, OR 1 TABLESPOON FRESH OREGANO LEAVES
SALT AND PEPPER TO TASTE
½ CUP EXTRA-VIRGIN OLIVE OIL

1. Put all but the olive oil into the blender and blend until smooth. Whisk in the oil slowly in a thin stream. Bottle and give it a good shake before you use it!

PER SERVING (2 TABLESPOONS): Fat: 7 g **Protein:** 0 g **Carbohydrates:** 0 g **Sugar:** 0 g

FRENCH DRESSING

CALORIES: 77
MAKES 1 CUP

⅓ CUP RED-WINE VINEGAR

½ TEASPOON WORCESTERSHIRE SAUCE

1 CLOVE GARLIC, CHOPPED

2 TABLESPOONS FRESH PARSLEY, CHOPPED

1 TEASPOON THYME, DRIED

1 TEASPOON ROSEMARY, DRIED

PINCH OF SUGAR

⅔ CUP EXTRA-VIRGIN OLIVE OIL

1. Mix all ingredients except the olive oil in the blender. Slowly add the oil in a thin stream so that the ingredients will emulsify.

PER SERVING (2 TABLESPOONS): Fat: 9 g **Protein:** 0 g **Carbohydrates:** 1 g **Sugar:** 1 g

BALSAMIC VINAIGRETTE AND MARINADE

CALORIES: 76
MAKES 1 CUP

2 SHALLOTS, MINCED

2 CLOVES GARLIC, MINCED

⅓ CUP BALSAMIC VINEGAR

JUICE OF ½ LEMON

SALT AND PEPPER TO TASTE

½ TEASPOON DIJON-STYLE MUSTARD

½ CUP OLIVE OIL

1. Place all but the olive oil in the jar of the blender. With the blender running on a medium setting, slowly pour the oil into the jar. Blend until very smooth. Cover and store in the refrigerator for up to 7 days.

PER SERVING (2 TABLESPOONS): Fat: 7 g **Protein:** 0 g **Carbohydrates:** 4 g **Sugar:** 0 g

The Condiment of Kings

Mustard is one of the oldest condiments, having been used for over 3,000 years! The first mustards were made from crushed black or brown mustard seeds mixed with vinegar. In 1856, the creator of Dijon mustard, Jean Naigeon, changed the recipe into what it is today—crushed mustard seeds mixed with sour juice made from unripe grapes.

CREAMY MUSTARD DIP

CALORIES: 42
SERVES 12

⅔ CUP PLAIN NONFAT YOGURT
½ CUP 1% COTTAGE CHEESE
⅓ CUP LOW-FAT MAYONNAISE
3 TABLESPOONS DIJON MUSTARD
1 TABLESPOON YELLOW MUSTARD
⅛ TEASPOON WHITE PEPPER

1. Combine all ingredients in a blender or food processor; blend or process until smooth. Cover and refrigerate for 2 to 3 hours to blend flavors before serving.

PER SERVING: Fat: 2.50 g **Protein:** 3 g **Carbohydrates:** 4 g **Sugar:** 1.5 g

CHILI BEAN DIP

CALORIES: 56
MAKES 1½ CUPS

1 (15-OUNCE) CAN KIDNEY BEANS, RINSED AND DRAINED
2 CHIPOTLE PEPPERS IN ADOBO SAUCE, MINCED
2 TABLESPOONS ADOBO SAUCE
1 TABLESPOON RED-WINE VINEGAR
2 TEASPOONS CHILI POWDER
¼ TEASPOON CUMIN
1 TABLESPOON MINCED ONION
2 TABLESPOONS MINCED FLAT-LEAF PARSLEY

1. Using a potato masher, mash the beans until smooth but some texture remains. Stir in remaining ingredients except parsley.

2. Transfer mixture to serving bowl and sprinkle with parsley. Cover and chill for 3 to 4 hours before serving.

PER SERVING (¼ CUP): Fat: 4 g **Protein:** 8 g **Carbohydrates:** 22 g **Sugar:** 2 g

HERBED CLAM DIP

CALORIES: 120
YIELDS 1½ CUPS

1 CUP LOW-FAT COTTAGE CHEESE

1 (10-OUNCE) CAN MINCED CLAMS

⅓ CUP CHOPPED FLAT-LEAF PARSLEY

3 TABLESPOONS YOGURT CHEESE (SEE CHAPTER 2)

2 TEASPOONS DRIED BASIL LEAVES

2 TABLESPOONS MINCED ONION

1 TABLESPOON LEMON JUICE

DASH TABASCO SAUCE

⅛ TEASPOON WHITE PEPPER

1. In a food processor or blender, process cottage cheese until smooth, then transfer to small bowl.

2. Drain clams, reserving 1 tablespoon of the juice. Add clams and reserved juice to cottage cheese mixture along with parsley, yogurt cheese, and basil; mix well. Stir in remaining ingredients.

3. Cover tightly and refrigerate for 2 to 3 hours before serving.

PER SERVING (¼ CUP): Fat: 3 g **Protein:** 3 g
Carbohydrates: 6 g **Sugar:** 4 g

BAKED MUSHROOM DIP WITH SPINACH

CALORIES: 83
SERVES 6

1 TABLESPOON OLIVE OIL

24 MEDIUM BUTTON MUSHROOMS, QUARTERED

1½ CUPS FROZEN SPINACH, THAWED AND DRAINED

½ CUP WHITE SAUCE

¼ CUP SHREDDED SHARP CHEDDAR CHEESE

¼ CUP SHREDDED PART-SKIM MOZZARELLA CHEESE

⅛ TEASPOON WHITE PEPPER

1. Preheat oven to 350°F. In a large skillet over medium heat, combine olive oil and mushrooms. Cook and stir until mushrooms are tender and lightly browned, about 5 to 6 minutes. Set aside.

2. Drain spinach very well by pressing between paper towels. Line bottom of a 1-quart baking dish with the spinach. Arrange mushrooms on top. Pour white sauce over mushrooms, then sprinkle with cheeses and pepper.

3. Bake until dip is hot and bubbly and cheeses melt and begin to brown, about 20 to 25 minutes. Serve immediately.

PER SERVING: Fat: 4 g **Protein:** 2 g **Carbohydrates:** 7 g
Sugar: 1 g

LEMON PEPPER DRESSING

CALORIES: 81
SERVES 8

7 OUNCES LOW-FAT MAYONNAISE

JUICE AND MINCED RIND OF ½ LEMON

1 TEASPOON DIJON-STYLE MUSTARD

1 TEASPOON BLACK PEPPER, FRESHLY GROUND

½ TEASPOON WHITE PEPPER

½ TEASPOON RED PEPPER FLAKES

SALT TO TASTE

¼ TEASPOON ANCHOVY PASTE

1. Whisk all ingredients together and serve with chicken, salad, or cold meats.

PER SERVING: Fat: 8 g **Protein:** 0 g **Carbohydrates:** 2 g **Sugar:** 0 g

Peppercorns and Chilies

Peppercorns and chilies offer different flavors in cooking. Peppercorns are dried berries, and chilies are the hot fruit of a plant and have spicy seeds. This recipe is a wonderful marriage of pepper flavors. Use it with grilled vegetables, as well as on salads.

HOLLANDAISE SAUCE

CALORIES: 161
SERVES 6

4 OUNCES SWEET UNSALTED BUTTER

1 WHOLE EGG

1 EGG YOLK

¼ TEASPOON DRY MUSTARD

JUICE OF ½ LEMON

⅛ TEASPOON CAYENNE PEPPER

SALT TO TASTE

IN THIS RECIPE YOU CAN SUBSTITUTE VEGAN BUTTER FOR REGULAR BUTTER TO CUT BACK ON SATURATED FAT.

1. Melt the butter over very low heat. While the butter is melting, blend all but the salt in the blender or food processor.

2. With the blender running on medium speed, slowly add the butter, a little at a time. Return the sauce to a low heat and whisk until thickened. Add salt and serve immediately.

PER SERVING: Fat: 17 g **Protein:** 2 g **Carbohydrates:** 0 g **Sugar:** 0 g

Bernaise Sauce and Sauce Maltaise

If you substitute white-wine vinegar for lemon juice and add chives in this recipe, you will have Bernaise Sauce, a classic for steaks. If you substitute orange juice for lemon juice, you'll have Sauce Maltaise, which is delicious with vegetables.

SWEET AND SOUR DRESSING

CALORIES: 22
SERVES 8

- 3 OUNCES SOY SAUCE
- 1 TEASPOON ASIAN SESAME SEED OIL
- 1 TEASPOON FRESH GINGER, MINCED
- 1 TABLESPOON MAPLE SYRUP OR HONEY
- 1 TABLESPOON CONCENTRATED ORANGE JUICE
- 1 TABLESPOON APRICOT PRESERVES OR JAM
- 1 CLOVE GARLIC, MINCED
- 1 TEASPOON TABASCO SAUCE, OR TO TASTE

1. Whisk all ingredients together over low heat until well blended and serve.

PER SERVING: Fat: 1 g **Protein:** 0 g **Carbohydrates:** 4 g **Sugar:** 4 g

AIOLI

CALORIES: 99
SERVES 16

- 2 PASTEURIZED EGGS, AT ROOM TEMPERATURE
- 1 TEASPOON LEMON JUICE
- 1 TEASPOON WHITE WINE VINEGAR
- ½ TEASPOON DIJON-STYLE MUSTARD
- 4 CLOVES GARLIC, OR TO TASTE
- ¾ CUP OLIVE OIL
- CHOICE OF: ½ TEASPOON OREGANO, TARRAGON, OR ROSEMARY
- SALT AND PEPPER TO TASTE

1. Place the eggs, lemon juice, vinegar, mustard, and garlic in the blender.

2. Add the olive oil a little at a time. When the mixture is creamy, taste; add herbs, salt, and pepper. Pulse to blend; store in the refrigerator or serve.

PER SERVING: Fat: 11 g **Protein:** 1 g **Carbohydrates:** 0 g **Sugar:** 0 g

Storing Aioli
Aioli will keep in the refrigerator for a day or two, but it's best made and used the same day.

MUSTARD CREAM SAUCE (HOT)

CALORIES: 111
SERVES 4

2 TABLESPOONS OLIVE OIL

2 SHALLOTS, MINCED

1 CLOVE GARLIC, MINCED

1 TEASPOON FLOUR

⅔ CUP CHICKEN BROTH

1 OUNCE DRY VERMOUTH

1 TABLESPOON DIJON-STYLE MUSTARD, PREPARED

2 OUNCES HEAVY CREAM

SALT AND PEPPER TO TASTE

1. Heat the olive oil over medium flame. Add the shallots and garlic; sauté for 5 minutes or until soft. Whisk in the flour and cook for another 2 to 3 minutes. Whisk in the chicken broth, vermouth, and mustard.

2. Bring the sauce to a boil. Whisk in the cream and turn off heat. Taste for salt and pepper and add accordingly.

PER SERVING: Fat: 0 g **Protein:** 0 g **Carbohydrates:** 1 g **Sugar:** 0 g

---

GRILLED PEACH CHUTNEY

CALORIES: 45
SERVES 16

6 MEDIUM-SIZED FREESTONE PEACHES, HALVED AND PITTED

½ RED ONION, MINCED

2 JALAPEÑO PEPPERS, CORED, SEEDED, AND MINCED

JUICE OF 1 LIME

½ TEASPOON GROUND CLOVES

½ TEASPOON GROUND ALLSPICE

½ TEASPOON CORIANDER SEEDS, GROUND

½ CUP LIGHT BROWN SUGAR, OR TO TASTE

¼ CUP WHITE WINE VINEGAR

1 TEASPOON SALT, OR TO TASTE

FRESHLY GROUND BLACK PEPPER TO TASTE

RED PEPPER FLAKES TO TASTE

¼ BUNCH FRESH CILANTRO, CHOPPED

1. Grill the peaches, cut side down, over low flame until they are soft but not falling apart, about 5 minutes.

2. Cool them and then slip off the skins. Using a knife, cut them into chunks and place in a bowl. This method retains the juice and some texture.

3. Mix the rest of the ingredients into the bowl with the peaches. Cool, cover, and refrigerate until ready to serve. Warm just before serving.

PER SERVING: Fat: 0 g **Protein:** 0 g **Carbohydrates:** 12 g **Sugar:** 8 g

CUCUMBER, DILL, AND SOUR CREAM SAUCE

CALORIES: 62
SERVES 4

1½ CUPS CUCUMBER, PEELED AND CHOPPED

½ CUP RED ONION, CHOPPED FINE

JUICE OF 1 LEMON

1 TEASPOON TABASCO SAUCE

½ CUP LOW-FAT SOUR CREAM

1 TEASPOON CELERY SALT, OR TO TASTE

½ CUP FRESH DILL, FINELY MINCED

2 TABLESPOONS MINCED CHIVES

½ TEASPOON SWEET PAPRIKA, OR TO TASTE

1. Mix all ingredients in a bowl. Cover and refrigerate for 1 hour. Serve chilled.

PER SERVING: Fat: 4 g **Protein:** 1 g **Carbohydrates:** 10 g **Sugar:** 1 g

CAJUN REMOULADE

CALORIES: 18
MAKES 2 CUPS

3 TABLESPOONS LEMON JUICE

1 CUP LOW-FAT PLAIN GREEK YOGURT

¼ LARGE ONION, MINCED

4 GREEN ONIONS, CHOPPED

3 CLOVES GARLIC, MINCED

1½ TABLESPOONS HORSERADISH

1 TABLESPOON RELISH

2 TABLESPOONS DIJON MUSTARD

2 TABLESPOONS TOMATO PASTE

½ TEASPOON SALT

CAYENNE AND BLACK PEPPER TO TASTE

1. Mix all ingredients in a bowl using a fork or a food processor.

PER SERVING (2 TABLESPOONS): Fat: 1 g **Protein:** 1 g **Carbohydrates:** 3 g **Sugar:** 3 g

MINT CHIMICHURRI SAUCE

CALORIES: 98
MAKES 2 CUPS

¾ CUP OLIVE OIL

3 TABLESPOONS RED-WINE VINEGAR

JUICE OF 1 LEMON

3 CLOVES GARLIC, MINCED

1 LARGE SHALLOT, QUARTERED

1 TEASPOON SALT

1 SMALL JALAPEÑO, SEEDED AND CHOPPED

2 CUPS FRESH PARSLEY

2 CUPS FRESH CILANTRO

1 CUP FRESH MINT

IN THIS RECIPE YOU CAN SUBSTITUTE LOW-FAT MAYONNAISE FOR REGULAR MAYONNAISE AND USE COOKING SPRAY INSTEAD OF CANOLA OIL.

1. Wash herbs, remove stems and chop leaves.

2. In a blender, add olive oil, vinegar, lemon juice, garlic, shallots, salt, and jalapeño; blend ingredients together. Add parsley, cilantro, and mint to the blender in batches and blend until sauce is smooth.

PER SERVING (¼ cup): Fat: 10 g **Protein:** 0 g **Carbohydrates:** 2 g **Sugar:** 0 g

TARTAR SAUCE

CALORIES: 84
SERVES 26

1 CUP CANOLA OIL

5 TABLESPOONS WHITE VINEGAR

1 TABLESPOON SCALLION TOPS, CHOPPED

2 TABLESPOONS LOW-FAT MAYONNAISE

2 HARD-BOILED EGG YOLKS

1. Beat canola oil and white vinegar. Add scallion tops, mayonnaise, and egg yolk mixture. Beat until smooth.

PER SERVING: Fat: 9 g **Protein:** 0 g **Carbohydrates:** 0 g **Sugar:** 0 g

Tartar Sauce History
Tartar sauce was invented by the French, who served it with raw steak. Over time, this raw steak became known as Steak Tartare because of the tartar sauce.

BEEF HORSERADISH

CALORIES: 13
SERVES 40

2 CUPS FAT-FREE SOUR CREAM

¼ CUP HORSERADISH, DRAINED

1 TEASPOON MINCED CHIVES

1 TEASPOON WHITE WINE VINEGAR

SALT AND PEPPER TO TASTE

1. Combine all ingredients in medium-size bowl and blend well. Chill until ready to serve.

PER SERVING: Fat: 0 g **Protein:** 1 g **Carbohydrates:** 2 g **Sugar:** 0 g

BAKED FISH SAUCE

CALORIES: 20
SERVES 27

1 TABLESPOON BUTTER

1 ONION, CHOPPED

1 TABLESPOON FLOUR

3 SLICES AMERICAN CHEESE

1½ CUPS SKIM MILK

1. Melt butter in a deep skillet over medium heat.

2. Add in the onion and flour, mixing as you go.

3. Add the cheese and milk. Cook until cheese is melted and sauce is thick.

PER SERVING: Fat: 2 g **Protein:** 1 g **Carbohydrates:** 1 g **Sugar:** 1 g

RED-WINE BUTTER SAUCE

CALORIES: 13
SERVES 18

½ CUP RED WINE
½ CUP LOW-SODIUM BEEF STOCK
1 TABLESPOON FLOUR
1 TABLESPOON BUTTER
½ CUP RED WINE
½ CUP LOW-SODIUM BEEF STOCK

1. Sauté butter and flour until smooth in a deep skillet over medium heat.

2. Blend in wine. Blend in beef stock. Thicken sauce, then remove from heat and serve.

PER SERVING: Fat: 1 g **Protein:** 0 g **Carbohydrates:** 1 g **Sugar:** 0 g

MINCEMEAT-STYLE CHUTNEY

CALORIES: 14
SERVES 48

1 CUP DICED SWEET ONION
1 CUP PEELED AND DICED GRANNY SMITH APPLES
1 CUP PEELED AND DICED BANANAS
1 CUP PEELED AND DICED PEACHES
¼ CUP RAISINS
¼ CUP DRIED CRANBERRIES
¼ CUP DRY WHITE WINE
¼ CUP APPLE CIDER VINEGAR
1 TEASPOON BROWN SUGAR
½ TEASPOON CINNAMON
½ TEASPOON PUMPKIN PIE SPICE
⅛ TEASPOON FRESHLY GROUND BLACK PEPPER
⅛ TEASPOON DRIED LEMON GRANULES, CRUSHED

1. In a large saucepan, combine all the ingredients and cook over low heat for about 1 hour, stirring occasionally. Let cool completely. Can be kept for 1 week in the refrigerator or in the freezer for 3 months.

PER SERVING: Fat: 0 g **Protein:** 0 g **Carbohydrates:** 4 g **Sugar:** 2 g

Chutney Choices

Chutney is also good if made with your choice of curry powder instead of the cinnamon and pumpkin pie spice. Or, for a zesty change of pace, you can substitute your choice of chili powder for the pumpkin pie spice.

ARTICHOKE PESTO

CALORIES: 37
SERVES 48

¾ CUP CANOLA OIL

3 TEASPOONS MINCED GARLIC

⅓ CUP LEMON JUICE

1 TEASPOON CRUSHED THYME

1 BAY LEAF

SALT AND PEPPER TO TASTE

1 (14-OUNCE) CAN ARTICHOKE HEARTS

½ CUP PACKED FRESH BASIL LEAVES, CHOPPED

1. Preheat oven to 350°F.

2. Combine ½ cup oil, lemon juice, garlic, thyme, bay leaf, salt, and pepper in a medium-size bowl. Add artichoke hearts and mix. Transfer ingredients to a deep skillet and cook over stove until boiling, stirring occasionally.

3. Transfer ingredients to an ovenproof dish or bake pan, cover with foil, and put into oven for 30 minutes. Allow mixture to cool and remove bay leaf.

4. Put all ingredients into blender with ¼ cup oil and basil leaves. Blend until smooth.

PER SERVING: Fat: 4 g **Protein:** 0 g **Carbohydrates:** 1 g **Sugar:** 0 g

Pesto Uses

This pesto tastes excellent spread over toasted ciabatta bread or mixed in with any type of pasta. Try baking homemade pizza with pesto sauce instead of tomato sauce for a tangier flavor. Commercial pesto sauce is easy to find in grocery stores, but it's almost as easy to make your own; making your own also gives you control over the ingredients and the calorie count.

COUNTRY BARBECUE SAUCE

CALORIES: 118
SERVES 8

- 4 CLOVES GARLIC, CHOPPED
- 2 LARGE YELLOW ONIONS, CHOPPED
- 2 SWEET RED PEPPERS, CORED, SEEDED, AND CHOPPED
- 2 SERRANO CHILI PEPPERS, CORED, SEEDED, AND MINCED (OPTIONAL)
- 2 TABLESPOONS OLIVE OIL
- 1 TEASPOON SALT, OR TO TASTE
- 2 TEASPOONS BLACK PEPPER
- 1 TEASPOON TABASCO SAUCE, OR TO TASTE
- 2 OUNCES CIDER VINEGAR
- 2 TABLESPOONS DIJON-STYLE PREPARED MUSTARD
- 1 (28-OUNCE) CAN TOMATO PURÉE
- 2 TABLESPOONS MOLASSES
- 1 TEASPOON LIQUID SMOKE
- 4 WHOLE CLOVES
- 1 CINNAMON STICK
- 1 TEASPOON HOT PAPRIKA
- 1 TABLESPOON SWEET PAPRIKA

1. In a large soup pot, sauté the garlic, onions, and peppers in olive oil. Stirring constantly, add the rest of the ingredients. Bring to a boil. Reduce heat.

2. Cover the pot and simmer for 2 hours. If you don't like the texture, purée in the blender.

PER SERVING: Fat: 4 g **Protein:** 3 g **Carbohydrates:** 18 g **Sugar:** 3 g

Sweet, Spicy, or Both

The amount of heat you add to barbeque sauce is a matter of personal taste, as is the amount of sweetness. Some people prefer the flavor of honey over molasses; others use brown sugar. Experiment!

CHIPOTLE-POBLANO SAUCE

CALORIES: 18
SERVES 10

6 CHIPOTLE PEPPERS
1 POBLANO PEPPER
½ CUP BOILING WATER
½ TEASPOON CUMIN SEED
½ TEASPOON DRIED MEXICAN
   OREGANO
1 TABLESPOON DRIED MINCED
   ONION
1 TEASPOON ONION POWDER
2 TEASPOONS ROASTED GARLIC
   POWDER
1 TABLESPOON OLIVE OIL
PINCH OF SALT

1. Remove the stems and seeds from the peppers, and slit the peppers lengthwise. Roast in a heavy skillet over medium-high heat, turning them occasionally; heat until puffed and just beginning to get brown, about 10 seconds each. (Do not burn the peppers or the resulting sauce will be bitter.) As they're done, put the peppers in a bowl.

2. Pour the boiling water over the peppers; let soak for 15 minutes. (If you wish to peel the peppers, remove them from the water with a slotted spoon and do so before completing step 4.)

3. Dry-roast the cumin and oregano in the skillet until fragrant, being careful that the oregano doesn't burn.

4. Add all the ingredients to the bowl of a food processor or blender container. Process until mixed, yet still chunky. Leftovers can be stored for several days in the refrigerator.

PER SERVING: Fat: 2 g **Protein:** 1 g **Carbohydrates:** 1 g
Sugar: 0 g

YOGURT CHEESE SPINACH DIP

CALORIES: 62
SERVES 8

2 CUPS PLAIN LOW-FAT YOGURT
½ CUP FINELY CHOPPED ONION
2 CLOVES GARLIC, MINCED
1 TABLESPOON OLIVE OIL
2 CUPS FRESH SPINACH
½ TEASPOON SALT
⅛ TEASPOON CAYENNE PEPPER
2 TABLESPOONS LEMON JUICE

1. The day before you want to serve the dip, place the yogurt in a strainer lined with cheesecloth or a coffee filter. Rest the strainer over a deep bowl, cover both with plastic wrap, and let stand in the refrigerator overnight.

2. The next day, remove the yogurt cheese from the strainer; save the whey for another use.

3. In a heavy saucepan, cook onion and garlic in olive oil over medium heat until tender, about 5 minutes. Coarsely chop the spinach and add to the pan; cook and stir until spinach is wilted and water has evaporated, about 3–4 minutes. Remove from heat and sprinkle with salt, cayenne pepper, and lemon juice. Remove to a medium-size mixing bowl; let stand until cool, about 45 minutes. Blend in the yogurt cheese. Serve immediately or cover and chill for up to 3 days.

PER SERVING: Fat: 3 g **Protein:** 4 g **Carbohydrates:** 6 g **Sugar:** 6 g

SPAGHETTI SAUCE

CALORIES: 125
SERVES 6

2 TABLESPOONS OLIVE OIL

1 ONION, CHOPPED

4 CLOVES GARLIC, MINCED

1 CUP CHOPPED CELERY

1 (8-OUNCE) PACKAGE SLICED MUSHROOMS

1 (6-OUNCE) CAN NO-SALT TOMATO PASTE

2 (14-OUNCE) CANS NO-SALT DICED TOMATOES, UNDRAINED

1 TABLESPOON DRIED ITALIAN SEASONING

½ CUP GRATED CARROTS

⅛ TEASPOON WHITE PEPPER

½ CUP DRY RED WINE

½ CUP WATER

1. In a large saucepan, heat olive oil over medium heat. Add onion and garlic; cook and stir until crisp-tender, about 4 minutes. Add celery and mushrooms; cook and stir for 2–3 minutes longer.

2. Add tomato paste; let paste brown a bit without stirring (this adds flavor to the sauce). Then add remaining ingredients and stir gently but thoroughly.

3. Bring sauce to a simmer, then reduce heat to low and partially cover. Simmer for 60–70 minutes, stirring occasionally, until sauce is blended and thickened. Serve over hot cooked pasta, couscous, or rice.

PER SERVING: Fat: 5 g **Protein:** 2 g **Carbohydrates:** 15 g **Sugar:** 5 g

Freezing Spaghetti Sauce

Spaghetti sauce freezes beautifully, and it is suitable for all sorts of casseroles and soups in addition to just serving it over spaghetti. To freeze, portion 4 cups into a hard-sided freezer container, leaving about 1" of head space for expansion. Seal, label, and freeze for up to 3 months. To thaw, let stand in fridge overnight, then heat in saucepan.

CHAPTER 4

Sides and Snacks

CRISP POLENTA WITH TOMATO SAUCE

CALORIES: 229
SERVES 8

- 1 RECIPE CHEESE POLENTA (SEE BELOW)
- 1 CUP SHREDDED PART-SKIM MOZZARELLA CHEESE
- 3 CUPS SPAGHETTI SAUCE, HEATED

1. Prepare polenta as directed, except when done, pour onto a greased cookie sheet; spread to a ½"-thick rectangle, about 9" × 15". Cover and chill until very firm, about 2 hours.

2. Preheat broiler. Cut polenta into fifteen 3" squares. Place on a broiler pan; broil for 4–6 minutes or until golden brown. Carefully turn polenta and broil for 3–5 minutes or until golden brown.

3. Remove from oven and sprinkle with mozzarella cheese. Top each with a dollop of the hot spaghetti sauce and serve immediately.

PER SERVING: Fat: 8 g **Protein:** 7 g **Carbohydrates:** 30 g **Sugar:** 3 g

CHEESE POLENTA

CALORIES: 131
SERVES 6

- ¼ TEASPOON SALT
- 3 CUPS WATER
- 1 CUP SKIM MILK
- 1¼ CUPS YELLOW CORNMEAL
- 1 TABLESPOON BUTTER OR PLANT STEROL MARGARINE
- ¼ CUP GRATED PARMESAN CHEESE
- ¼ CUP SHREDDED HAVARTI CHEESE
- ½ TEASPOON CRUSHED RED PEPPER FLAKES

1. In large saucepan, combine salt and water and bring to a boil. In small bowl, combine milk with cornmeal and mix until smooth.

2. Slowly add the cornmeal mixture to the boiling water, stirring constantly with a wire whisk. Cook over medium-low heat, stirring constantly, until polenta is very thick, about 5–10 minutes. Stir in butter, cheeses, and red pepper flakes. Serve immediately.

PER SERVING: Fat: 5 g **Protein:** 6 g **Carbohydrates:** 21 g **Sugar:** 2 g

CHILI FRIES

CALORIES: 225
SERVES 4

4 RUSSET POTATOES
2 TABLESPOONS OLIVE OIL
2 TABLESPOONS CHILI POWDER
1 TABLESPOON GRILL SEASONING
1 TEASPOON GROUND CUMIN
1 TEASPOON PAPRIKA
¼ TEASPOON PEPPER

1. Preheat oven to 425°F. Scrub potatoes and pat dry; cut into ½" strips, leaving skin on. A few strips won't have any skin. Toss with olive oil and arrange in a single layer on a large cookie sheet.

2. In small bowl, combine remaining ingredients and mix well. Sprinkle over potatoes and toss to coat. Arrange in single layer.

3. Bake for 35–45 minutes, turning once during baking time, until potatoes are deep golden brown and crisp. Serve immediately.

PER SERVING: Fat: 5 g **Protein:** 4 g **Carbohydrates:** 30 g **Sugar:** 0 g

Grill Seasoning
Grill seasoning mixes usually contain pepper, garlic, salt, and a bit of sugar, along with spices like oregano and rosemary. There are quite a few different varieties, from Cajun spice to chili lime to chipotle.

EDAMAME

CALORIES: 115
SERVES 6

6 CUPS OF WATER
½ TEASPOON SALT
1 POUND FROZEN EDAMAME IN PODS

1. Bring the water and the salt to a boil in a saucepan.

2. Add the edamame and let the water come back to a boil.

3. Cook on medium-high for 5 minutes.

4. Drain the edamame and rinse with cold water.

5. Drain again and serve either warm or cool.

PER SERVING: Fat: 5 g **Protein:** 10 g **Carbohydrates:** 8 g **Sugar:** 0 g

SESAME GREEN BEANS

CALORIES: 119
SERVES 4

1 POUND FRESH GREEN BEANS 1
TABLESPOON SESAME OIL
1 TEASPOON SALT
¼ TEASPOON PEPPER
¼ CUP SESAME SEEDS

1. Trim the stem ends off the green beans.

2. Add the green beans to boiling water and cook them for 5 minutes.

3. Drain the beans and plunge them into ice water. Drain them again.

4. Heat a sauté pan over medium heat and add the sesame oil to it. Sauté the beans in the sesame oil for 3 minutes.

5. Season the beans with salt and pepper and sprinkle the sesame seeds over them. Serve hot.

PER SERVING: Fat: 8 g **Protein:** 4 g **Carbohydrates:** 10 g **Sugar:** 2 g

PEAS WITH BUTTER LETTUCE

CALORIES: 111
SERVES 4

2 CUPS FRESH OR FROZEN BABY
PEAS
6 BUTTER LETTUCE LEAVES
2 TABLESPOONS BUTTER
SALT TO TASTE
¼ TEASPOON WHITE PEPPER

1. Cook the peas in boiling water until tender.

2. Cut the butter lettuce into shreds and sauté it in the butter until limp.

3. Add the peas to the lettuce and season with salt and pepper.

PER SERVING: Fat: 6 g **Protein:** 4 g **Carbohydrates:** 10 g **Sugar:** 1 g

ROASTED GARLIC SPINACH

CALORIES: 104
SERVES 4

¼ CUP PEELED GARLIC CLOVES
1 TABLESPOON OLIVE OIL
2 TABLESPOONS BUTTER
4 CUPS FRESH BABY SPINACH LEAVES
1 TEASPOON SALT
¼ TEASPOON PEPPER
PINCH OF NUTMEG

1. Preheat oven to 400°F. Toss the garlic cloves in olive oil. Put them on a piece of foil in a baking dish and roast in the oven for about 30 minutes.

2. When the garlic is done, melt the butter in a sauté pan and add the spinach. Sauté the spinach in the butter for about 10 minutes over medium-high heat.

3. Add the roasted garlic cloves to the spinach and season with salt, pepper, and nutmeg. Serve hot.

PER SERVING: Fat: 9 g **Protein:** 2 g **Carbohydrates:** 4 g
Sugar: 0 g

SWEET AND SOUR RED CABBAGE

CALORIES: 206
SERVES 4

1 RED CABBAGE, SHREDDED
1 LARGE ONION, SLICED
2 PEELED APPLES, SLICED
2 TABLESPOONS BACON FAT
1 TABLESPOON SUGAR
1 CUP APPLE JUICE
1 CUP RED-WINE VINEGAR
2 TEASPOONS SALT
1 TEASPOON PEPPER

1. Preheat oven to 350°F.

2. Layer cabbage, onion, and apples in a baking dish.

3. Heat bacon fat, sugar, juice, and vinegar in a saucepan to a simmer.

4. Pour hot liquid over cabbage; then sprinkle cabbage with salt and pepper. Toss to combine.

5. Cover and bake cabbage in oven for 2 hours, until tender.

PER SERVING: Fat: 7 g **Protein:** 4 g **Carbohydrates:** 37 g
Sugar: 8 g

SUMMER SWISS CHARD

CALORIES: 132
SERVES 4

- 1 POUND SWISS CHARD
- 3 TABLESPOONS OLIVE OIL
- 1 CUP DICED ONION
- PINCH OF SALT
- ½ TEASPOON OREGANO
- 3 TABLESPOONS RED-WINE VINEGAR
- SALT AND PEPPER TO TASTE

1. Chop the chard and set aside.

2. Heat the olive oil in a skillet over medium heat.

3. Add the diced onion, a pinch of salt, and oregano and cook until the onions are tender.

4. Add the chopped chard and sauté for a few minutes and then remove from heat.

5. Stir in the vinegar and season with salt and pepper.

PER SERVING: Fat: 11 g **Protein:** 3 g **Carbohydrates:** 8 g **Sugar:** 0 g

BEETS WITH BEET GREENS

CALORIES: 238
SERVES 4

- 16 BABY BEETS, GREENS ATTACHED
- 2 TABLESPOONS BUTTER
- 1 TABLESPOON FRESH LEMON JUICE
- ½ TEASPOON SALT

1. Wash beets but don't peel them.

2. Bring about 3 inches of water to a boil and then put the beets, root down, into boiling water. The beet roots will be in the water and the greens will cook in the steam above the water.

3. Cover and cook for 12 minutes. Drain and cut the greens off the roots.

4. Chop the greens and peel the roots. The skin will slip off easily.

5. Put the beets, greens, and roots in a saucepan and add butter, lemon juice, and salt. Warm them over low heat and serve hot.

PER SERVING: Fat: 7 g **Protein:** 10 g **Carbohydrates:** 41 g **Sugar:** 12 g

BAKED FENNEL

CALORIES: 75
SERVES 6

3 FENNEL BULBS
1 CUP CHICKEN BROTH
¼ CUP CRUMBLED GORGONZOLA CHEESE
¼ CUP PANKO BREAD CRUMBS
SALT AND PEPPER TO TASTE

1. Cut the fennel bulbs in half lengthwise through the root end.

2. Put the fennel cut-side down in a skillet and add the chicken broth. Cover and simmer for 20 minutes.

3. Preheat oven to 375°F. Place cooked fennel bulbs in a baking dish, cut-sides up.

4. Mix the Gorgonzola with the bread crumbs and divide the mixture evenly on the top of each fennel bulb.

5. Bake for 25 minutes, season with salt and pepper, and serve hot.

PER SERVING: Fat: 2 g **Protein:** 3 g **Carbohydrates:** 12 g **Sugar:** 1 g

YAMS WITH COCONUT MILK

CALORIES: 266
SERVES 4

3 POUNDS SWEET POTATOES
1 CUP COCONUT MILK
¼ CUP SHREDDED COCONUT
½ CUP CHOPPED MACADAMIA NUTS

1. Preheat the oven to 350°F.

2. Peel sweet potatoes and slice them into ½"-thick rounds.

3. Overlap the sweet potato slices in one layer in a baking dish.

4. Pour the coconut milk over the sweet potatoes, then sprinkle them with coconut and macadamia nuts.

5. Bake them uncovered for 60 minutes.

PER SERVING: Fat: 15 g **Protein:** 4 g **Carbohydrates:** 32 g **Sugar:** 5 g

Yams versus Sweet Potatoes

Yams and sweet potatoes are so close that they can be used interchangeably in cooking. Sweet potatoes are a rich orange inside and have a deeper brown skin. They're also by far the sweeter of the two. To add extra flavor and nutrition, sprinkle them with nuts, cook them with apples, and mix them with sweet green peas.

BROCCOLI RABE WITH LEMON AND CHEESE

CALORIES: 81
SERVES 4

- 1 QUART WATER
- 1 TEASPOON SALT
- ½ CUP LOOSELY PACKED BROCCOLI RABE, ENDS TRIMMED
- 2 TABLESPOONS OLIVE OIL
- 2 CLOVES GARLIC, CHOPPED
- 1 TABLESPOON LEMON JUICE
- SALT AND PEPPER TO TASTE
- 2 TABLESPOONS PARMESAN CHEESE

1. Bring the water to a boil; add salt and broccoli rabe. Reduce heat and simmer for 6 to 8 minutes. Drain and shock under cold water and dry on paper towels.

2. Heat olive oil over medium-low heat and sauté the garlic for 5 minutes. Cut the broccoli rabe stems in 2" pieces and add to the garlic and olive oil. Sprinkle with lemon juice, salt, and pepper. Serve the Parmesan cheese at the table.

PER SERVING: Fat: 8 g **Protein:** 2 g **Carbohydrates:** 2 g
Sugar: 0 g

WILD RICE WITH WALNUTS AND APPLES

CALORIES: 417
SERVES 4

- 2 CUPS WILD RICE, COOKED TO PACKAGE DIRECTIONS
- 2 SHALLOTS
- 1 TART APPLE, PEELED, CORED, AND CHOPPED
- ¼ CUP OLIVE OIL
- ½ CUP WALNUTS, TOASTED
- SALT AND PEPPER TO TASTE

1. While the rice is cooking, sauté the shallots and apple in the olive oil over medium heat for 5 minutes. Just before serving, mix all ingredients together.

PER SERVING: Fat: 32 g **Protein:** 8 g **Carbohydrates:** 31 g
Sugar: 3 g

LIMA BEAN SUCCOTASH

CALORIES: 248
SERVES 4

¾ CUP CREAM
1 CUP FROZEN COOKED BABY LIMA BEANS
1½ CUPS CORN KERNELS
1 TABLESPOON BUTTER
SALT AND PEPPER TO TASTE

1. Heat the cream in a saucepan over medium-high heat and reduce by half.

2. Add the lima beans and corn and turn the heat to low.

3. Cover and cook for 10 minutes.

4. Stir in butter and season to taste with salt and pepper.

5. Remove from heat and serve hot.

PER SERVING: Fat: 15 g **Protein:** 6 g **Carbohydrates:** 25 g **Sugar:** 10 g

COUSCOUS TABOULI

CALORIES: 332
SERVES 4

1½ CUPS WATER
1 CUP COUSCOUS
⅓ CUP LEMON JUICE
2 TABLESPOONS CHOPPED FRESH MINT
1 TEASPOON SALT
1 TEASPOON PEPPER
¼ CUP EXTRA-VIRGIN OLIVE OIL
1 CUP CHOPPED FRESH PARSLEY
½ CUP CHOPPED GREEN ONIONS
2 LARGE TOMATOES, DICED
½ CUP DICED CUCUMBER
1 TABLESPOON MINCED GARLIC

1. Bring the water to a boil in a saucepan, add the couscous, cover, remove from heat, and let sit 5 minutes to absorb the liquid.

2. Fluff the couscous with a fork and put it in a large bowl to let it cool.

3. Add the remaining ingredients to the couscous and mix well.

4. Let sit at room temperature for 60 minutes or refrigerate overnight.

5. Serve chilled or at room temperature.

PER SERVING: Fat: 12 g **Protein:** 7 g **Carbohydrates:** 42 g **Sugar:** 2 g

BAKED SWEET POTATOES

CALORIES: 441
SERVES 4

- **4 MEDIUM SWEET POTATOES**
- **4 OUNCES SOFT UNSALTED BUTTER**
- **½ TEASPOON SALT**
- **¼ TEASPOON WHITE PEPPER**
- **¼ TEASPOON CINNAMON**
- **½ CUP CHOPPED PEANUTS**
- **¼ CUP CHOPPED CHIVES**

1. Preheat oven to 400°F. Scrub the sweet potatoes and poke them all over with a fork or paring knife. Bake directly on the oven rack for 45–60 minutes.

2. Mix the soft butter with the salt, white pepper, and cinnamon.

3. Split the baked potatoes and top with the butter, peanuts, and chives.

PER SERVING: Fat: 31 g **Protein:** 7 g **Carbohydrates:** 37 g **Sugar:** 5 g

---

BAGEL CHIPS

CALORIES: 26
MAKES 12 CHIPS

- **2 WHOLE-WHEAT OR PUMPERNICKEL BAGELS**
- **OLIVE OIL SPRAY**
- **GARLIC SALT AND PEPPER TO TASTE**

1. Thinly slice the bagels crosswise, discarding the tiny ends.

2. Spread the pieces on a baking sheet. Spray with olive oil and sprinkle with garlic salt and pepper.

3. Bake at 350°F for 10 minutes. Serve as crackers.

PER SERVING: Fat: 0 g **Protein:** 1 g **Carbohydrates:** 5 g **Sugar:** 0 g

Fresh Garlic Rub
Try this: Take a large clove of garlic, cut it in half, and rub the cut side all over the surface of the bagels. Rubbing garlic is a technique that can be used on breads as well as chicken and beef.

POLENTA WITH BROCCOLI RABE

CALORIES: 74
SERVES 4

1 POUND BROCCOLI RABE
1 QUART BOILING, SALTED WATER
2 TABLESPOONS OLIVE OIL
2 CLOVES GARLIC, MINCED
JUICE OF ½ LEMON
RED PEPPER FLAKES TO TASTE
BASIC POLENTA

1. Rinse the broccoli rabe and cut in 1½" pieces, trimming off very bottoms of stems.

2. Drop the broccoli rabe into the boiling water and cook for 5 minutes. Shock in cold water. Drain thoroughly.

3. Heat the olive oil and add garlic; sauté over medium heat for a few minutes; add the lemon juice, pepper flakes, and drained broccoli rabe. Cook and stir until well coated.

4. Serve over hot polenta.

PER SERVING: Fat: 7 g **Protein:** 1 g **Carbohydrates:** 3 g **Sugar:** 0 g

ROASTED CHICKPEAS WITH PARMESAN

CALORIES: 100
SERVES 2

½ CUP CANNED CHICKPEAS, DRAINED
2 TABLESPOONS FRESHLY GRATED PARMESAN CHEESE
FEW DROPS HOT SAUCE
PITA BREAD CRISPS

1. Mash chickpeas with fork in a small bowl or mix in a blender until smooth.

2. Mix Parmesan cheese with chickpea mixture.

3. Add hot sauce and blend well. Serve with pita bread crisps.

PER SERVING: Fat: 3 g **Protein:** 6 g **Carbohydrates:** 14 g **Sugar:** 2 g

Roasted Chickpeas

Roasted chickpeas make a tasty snack on their own. They come in many flavors, and they are good sources of iron, calcium, antioxidants, and protein. They have less fat than peanuts, but be careful to buy low-sodium chickpeas to avoid excess salt.

BROCCOLI CHEDDAR RICE

CALORIES: 437
SERVES 4

- ¼ CUP OLIVE OIL
- ½ CUP DICED ONION
- 1 CUP LONG-GRAIN WHITE RICE
- 2 CUPS CHOPPED FRESH BROCCOLI
- 1¾ CUPS CHICKEN BROTH
- ½ TEASPOON SALT
- ¼ TEASPOON GROUND PEPPER
- 1 CUP GRATED CHEDDAR CHEESE

1. Preheat oven to 350°F.

2. Heat olive oil in a saucepan and sauté the onion in it until tender.

3. Add rice and sauté for 3–5 minutes with the onion. Stir the broccoli into the rice mixture.

4. Pour the rice mixture into a 9" × 13" glass baking dish. Add chicken broth, salt, pepper, and cheese. Stir to incorporate. Cover with foil and bake for 45 minutes.

PER SERVING: Fat: 24 g **Protein:** 12 g **Carbohydrates:** 42 g **Sugar:** 1 g

---

SKINNY BAKED POTATO

CALORIES: 190
SERVES 1

- 1 SMALL BAKED POTATO
- 2 TABLESPOONS FAT-FREE SOUR CREAM
- ½ CUP SALSA

1. Prick the potato several times with a fork, then place on a plate.

2. Bake potato in microwave for about 5 minutes on each side until soft.

3. Cut potato in half lengthwise and place 1 tablespoon of sour cream on each half.

4. Top with salsa.

PER SERVING: Fat: 1 g **Protein:** 7 g **Carbohydrates:** 42 g **Sugar:** 4 g

OVEN-FRIED POTATO WEDGES

CALORIES: 328
SERVES 4

OLIVE OIL SPRAY

4 LARGE BAKING POTATOES, WASHED AND CUT INTO 6 WEDGES EACH

¾ TEASPOON FRESHLY GROUND BLACK PEPPER

1 TEASPOON GARLIC POWDER

½ TEASPOON DRIED ROSEMARY, CRUSHED

½ TEASPOON DRIED LEMON GRANULES, CRUSHED

1. Preheat the oven to 400°.

2. Spray a baking sheet with the olive oil spray. Arrange the potato wedges on the sheet. Spray the potatoes with a thin layer of the olive oil spray. Sprinkle the potatoes with the pepper, garlic powder, rosemary, and lemon granules.

3. Bake for 30 to 35 minutes, turning the potatoes to the other cut side after 20 minutes. Bake until the potatoes are lightly browned, crisp outside, and tender inside.

PER SERVING: Fat: 1 g **Protein:** 7 g **Carbohydrates:** 60 g **Sugar:** 3 g

---

CARROTS WITH AN ENGLISH ACCENT

CALORIES: 70
SERVES 4

SPRAY OIL WITH BUTTER FLAVOR

¼ CUP WATER

1 TEASPOON LEMON JUICE

4 CUPS BABY CARROTS, SLICED

1 TEASPOON ENGLISH SPICE BLEND

1. Preheat oven to 350°.

2. Treat an ovenproof casserole dish with the spray oil. Add the water and lemon juice, and stir to combine. Spread the carrot slices over the water-lemon mixture. Mist the carrots with the spray oil. Sprinkle the seasoning over the carrots. Cover and bake for 45 minutes. Mist the carrots again with the spray oil, if desired. Uncover and bake for an additional 10 minutes or until the carrots are tender.

PER SERVING: Fat: 0 g **Protein:** 2 g **Carbohydrates:** 15 g **Sugar:** 3 g

SWEET POTATO MASH

CALORIES: 204
SERVES 4

- **4 MEDIUM-SIZE SWEET POTATOES, PEELED AND CUBED**
- **2 TEASPOONS LEMON JUICE**
- **4 TEASPOONS UNSALTED BUTTER**
- **¼ TEASPOON GROUND CUMIN**
- **¼ TEASPOON GROUND CINNAMON**
- **¼ TEASPOON DRIED GINGER**
- **¼ TEASPOON CHIPOTLE POWDER OR OTHER SALT-FREE CHILI POWDER (OPTIONAL)**
- **½ CUP SKIM MILK**

1. Put the sweet potatoes in a saucepan. Cover with cold water. Add the lemon juice. Bring to a boil over medium heat. Cover and cook for 7–10 minutes, until the potatoes are fork tender. Once the sweet potatoes are fully cooked, drain the water from the pot and place them in a medium-size bowl.

2. Melt the butter in the saucepan over medium heat. Add the cumin, cinnamon, ginger, and chipotle powder; sauté the spices for 30 seconds. Add the milk and bring to a boil. Pour over the cooked sweet potatoes. Mix together using a masher or wooden spoon. Serve immediately.

PER SERVING: Fat: 4 g **Protein:** 4 g **Carbohydrates:** 38 g **Sugar:** 3 g

HERB-SEASONED ROASTED RED ONIONS

CALORIES: 68
SERVES 4

- **4 MEDIUM-SIZE RED ONIONS**
- **NONSTICK COOKING SPRAY**
- **¼ TEASPOON SALT**
- **4 TEASPOONS UNSALTED BUTTER**
- **⅛ TEASPOON DRIED THYME**
- **⅛ TEASPOON DRIED PARSLEY**
- **⅛ TEASPOON DRIED BASIL**
- **⅛ TEASPOON DRIED ROSEMARY**

1. Preheat oven to 400°.

2. Remove the first layer of skin from the onions. Use a knife to cut off the bottom of the core end of the onion to give it a flat base. Make two cross-shaped cuts in the top of each onion, cutting halfway down. Stand the onions up in a ovenproof baking pan treated with nonstick spray. Sprinkle the onions with the salt, trying to get some into each "gap."

3. In a small bowl, mix together the butter, thyme, parsley, basil, and rosemary. Divide the butter between the onions, placing it in the cross-cut slits of each onion.

4. Bake for 30–35 minutes or until the onions are tender.

PER SERVING: Fat: 4 g **Protein:** 2 g **Carbohydrates:** 10 g **Sugar:** 0 g

FRENCH-GLAZED GREEN BEANS

CALORIES: 127
SERVES 4

¼ CUP CHOPPED WALNUTS

4 TEASPOONS COLD-PRESSED WALNUT OR CANOLA OIL

2 (15-OUNCE) CANS FRENCH-CUT GREEN BEANS

1 TEASPOON LEMON JUICE

1 TEASPOON HONEY

1 TEASPOON FRENCH SPICE BLEND

⅛ TEASPOON DRIED LEMON GRANULES, CRUSHED

⅛ TEASPOON MUSTARD POWDER

⅛ TEASPOON FRESHLY GROUND BLACK PEPPER

1. Bring a large, deep nonstick sauté pan to temperature over medium heat. Add the walnuts. Toast for 3 minutes, stirring frequently so the walnuts don't burn. Transfer to a bowl and set aside.

2. Add the walnut oil to the pan. Drain the green beans and add to the pan; stir to toss in the oil. Once the green beans are brought to temperature, push them to the sides of the pan. Add the lemon juice, honey, spice blend, lemon granules, mustard powder, and pepper; stir to combine. Toss the green beans in the lemon juice mixture. Pour into a serving bowl and top with the toasted walnuts.

PER SERVING: Fat: 10 g **Protein:** 3 g **Carbohydrates:** 10 g **Sugar:** 2 g

---

SPICE AND HONEY NUTS

CALORIES: 220
SERVES 16

2 CUPS WALNUT HALVES

2 CUPS PECAN HALVES

3 TABLESPOONS BUTTER

¼ CUP HONEY

⅓ CUP BROWN SUGAR

1 TEASPOON CINNAMON

1 TEASPOON GINGER

½ TEASPOON CARDAMOM

⅛ TEASPOON CAYENNE PEPPER

1. Preheat oven to 375°F. Spread walnuts and pecans on large cookie sheet and toast for 8–12 minutes or until the nuts are fragrant, stirring once during cooking time.

2. In small saucepan, combine butter, honey, and remaining ingredients over medium heat. Cook, stirring frequently, just until mixture comes to a boil. Drizzle over nuts, tossing to coat. Reduce oven temperature to 325°F. Bake nuts for 15–20 minutes, stirring every 5 minutes, until glazed. Cool completely, then break apart and store in airtight container.

PER SERVING: Fat: 19 g **Protein:** 3 g **Carbohydrates:** 12 g **Sugar:** 11 g

Nut Nutrition

Some nuts are better than others! The type of nuts that may help reduce the risk of heart disease include almonds, peanuts, pecans, pistachio nuts, walnuts, and hazelnuts. They are a high-fat food, but the type of fat is monounsaturated, which can help lower LDL ("bad") cholesterol.

POTATO SOUFFLÉ

2 YUKON GOLD POTATOES
WATER, AS NEEDED
1 TABLESPOON OLIVE OIL
⅛ TEASPOON NUTMEG
¼ TEASPOON ONION SALT
⅛ TEASPOON CAYENNE PEPPER
⅓ CUP FAT-FREE HALF-AND-HALF
¼ CUP GRATED PARMESAN CHEESE
4 EGG WHITES
¼ TEASPOON CREAM OF TARTAR
NONSTICK COOKING SPRAY
1 CUP CHOPPED GRAPE TOMATOES
¼ CUP CHOPPED FRESH BASIL

1. Preheat oven to 450°F. Peel and thinly slice potatoes, adding to a pot of cold water as you work. Bring potatoes to a boil over high heat, reduce heat, and simmer until tender, about 12–15 minutes.

2. Drain potatoes and return to hot pot; shake for 1 minute. Add olive oil, nutmeg, onion salt, and pepper and mash until smooth. Beat in the half-and-half and Parmesan cheese.

3. In large bowl, combine egg whites with cream of tartar and beat until stiff peaks form. Stir a dollop of the egg whites into the potato mixture and stir. Then fold in remaining egg whites.

4. Spray the bottom of a 2-quart casserole dish with nonstick cooking spray. Spoon potato mixture into casserole. Bake for 20 minutes, then reduce heat to 375°F and bake for another 12–17 minutes or until soufflé is golden brown and puffed.

5. While soufflé is baking, combine tomatoes and basil in small bowl and mix gently. Serve immediately with tomato mixture for topping the soufflé.

PER SERVING: Fat: 9 g **Protein:** 9 g **Carbohydrates:** 15 g
Sugar: 1 g

Cooking Potatoes

When cooking potatoes, place them in cold water to cover as you are peeling or chopping them. Potatoes can turn brown very quickly, and this slows the process. Do not overcook potatoes; cook them just until they are tender when pierced with a knife. Drain well and shake in the hot pot to remove excess moisture.

MINI HOT-PEPPER PIZZAS

CALORIES: 242
SERVES 4

4 WHOLE-WHEAT ENGLISH MUFFINS, SPLIT

1 TABLESPOON OLIVE OIL

2 CLOVES GARLIC, MINCED

1 RED BELL PEPPER, DICED

2 JALAPEÑO PEPPERS, MINCED

⅛ TEASPOON PEPPER

½ TEASPOON DRIED OREGANO LEAVES

½ CUP PART-SKIM RICOTTA CHEESE

¼ CUP GRATED PARMESAN CHEESE

1. Preheat oven to broil. Place English muffins, split side up, on a broiler pan. Broil 6" from heat source until lightly toasted, about 3–5 minutes. Remove from oven and set aside.

2. In medium skillet, heat olive oil over medium heat. Add garlic, red pepper, and jalapeño peppers. Cook and stir until tender, about 5 minutes. Sprinkle with pepper and oregano.

3. Stir ricotta into vegetable mixture; spread on the English muffin halves. Sprinkle with Parmesan. Broil 6" from heat source for 5–8 minutes or until pizzas are hot and topping bubbles and begins to brown. Let cool for 5 minutes, then serve.

PER SERVING: Fat: 9 g **Protein:** 3 g **Carbohydrates:** 15 g **Sugar:** 2 g

English Muffins

English muffins are a great choice for sandwiches or a pizza base. Split the muffins with a fork to create peaks and ridges that hold ingredients and become crunchy when toasted or grilled. Whole-wheat or whole-grain English muffins are readily available. They do spoil rather quickly, so freeze them after the first day.

STUFFED ONIONS

CALORIES: 235
SERVES 4

- 2 LARGE SWEET ONIONS
- 1 TABLESPOON OLIVE OIL
- 2 OUNCES COOKED AND CRUMBLED BREAKFAST SAUSAGE
- 2 OUNCES SHREDDED MONTEREY JACK CHEESE
- 3 TABLESPOONS BREAD CRUMBS
- 1 TABLESPOON CHOPPED FRESH HERBS
- 2 TABLESPOONS CHOPPED GREEN CHILIES
- SALT AND PEPPER TO TASTE
- 1 EGG, BEATEN
- 1 CUP ENCHILADA OR TOMATO SAUCE, WARMED

1. Preheat the oven to 350°F. Cut the onions in half horizontally and peel them.

2. Bring a pot of salted water to boil and cook the onions for 12 minutes. Drain and take out the center of each onion, creating four onion cups. Put the cups in a baking dish that has been brushed with olive oil. Set aside.

3. Chop the centers of the onions and sauté them in olive oil. Transfer them to a bowl and add the sausage, cheese, bread crumbs, herbs, green chilies, salt, and pepper. Mix well, add the egg, and mix again.

4. Make four balls out of the stuffing and put one in each onion cup.

5. Cover and bake for 20 minutes. Uncover and bake for 10 more minutes. Serve hot with enchilada or tomato sauce spooned on top.

PER SERVING: Fat: 14 g **Protein:** 11 g **Carbohydrates:** 17 g **Sugar:** 1 g

Herbs and Crumbs

For toppings of broiled, grilled, or baked vegetables, herbs and crumbs are absolutely the most interesting and versatile ways to turn ho-hum into mouthwateringly delicious. Take some left-over whole-grain bread and put it in the food processor with seasoned salt, oregano, and Parmesan cheese, and let it grind away. Sprinkle over grilled vegetables.

COLCANNON

1 POUND KALE

1 TABLESPOON OLIVE OIL

3 LARGE POTATOES, ABOUT 3 POUNDS

2 TEASPOONS KOSHER SALT

4 TABLESPOONS BUTTER

⅓ CUP MILK

½ TEASPOON WHITE PEPPER

1. Pull the stems off the kale and discard. Chop the greens and sauté them in olive oil over medium heat for 15 minutes. Take them off the heat and reserve.

2. Peel potatoes and cut them into 2" pieces. Put potato pieces in a pot with cold water to cover and 1 teaspoon salt.

3. Turn heat to medium-high and bring potatoes and water to a boil. Turn down to a simmer and cook until the potatoes can be easily pierced with a fork, about 15 minutes.

4. Drain potatoes in a colander, then put them in a bowl and mash them with a potato masher, or put them through a ricer. Add butter and milk and mix to a creamy consistency. Season with 1 teaspoon salt and the white pepper.

5. Add the sautéed kale to the mashed potatoes and fold it in. Serve hot.

PER SERVING: Fat: 17 g **Protein:** 8 g **Carbohydrates:** 37 g **Sugar:** 1 g

ROASTED CORN ON THE COB

CALORIES: 198
SERVES 8

8 EARS OF FRESH SWEET CORN, UNSHUCKED
¼ TEASPOON GARLIC SALT
PINCH OF LEMON PEPPER SEASONING
PINCH OF SEASONED SALT
PINCH OF CHILI POWDER
PINCH OF DRIED MIXED HERBS
½ CUP MELTED BUTTER
¼ CUP KOSHER SALT

1. Pull the corn silk out of the tops of the corn and then peel the husks down far enough to clean the rest of the silk, but leave the husks attached. Pull the husks back up around the corn. Put them in a roasting pan and fill it with water. Let the corn soak for 10 minutes so the husks won't burn in the oven. The moisture will also help create steam.

2. Preheat the oven to 400°F.

3. Drain the water from the corn and put it in a single layer on cookie sheets.

4. Roast the corn in the oven for 45 minutes. Remove from the oven and peel the husks back from the cobs to make a handle at the bottom.

5. Add the garlic salt, lemon pepper, seasoned salt, chili powder, and mixed herbs to the melted butter. Brush the corn with butter-spice mixture and place on a platter. Serve hot with kosher salt for sprinkling.

PER SERVING: Fat: 13 g **Protein:** 5 g **Carbohydrates:** 35 g **Sugar:** 6 g

Corn
Try stuffing a tomato with corn and baking it, melting some Cheddar cheese on top and into the corn filling. Make corn relish with vinegar, honey, and spices. You can easily add this special vegetable to your diet regularly.

EGGPLANT WITH ROMESCO SAUCE

CALORIES: 335
SERVES 4

- 1 EGGPLANT
- 3 TABLESPOONS KOSHER SALT
- 6 OUNCES ROASTED RED BELL PEPPER
- ¼ CUP TOASTED SLICED ALMONDS
- 1 CLOVE PEELED GARLIC
- 1½ TEASPOONS RED-WINE VINEGAR
- 1½ TEASPOONS PAPRIKA
- ¼ TEASPOON CAYENNE PEPPER
- ½ TEASPOON SALT
- ½ CUP OLIVE OIL, DIVIDED USE

1. Slice the eggplant into ½"-thick rounds and place them in a colander over a bowl or in the sink. Sprinkle kosher salt over the eggplant and let sit for 30 minutes.

2. Meanwhile, make the romesco sauce by putting the roasted red bell peppers in a food processor with the almonds, garlic, vinegar, paprika, cayenne pepper, and salt. Purée and then add ¼ cup olive oil while the motor is running.

3. Rinse the eggplant rounds and drain them on paper towels. Blot them dry and brush them with remaining olive oil.

4. Grill the eggplant on a preheated grill or grill pan for about 5 minutes per side.

5. Place half of the grilled eggplant on a platter and spoon half of the sauce over it. Top with the remaining eggplant rounds and spoon the remaining sauce over the top.

PER SERVING: Fat: 31 g **Protein:** 3 g **Carbohydrates:** 11 g **Sugar:** 0 g

Eggplant Facts

Any big eggplant will do for frying or baking. Most cooks today find the tiny eggplants and their wonderful range of colors easier to deal with because they don't need soaking to reduce the bitterness of large eggplants.

QUINOA PILAF

CALORIES: 280
SERVES 4

¼ CUP UNSALTED BUTTER
½ CUP DICED ONION
¼ CUP DICED CARROTS
¼ CUP DICED CELERY
1 CUP QUINOA
1 ½ CUPS CHICKEN BROTH
½ TEASPOON SALT
¼ TEASPOON WHITE PEPPER
1 BAY LEAF

1. Preheat oven to 350°F.

2. Melt butter in a saucepan and sauté the onion, carrots, and celery in it until tender.

3. Add quinoa and sauté for 3–5 minutes with the vegetables.

4. Pour mixture into a baking dish, add chicken broth, salt, pepper, and bay leaf and stir to incorporate.

5. Cover and bake for 45 minutes. Remove bay leaf before serving.

PER SERVING: Fat: 14 g **Protein:** 6 g **Carbohydrates:** 32 g
Sugar: 0 g

Quinoa

South American natives cultivated quinoa and had rituals to thank their creator for the miraculously sustaining food. This led the Spanish to prohibit the people from growing it in the seventeenth and eighteenth centuries. Terraced mountain slopes covered with cultivated quinoa were burned, and people starved. Enough seeds were secretly stored that quinoa, prized for its ability to grow on the chilly slopes of the Andes, is back.

98   500 UNDER 500

ROASTED GREEN BEANS WITH PINE NUTS

CALORIES: 99
SERVES 6

2 POUNDS GREEN BEANS, TRIMMED

NONSTICK COOKING SPRAY

2 OUNCES PROSCIUTTO OR BACON, THINLY SLICED

2 TEASPOONS OLIVE OIL

4 CLOVES GARLIC, MINCED

2 TEASPOONS FRESH SAGE, MINCED

¼ TEASPOON SALT

FRESH GROUND PEPPER TO TASTE

¼ CUP PINE NUTS, TOASTED

1 TEASPOON LEMON ZEST

1. Boil water in a large pot. Add green beans to pot and simmer until crisp-tender, about 4 minutes. Drain green beans and set aside.

2. Spray a large pan with cooking spray and place over medium heat. Add prosciutto and cook, stirring, until crisp. Transfer prosciutto to a paper towel to blot excess oil.

3. Add 2 teaspoons oil to the large pan and return to medium heat. Add green beans, garlic, sage, half of the salt, and pepper to the pan. Cook until the green beans begin to slightly brown.

4. Add in the pine nuts, lemon zest, and prosciutto; season with remaining salt and additional pepper.

PER SERVING: Fat: 5 g **Protein:** 5 g **Carbohydrates:** 10 g
Sugar: 2 g

Toasting Nuts and Seeds

Place nuts or seeds in a dry skillet over medium-low heat and cook for 3 to 5 minutes. Nuts will have a nutty scent and be slightly browned.

SESAME CORN WAFERS

CALORIES: 89
SERVES 16

- 1 CUP MASA HARINA
- 2 TABLESPOONS WHITE CORNMEAL
- 1 TEASPOON SALT
- ½ CUP BOILING WATER
- 1 TABLESPOON BUTTER
- ½ CUP SESAME SEEDS
- 2 CUPS CANOLA OIL
- MORE SALT, IF DESIRED

1. Combine masa harina, cornmeal, and salt in large bowl. Add boiling water and butter and stir until a soft dough forms. You may need to add another tablespoon or so of boiling water. Divide dough into 5 equal pieces. Roll out each piece to ⅛" thickness, about a 6" x 6" rectangle, between two sheets of plastic wrap. Remove the top sheet of plastic wrap, sprinkle with some of the sesame seeds and press seeds into the dough. Cut the dough into 1" x ½" pieces. Repeat with remaining dough.

2. Place oil in heavy saucepan and heat over medium high heat to 375°F. Fry chips, about a fourth at a time, until light golden brown. Remove to paper towels, sprinkle with salt, and let cool. Store covered in airtight container.

3. These can also be baked. Add another 1½ to 2 cups of boiling water to the masa harina mixture to make a batter. Drop by teaspoonfuls onto silicone-lined cookie sheets and sprinkle with sesame seeds. Bake at 450°F for 11–14 minutes or until chips are golden brown.

PER SERVING: Fat: 7 g **Protein:** 2 g **Carbohydrates:** 7 g **Sugar:** 2 g

Masa Harina

Masa harina is not cornmeal; it is corn flour. You can find it in the ethnic foods aisle of most supermarkets and in Mexican and Hispanic markets. It is very finely ground so the dough will hold together. There is no gluten in corn flour, so you can reroll scraps as long as you want to; they won't get tough.

CURRIED COUSCOUS

CALORIES: 365
SERVES 6

1 TABLESPOON UNSALTED BUTTER
1 TEASPOON CURRY POWDER
1½ CUPS COUSCOUS
1½ CUPS BOILING WATER
¼ CUP PLAIN NONFAT YOGURT
¼ CUP EXTRA-VIRGIN OLIVE OIL
1 TEASPOON WHITE WINE VINEGAR
¼ TEASPOON GROUND TURMERIC
¼ TEASPOON LEMON ZEST
1 TEASPOON FRESHLY GROUND BLACK PEPPER
½ CUP DICED CARROTS
½ CUP MINCED FRESH PARSLEY
½ CUP RAISINS
¼ CUP BLANCHED, SLICED ALMONDS
2 SCALLIONS, WHITE AND GREEN PARTS THINLY SLICED
¼ CUP DICED RED ONION
1½ TEASPOONS SESAME SALT

1. In a small nonstick skillet, melt the butter until sizzling, then add the curry powder. Stir for several minutes, being careful not to burn the butter. Place the couscous in a medium-size bowl. Pour enough of the boiling water into the pan with the sautéed curry powder to mix it with the water and rinse out the pan. Pour that and the remaining boiling water over the couscous. Cover tightly and allow the couscous to sit for 5 minutes. Fluff with a fork.

2. Mix together the yogurt, olive oil, vinegar, turmeric, lemon zest, and pepper; pour over the fluffed couscous, and mix well. Add the carrots, parsley, raisins, almonds, scallions, red onion, and sesame salt; mix well. Serve at room temperature.

PER SERVING: Fat: 14 g **Protein:** 10 g **Carbohydrates:** 46 g **Sugar:** 4 g

Curry It Up

There's a big difference in taste between "raw" curry powder and that which has been toasted or sautéed. Sautéing curry powder boosts the flavors, releasing the natural aromatic oils in the spices.

GOLDEN DELICIOUS RISOTTO

CALORIES: 345
SERVES 4

4–5 CUPS WATER

NONSTICK COOKING SPRAY

2 TABLESPOONS EXTRA-VIRGIN OLIVE OIL

2 TABLESPOONS MINCED ONION OR SHALLOT

1 CUP ARBORIO RICE (SHORT-GRAIN WHITE RICE)

2 MEDIUM-SIZE GOLDEN DELICIOUS APPLES, PEELED, CORED, AND DICED

¾ TEASPOON LOW-SODIUM CHICKEN BASE

¼ TEASPOON SAUTÉED VEGETABLE BASE

⅓ CUP DRY WHITE WINE

2 TABLESPOONS UNSALTED BUTTER

2 TABLESPOONS GRATED PARMESAN CHEESE

FRESHLY GRATED NUTMEG (OPTIONAL)

1. In medium-size saucepan, heat the water to boiling; reduce heat to maintain a steady simmer.

2. In large nonstick sauté pan treated with nonstick spray, bring the olive oil to temperature over medium heat; add the onion (or shallot) and sauté for 3 minutes. Add the rice and half of the diced apple; sauté, stirring well, for 3 minutes. Add the bases and stir to dissolve. Add the wine and stir until the wine evaporates.

3. Stirring, ladle in enough of the water to just cover the rice (about ¾ cup). Lower the heat to maintain a steady simmer and cook the rice, stirring constantly, until almost all of the water has been absorbed, about 4 minutes.

4. Continue adding water ½ cup at a time, stirring, and cooking until absorbed. (The simmering water is added in small increments because you only want to use as much as is necessary for the rice to absorb before it's cooked; humidity and differences in burner temperature can make the difference in the amount of water needed.) After 15 minutes, stir in the remaining diced apples. The rice is done when it is creamy yet firm in the center (al dente). Total cooking time will be around 25 to 30 minutes.

5. Remove pan from heat; stir in the butter and Parmesan cheese. Serve immediately; grate nutmeg over the top of each serving.

PER SERVING: Fat: 13 g **Protein:** 5 g **Carbohydrates:** 45 g **Sugar:** 2 g

Rice and Broth Basics

When you prepare traditional rice, the ratio of liquid to rice is usually 2 parts to 1. It's more than double that for risotto, so it's important to keep that in mind. Even using all low-sodium broth may make the risotto too salty when you consider that the liquid from 4 or more cups of it are being absorbed or evaporated for each cup of rice you prepare. While you can use low-sodium chicken, mushroom, vegetable, or any other broth that will complement the rice and the rest of your meal, it's usually sufficient to use 1 cup of broth and 3 cups of water for every cup of rice when preparing risotto.

BUTTERNUT SQUASH CHEESE MUFFINS

CALORIES: 85
SERVES 12

- **1 TABLESPOON UNSALTED BUTTER**
- **1 TABLESPOON EXTRA-LIGHT OLIVE OIL OR CANOLA OIL**
- **1 CUP CHOPPED SWEET ONION**
- **1 CUP SLICED BUTTON MUSHROOMS**
- **¼ CUP WATER**
- **2 CUPS BUTTERNUT SQUASH, ROASTED AND CUBED**
- **6 TABLESPOONS UNBLEACHED ALL-PURPOSE FLOUR**
- **3 TABLESPOONS OAT BRAN OR WHEAT GERM**
- **2 LARGE EGGS**
- **¼ TEASPOON FRESHLY GROUND BLACK PEPPER**
- **½ CUP GRATED JARLSBERG CHEESE**
- **1 TABLESPOON HULLED SESAME SEEDS**

1. Preheat oven to 400°F.

2. Add the butter and oil to a nonstick sauté pan over high heat. When the butter begins to sizzle, reduce heat to medium and add the onion and mushrooms. Sauté until the onion is transparent. Set aside to cool.

3. In the bowl of a food processor or in a blender, combine the cooled sautéed mixture and all of the remaining ingredients *except* the cheese and sesame seeds; pulse until mixed.

4. Fold the cheese into the squash mixture. Spoon the resulting batter into muffin cups treated with nonstick spray (or lined with foil muffin liners), filling each muffin section to the top. Evenly divide the sesame seeds over the top of the batter. Bake for 35–40 minutes. (For savory appetizers, make 24 mini-muffins; bake for 20 to 25 minutes.)

PER SERVING: Fat: 5 g **Protein:** 4 g **Carbohydrates:** 9 g **Sugar:** 3 g

BAKED STUFFED TOMATOES

CALORIES: 114
SERVES 4

- 1 ¼ CUPS CHOPPED PARSLEY
- 3 SMALL CLOVES GARLIC, FINELY CHOPPED
- PINCH OF RED PEPPER FLAKES
- ¾ CUP BREAD CRUMBS
- OLIVE OIL SPRAY
- 10 PLUM TOMATOES, CUT IN HALF LENGTHWISE AND SEEDED
- ½ TEASPOON FRESHLY GROUND BLACK PEPPER
- ¼ TEASPOON DRIED LEMON GRANULES, CRUSHED
- ½ CUP WATER

1. Preheat oven to 400°.

2. In the bowl of a food processor, combine the parsley, garlic, red pepper flakes, and bread crumbs; pulse to chop and mix. Set aside.

3. Prepare a casserole dish or baking pan large enough to hold the tomato halves side by side by spraying it with the olive oil spray. Fill the tomato halves with the bread crumb mixture and place them in the dish or pan. Spray a light layer of the olive oil spray over the tops of the filled tomatoes. Sprinkle the pepper and lemon granules over the top of the bread crumbs.

4. Add ½ cup water to the bottom of the pan. Cover tightly with an aluminum foil tent. Bake for 45 minutes or until the tomatoes are tender.

5. Remove the aluminum foil. Place the pan under the broiler and broil until crisp and slightly browned, about 2 minutes. (Watch closely so the bread crumbs don't burn!)

PER SERVING: Fat: 2 g **Protein:** 5 g **Carbohydrates:** 24 g **Sugar:** 2 g

Using Less Fat

When you use cold-pressed vegetable oil in a recipe that calls for butter, you can usually reduce the amount of oil you use by 25 percent. In other words, if the recipe calls for 1 teaspoon of butter, you'll only need to use ¾ teaspoon of oil.

CHAPTER 5

Salads

WILD RICE SALAD

CALORIES: 232
SERVES 4

- 2 CUPS COOKED WILD RICE, WARM
- ¼ CUP DICED YELLOW BELL PEPPER
- 1 TABLESPOON MINCED SHALLOTS
- ¼ CUP DRIED CRANBERRIES
- ½ CUP CHOPPED WALNUTS
- 2 TABLESPOONS BALSAMIC VINEGAR
- 1 TABLESPOON WALNUT OIL
- SALT AND PEPPER TO TASTE

1. Mix everything together while the wild rice is still warm. This allows the rice to absorb more flavor.

2. Chill mixture.

3. Adjust seasoning and serve cold.

PER SERVING: Fat: 12 g **Protein:** 7 g **Carbohydrates:** 26 g **Sugar:** 5 g

Wild Rice

For years wild rice was harvested by hand by Native Americans in the lake country of northwestern United States and Canada. Watch for the rice to go from spikes to blooms. It's loaded with fiber and flavor. Plus, you can add dried berries, prunes, apricots, and nuts to give it extra flavor.

ORANGE AND ONION SALAD

CALORIES: 116
SERVES 4

- 2 NAVEL ORANGES
- 1 BLOOD ORANGE
- 1 SMALL RED ONION, PEELED
- 2 TABLESPOONS OLIVE OIL
- 2 TEASPOONS LIME JUICE
- SALT AND PEPPER TO TASTE
- 1 TABLESPOON CHOPPED FRESH PARSLEY

1. Cut the top and bottom off the oranges and stand them up on their cut ends. With a small serrated knife, cut away the rind in strips. Remove as much white pith as you can.

2. Turn the oranges on their sides and cut crosswise into the slices. Arrange the orange slices on a plate.

3. Cut slices from the onion crosswise and scatter them across the orange slices.

4. Put the olive oil, lime juice, salt, pepper, and parsley in a jar with a lid and shake the ingredients to combine.

5. Pour the vinaigrette over the oranges and onions and serve at room temperature or chilled.

PER SERVING: Fat: 7 g **Protein:** 2 g **Carbohydrates:** 16 g **Sugar:** 1 g

FIG AND PARMESAN CURL SALAD

CALORIES: 284
SERVES 2

- 4 FRESH FIGS, CUT IN HALVES OR 4 DRIED FIGS, PLUMPED IN 1 CUP BOILING WATER AND SOAKED FOR ½ HOUR
- 2 CUPS FRESH BABY SPINACH, STEMS REMOVED
- ¼ CUP OLIVE OIL
- JUICE OF ½ LEMON
- 2 TABLESPOONS BALSAMIC VINEGAR
- 1 TEASPOON HONEY
- 1 TEASPOON DARK BROWN MUSTARD
- SALT AND PEPPER TO TASTE
- 4 LARGE CURLS OF PARMESAN CHEESE

1. When the figs (if dried) are softened, prepare the spinach and arrange both on serving dishes.

2. Whisk the olive oil, lemon juice, balsamic vinegar, honey, mustard, salt, and pepper together. Make Parmesan curls with a vegetable peeler and drizzle with dressing.

PER SERVING: Fat: 16 g **Protein:** 11 g **Carbohydrates:** 30 g **Sugar:** 12 g

A Hidden Gem
Figs are a wonderfully nutritious food. Not only are they high in fiber and minerals, they also add tons of flavor to any recipe. Some cultures even claim that figs have medicinal value and healing potential.

BROCCOLI SLAW

CALORIES: 169
SERVES 4

- 3 CUPS BLANCHED BROCCOLI FLORETS
- ¼ CUP SHREDDED CARROT
- 2 TABLESPOONS MAYONNAISE
- 1 TEASPOON DIJON MUSTARD
- 1 TABLESPOON RED-WINE VINEGAR
- 1 TABLESPOON MINCED SHALLOTS
- ¼ CUP GOLDEN RAISINS
- ½ CUP TOASTED SLICED ALMONDS
- SALT AND PEPPER, TO TASTE

1. Mix all ingredients together.

2. Refrigerate at least 60 minutes before serving.

PER SERVING: Fat: 11 g **Protein:** 4 g **Carbohydrates:** 15 g **Sugar:** 2 g

LENTIL SALAD

CALORIES: 287
SERVES 4

- 1 (1-POUND) BAG LENTILS (GREEN, YELLOW, OR RED)
- 1 MEDIUM ONION, CHOPPED
- ½ CUP WINE VINEGAR
- SALT
- 1 DICED CARROT
- 2 STALKS CELERY, CHOPPED
- 2 MEDIUM TOMATOES, SLICED
- 1 CUP FRENCH DRESSING (SEE CHAPTER 3)

1. Cover the lentils with water and add onion and wine vinegar. Bring to a boil, lower heat, and simmer until soft. Sprinkle with salt.

2. Toss with diced carrot and chopped celery and arrange tomatoes around mound of lentils. Sprinkle with French dressing and serve warm or at room temperature.

PER SERVING: Fat: 20 g **Protein:** 7 g **Carbohydrates:** 25 g **Sugar:** 2 g

A Note About Lentils
Due to their small size, lentils cook faster than other beans and legumes. Dried lentils can keep well in the pantry for up to one year.

COLESLAW

CALORIES: 167
SERVES 4

- 3 CUPS SHREDDED CABBAGE
- ¼ CUP SHREDDED CARROT
- ¼ CUP GREEN ONION, SLICED ON THE BIAS
- ¼ CUP CANOLA OIL
- 1 TEASPOON SESAME OIL
- 2 TABLESPOONS RICE VINEGAR
- 1 TABLESPOON SESAME SEEDS
- SALT AND PEPPER, TO TASTE

1. Mix all ingredients together.

2. Refrigerate at least 60 minutes before serving.

PER SERVING: Fat: 16 g **Protein:** 1 g **Carbohydrates:** 4 g **Sugar:** 1 g

CUCUMBER SALAD WITH YOGURT AND DILL

CALORIES: 109
SERVES 2

2 LARGE CUCUMBERS

1 CUP PLAIN LOW-FAT YOGURT

1 TABLESPOON WHITE-WINE VINEGAR

2 TABLESPOONS FRESH DILL, FINELY CHOPPED

SALT AND PEPPER TO TASTE

1. Wash and peel cucumbers; chop into ¼" thick slices.

2. Combine cucumber with yogurt, vinegar, dill, salt, and pepper.

3. Serve chilled.

PER SERVING: Fat: 2 g **Protein:** 8 g **Carbohydrates:** 15 g **Sugar:** 5 g

Making a Cucumber Raita

This recipe may be modified to make raita, an Indian cuisine condiment. Chop the cucumber into ¼" cubes. Substitute the dill with 2 tablespoons chopped mint leaves; add a minced garlic clove and cayenne pepper to taste.

AVOCADO AND SHRIMP SALAD

CALORIES: 200
SERVES 4

24 RAW SHRIMP

2 TABLESPOONS OLIVE OIL

4 WHOLE GREEN ONIONS, SLICED

2 GARLIC CLOVES, FINELY MINCED

2 TABLESPOONS DRY WHITE WINE

SALT AND PEPPER TO TASTE

1 RED GRAPEFRUIT

8 OUNCES OF BUTTER LETTUCE, WASHED AND TORN INTO BITE-SIZE PIECES

1 RIPE AVOCADO, SLICED

1. Peel and devein the shrimp.

2. In a pan set over medium-high heat, add the olive oil. Add shrimp and half of the green onions to hot pan. Cook stirring frequently until shrimp are cooked half through. Add minced garlic and white wine to the pan; cook for an additional minute; adding salt and pepper.

3. Cut grapefruit in half and set one half to the side. Add in juice of half grapefruit to the pan; cook for 2 to 3 minutes. Cut the peel off the remaining grapefruit half and slice fruit into bite-size pieces.

4. Place lettuce, avocado slices, and remaining green onions on salad plates for serving. Transfer cooked shrimp to plates.

5. Drizzle sauce from pan over top and garnish with remaining grapefruit slices.

PER SERVING: Fat: 13 g **Protein:** 10 g **Carbohydrates:** 13 g **Sugar:** 2 g

ARUGULA AND FENNEL SALAD WITH POMEGRANATE

CALORIES: 224
SERVES 4

- 2 LARGE NAVEL ORANGES
- 1 POMEGRANATE
- 4 CUPS ARUGULA
- 1 CUP FENNEL, THINLY SLICED
- 4 TABLESPOONS OLIVE OIL
- SALT AND PEPPER TO TASTE

1. Cut the tops and bottoms off of the oranges and then cut the remaining peel away from the oranges. Slice each orange into 10–12 small pieces.

2. Remove seeds from the pomegranate.

3. Place arugula, orange pieces, pomegranate seeds, and fennel slices into a large bowl.

4. Coat the salad with olive oil and season with salt and pepper as desired.

PER SERVING: Fat: 15 g **Protein:** 3 g **Carbohydrates:** 24 g **Sugar:** 7 g

Fennel

Fennel, a crunchy and slightly sweet vegetable, is a popular Mediterranean ingredient. Fennel has a white or greenish-white bulb and long stalks with feathery green leaves stemming from the top. Fennel is closely related to cilantro, dill, carrots, and parsley.

FLANK STEAK SALAD

CALORIES: 253
SERVES 4

- 1 POUND FLANK STEAK, THINLY SLICED
- SALT AND PEPPER TO TASTE
- 1 TABLESPOON CANOLA OIL
- 1 TEASPOON GARLIC, MINCED
- 1 TEASPOON OREGANO
- 2 TABLESPOONS RED-WINE VINEGAR
- 1 TABLESPOON MARGARINE
- 1 (12-OUNCE) BAG ITALIAN SALAD BLEND

1. Season the flank steak pieces with salt and pepper.

2. Heat the canola oil in a skillet. Sauté flank steak pieces until cooked through.

3. Stir in the garlic, oregano, and vinegar.

4. Add the margarine to the skillet and let it melt.

5. Add the salad greens to the skillet. Stir for about 30 seconds.

6. Transfer all ingredients to a plate and serve.

PER SERVING: Fat: 15 g **Protein:** 25 g **Carbohydrates:** 4 g **Sugar:** 0 g

SINFULLY THIN SALAD

CALORIES: 213
SERVES 4

1 HEAD BOSTON LETTUCE

2 TABLESPOONS ARTIFICIAL BACON PIECES

1 TEASPOON SPLENDA

4 TABLESPOONS RED-WINE VINEGAR

6 TABLESPOONS CANOLA OIL

SALT AND PEPPER TO TASTE

1. Wash, dry, and separate leaves of Boston lettuce.

2. Combine lettuce with the rest of the ingredients.

3. Serve immediately.

PER SERVING: Fat: 22 g **Protein:** 2 g **Carbohydrates:** 4 g
Sugar: 0 g

Serving Lettuce

It's not a good idea to marinate anything with lettuce because the leaves will take on too much water and oil and get soggy. Dress the lettuce immediately before serving or leave the salad naked and let people add as much or as little dressing as they like.

CUCUMBER AND RED ONION SALAD

CALORIES: 288
SERVES 4

2 LARGE CUCUMBERS

2 CUPS SALTED WATER

1 LARGE RED ONION, SLICED INTO THIN RINGS

¼ CUP CIDER VINEGAR

½ CUP CANOLA OIL

SALT AND PEPPER TO TASTE

1 TEASPOON SPLENDA

1. Peel cucumbers, halve them, and scoop out the seeds.

2. Slice cucumber and place in a bowl with salted water for 20 minutes.

3. Drain cucumber slices.

4. Combine cucumber slices and onion slices.

5. Add the rest of the ingredients; refrigerate until ready to serve.

PER SERVING: Fat: 28 g **Protein:** 1 g **Carbohydrates:** 10 g
Sugar: 1 g

TEXAS CAVIAR

CALORIES: 224
SERVES 8

- 1 POUND BLACK-EYED PEAS
- 1½ CUPS ITALIAN SALAD DRESSING
- 1 CUP WHITE CORN
- 2 CUPS RED BELL PEPPERS, DICED
- 1½ CUPS ONION, DICED
- 1 CUP GREEN ONIONS, FINELY CHOPPED
- ½ CUP JALAPEÑO PEPPERS, FINELY CHOPPED
- 1 TABLESPOON GARLIC, FINELY CHOPPED
- SALT AND HOT PEPPER SAUCE TO TASTE

1. Soak peas in enough water to cover for 6 hours or overnight. Drain well.

2. Transfer peas to saucepan. Add water to cover. Place over high heat and bring to boil. Let boil until tender, about 40 minutes; do not overcook.

3. Drain peas well. Transfer peas to a large bowl. Stir in dressing and let cool.

4. Add all remaining ingredients and mix well.

PER SERVING: Fat: 13 g **Protein:** 4 g **Carbohydrates:** 25 g **Sugar:** 3 g

Time-Saving Tip
You can substitute 2 (12-ounce) cans of black-eyed peas for one pound of dried peas and use your favorite bottled salad dressing to speed up the preparation time. The final result will turn out just as well.

EXOTIC FRUIT SALAD

CALORIES: 110
SERVES 6

- 1 BLOOD ORANGE, RIND REMOVED AND CUT INTO SEGMENTS
- ½ CUP POMEGRANATE SEEDS
- 1 KIWI FRUIT, PEELED AND CUT INTO ROUNDS
- ½ CUP BLUEBERRIES
- ½ CUP QUARTERED STRAWBERRIES
- ½ CUP FRESH PINEAPPLE CHUNKS
- ½ CUP PEELED MANGO CHUNKS
- ¼ CUP CHOPPED CANDIED GINGER
- ¼ CUP SHREDDED COCONUT

1. Gently toss everything but the ginger and coconut in a large bowl.

2. Chill salad before serving.

3. Sprinkle the ginger and coconut on the salad and serve on individual plates or in one large bowl.

PER SERVING: Fat: 2 g **Protein:** 1 g **Carbohydrates:** 24 g **Sugar:** 5 g

SOUTHWESTERN CORN SALAD

CALORIES: 383
SERVES 4

- 2 CUPS FROZEN OR CANNED CORN
- ¾ CUP CUCUMBER, SEEDED AND DICED
- ½ CUP RED ONION, MINCED
- 1 (14-OUNCE) CAN DICED TOMATOES
- 6 SCALLIONS, CHOPPED
- 4 TABLESPOONS NONFAT SOUR CREAM
- ¼ CUP CIDER VINEGAR
- ½ CUP CANOLA OIL
- SALT AND PEPPER TO TASTE

1. Combine corn, cucumbers, onions, and tomatoes in a salad bowl.

2. Separately combine the rest of the ingredients.

3. Add the dressing to the salad and toss.

4. Cover and refrigerate until cooled.

PER SERVING: Fat: 29 g **Protein:** 5 g **Carbohydrates:** 32 g
Sugar: 6 g

PEAR AND WATERCRESS SALAD

CALORIES: 198
SERVES 4

- 2 PEARS
- 3 TABLESPOONS CANOLA OIL
- 1½ TABLESPOONS APPLE CIDER VINEGAR
- SALT AND PEPPER TO TASTE
- 1 TEASPOON WHOLE-GRAIN MUSTARD
- ½ CUP WATERCRESS, WASHED, DRIED, STEMS TRIMMED
- 1 CUP ARUGULA, WASHED, DRIED, STEMS TRIMMED
- 2 OUNCES BLEU CHEESE, CRUMBLED

1. Core the pears. Cut into ¾" slices.

2. In 1 teaspoon of canola oil, sauté the pears until brown.

3. Mix the remaining oil with the vinegar, salt, and pepper.

4. Add mustard, whisking until dressing is slightly thick.

5. Mix watercress and arugula in a plastic bag.

6. Put into salad bowl; add bleu cheese.

7. Add pears to salad bowl. Drizzle with dressing and serve immediately.

PER SERVING: Fat: 15 g **Protein:** 4 g **Carbohydrates:** 14 g
Sugar: 3 g

CRISPY COBB SALAD

CALORIES: 295
SERVES 4

- 4 OUNCES ARUGULA
- 2 CUPS SHREDDED WHITE MEAT CHICKEN, BOILED
- 1 LARGE TOMATO
- 2 HARD-BOILED EGGS, FINELY CHOPPED
- 1 RIPE AVOCADO, PITTED AND SLICED INTO SMALL PIECES
- 3 SLICES COOKED BACON
- ½ CUP BOTTLED LOW-CALORIE BLEU CHEESE DRESSING

1. Layer shallow salad bowl as follows: arugula, chicken, tomato, eggs, avocado, and bacon.

2. Cover with bleu cheese dressing and serve immediately.

PER SERVING: Fat: 17 g **Protein:** 29 g **Carbohydrates:** 7 g **Sugar:** 2 g

Chopping versus Layering

Many people prefer their salad chopped as opposed to layered. Layering is a fun and different way to serve a salad, with a surprise as you dig in. It also provides a nicer, more ordered presentation, and it's easy to prepare since you don't have to fuss over mixing the salad perfectly.

CRABMEAT AND SHRIMP SALAD

CALORIES: 170
SERVES 4

- ¾ POUND LUMP CRABMEAT, COOKED
- ½ POUND SHRIMP, COOKED AND DICED
- 4 TEASPOONS DRIED CHIVES
- 1 STALK CELERY, DICED
- ¼ CUP FAT-FREE SOUR CREAM
- 1 TEASPOON LEMON JUICE
- 1 TEASPOON DIJON MUSTARD
- SALT AND PEPPER TO TASTE
- 1 TEASPOON SPLENDA
- 1 HEAD ICEBERG LETTUCE

1. Combine all ingredients. Cover salad and refrigerate until chilled. Serve salad on iceberg lettuce leaves.

PER SERVING: Fat: 2 g **Protein:** 32 g **Carbohydrates:** 7 g **Sugar:** 1 g

ASIAN BEEF SALAD

CALORIES: 150
SERVES 4

- ¾ **POUND FLANK STEAK, THINLY SLICED AND ROLLED IN BLACK PEPPER**
- 3 **TABLESPOONS LIME JUICE**
- 1 **TABLESPOON ASIAN FISH SAUCE**
- ½ **TEASPOON SPLENDA**
- 1 **GREEN THAI CHILI, SEEDED AND MINCED**
- 2 **SCALLIONS, DICED**
- 2 **TEASPOONS CORIANDER, CRUSHED**
- ½ **SEEDLESS CUCUMBER, DICED**
- 1 **TEASPOON MINT LEAVES, FINELY CHOPPED**

1. Preheat broiler.

2. Broil flank steak strip for 5 minutes on each side.

3. Mix lime juice, fish sauce, Splenda, and chilies in a bowl.

4. Add the scallions, coriander, cucumber, and steak to the dressing.

5. Arrange on a platter and garnish with mint leaves; serve.

PER SERVING: Fat: 6 g **Protein:** 19 g **Carbohydrates:** 4 g **Sugar:** 0 g

HOLLYWOOD LOBSTER SALAD

CALORIES: 225
SERVES 4

- ¾ **POUND LOBSTER MEAT, COOKED AND TORN INTO CHUNKS**
- 4 **TABLESPOONS EXTRA-VIRGIN OLIVE OIL**
- 1 **TEASPOON LEMON JUICE**
- 3 **TABLESPOONS CHOPPED CHIVES**
- ⅓ **CUP FAT-FREE MIRACLE WHIP SALAD DRESSING**
- **SALT AND PEPPER TO TASTE**
- 1 **HEAD BOSTON LETTUCE**

1. Gently fold all ingredients except the lettuce together.

2. Cover and refrigerate until chilled.

3. Arrange salad on a bed of salad greens and serve immediately.

PER SERVING: Fat: 15 g **Protein:** 18 g **Carbohydrates:** 6 g **Sugar:** 1 g

WALDORF SALAD

CALORIES: 275
SERVES 4

1 CUP DICED RED APPLE, SKIN ON
1 CUP DICED GRANNY SMITH APPLE, SKIN ON
1 CUP DICED CELERY
½ CUP HALVED SEEDLESS GRAPES
½ CUP CHOPPED WALNUTS
¼ CUP MAYONNAISE
¼ CUP PLAIN YOGURT
4 BUTTER LETTUCE LEAVES

1. Combine apples, celery, grapes, walnuts, mayonnaise, and yogurt in a bowl.

2. Spoon salad onto lettuce, either on a platter or individual plates.

3. Serve chilled.

PER SERVING: Fat: 18 g **Protein:** 4 g **Carbohydrates:** 24 g **Sugar:** 4 g

Sesame Twist

To add a distinctly Asian flavor and even more fiber to this recipe, stir about 1 teaspoon of toasted sesame oil into the mayonnaise first and then sprinkle the finished salad with a generous amount of sesame seeds.

CRABMEAT SALAD WITH RICE AND ASIAN SPICES

CALORIES: 451
SERVES 4

2 CUPS NAPA CABBAGE, SHREDDED
2 CUPS COOKED RICE, BROWN OR BASMATI
1 POUND LUMP CRABMEAT, FRESH (ANY KIND)
1 CUP LOW-FAT MAYONNAISE
2 TABLESPOONS CHAMPAGNE VINEGAR
2 TABLESPOONS LEMON JUICE
1 TABLESPOON SESAME SEED OIL
¼ TEASPOON ASIAN FIVE-SPICE POWDER
SALT AND PEPPER TO TASTE

1. In a large serving bowl, toss the cabbage, rice, and crabmeat. Mix together the rest of the ingredients for dressing and coat the contents of the bowl. Serve chilled.

PER SERVING: Fat: 25 g **Protein:** 27 g **Carbohydrates:** 35 g **Sugar:** 1 g

Exploring Vinegar

Champagne vinegar is made from the same champagne used for drinking. It is aged in oak barrels, and because it is made from light, sparkling wine, it has a bright, crisp taste that is delicious in vinaigrettes.

CORN AND TOMATO SALAD

CALORIES: 183
SERVES 4

2 CUPS FRESH SWEET CORN

2 TABLESPOONS OLIVE OIL

½ TEASPOON GRATED LEMON ZEST

1 TABLESPOON FRESH LEMON JUICE

PINCH OF GROUND CUMIN

¼ TEASPOON SALT

¼ TEASPOON PEPPER

2 TABLESPOONS MINCED GREEN ONIONS

¼ CUP DICED RED BELL PEPPER

¼ CUP DICED GREEN BELL PEPPER

¼ CUP PITTED BLACK OLIVES

¼ CUP CHOPPED ARUGULA

2 MEDIUM TOMATOES

1. Steam the corn for 2 minutes and then spread it on a sheet pan to cool.

2. Put the olive oil, lemon zest, lemon juice, cumin, salt, and pepper in a jar and shake to combine.

3. Toss the corn, green onions, bell peppers, black olives, and arugula together in a large bowl.

4. Pour the dressing over the corn salad and toss to combine. Chill for 60 minutes.

5. Slice the tomatoes and serve the corn salad on top.

PER SERVING: Fat: 6 g **Protein:** 3 g **Carbohydrates:** 24 g **Sugar:** 1 g

---

CHICKEN SALAD

CALORIES: 281
SERVES 4

1 HEAD ROMAINE LETTUCE

¼ CUP RED-WINE VINEGAR

2 CLOVES GARLIC, MINCED

2 TABLESPOONS DIJON MUSTARD

1 TEASPOON ROSEMARY, DRIED

SALT AND PEPPER TO TASTE

¼ CUP OLIVE OIL

¼ CUP CARROT, DICED

1 MEDIUM RED BELL PEPPER, CUT LENGTHWISE, CORED, SEEDED, AND MINCED

¼ CUP RADISH, SLICED

2 CUPS SHREDDED COOKED CHICKEN BREAST

1. Wash romaine lettuce, remove core, and chop leaves into 1"-size pieces.

2. Combine vinegar, garlic, mustard, rosemary, salt, and pepper in small bowl. Whisk olive oil into vinegar mixture.

3. Place romaine, carrot, bell pepper, radish, and chicken in a large bowl. Pour dressing over top salad and coat well.

PER SERVING: Fat: 17 g **Protein:** 24 g **Carbohydrates:** 9 g **Sugar:** 2 g

Not Your Typical Chicken Salad
Using herbs and vegetables brightens up the typical deli-style chicken salad. The purpose of carrots, radishes, bell pepper, and herbs is to spruce up the color on your plate, add crunch, and increase the amount of essential vitamins and fiber.

AVOCADO GRAPEFRUIT SALAD

CALORIES: 335
SERVES 4

2 AVOCADOS
1 RUBY RED GRAPEFRUIT
¼ CUP POMEGRANATE SEEDS
1 TABLESPOON MINCED SHALLOT
¼ CUP OLIVE OIL
1 TABLESPOON POMEGRANATE JUICE
SALT AND PEPPER, TO TASTE

1. Cut the avocados in half and remove the pits. Cut the avocado halves, still in the skin, into long thin strips. Scoop the meat out of the skin with a large spoon. Fan the strips out on a serving plate.

2. Peel the grapefruit skin. Cut sections off the grapefruit with a sharp knife.

3. Squeeze the juice from some of the grapefruit sections onto the avocados. Scatter the remaining grapefruit sections over the avocados. Sprinkle pomegranate seeds over the salad.

4. Whisk the shallot, olive oil, pomegranate juice, salt, and pepper together in a bowl.

5. Drizzle the mixture over the salad and serve at room temperature.

PER SERVING: Fat: 18 g **Protein:** 3 g **Carbohydrates:** 28 g **Sugar:** 12 g

Grenadine

The pomegranate used in this salad recipe is a source of ruby red juice. Grenadine is a tart-sweet syrup that is made from pomegranate juice and sugar. It is used to make mixed drinks, including the nonalcoholic Shirley Temple and Roy Rogers. Try mixing a little grenadine in your lemonade.

TABOULI SALAD

CALORIES: 141
SERVES 6

½ CUP MEDIUM BULGUR WHEAT
½ CUPS WATER
⅓ CUP LEMON JUICE
2 TABLESPOONS CHOPPED FRESH MINT
1 TEASPOON SALT
1 TEASPOON PEPPER
¼ CUP EXTRA-VIRGIN OLIVE OIL
1 CUP CHOPPED FRESH PARSLEY
½ CUP CHOPPED GREEN ONIONS
2 LARGE TOMATOES, DICED
1 TABLESPOON MINCED GARLIC

1. Soak the bulgur in the water for at least 2 hours.

2. Drain the excess water and put the bulgur in a large bowl.

3. Add the remaining ingredients to the bulgur and mix well.

4. Let sit at room temperature for 60 minutes or refrigerate overnight.

5. Serve chilled or at room temperature.

PER SERVING: Fat: 8 g **Protein:** 2 g **Carbohydrates:** 15 g **Sugar:** 2 g

Prepare Your Own Bulgur

If you soak 2 cups of wheat berries in 4 cups of water overnight, you can make your own bulgur the next day. Drain the wheat berries, simmer them in 4 cups of water for 60 minutes, and drain. Dry the wheat berries on a baking sheet pan in a 250°F oven for 45 minutes or until dry. Chop up the dried, cooked wheat berries in a food processor and store in a large jar.

CARROT SALAD

CALORIES: 305
SERVES 4

- ½ **CUP SALAD OIL**
- 2 **TABLESPOONS HONEY MUSTARD**
- 1 **TABLESPOON WHITE WINE VINEGAR**
- **SALT TO TASTE**
- **PEPPER TO TASTE**
- 4 **MEDIUM CARROTS**
- 2 **GREEN ONIONS**

1. In a blender combine salad oil, honey mustard, and vinegar and blend until smooth. Add salt and pepper to your taste. Set aside.

2. Peel and shred the carrots and put them in a mixing bowl.

3. Slice the green onions and toss them with the shredded carrots.

4. Pour the dressing over the carrot mixture and toss well to combine.

5. Refrigerate overnight to let the flavors develop.

PER SERVING: Fat: 24 g **Protein:** 1.20 g
Carbohydrates: 12 g **Sugar:** 3 g

CURRIED SHRIMP SALAD IN A PAPAYA

CALORIES: 312
SERVES 2

- 2 **TABLESPOONS OLIVE OIL**
- ¼ **CUP PLAIN YOGURT**
- 1 **TABLESPOON LEMON JUICE**
- 1 **TEASPOON GRATED LEMON ZEST**
- ½ **TEASPOON CURRY POWDER**
- **SALT AND PEPPER TO TASTE**
- 1 **CUP COOKED PEELED SHRIMP, CHILLED**
- ¼ **CUP DICED CELERY**
- ¼ **CUP DICED CUCUMBER**
- ¼ **CUP SEEDLESS GREEN GRAPES, HALVED**
- 1 **MEDIUM PAPAYA**
- ¼ **CUP TOASTED SLICED ALMONDS**

1. Whisk together olive oil, yogurt, lemon juice, lemon zest, curry powder, salt, and pepper in a mixing bowl.

2. Add the shrimp, celery, cucumber, and grapes and toss to coat with the dressing. Chill salad until ready to serve.

3. Cut the papaya in half lengthwise through the stem area and scoop out the seeds.

4. Fill the papaya with the shrimp salad, mounding it up on top.

5. Sprinkle the almonds on top of the shrimp salad. Serve with a fork and spoon so the papaya flesh can be scooped and eaten after the salad is gone.

PER SERVING: Fat: 20 g **Protein:** 9 g **Carbohydrates:** 24 g
Sugar: 3 g

SHAVED FENNEL, KUMQUAT, AND FRISÉE SALAD

CALORIES: 360
SERVES 4

½ CUP OLIVE OIL

2 TABLESPOONS ORANGE JUICE

1 TEASPOON GRATED ORANGE ZEST

1 TABLESPOON MINCED SHALLOT

1 TEASPOON WHOLE-GRAIN MUSTARD

1 TEASPOON FENNEL SEEDS

SALT TO TASTE

PEPPER TO TASTE

2 FENNEL BULBS

6 KUMQUATS

2 LARGE HANDFULS FRISÉE

1. Combine olive oil, orange juice, orange zest, shallot, whole-grain mustard, and fennel seeds in a blender and blend until smooth. Add salt and pepper to taste.

2. Thinly slice the fennel bulbs and kumquats and toss them together in a bowl. Remove any kumquat seeds.

3. Divide the frisée among four salad plates and top with the fennel/kumquat mélange. Drizzle the dressing over the salad.

PER SERVING: Fat: 28 g **Protein:** 3 g **Carbohydrates:** 24 g **Sugar:** 1 g

Kumquats

Kumquats are great snacks to pack in a lunch. The olive-sized orange citrus fruits are entirely edible, skins, seeds, and all. The skin is sweet and the interior is sour. Try adding them to your next relish tray along with black and green olives. The only problem with kumquats is that they are only available during the fall-winter season.

CELERY ROOT SALAD

CALORIES: 145
SERVES 4

½ POUND CELERY ROOTS

¼ CUP MINCED SHALLOTS

¼ CUP OLIVE OIL

2 TABLESPOONS LEMON JUICE

1 TEASPOON GRATED LEMON ZEST

1 TEASPOON DIJON MUSTARD

SALT AND PEPPER TO TASTE

2 TABLESPOONS CHOPPED CHIVES

1. Peel the celery roots and cut them into ¼"-thick slices. Stack the slices a few at a time and cut them into matchstick strips (julienne). Place the sticks in a large bowl.

2. Put the shallots, olive oil, lemon juice, lemon zest, mustard, salt, pepper, and chives in a jar with a lid and shake to combine.

3. Pour the dressing over the celery root and toss to combine. Cover and refrigerate for at least 60 minutes.

4. Serve as part of a salad sampler plate or as a side salad.

PER SERVING: Fat: 13 g **Protein:** 2 g **Carbohydrates:** 7 g **Sugar:** 0 g

Raw or Cooked?

The celery root in this recipe is not cooked but served raw. You may blanch the celery root if you prefer a less crunchy salad. Bring a large pot of water to a boil and plunge the peeled and julienned celery root into it for 5 minutes, then shock them in a large bowl of ice water. Drain them in a colander when they have chilled and proceed with the recipe.

GREEN LENTIL SALAD

CALORIES: 286
SERVES 4

- 1 CUP DRIED FRENCH GREEN LENTILS
- 5 CUPS WATER
- 1 BAY LEAF
- 2 TABLESPOONS OLIVE OIL
- 1 CARROT, FINELY CHOPPED
- 1 STALK CELERY, FINELY CHOPPED
- 2 TABLESPOONS MINCED SHALLOTS
- 1 TEASPOON MINCED GARLIC
- 2 TABLESPOONS EXTRA-VIRGIN OLIVE OIL
- ¼ CUP LEMON JUICE
- 1 TEASPOON GRATED LEMON ZEST
- 1 TABLESPOON CHOPPED FRESH THYME
- 1 TABLESPOON CHOPPED FRESH PARSLEY
- ¼ TEASPOON GROUND CORIANDER
- SALT AND PEPPER TO TASTE

1. Put the lentils, water, and bay leaf in a saucepan. Bring to a boil, reduce heat, and simmer for 20 minutes. Drain in a colander, remove the bay leaf, and let the lentils cool. Put them in a large bowl and set aside.

2. Heat the olive oil in a sauté pan and cook the carrot, celery, and shallots over medium heat until tender, about 5 minutes. Add to the lentils.

3. Add the garlic, extra-virgin olive oil, lemon juice, lemon zest, thyme, parsley, coriander, salt, and pepper to the lentils. Toss to combine and chill.

4. Serve chilled or at room temperature.

PER SERVING: Fat: 13 g **Protein:** 11 g **Carbohydrates:** 30 g **Sugar:** 2 g

Beans Count

You can soak them overnight and then cook them or buy them canned without losing much of their nutritional makeup. Beans are a substitute for animal proteins in vegetarian cooking, and they add to any meal, vegetarian or not.

GREEK SALAD

4 CUPS ROMAINE LETTUCE, CHOPPED INTO SMALL PIECES

1 LARGE TOMATO, SEEDS REMOVED AND CHOPPED

1 SMALL CUCUMBER, SLICED

1 GREEN BELL PEPPER, CORED, SEEDED, CUT INTO RINGS

½ CUP FETA CHEESE

¼ CUP RED-WINE VINEGAR

JUICE OF 1 LEMON

1 TABLESPOON ITALIAN SEASONING

SALT AND PEPPER TO TASTE

¼ CUP EXTRA-VIRGIN OLIVE OIL

2 TEASPOONS CAPERS

16 KALAMATA OLIVES

1. Place lettuce, tomato, cucumber, bell pepper, and feta in a large bowl.

2. To make dressing, whisk vinegar, lemon juice, Italian seasoning, salt, and pepper in a small bowl; mix in olive oil.

3. Coat vegetables with dressing.

4. Place salad on plates. Top salad plates with capers and olives.

PER SERVING: Fat: 7 g **Protein:** 5 g **Carbohydrates:** 20 g **Sugar:** 1 g

Feta Is Betta'!

Feta cheese has been made by Greek shepherds for many centuries. Originally it was made from goat's or sheep's milk; today feta cheese is made from pasteurized cow's milk. In Greece feta cheese is served in restaurants and homes as a garnish on various types of fresh salads.

BLOOD ORANGE SALAD WITH SHRIMP AND BABY SPINACH

CALORIES: 314
SERVES 4

- **2 BAGS BABY SPINACH (TRY TO FIND PREWASHED)**
- **2 BLOOD ORANGES**
- **1¼ POUNDS SHRIMP, PEELED, DEVEINED, COOKED, AND CHILLED**
- **JUICE OF ½ LEMON**
- **¼ CUP EXTRA-VIRGIN OLIVE OIL**
- **¼ TEASPOON DRY MUSTARD**
- **SALT AND PEPPER TO TASTE**
- **¼ CUP STEMMED, LOOSELY PACKED PARSLEY OR CILANTRO (WHICHEVER YOU LIKE)**

1. Just before serving, place the spinach on individual serving plates.

2. Peel the oranges. Slice them crossways, about ¼" thick, picking out any seeds. Arrange on top of the spinach. Arrange the shrimp around the oranges.

3. Place the rest of the ingredients in the blender and purée until the dressing is a bright green. Pour over the salads. Serve chilled.

PER SERVING: Fat: 16 g **Protein:** 32 g **Carbohydrates:** 14 g **Sugar:** 0 g

Fresh Spinach—Not Lettuce

Substitute fresh baby spinach for less nutritious iceberg lettuce. White or pale green lettuce can be used as accents but have less nutritional substance than such greens as spinach, escarole, chicory, and watercress.

PORTOBELLO MUSHROOM SALAD WITH GORGONZOLA, PEPPERS, AND BACON

CALORIES: 365
SERVES 4

2 LARGE PORTOBELLO MUSHROOMS

½ CUP FRENCH DRESSING (SEE CHAPTER 3)

4 STRIPS BACON, FRIED CRISP

4 OUNCES GORGONZOLA CHEESE, CRUMBLED

½ CUP LOW-FAT MAYONNAISE

2 CUPS ROMAINE LETTUCE, CHOPPED

½ CUP SWEET RED ROASTED PEPPERS, CHOPPED (FROM A JAR IS FINE)

IN THIS RECIPE YOU CAN SUBSTITUTE YOUR FAVORITE LOW-FAT CHEESE FOR THE GORGONZOLA AND VEGETARIAN BACON OR CANADIAN BACON FOR THE REGULAR BACON.

1. Marinate mushrooms for 1 hour in the French dressing. Fry the bacon; set on paper towels and crumble.

2. On a hot grill or broiler, grill the mushrooms for 3 minutes per side. Cut them in strips.

3. While the mushrooms are cooking, heat the Gorgonzola cheese and mayonnaise in a small saucepan until the cheese melts.

4. Place the mushrooms on the bed of lettuce. Sprinkle with bacon. Drizzle with the cheese mixture and garnish with red roasted peppers.

PER SERVING: Fat: 27 g **Protein:** 11 g **Carbohydrates:** 12 g **Sugar:** 3 g

Mushroom Choices
There are many varieties of mushrooms now available. Brown mushrooms have a robust flavor. White button mushrooms are delicious in sauces, and the big ones work well when stuffed or grilled. Get wild mushrooms from a reputable mycologist. Never guess if a wild mushroom that you find in the woods is safe. It may be poisonous!

GRILLED TUNA SALAD WITH ASIAN VEGETABLES AND SPICY DRESSING

CALORIES: 388
SERVES 4

- 3 TABLESPOONS SESAME OIL
- ½ CUP OLIVE OIL
- 2 CLOVES GARLIC, MINCED
- 1 TEASPOON FRESH GINGER, MINCED
- 2 TEASPOONS SHERRY VINEGAR
- 1 TABLESPOON SOY SAUCE
- 2 TO 3 CUPS NAPA CABBAGE, SHREDDED
- 1 RED ONION, CUT IN WEDGES
- 2 JAPANESE EGGPLANTS, CUT LENGTHWISE
- 4 (¼-POUND) TUNA STEAKS

1. In a bowl, whisk together the sesame oil, olive oil, garlic, ginger, sherry vinegar, and soy sauce and set aside.

2. Place the cabbage on serving plates. Paint the onion, eggplants, and tuna with the dressing.

3. Grill the vegetables and tuna for 3 to 4 minutes per side. Arrange the vegetables and fish over the cabbage. Drizzle with the rest of the dressing.

PER SERVING: Fat: 32 g **Protein:** 3 g **Carbohydrates:** 13 g **Sugar:** 0 g

A Quick Meal

Tuna is a large fish in the mackerel family that has a unique circulatory system that allows them to retain a higher body temperature than the cool waters they inhabit. This provides tuna with an extra burst of energy that allows them to reach short-distance swimming speeds of over 40 miles per hour!

MARINATED CHICKEN AND BROWN RICE SALAD WITH WATER CHESTNUTS

CALORIES: 333
SERVES 4

½ CUP RED-WINE VINEGAR

1 CUP LOW-FAT MAYONNAISE

1 TEASPOON DIJON-STYLE MUSTARD

½ TEASPOON CELERY SALT

4 SKINLESS AND BONELESS CHICKEN BREASTS, ABOUT 4 OUNCES EACH

2 CUPS BROWN RICE, COOKED

4 SCALLIONS, CHOPPED

1 CARROT, JULIENNE

1 (8-OUNCE) CAN WATER CHESTNUTS, DRAINED AND SLICED

SALT AND PEPPER TO TASTE

1 BAG MIXED GREENS, WASHED AND READY TO USE

1. Mix the red-wine vinegar, mayonnaise, mustard, and celery salt together in a bowl. Spread 4 teaspoons of the mixture on the chicken breasts, being careful not to contaminate the dressing with a spoon that touched the chicken.

2. Combine the rest of the dressing with the cooked rice. Mix in the scallions, carrot, water chestnuts, salt, and pepper. Set aside.

3. Grill the chicken for about 4 to 5 minutes per side over high heat. Let rest for 5 minutes and slice.

4. Place the mixed greens on serving plates, mound the rice, and decorate with the warm chicken.

PER SERVING: Fat: 21 g **Protein:** 5 g **Carbohydrates:** 33 g **Sugar:** 2 g

What Is a Water Chestnut?

A water chestnut is not a nut at all, but a tuber. Commonly referred to as a Chinese water chestnut, they get their name from a resemblance to the chestnut's shape and color. They grow in freshwater ponds, lakes, and slow-running streams in Japan, China, Thailand, and Australia. Water chestnuts are useful for adding a crunchy texture to recipes such as stir-fries, salads, and stuffing.

WHEAT BERRY SALAD

CALORIES: 205
SERVES 6

- 4 CUPS WATER
- 1 TEASPOON KOSHER SALT
- 1 CUP WHEAT BERRIES
- 1 CUP FRENCH DRESSING (SEE CHAPTER 3)
- 2 CUPS JICAMA (MEXICAN TURNIP), PEELED AND DICED
- 1 GREEN APPLE, PEELED, CORED, AND DICED
- ½ POUND SMALL RED GRAPES, SEEDLESS
- 2 CUPS LEAVES OF MIXED BABY GREENS (FROM A PREWASHED BAG IS FINE)
- FRESHLY GROUND BLACK PEPPER TO TASTE

1. Bring the water to a boil. Add salt and wheat berries.

2. Cook the wheat berries until crisp-tender, following package direction.

3. Place cooked wheat berries in a large serving bowl. While still warm, toss with the French dressing. Add jicama, apple, and grapes. Toss and chill. Place mixture on plates over mixed baby greens. Add pepper to taste.

PER SERVING: Fat: 13 g **Protein:** 2 g **Carbohydrates:** 17 g **Sugar:** 5 g

The Homely Legume

Jicama, also known as a Mexican turnip, is a lumpy root vegetable with a unique and versatile taste. The jicama's peel is inedible, but like a potato, it can be fried, baked, boiled, steamed, or mashed. The jicama can also be eaten raw. Try it as a vehicle for guacamole or use its mild flavor and crunchy texture in fruit salad.

BABY VEGETABLE SALAD

CALORIES: 346
SERVES 4

¼ CUP OLIVE OIL

2 CLOVES GARLIC, MINCED

12 TINY FRESH WHITE ONIONS

1 POUND TINY HARICOTS VERTS (BABY GREEN BEANS)

1 BULB FENNEL, RIMMED OF ANY BROWN AND SLICED THINLY

5 OUNCES SMALL WHITE BUTTON MUSHROOMS

8 BABY CARROTS

¼ CUP CHAMPAGNE VINEGAR

¼ CUP FRESH BASIL, SHREDDED

¼ CUP FRESH PARSLEY, SHREDDED

SALT AND PEPPER TO TASTE

½ CUP STEMMED, LOOSELY PACKED WATERCRESS

1 HEAD BOSTON LETTUCE, SHREDDED

½ POUND CURRANT OR GRAPE TOMATOES

½ POUND BLACK FOREST HAM, CHOPPED

1. Heat the olive oil over medium-low flame and sauté the garlic, onions, haricots verts, fennel, mushrooms, and carrots until the haricots verts and carrots are crisp-tender.

2. Stir in the champagne vinegar, basil, and parsley. Sprinkle with salt and pepper to taste.

3. When the vegetables are at room temperature, arrange the watercress and lettuce on serving plates and spoon on the veggies. Add tomatoes. Sprinkle with the ham and serve.

PER SERVING: Fat: 20 g **Protein:** 19 g **Carbohydrates:** 18 g **Sugar:** 3 g

POACHED SALMON SALAD WITH HARD-BOILED EGGS

CALORIES: 480
SERVES 4

- 1⅓ POUNDS SALMON FILET, SKIN AND BONES REMOVED
- ½ CUP COLD WATER
- ¼ CUP DRY WHITE WINE
- JUICE OF ½ LEMON
- 1 TABLESPOON JUNIPER BERRIES, BRUISED WITH A MORTAR AND PESTLE
- 4 EGGS
- 1 CUP LOW-FAT MAYONNAISE
- ¼ CUP STEMMED, LOOSELY PACKED FRESH PARSLEY
- 2 SPRIGS FRESH DILL WEED, OR 2 TEASPOONS DRIED
- ZEST AND JUICE OF ½ LEMON
- 4 DROPS OF TABASCO SAUCE, OR TO TASTE
- WATERCRESS OR LETTUCE FOR ARRANGEMENT ON PLATTER
- GARNISH OF CAPERS

1. Place the salmon in a pan that will hold it without curling the ends. Add the water, wine, lemon juice, and juniper berries. Over medium-low heat, poach the fish until it flakes, about 12 minutes depending on thickness. Do not turn. Drain and cool; refrigerate until just before serving.

2. In cold water to cover, bring the eggs to a boil and simmer for 10 minutes. Place under cold running water, crack, and peel. Slice just before serving.

3. Put the mayonnaise, parsley, dill, lemon zest and juice, and Tabasco in the blender. Purée until very smooth.

4. Arrange the salmon on a serving platter. Surround with watercress or lettuce and eggs. Dot with capers and serve green mayonnaise on the side.

PER SERVING: Fat: 33 g **Protein:** 36 g **Carbohydrates:** 7 g **Sugar:** 0 g

FRESH TUNA SALAD A LA NIÇOISE

CALORIES: 370
SERVES 2

- ¼ POUND GREEN BEANS, TRIMMED
- 2 (4-OUNCE) TUNA STEAKS
- 2 TABLESPOONS OLIVE OIL
- SALT AND PEPPER TO TASTE
- 1 HEAD BUTTER LETTUCE
- 1½ TABLESPOONS CAPERS
- ¼ CUP NIÇOISE OLIVES
- ½ CUP CHERRY TOMATOES
- 2 HARD-BOILED EGGS, QUARTERED

1. Cook green beans in a pot of boiling water, uncovered, until crisp-tender, about 4 minutes, then transfer immediately to a bowl of ice water to stop cooking. Drain green beans and pat dry.

2. Brush tuna with olive oil and season with salt and pepper as desired. Grill on lightly oiled rack or grill pan, uncovered, turning over once, until browned on outside and pink in the center, 6 to 8 minutes total. Slice tuna unto quarter-inch thick pieces.

3. Wash lettuce and tear into bite-sized pieces; place in large bowl. Add green beans, capers, olives, and tomatoes to bowl; coat with Italian dressing.

4. Divide salad onto two plates. Top with tuna and egg quarters.

PER SERVING: Fat: 22 g **Protein:** 32 g **Carbohydrates:** 30 g **Sugar:** 1 g

Time-Saving Tip

If you are tight on time and money, try substituting the tuna steaks with a large can of albacore tuna. Canned albacore usually contains more omega-3 fats than chunk light tuna. The salad will still taste authentic without spending extra cash and time grilling the fish.

CHAPTER 6

Soups and Stews

SPLIT PEA SOUP

CALORIES: 238
SERVES 6

8 CUPS WATER
2 CUPS SPLIT PEAS
1 HAM BONE
½ CUP DICED CARROT
¼ CUP DICED CELERY
1 CUP DICED ONION
SALT AND PEPPER TO TASTE

1. Simmer water, split peas, and ham bone for 60 minutes.

2. Add carrot, celery, and onion and simmer for another hour.

3. Remove the ham bone, season the soup with salt and pepper, and serve hot.

PER SERVING: Fat: 1 g **Protein:** 17 g **Carbohydrates:** 41 g
Sugar: 5 g

WHITE BEAN SOUP

CALORIES: 233
SERVES 4

½ CUP DICED CARROTS
½ CUP DICED ONION
¼ CUP DICED CELERY
2 TABLESPOONS OLIVE OIL
1 TABLESPOON TOMATO PASTE
4 CUPS CHICKEN BROTH
2 CUPS COOKED WHITE BEANS
1 SPRIG FRESH THYME
SALT AND PEPPER TO TASTE

1. Sauté the carrots, onion, and celery in the olive oil for 10 to 15 minutes.

2. Add tomato paste and stir to combine.

3. Add chicken broth, beans, and thyme, bring to a boil, and simmer for 25 minutes.

4. Remove the thyme sprig and purée half of the soup in a blender.

5. Return the purée to the pot. Stir and season the soup with salt and pepper. Serve hot.

PER SERVING: Fat: 4 g **Protein:** 16 g **Carbohydrates:** 31 g
Sugar: 7 g

RED LENTIL SOUP

CALORIES: 275
SERVES 4

2 TABLESPOONS OLIVE OIL
4 CLOVES GARLIC, MINCED
1 CUP CHOPPED ONION
2 TABLESPOONS MINCED GINGER ROOT
2 PARSNIPS, PEELED AND CHOPPED
3 CARROTS, PEELED AND CHOPPED
2 CUPS VEGETABLE BROTH
2 CUPS WATER
2 SPRIGS FRESH THYME
1 CUP RED LENTILS

1. In a large soup pot, heat olive oil over medium heat. Add garlic and onion; cook and stir until crisp-tender, about 4 minutes. Add ginger root, parsnips, and carrots and cook for 2 minutes. Then stir in vegetable broth, water, and thyme sprigs and bring to a boil. Reduce heat, cover, and simmer for 10 minutes.

2. Meanwhile, pick over lentils and wash thoroughly. Add lentils to pot and bring back to a simmer. Simmer for 15–25 minutes or until lentils and vegetables are tender. Remove the thyme stems and discard. You can purée this soup if you'd like, but you can also serve just as it is.

PER SERVING: Fat: 8 g **Protein:** 18 g **Carbohydrates:** 34 g **Sugar:** 3 g

GAZPACHO MARY

CALORIES: 165
SERVES 4

3 LARGE TOMATOES
5 CELERY HEARTS
½ YELLOW BELL PEPPER
1 SHALLOT
½ CUCUMBER
¼ CUP LEMON JUICE
¼ CUP EXTRA-VIRGIN OLIVE OIL
¾ CUP TOMATO JUICE
½ TEASPOON CAYENNE PEPPER SAUCE
1 TEASPOON WORCESTERSHIRE SAUCE
1 TABLESPOON GRATED HORSERADISH
1 TEASPOON CELERY SALT
½ TEASPOON BLACK PEPPER

1. Chop the tomatoes and place them in a blender. Chop up one celery heart and save the others for garnish. Add the chopped one to the blender.

2. Chop the pepper, shallot, and cucumber and add them to the blender.

3. Add the remaining ingredients to the blender and purée until smooth and there are no large chunks.

4. Pour into glass tumblers and garnish with celery hearts. Serve chilled.

PER SERVING: Fat: 6 g **Protein:** 5 g **Carbohydrates:** 21 g **Sugar:** 8 g

SCANDINAVIAN SUMMER FRUIT SOUP

CALORIES: 232
SERVES 6

4 CUPS APPLE CIDER

1 CUP CRANBERRY JUICE

½ CUP ORANGE JUICE

¼ CUP LEMON JUICE

¼ CUP SUGAR

¼ TEASPOON SALT

4 PEACHES, PEELED AND CHOPPED

1 PINT STRAWBERRIES, CHOPPED

2 PEARS, PEELED AND CHOPPED

2 CINNAMON STICKS

½ TEASPOON GROUND CARDAMOM

1 BUNCH FRESH MINT

6 TABLESPOONS LOW-FAT SOUR CREAM

1. Make the soup the day before. In a large bowl, combine apple cider, cranberry juice, orange juice, lemon juice, sugar, and salt.

2. Place half of the peaches, strawberries, and pears in a food processor or blender. Add 1 cup of the apple cider mixture and blend or process until smooth. Add to apple cider mixture along with remaining ingredients except mint and sour cream. Cover and chill for at least 8 hours.

3. Remove cinnamon sticks and stir soup. Then spoon soup into chilled bowls and garnish with mint and sour cream.

PER SERVING: Fat: 3 g **Protein:** 2 g **Carbohydrates:** 30 g **Sugar:** 10 g

THREE BEAN CHILI

CALORIES: 326
SERVES 6

1 CUP DRIED BLACK BEANS

1 CUP DRIED KIDNEY BEANS

1 CUP DRIED PINTO BEANS

WATER, AS NEEDED, PLUS 4 CUPS

2 JALAPEÑO PEPPERS, MINCED

2 ONIONS, CHOPPED

4 CLOVES GARLIC, MINCED

4 CUPS LOW-SODIUM BEEF BROTH, DIVIDED

2 (14-OUNCE) CANS LOW-SODIUM DICED TOMATOES, UNDRAINED

1 (6-OUNCE) CAN LOW-SODIUM TOMATO PASTE

⅛ TEASPOON PEPPER

1. Pick over beans and rinse well; drain and place in large bowl. Cover with water and let stand overnight. In the morning, drain and rinse the beans and place them into a 4- to 5-quart slow cooker.

2. Add peppers, onions, and garlic to slow cooker. Add 4 cups water and 3 cups broth to the slow cooker. Stir well. Cover and cook on low for 8 hours, or until beans are tender.

3. Add canned tomatoes to slow cooker. In a small bowl, combine remaining 1 cup broth with the tomato paste; stir with whisk to dissolve the tomato paste. Add to slow cooker along with pepper. Cover and cook on low for 1–2 hours longer or until chili is thick.

PER SERVING: Fat: 1 g **Protein:** 10 g **Carbohydrates:** 32 g **Sugar:** 5 g

HARVEST STEW

CALORIES: 358
SERVES 6

1 POUND STEWING BEEF CUBES
2 TABLESPOONS OLIVE OIL
¼ CUP FLOUR
¾ CUP DICED ONIONS
½ CUP SLICED CARROTS
½ CUP DICED CELERY
1 LEEK, CLEANED AND DICED
6 GARLIC CLOVES, PEELED
2 CUPS DICED ZUCCHINI
1 POTATO, PEELED AND DICED
3 TURNIPS, DICED
2 TOMATOES, CHOPPED
1 BAY LEAF
3 SPRIGS FRESH THYME
4 CUPS BEEF BROTH
2 TABLESPOONS
  WORCESTERSHIRE SAUCE
SALT AND PEPPER TO TASTE

1. Brown the beef cubes in olive oil. Sprinkle the flour over the meat and stir to coat and distribute.

2. Add the onions, carrots, celery, leek, garlic, zucchini, potato, turnips, tomatoes, bay leaf, thyme sprigs, and beef broth. Bring to a boil, then lower the heat and simmer for 60 minutes.

3. Remove the bay leaf and thyme sprigs. Add the Worcestershire sauce, salt, and pepper. Serve hot.

PER SERVING: Fat: 22 g **Protein:** 36 g **Carbohydrates:** 13 g
Sugar: 5 g

CREAMY CAULIFLOWER SOUP

CALORIES: 291
SERVES 4

2 TABLESPOONS OLIVE OIL
½ CUP ONION, FINELY CHOPPED
½ CUP CELERY, CHOPPED
1 CUP CAULIFLOWER
4 CUPS CHICKEN STOCK
1 CUP CHEDDAR CHEESE,
  SHREDDED
SALT AND PEPPER TO TASTE
1 CUP LOW-FAT MILK

1. Heat oil in a large pot, sauté onion and celery until translucent, add cauliflower and chicken stock, and bring to a boil. Reduce heat, cover, and simmer for 25 minutes, stirring occasionally.

2. Purée soup in food processor or blender until smooth.

3. Return soup to pot and bring temperature to medium-low heat. Add cheese, salt, and pepper, continue to cook and stir until cheese is melted and well integrated.

4. Add milk and stir into the soup. Add more chicken stock if the consistency of the soup is too thick.

PER SERVING: Fat: 18 g **Protein:** 17 g **Carbohydrates:** 16 g
Sugar: 2 g

COLD BASIL AND FRESH TOMATO SOUP

CALORIES: 60
SERVES 4

2 POUNDS RED, RIPE TOMATOES, HALVED AND CORED

1 CUP BEEF BROTH

¼ CUP RED WINE

1 TEASPOON GARLIC POWDER

20 BASIL LEAVES

SALT AND PEPPER TO TASTE

CHOPPED CHIVES FOR GARNISH

CHEDDAR OR PARMESAN CHEESE, FOR GARNISH

1. In the blender, purée tomatoes, beef broth, wine, garlic powder, basil, salt, and pepper. Chill overnight. Add garnish at the last minute.

2. If serving the soup hot, garnish with grated Cheddar or Parmesan cheese.

PER SERVING: Fat: 0 g **Protein:** 2 g **Carbohydrates:** 11 g **Sugar:** 1 g

AVOCADO SOUP, CHILLED WITH LIME FLOAT

CALORIES: 487
SERVES 2

2 RIPE AVOCADOS, PEELED

½ CUP CHICKEN BROTH

½ CUP BUTTERMILK (NONFAT IS FINE)

JUICE OF ½ LIME

2 SHALLOTS, MINCED

½ TEASPOON SALT, OR TO TASTE

½ CUP SOUR CREAM

1 TEASPOON LIME JUICE

ZEST OF ½ LIME

TABASCO SAUCE TO TASTE

IN THIS RECIPE YOU CAN SUBSTITUTE LOW-FAT SOUR CREAM FOR REGULAR SOUR CREAM.

1. In the blender, purée the avocados with chicken broth, buttermilk, lime juice, shallots, and salt. Taste for seasoning.

2. Whisk the sour cream, lime juice, lime zest, and Tabasco together. Float on top of the soup.

3. Serve icy cold.

PER SERVING: Fat: 45 g **Protein:** 6 g **Carbohydrates:** 23 g **Sugar:** 2 g

Zesty!
While zests are a fabulous way to add a kick of citrus flavor to almost any dish, be careful of lime zest—it gets very bitter when cooked. However, it is still a wonderful addition to fresh and uncooked dishes.

BROCCOLI SOUP WITH CHEESE

CALORIES: 297
SERVES 4

¼ CUP OLIVE OIL

1 MEDIUM SWEET ONION, CHOPPED

2 CLOVES GARLIC, CHOPPED

1 LARGE BAKING POTATO, PEELED AND CHOPPED

1 LARGE BUNCH BROCCOLI, COARSELY CHOPPED

½ CUP DRY WHITE WINE

3 CUPS CHICKEN BROTH

SALT AND PEPPER TO TASTE

PINCH OF GROUND NUTMEG

4 HEAPING TABLESPOONS EXTRA SHARP CHEDDAR CHEESE, GRATED, FOR GARNISH

1. Heat the olive oil in a large soup kettle. Sauté the onion, garlic, and potato over medium heat until softened slightly. Add the broccoli, liquids, and seasonings.

2. Cover the soup and simmer over low heat for 45 minutes.

3. Cool slightly. Purée in the blender. Reheat and place in bowls.

4. Spoon the cheese over the hot soup.

PER SERVING: Fat: 19 g **Protein:** 8 g **Carbohydrates:** 22 g **Sugar:** 2 g

Save the Stalks

When you prepare broccoli, save the stems. They can be grated and mixed with carrots in a slaw, cut into coins and served hot, or cooked and puréed as a side. Broccoli marries well with potatoes and carrots and is good served raw with a dipping sauce.

CUCUMBER SOUP

CALORIES: 145
SERVES 2

1 SLENDER ENGLISH CUCUMBER, PEELED AND CHOPPED

JUICE OF 1 LEMON

1 CUP NONFAT BUTTERMILK

1 CUP LOW-FAT YOGURT

2 TABLESPOONS FRESH DILL WEED, SNIPPED

SALT AND FRESHLY GROUND WHITE PEPPER TO TASTE

1 TEASPOON TABASCO SAUCE (OPTIONAL)

GARNISH OF EXTRA SNIPPETS OF DILL OR CHIVES

1. Mix all ingredients together and purée in the blender until smooth. Place in a glass or other nonreactive bowl (to avoid staining a reactive bowl with the acidic citrus).

2. Let rest in the refrigerator for 4 hours or overnight.

3. Taste and add seasonings if necessary before serving in chilled bowls.

PER SERVING: Fat: 3 g **Protein:** 11 g **Carbohydrates:** 21 g **Sugar:** 2 g

COLD TOMATO SOUP WITH TOFU

CALORIES: 35
SERVES 2

6 OUNCES SATIN TOFU

8 OUNCES TOMATO JUICE

½ CUP SWEET ONION, COARSELY CHOPPED

1 TO 2 CLOVES GARLIC

½ TEASPOON DRIED OREGANO

1 TEASPOON CHILI POWDER

CELERY SALT AND PEPPER TO TASTE

1 TEASPOON WORCESTERSHIRE SAUCE

½ CUP CRUSHED ICE

1. Place all ingredients in the blender and purée until smooth.

PER SERVING: Fat: 0 g **Protein:** 1 g **Carbohydrates:** 9 g **Sugar:** 1 g

SAVORY FISH STEW

CALORIES: 157
SERVES 6

1 TABLESPOON OLIVE OIL

1 ONION, FINELY CHOPPED

½ CUP DRY WHITE WINE

3 LARGE TOMATOES, CHOPPED

2 CUPS LOW-SODIUM CHICKEN BROTH

8 OUNCES CLAM JUICE

3 CUPS FRESH SPINACH

1 POUND HALIBUT FILETS, CUT INTO 1" PIECES

WHITE PEPPER TO TASTE

1 TABLESPOON FRESH CILANTRO, CHOPPED

1. Place large pan over medium heat. Add oil to the pan and sauté onions for 2–3 minutes. Add wine to deglaze the pan. Scrape the pan to loosen small bits of onion.

2. Add tomatoes and cook for 3–4 minutes, then add broth and clam juice to the pan. Stir in spinach and allow to wilt while continuing to stir.

3. Season fish with pepper. Place fish in the pan and cook for 5–6 minutes until opaque. Mix in cilantro before serving.

PER SERVING: Fat: 7 g **Protein:** 19 g **Carbohydrates:** 7 g **Sugar:** 1 g

ONION SOUP WITH POACHED EGG FLOAT

CALORIES: 392
SERVES 2

- 2 TABLESPOONS OLIVE OIL
- ½ SWEET RED ONION, CHOPPED
- ½ SWEET WHITE ONION, CHOPPED
- 2 SHALLOTS, CHOPPED
- 2¾ CUPS RICH BEEF BROTH
- 2 TABLESPOONS PORT WINE
- 1 BAY LEAF
- 1 TEASPOON WORCESTERSHIRE SAUCE
- SALT AND PEPPER TO TASTE
- 4 EGGS

1. Heat the olive oil in a large saucepan. Add the onions and shallots. Sauté for 6 minutes. Add the beef broth, wine, bay leaf, and Worcestershire sauce. Cover and reduce heat to low. Simmer for 30 minutes.

2. Add salt and pepper to taste. You can chill the soup until just before serving.

3. Heat the soup. Carefully drop in the eggs and poach for 2 minutes. Serve soup with eggs floating on top.

PER SERVING: Fat: 15 g **Protein:** 9 g **Carbohydrates:** 23 g **Sugar:** 2 g

Onions, Shallots, and Chives

When it comes to onions, the more varieties the merrier! When you use several different varieties, you get a depth of flavor that would not be possible if you just use one kind of onion—so mix it up!

EGG DROP SOUP WITH LEMON

CALORIES: 158
SERVES 2

- 1 TABLESPOON PEANUT OIL
- 1 CLOVE GARLIC, MINCED
- 2 CUPS CHICKEN BROTH
- JUICE OF ½ LEMON
- 1 TABLESPOON HOISIN SAUCE
- 1 TEASPOON SOY SAUCE
- 1 TEASPOON ASIAN FISH SAUCE
- ½ TEASPOON CHILI OIL, OR TO TASTE
- 1" FRESH GINGER ROOT, PEELED AND MINCED
- 2 EGGS

1. Heat the peanut oil in a large saucepan. Sauté the garlic over medium heat until softened, about 5 minutes.

2. Add chicken broth, lemon juice, hoisin sauce, soy sauce, fish sauce, chili oil, and ginger root. Stir and cover. Cook over low heat for 20 minutes.

3. Just before serving, whisk the eggs with a fork. Add to the boiling soup and continue to whisk until the eggs form thin strands.

PER SERVING: Fat: 13 g **Protein:** 5 g **Carbohydrates:** 2 g **Sugar:** 0 g

PUMPKIN SOUP

CALORIES: 326
SERVES 4

½ CUP CHOPPED SHALLOTS

2 TABLESPOONS CHOPPED FRESH SAGE

2 TABLESPOONS OLIVE OIL

4 CUPS VEGETABLE BROTH

2 CUPS CANNED PUMPKIN, PEELED AND CHOPPED

½ CUP PLAIN YOGURT

SALT TO TASTE

WHITE PEPPER TO TASTE

½ CUP DRIED CRANBERRIES

½ CUP ROASTED PUMPKIN SEEDS

1. Sauté shallots and sage in olive oil in a soup pot 5 minutes over medium heat. Add vegetable broth and pumpkin.

2. Bring to a boil, then simmer until pumpkin is cooked, about 45 minutes.

3. Purée soup in a blender until smooth.

4. Stir in yogurt and season with salt and white pepper.

5. Serve garnished with dried cranberries and roasted pumpkin seeds sprinkled on top.

PER SERVING: Fat: 11 g **Protein:** 9 g **Carbohydrates:** 22 g **Sugar:** 9 g

BEEF, BARLEY, AND VEGETABLE SOUP

CALORIES: 290
SERVES 8

1 TABLESPOON OLIVE OIL

1 POUND TOP ROUND BEEF, CUBES

8 CUPS BEEF BROTH

1 (8-OUNCE) CAN TOMATO SAUCE

1½ CUPS CARROTS, CHOPPED

1½ CUPS PEAS

1½ CUPS GREEN BEANS, TRIMMED

1½ CUPS BARLEY

4 CLOVES GARLIC, MINCED

1 TABLESPOON ONION POWDER

SALT AND PEPPER TO TASTE

1. Heat olive oil in a large pot over medium heat. Add beef cubes to pot and brown.

2. Add broth and tomato sauce and simmer for 1 hour.

3. Add carrots, peas, green beans, barley, garlic, and onion powder to the pot.

4. Simmer for 45 minutes, until barley is cooked. Add salt and pepper as desired.

PER SERVING: Fat: 6 g **Protein:** 28 g **Carbohydrates:** 30 g **Sugar:** 2 g

BUTTERNUT SQUASH SOUP

CALORIES: 120
SERVES 4

¼ TEASPOON EXTRA-VIRGIN OLIVE OIL

4 CUPS DICED, PEELED BUTTERNUT SQUASH

1 LARGE YELLOW ONION, CHOPPED

4 STALKS CELERY, CHOPPED

1 BAY LEAF

2 TEASPOONS DRIED OREGANO

¼ TEASPOON GROUND NUTMEG

⅓ TEASPOON SALT

¼ TEASPOON FRESHLY GROUND BLACK PEPPER

4 CUPS VEGETABLE STOCK

1. Heat the olive oil in a stockpot over medium heat. Add the squash, onion, and celery; sauté until the onion has softened, about 2 minutes. Add the bay leaf, oregano, nutmeg, salt, and pepper; sauté for an additional 2 minutes.

2. Add the stock and bring to a boil. Reduce heat and simmer until the squash is soft, about 20 to 25 minutes.

3. If desired, use a hand blender to cream the soup. Serve warm.

PER SERVING: Fat: 1 g **Protein:** 3 g **Carbohydrates:** 30 g **Sugar:** 2 g

LEEK AND POTATO SOUP (HOT OR COLD)

CALORIES: 491
SERVES 4

¼ CUP OLIVE OIL

2 LEEKS, COARSELY CHOPPED

1 LARGE SWEET ONION, CHOPPED

2 LARGE BAKING POTATOES, PEELED AND CHOPPED

2 CUPS CHICKEN BROTH

1 TEASPOON SALT

1 CUP 2% MILK

1 CUP WHIPPING CREAM

¼ CUP CHOPPED CHIVES

SALT AND FRESHLY GROUND PEPPER TO TASTE

GARNISH OF ¼ CUP CHOPPED WATERCRESS

IN THIS RECIPE YOU CAN SUBSTITUTE 2% MILK WITH NONFAT MILK.

1. Heat the olive oil in a large soup kettle. Be sure to rinse the sand out of your leeks! Add the leeks and onion and sauté for 5 minutes over medium heat.

2. Add the potatoes, chicken broth, and salt. Simmer until the potatoes are tender. Set aside and cool.

3. Put the soup through a ricer or purée in the blender until smooth.

4. Pour the soup back into the pot, add the milk, whipping cream, and chives and reheat. Add salt and pepper to taste. Float the watercress on top for garnish.

PER SERVING: Fat: 33 g **Protein:** 8 g **Carbohydrates:** 40 g **Sugar:** 5 g

CORN POLENTA CHOWDER

CALORIES: 276
SERVES 6

- 2 STRIPS TURKEY BACON
- 1 TABLESPOON OLIVE OIL
- 1 RED ONION, CHOPPED
- 3 CLOVES GARLIC, MINCED
- 1 RED BELL PEPPER, CHOPPED
- 2 JALAPEÑO PEPPERS, MINCED
- 2 YUKON GOLD POTATOES, CHOPPED
- 5 CUPS LOW-SODIUM CHICKEN BROTH
- ⅓ CUP CORNMEAL
- 2 TABLESPOONS ADOBO SAUCE
- 2 (10-OUNCE) PACKAGES FROZEN CORN, THAWED
- 1 CUP FAT-FREE HALF-AND-HALF
- ¼ CUP CHOPPED CILANTRO
- ⅛ TEASPOON CAYENNE PEPPER

1. In a large soup pot, cook bacon until crisp. Remove from heat, crumble, and set aside. To drippings remaining in pot, add olive oil, then onion and garlic; cook and stir until tender, about 5 minutes.

2. Stir in bell peppers, jalapeños, potatoes, and 3 cups of the broth. Bring to a boil, then reduce heat, cover, and simmer for 20 minutes until potatoes are tender.

3. Meanwhile, in a small microwave-safe bowl, combine cornmeal and 1 cup chicken broth. Microwave on high for 2 minutes, remove and stir, then microwave for 2–4 minutes longer or until mixture thickens; stir in adobo sauce and remaining 1 cup chicken broth. Add to soup along with corn. Simmer for another 10 minutes.

4. Add the half-and-half, cilantro, and cayenne pepper and stir well. Heat until steam rises, then sprinkle with reserved bacon and serve immediately.

PER SERVING: Fat: 10 g **Protein:** 27 g **Carbohydrates:** 69 g **Sugar:** 14 g

BEANS FOR SOUP

CALORIES: 190
SERVES 10

1 POUND DRIED BEANS
WATER, AS NEEDED

1. Sort beans, then rinse well and drain. Combine in a large pot with water to cover by 1". Bring to a boil over high heat, then cover pan, remove from heat, and let stand for 2 hours.

2. Place pot in refrigerator and let beans soak overnight. In the morning, drain beans and rinse; drain again. Place in a 5- to 6-quart slow cooker with water to just cover. Cover and cook on low for 8–10 hours until beans are tender. Do not add salt or any other ingredient.

3. Package beans in 1-cup portions into freezer bags, including a bit of the cooking liquid in each bag. Seal, label, and freeze for up to 3 months. To use, defrost in refrigerator overnight, or open bag and microwave on defrost until beans begin thawing, then stir into soup to heat.

PER SERVING: Fat: 1 g **Protein:** 11 g **Carbohydrates:** 29 g
Sugar: 1 g

Sodium in Canned Beans

A cup of canned beans, even after rinsing and draining, contains about 300 to 500 mg of sodium. A cup of dried beans, cooked until tender, has about 7 mg of sodium. Let your slow cooker do the cooking, and dramatically reduce your sodium intake. Cooking a large batch of beans all at once makes them almost as convenient as canned.

FRESH YELLOW TOMATO SOUP

CALORIES: 197
SERVES 6

WATER, AS NEEDED

8 YELLOW TOMATOES

1 TABLESPOON OLIVE OIL

1 TABLESPOON BUTTER

4 CLOVES GARLIC, PEELED AND MINCED

1 YELLOW BELL PEPPER, CHOPPED

1 RED BELL PEPPER, CHOPPED

4 CUPS LOW-SODIUM CHICKEN BROTH

1 TABLESPOON LEMON JUICE

⅛ TEASPOON WHITE PEPPER

1 LARGE BUNCH BASIL, TORN

¼ CUP TOASTED SLICED ALMONDS

1. Prepare a large bowl of ice water. Bring large pot of water to a boil. Cut an X into the bottom of each tomato and drop tomatoes into boiling water. Bring water back to a boil and simmer for 1 minute, then remove each tomato and drop into ice water. Let cool for 5 minutes, then peel tomatoes; discard skin.

2. Heat a large soup pot over medium heat and add olive oil and butter and let melt. Add garlic; cook and stir for 3 minutes. Cut tomatoes into quarters and add to pot along with peppers. Cook and stir for 4 minutes.

3. Add the broth, lemon juice, and pepper. Bring to a boil and cook for 10 minutes, then add half of the basil.

4. Using an immersion blender, purée soup. Or purée soup in batches in a blender or food processor. Garnish with remaining basil and toasted almonds and serve.

PER SERVING: Fat: 11 g **Protein:** 4 g **Carbohydrates:** 24 g **Sugar:** 3 g

VEGETABLE-BARLEY STEW

CALORIES: 295
SERVES 8

- ¾ POUND BEEF ROUND STEAK
- 2 TABLESPOONS FLOUR
- 1 TEASPOON PAPRIKA
- 2 TABLESPOONS OLIVE OIL
- 2 ONIONS, CHOPPED
- 4 CUPS LOW-SODIUM BEEF BROTH, DIVIDED
- 4 CARROTS, THICKLY SLICED
- 3 POTATOES, CUBED
- 1 (8-OUNCE) PACKAGE SLICED MUSHROOMS
- 3 CUPS WATER
- 1 TEASPOON DRIED MARJORAM LEAVES
- 1 BAY LEAF
- ¼ TEASPOON SALT
- ¼ TEASPOON PEPPER
- ¾ CUP HULLED BARLEY

1. Trim beef and cut into 1" pieces. Sprinkle with flour and paprika and toss to coat. In a large skillet, heat olive oil over medium heat. Add beef; brown beef, stirring occasionally, for about 5–6 minutes. Remove to a 4- to 5-quart slow cooker.

2. Add onions to skillet along with ½ cup beef broth. Bring to a boil, then simmer, scraping the bottom of the skillet, for 3–4 minutes. Add to slow cooker along with all remaining ingredients.

3. Cover and cook on low for 8–9 hours, or until barley and vegetables are tender. Stir, remove bay leaf, and serve immediately.

PER SERVING: Fat: 9 g **Protein:** 14 g **Carbohydrates:** 10 g
Sugar: 2 g

Barley

Barley contains a substance called beta-glucan that has proved effective in reducing cholesterol levels in clinical studies. You can buy barley in several forms. Hulled barley is the most nutritious, while pearl barley is more polished and cooks more quickly. Barley flakes and grits are also available for quick-cooking recipes.

RATATOUILLE

CALORIES: 104
SERVES 6

3 TABLESPOONS OLIVE OIL
2 ONIONS, CHOPPED
4 CLOVES GARLIC, MINCED
1 GREEN BELL PEPPER, SLICED
1 YELLOW BELL PEPPER, SLICED
1 EGGPLANT, PEELED AND CUBED
¼ TEASPOON SALT
⅛ TEASPOON PEPPER
2 TABLESPOONS FLOUR
2 ZUCCHINI, SLICED
1 TABLESPOON RED-WINE VINEGAR
2 TABLESPOONS CAPERS, RINSED
¼ CUP CHOPPED FLAT-LEAF PARSLEY

1. In a large saucepan, heat olive oil over medium heat. Add onion and garlic; cook and stir until crisp-tender, about 3 minutes. Add bell peppers; cook and stir until crisp-tender, about 3 minutes.

2. Sprinkle eggplant with salt, pepper, and flour. Add to saucepan; cook and stir until eggplant begins to soften. Add remaining ingredients except parsley; cover, and simmer for 30–35 minutes or until vegetables are soft and mixture is blended. Sprinkle with parsley and serve.

PER SERVING: Fat: 5 g **Protein:** 1 g **Carbohydrates:** 6 g **Sugar:** 2 g

Eggplant

Eggplant is very low in calories and sodium and has a fairly high fiber content, about 2 grams per cup. It has lots of minerals, but a low vitamin content. It does contain the phytochemical monoterpene, which may help prevent cancer. To reduce bitterness, choose smaller eggplants that are firm and heavy for their size.

BLACK BEAN SOUP

SERVES 6

¼ CUP MINCED SHALLOT

2 TABLESPOONS OLIVE OIL

1 LARGE POTATO, PEELED AND DICED

4 CUPS CHICKEN BROTH

2 CUPS COOKED BLACK BEANS

1 TEASPOON DRIED THYME

½ TEASPOON GROUND CORIANDER

1 TABLESPOON DRY SHERRY

2 TEASPOONS SALT

6 LEMON SLICES

2 TABLESPOONS CHOPPED CHIVES

1. Sauté shallots in olive oil. Add potato and chicken broth and simmer for 30 minutes.

2. Add black beans, thyme, and coriander and simmer 45 minutes.

3. Purée $1/3$ of the soup in a blender and return it to the pot.

4. Stir in the sherry and salt.

5. Serve hot, garnished with lemon slices and chives.

PER SERVING: Fat: 4 g **Protein:** 11 g **Carbohydrates:** 24 g **Sugar:** 1 g

Soaking Beans

To help keep the gas factor down, dried beans need a soak. Fill a saucepan with 1½ quarts water and add 1 cup beans. Bring the water and beans to a boil and simmer for 2 minutes. Turn the heat off and let the beans sit in the water overnight, at least 8 hours. Most of the gas-causing elements will dissolve into the water. Discard the soaking water and add fresh water to cook the beans.

CHAPTER 6: SOUPS AND STEWS   149

CELERY SOUP

2 TABLESPOONS OLIVE OIL
2 CUPS CHOPPED CELERY
1 MEDIUM ONION, CHOPPED
3 TABLESPOONS FLOUR
½ TEASPOON SALT
½ TEASPOON PEPPER
3 CUPS VEGETABLE BROTH
½ CUP CREAM
1 TABLESPOON BUTTER
1 CUP THINLY SLICED CELERY

1. Put the olive oil in a soup pot. Sauté the chopped celery and onion over medium heat for 5 minutes. Sprinkle the flour, salt, and pepper over the vegetables and continue cooking for 2 minutes.

2. Gradually add the vegetable broth and bring to a boil. Turn the heat down and simmer for 15 minutes. Purée the soup in a blender and return it to the pot.

3. Stir in the cream and keep the soup warm on low heat.

4. Melt the butter in a sauté pan and sauté the sliced celery until tender, about 5 minutes.

5. Stir the sautéed celery slices into the soup and serve hot.

PER SERVING: Fat: 12 g **Protein:** 2 g **Carbohydrates:** 11 g
Sugar: 0 g

Creamy Soups

Creamy soups are the most elegant of offerings, suitable for a first course at a sit-down dinner party—and it doesn't take much cream to enrich them. The fiber in these soups is especially digestible for people with diverticulosis or diverticulitis who cannot have seeds or the shells on corn or beans. Fiber is added with a garniture of fresh herbs or grated raw vegetables, such as radishes.

BEET AND CABBAGE BORSCHT

CALORIES: 120
SERVES 8

2 TABLESPOONS OLIVE OIL

1 TEASPOON CARAWAY SEEDS

½ CUP DICED ONION

½ CUP PEELED AND DICED CARROTS

½ CUP DICED CELERY

2 CUPS SHREDDED CABBAGE

½ CUP PEELED, DICED POTATOES

1 CUP PEELED, DICED TOMATOES (CANNED)

2 TABLESPOONS TOMATO PASTE

6 CUPS BEEF BROTH

2 CUPS DICED BEETS (CANNED)

2 TABLESPOONS DRIED DILL WEED

¼ CUP RED-WINE VINEGAR

SALT AND PEPPER TO TASTE

½ CUP SOUR CREAM

3 TABLESPOONS CHOPPED FRESH DILL

1 LOAF PUMPERNICKEL BREAD

1. Put the olive oil in a soup pot and sauté the caraway seeds, onion, carrots, and celery in it over medium heat until tender, about 15 minutes.

2. Add cabbage, potatoes, tomatoes (with liquid), tomato paste, and beef broth, bring to a boil, and simmer 45 minutes.

3. Add the beets (with liquid), dill, and vinegar and simmer 10–15 minutes.

4. Season with salt and pepper to taste.

5. Serve hot garnished with sour cream and chopped fresh dill and sliced pumpernickel bread.

PER SERVING: Fat: 7 g **Protein:** 4 g **Carbohydrates:** 11 g **Sugar:** 3 g

Red or Green?

Either red or green head cabbage may be used for this recipe since the beets color the soup dark red. The cabbage has a goodly amount of fiber if it's not overcooked. You can also add shredded raw cabbage as a garnish.

COCONUT CURRIED
BAN-APPLE SOUP

CALORIES: 255
SERVES 4

2 CUPS VEGETABLE BROTH
1 RIPE BANANA
1 LARGE POTATO
1 GRANNY SMITH APPLE
1 CELERY HEART
1 SWEET ONION
1 CUP COCONUT MILK
1 TEASPOON CURRY POWDER
1 TEASPOON SALT
¼ CUP TOASTED COCONUT
2 TABLESPOONS CHOPPED FRESH CILANTRO

1. Put the vegetable broth in a soup pot.

2. Peel the banana and potato, chop them, and put them in the soup pot. Core the apple, chop it, and add it to the soup pot. Chop the celery heart and onion and add them to the soup pot.

3. Bring the soup to a boil, then lower the heat and simmer for 10 to 15 minutes. Add the coconut milk, curry powder, and salt.

4. Put the hot soup in a blender and purée.

5. Serve the soup hot. Garnish with toasted coconut and cilantro.

PER SERVING: Fat: 13 g **Protein:** 3 g **Carbohydrates:** 34 g **Sugar:** 6 g

Cut the Fat

Coconut milk does add a rich and exotic flavor to the soup, but if you want to cut the fat in this recipe, substitute some other creamy liquid for the coconut milk. Try unsweetened soy milk, half-and-half, milk, or plain yogurt.

MINESTRONE VEGETABLE SOUP

CALORIES: 202
SERVES 6

½ CUP CHOPPED ONION

½ CUP CHOPPED CARROTS

¼ CUP CHOPPED CELERY

2 TABLESPOONS OLIVE OIL

2 CLOVES GARLIC, MINCED

1 CUP CHOPPED CABBAGE

4 CUPS CHICKEN BROTH

1 CUP CHOPPED, PEELED TOMATOES

2 CUPS CHOPPED ZUCCHINI

½ CUP COOKED NAVY BEANS

½ CUP COOKED GARBANZO BEANS

½ CUP BROKEN WHOLE-WHEAT SPAGHETTI

SALT AND PEPPER TO TASTE

¼ CUP BASIL PESTO

½ CUP GRATED PARMESAN CHEESE

1. Sauté the onions, carrots, and celery in the olive oil for 15 minutes.

2. Add garlic and cabbage and cook until cabbage is wilted.

3. Add chicken broth, tomatoes, zucchini, navy beans, and garbanzo beans and bring to a boil.

4. Simmer for 15 minutes. Add the broken spaghetti and simmer 15 minutes longer; then season with salt and pepper.

5. Serve hot with pesto and Parmesan cheese in each serving.

PER SERVING: Fat: 9 g **Protein:** 12 g **Carbohydrates:** 36 g **Sugar:** 6 g

CORN SOUP

- 4 EARS CORN, KERNELS CUT FROM COB AND COBS SAVED
- 5 CUPS WATER
- 1 CARROT, PEELED AND DICED
- 1 STALK CELERY, SLICED
- 1 SMALL ONION, DICED
- 2 TABLESPOONS OLIVE OIL
- 1 TABLESPOON CORNSTARCH
- 1 CUP MILK
- SALT AND PEPPER TO TASTE
- ½ CUP ROASTED RED BELL PEPPERS, DICED
- ¼ CUP BABY CORN
- 2 TABLESPOONS CHOPPED CHIVES

1. Simmer the corn cobs in the water for 15 minutes.

2. Meanwhile, sauté the carrot, celery, and onion in olive oil in a separate pan until tender. Add the corn kernels and sauté 5 minutes.

3. Remove the corn cobs from the water in the soup pot and discard them. Add the sautéed vegetables to the soup pot and simmer 15 minutes. Purée soup in a blender; then return to the pot.

4. Dissolve cornstarch in ¼ cup cold milk. Add remaining milk to soup pot and bring to a simmer. Stir in the cornstarch mixture and cook, stirring until thickened, about 3 minutes. Remove from heat and season with salt and pepper.

5. Serve hot. Garnish with roasted red bell peppers, baby corn, and chives.

PER SERVING: Fat: 6 g **Protein:** 5 g **Carbohydrates:** 24 g
Sugar: 7 g

Summer Soups in Winter

During the chilly season when farmers' markets are closed and your garden is brown, you can still get wonderful fresh produce and an abundance of excellent frozen vegetables. Of course, you can always find cabbage, zucchini, and tomatoes. The nutrition of brightly colored food is undisputed.

COLD FENNEL SOUP

2 TABLESPOONS OLIVE OIL

2 CUPS CHOPPED CELERY

1 MEDIUM SWEET ONION, CHOPPED

1 TEASPOON FENNEL SEEDS

3 TABLESPOONS FLOUR

½ TEASPOON SALT

½ TEASPOON PEPPER

3 CUPS VEGETABLE BROTH

1 CUP DICED FENNEL BULB

½ CUP DICED PEAR

1 TABLESPOON CHOPPED FENNEL FRONDS

1 TABLESPOON ANISE LIQUEUR

½ CUP PLAIN YOGURT

1. Heat the olive oil in a soup pot. Sauté the chopped celery and onion over medium heat for 5 minutes. Sprinkle the fennel seeds, flour, salt, and pepper over the vegetables and continue cooking for 2 minutes.

2. Gradually add the vegetable broth and bring to a boil. Turn the heat down and simmer for about 15 minutes. Purée the soup in a blender.

3. Chill the soup completely.

4. Stir the diced fennel bulb, pear, and chopped fennel fronds with the liqueur.

5. Whisk the yogurt into the chilled soup and adjust the seasoning with salt and pepper. Serve it in coffee mugs garnished with the diced fennel mixture.

PER SERVING: Fat: 5 g **Protein:** 2 g **Carbohydrates:** 13 g **Sugar:** 2 g

SOUTHWEST TORTILLA SOUP

CALORIES: 485
SERVES 6

1 SMALL ONION, DICED

1 CELERY STALK, DICED

2 TABLESPOONS OLIVE OIL

2 GARLIC CLOVES, MINCED

1 CUP CORN KERNELS

4 CUPS CHICKEN BROTH

½ CUP DICED ROASTED RED BELL PEPPER

1 CUP DICED, PEELED TOMATOES

½ CUP TOMATO PURÉE

3 BLUE CORN TORTILLAS, CUT IN ¼" STRIPS

1 TEASPOON GROUND CUMIN

1 TABLESPOON CHILI POWDER

2 TEASPOONS PURÉED CHIPOTLE PEPPERS IN ADOBO SAUCE

SALT AND PEPPER TO TASTE

¼ CUP CHOPPED CILANTRO

2 AVOCADOS, DICED

1 CUP CRUSHED BLUE CORN TORTILLA CHIPS

1 CUP SHREDDED MONTEREY JACK CHEESE

1. Sauté the onion and celery in olive oil until translucent. Add the garlic, corn, chicken broth, bell pepper, tomatoes, and tomato purée.

2. Bring to a boil, add the tortilla strips, cumin, chili powder, and chipotle purée, and simmer for 30 minutes. Remove from heat.

3. Season the soup with salt, pepper, and cilantro.

4. Serve the soup hot garnished with diced avocado, blue corn tortilla chips, and cheese.

PER SERVING: Fat: 24 g **Protein:** 12 g **Carbohydrates:** 59 g **Sugar:** 10 g

Creamy Tortilla Soup

This recipe is for a brothy version of tortilla soup. To transform this recipe into a creamy style of tortilla soup, simply purée the corn kernels before adding them. The starch in the puréed corn will thicken the soup into a creamy yellow version studded with a colorful confetti of vegetables.

CHICKEN AND RICE SOUP

CALORIES: 263
SERVES 6

3 BONELESS, SKINLESS CHICKEN BREASTS
SALT AND PEPPER TO TASTE
4 TABLESPOONS OLIVE OIL
1 SMALL ONION
2 CLOVES GARLIC
3 STALKS CELERY, CHOPPED
2 CARROTS, PEELED AND CHOPPED
44 OUNCES CHICKEN BROTH
¾ TABLESPOON THYME
2 CUPS CABBAGE, SHREDDED
2 BAY LEAVES
1 CUP WATER
¾ CUP LONG-GRAIN BROWN RICE

1. Wash chicken and pat dry. Season with salt and pepper and chop into 1"-thick pieces.

2. Heat 2 tablespoons oil in pan and sauté chicken pieces for 6 to 8 minutes, until chicken is well done. Set chicken aside for later.

3. Heat oil in a large pot, sauté onion and garlic over medium heat until translucent. Add celery and carrot to pot and cook for 5 minutes.

4. Add chicken broth, thyme, cooked chicken, cabbage, bay leaves, water, and rice to the pot. Simmer soup for 30 minutes or until rice is completely cooked.

PER SERVING: Fat: 10 g **Protein:** 24 g **Carbohydrates:** 19 g **Sugar:** 2 g

YELLOW PEPPER AND TOMATO SOUP

CALORIES: 176
SERVES 4

¼ CUP PEANUT OIL

½ CUP SWEET WHITE ONION, CHOPPED

2 CLOVES GARLIC, MINCED

1 SWEET YELLOW BELL PEPPER, SEEDED, FINELY CHOPPED

1½ CUPS CHICKEN BROTH

4 MEDIUM-SIZED YELLOW TOMATOES, CORED AND PURÉED

½ TEASPOON CUMIN, GROUND

½ TEASPOON CORIANDER, GROUND

JUICE OF ½ LEMON

SALT AND PEPPER TO TASTE

GARNISH OF FRESH BASIL LEAVES, TORN

1. In a soup kettle, heat the oil over medium flame and sauté the onion, garlic, and yellow pepper. After about 5 minutes add the chicken broth and tomatoes.

2. Stir in the seasonings, lemon juice, salt, and pepper.

3. Cover and simmer. You can purée the soup if you wish or leave some bits of texture in it.

4. Serve hot or cold and sprinkle with basil.

PER SERVING: Fat: 14 g **Protein:** 2 g **Carbohydrates:** 12 g **Sugar:** 3 g

Colorful Veggies

Yellow fruits and vegetables are loaded with vitamin A, or retinol, which keeps your skin moist and helps your eyes adjust to changes in light. It is important to eat a variety of different-colored fruits and vegetables every day.

SPINACH AND SAUSAGE SOUP WITH PINK BEANS

CALORIES: 344
SERVES 4

8 OUNCES ITALIAN SWEET SAUSAGE, CUT IN BITE-SIZE CHUNKS

2 CUPS WATER

¼ CUP OLIVE OIL

2 WHITE ONIONS, CHOPPED

4 CLOVES GARLIC, CHOPPED

2 STALKS CELERY, CHOPPED, LEAVES INCLUDED

2 CUPS BEEF BROTH

BUNCH FRESH SPINACH, KALE, OR ESCAROLE, OR 1 (10-OUNCE) PACKAGE FROZEN, CHOPPED SPINACH

1 TEASPOON DRIED OREGANO

1 TEASPOON RED PEPPER FLAKES

1 (13-OUNCE) CAN PINK OR RED KIDNEY BEANS, DRAINED

SALT TO TASTE

GRATED PARMESAN CHEESE

1. Place the sausage in a soup kettle. Add ¾ cup water and bring to a boil; let water boil off. Add the oil if dry and sauté the onions, garlic, and celery for 10 minutes over medium-low heat.

2. Stir in the rest of the ingredients except the cheese; cover and simmer for 35 minutes. Serve in heated bowls. Garnish with grated Parmesan cheese.

PER SERVING: Fat: 20 g **Protein:** 19 g **Carbohydrates:** 28 g
Sugar: 2 g

Vegetarian Option

This recipe can easily be transformed into a vegetarian-friendly soup. Substitute vegetarian sausage for Italian sausage and use vegetable broth instead of beef broth.

MEDITERRANEAN SEAFOOD SOUP

CALORIES: 450
SERVES 2

- 2 TABLESPOONS OLIVE OIL
- ½ CUP SWEET ONION, CHOPPED
- 2 CLOVES GARLIC, CHOPPED
- ½ BULB FENNEL, CHOPPED
- ½ CUP DRY WHITE WINE
- 1 CUP CLAM BROTH (CANNED IS FINE)
- 2 CUPS TOMATOES, CHOPPED
- 6 LITTLENECK CLAMS, TIGHTLY CLOSED
- 6 MUSSELS, TIGHTLY CLOSED
- 8 RAW SHRIMP, JUMBO, PEELED AND DEVEINED
- 1 TEASPOON DRIED BASIL, OR 5 LEAVES FRESH BASIL, TORN
- SALT AND RED PEPPER FLAKES TO TASTE

1. Heat the oil over medium flame and add onion, garlic, and fennel. After 10 minutes, stir in the wine and clam broth and add the tomatoes. Bring to a boil.

2. Drop clams into the boiling liquid. When clams start to open, add the mussels. When mussels start to open, put in the shrimp, basil, salt, and pepper flakes. Serve when shrimp turns pink.

PER SERVING: Fat: 18 g **Protein:** 48 g **Carbohydrates:** 19 g **Sugar:** 1 g

Littleneck Clams

Littleneck clams are the smallest variety of hard-shell clams and can be found on the northern East and West Coasts of the United States. They have a sweet taste and are delicious steamed and dipped in melted butter, battered and fried, or baked.

CASHEW ZUCCHINI SOUP

CALORIES: 117
SERVES 4

- **4 MEDIUM ZUCCHINI**
- **1 LARGE VIDALIA ONION, CHOPPED**
- **4 CLOVES GARLIC, CHOPPED**
- **½ TEASPOON SALT**
- **¼ TEASPOON GROUND PEPPER**
- **3 CUPS VEGETABLE BROTH**
- **½ CUP RAW CASHEWS**
- **½ TEASPOON DRIED TARRAGON**
- **ADDITIONAL SALT AND PEPPER TO TASTE**

1. Coarsely chop zucchini.

2. Cook onion in a large saucepan for 5 minutes, until soft and translucent. Add garlic and cook for 1 minute. Stir in chopped zucchini, salt, and pepper and cook over medium heat, covered, occasionally stirring, for 5 minutes.

3. Add the broth and simmer for 15 minutes.

4. Add cashews and tarragon. Purée soup in blender in 1 to 2 batches. Fill blender up to halfway to avoid burns from the hot liquid.

5. Return soup to the pot, season with additional salt and pepper as desired.

PER SERVING: Fat: 8 g **Protein:** 6 g **Carbohydrates:** 23 g **Sugar:** 1 g

Cashew Nut Butter

To save time, you may substitute whole raw cashews with cashew nut butter. You will enjoy using the leftover cashew nut butter as a spread on sandwiches and as a dip for fresh fruit. Remember when snacking on nut butters that they are high in calories, so limit the portion size.

BAKED POTATO SOUP

CALORIES: 177
SERVES 4

NONSTICK COOKING SPRAY

1 (16-OUNCE) BAG FROZEN COUNTRY-STYLE POTATOES

½ CUP SHREDDED SHARP CHEDDAR CHEESE

¼ TEASPOON BACON BASE

¼ TEASPOON HAM BASE

½ TEASPOON LOW-SODIUM CHICKEN BASE

¼ CUP NONFAT YOGURT

¼ CUP INSTANT NONFAT DRY MILK

1 CUP GARLIC BROTH

¼ CUP HERB BROTH

2½ CUPS WATER

FRESHLY GROUND PEPPER, TO TASTE

FRESH CHIVES, SNIPPED (OPTIONAL)

1. Preheat oven to 350°.

2. Treat a deep (3-quart or larger) Pyrex casserole dish with nonstick spray. Spread the frozen potatoes over the bottom of the pan. Cover with microwave-safe plastic wrap and microwave for 3 minutes at 50 percent power to defrost the potato mixture. Remove and discard the plastic wrap. Top with the cheese.

3. In a blender or food processor, combine the bases, yogurt, dry milk, broths, and water; pulse until well mixed. Pour the mixture over the cheese and potatoes. Bake for 45 minutes or until the cheese is melted and bubbly. Sprinkle with the freshly ground pepper and snipped chives, if desired, and serve.

PER SERVING: Fat: 5 g **Protein:** 9 g **Carbohydrates:** 26 g **Sugar:** 5 g

PEPPER POT SOUP

CALORIES: 285
SERVES 4

- 2 TEASPOONS OLIVE OIL
- 1 MEDIUM-SIZED SWEET ONION, CHOPPED
- 1 LARGE GREEN BELL PEPPER, CLEANED, SEEDED, AND CHOPPED
- 1 LEEK, CLEANED AND CHOPPED (OPTIONAL)
- 1 GREEN ONION, CLEANED AND CHOPPED (OPTIONAL)
- 1 SHALLOT, CLEANED AND CHOPPED (OPTIONAL)
- ¼ TEASPOON DRIED THYME
- ¼ TEASPOON DRIED MARJORAM
- ¼ TEASPOON GROUND CLOVES
- PINCH OF DRIED RED PEPPER FLAKES
- ½ TEASPOON FRESHLY GROUND BLACK PEPPER
- 4-OUNCE BONELESS SIRLOIN STEAK, THINLY SLICED AGAINST THE GRAIN, THEN CUT INTO SMALL PIECES
- ¼ TEASPOON HAM BASE
- ¼ TEASPOON BACON BASE
- 1 TEASPOON LOW-SODIUM BEEF BASE
- 4 MEDIUM-SIZED POTATOES, PEELED AND DICED
- 1 BAY LEAF
- 4 CUPS WATER

1. In a large, deep nonstick sauté pan, heat the oil over medium heat. Add the chopped onion, green pepper, and the leek, green onion, and shallot (if using); sauté until the onion is transparent.

2. Add the thyme, marjoram, cloves, red pepper flakes, and black pepper. Stir to mix with the green peppers and onions. Push the vegetables to the side of the pan and add the beef; stir-fry for 2 minutes.

3. Add the bases and stir to dissolve. Add the potatoes; stir and lightly sauté in the onion-beef mixture for about 1 minute.

4. Add the bay leaf and water; bring to a boil. Reduce heat, cover, and simmer for 20 minutes or until the potatoes are tender. Remove and discard the bay leaf before serving. Optional step: For a thicker soup, use a hand blender to cream the soup. The starch from the potatoes acts as a natural roux (without adding the fat and calories of a roux made with butter and flour). Serve warm garnished with an additional grind of freshly ground black pepper on top.

PER SERVING: Fat: 5 g **Protein:** 12 g **Carbohydrates:** 47 g **Sugar:** 2 g

ORIENTAL TUNA-MUSHROOM SOUP

CALORIES: 145
SERVES 4

- **5 CUPS WATER**
- **1 OUNCE DRIED WHOLE SHIITAKE MUSHROOMS**
- **½ TEASPOON BRAGG LIQUID AMINOS**
- **1 TEASPOON HONEY**
- **2 CUPS FRESH BUTTON MUSHROOMS, SLICED**
- **2 TEASPOONS LOW-SODIUM CHICKEN BASE**
- **4 TEASPOONS ORGANIC MISO (YELLOW, SHINSHU MISO)**
- **2 SLICES PEELED GINGER**
- **4 (¼") SLICES SOFT, SILKEN TOFU**
- **1 (6-OUNCE) CAN LOW-SODIUM TUNA, DRAINED**
- **4 LARGE GREEN SCALLIONS, WHITE AND GREEN PART FINELY CHOPPED**

1. In a saucepan or teakettle, bring the water to a boil. Place the dried mushrooms in a bowl and pour enough boiling water over them to cover generously; set aside.

2. Add about ½ cup of the boiling water to a large, heavy nonstick skillet. Stir in the Bragg Liquid Aminos and honey. Add the sliced fresh mushrooms to the skillet, cover, and simmer on medium-low until tender, about 2 minutes. Remove from heat and set aside.

3. Use a slotted spoon to remove the reconstituted dried mushrooms from the water. Add the mushrooms to the skillet with the fresh mushrooms. Strain the liquid from the dried mushrooms to remove any sediment.

4. In another saucepan, whisk together the remaining water and the strained mushroom liquid with the chicken base, miso, and ginger. Bring to a simmer over medium heat for 5 minutes. Remove the ginger and keep the liquid hot.

5. To serve, place a slice of the tofu in each of 4 warmed soup bowls and top with the cooked mushrooms and tuna. Evenly ladle the chicken broth–miso soup on top and garnish with the chopped scallions.

PER SERVING: Fat: 3 g **Protein:** 16 g **Carbohydrates:** 14 g **Sugar:** 2 g

QUICK THICK PEANUT SOUP

CALORIES: 282
SERVES 4

- ½ CUP CREAMY NO-SALT-ADDED PEANUT BUTTER
- 1 TEASPOON ONION POWDER
- 1 TEASPOON DRIED CELERY FLAKES
- PINCH OF DRIED RED PEPPER FLAKES
- 1 TEASPOON LOW-SODIUM CHICKEN BASE
- ¼ TEASPOON HAM BASE
- 3 CUPS WATER
- ¼ CUP INSTANT NONFAT DRY MILK
- ½ CUP UNSEASONED, NO-SALT-ADDED INSTANT POTATO FLAKES OR POTATO FLOUR

1. Heat the peanut butter in a nonstick saucepan over medium heat. Add the onion powder, celery flakes, dried peppers, and bases, stirring constantly until the bases are dissolved and well mixed.

2. In a blender or food processor, combine the water, dry milk, and potato granules; process until blended.

3. Slowly pour the water mixture into the peanut butter, whisking to combine. Lower the heat and simmer until the mixture is heated through and thickened, stirring gently. Serve immediately.

PER SERVING: Fat: 16 g **Protein:** 11 g **Carbohydrates:** 25 g **Sugar:** 3 g

Compost Broth

This isn't as yucky as it sounds. Rather, it's a frugal way to use the peelings from vegetables that you'd probably otherwise just throw away. Instead, wash vegetables before you peel them and place the peelings in a 1-gallon sealable plastic bag. Store the bag in the refrigerator for few days until you've got enough peelings and you're ready to make the broth. Include stuff you'd usually never dream of using, like onion and garlic peel! Simmer the peelings in at least 1 gallon of water for 1 hour. Strain the broth, and voilà! You have veggie broth.

CHAPTER 7

Sandwiches and Wraps

"EGG" SALAD SANDWICH SPREAD

CALORIES: 105
SERVES 6

½ (12-OUNCE) PACKAGE FIRM TOFU

⅓ CUP LOW-FAT MAYONNAISE

2 TABLESPOONS PLAIN YOGURT

2 TABLESPOONS DIJON MUSTARD

⅛ TEASPOON PEPPER

½ TEASPOON DRIED OREGANO LEAVES

1 CUP CHOPPED CELERY

1 RED BELL PEPPER, CHOPPED

¼ CUP GRATED PARMESAN CHEESE

1. Drain tofu and drain again on paper towels, pressing to remove moisture. Set aside.

2. In medium-size bowl, combine remaining ingredients and stir gently to combine. Crumble tofu into bowl and mix until mixture looks like egg salad. Cover tightly and refrigerate for 2–3 hours before serving. Store, covered, in the refrigerator for 3–4 days.

PER SERVING (½ CUP): Fat: 7 g **Protein:** 12 g **Carbohydrates:** 12 g **Sugar:** 2 g

Tofu

The best tofu to use for fake egg-salad sandwich spread is firm or extra-firm, depending on the consistency you like. Be sure to drain it very well; in fact, you can let it stand in a strainer for 30–40 minutes before using. If you don't, the excess liquid in the tofu will ruin the sandwich spread.

BROILED SWORDFISH CLUB

CALORIES: 419
SERVES 2

4 SLICES LEAN BACON OR TURKEY BACO

2 SWORDFISH FILETS, ABOUT 5 OUNCES EACH

2 TABLESPOONS LEMON JUICE

SALT AND PEPPER TO TASTE

2 TEASPOONS LOW-FAT MAYONNAISE

1 TEASPOON DRIED DILL, OR 2 TEASPOONS FRESH DILL WEED

4 SLICES WHOLE GRAIN BREAD

8 THIN SLICES CUCUMBER

4 SLICES FRESH TOMATO

IN THIS RECIPE YOU CAN SUBSTITUTE CANADIAN BACON OR VEGETARIAN BACON FOR REGULAR BACON.

1. Fry the bacon and drain on a paper towel. Sprinkle the fish with lemon juice, salt, and pepper. Run under a hot (450°F) broiler for 3 minutes per side.

2. Mix the mayonnaise and dill. Spread on the bread. Stack the bacon, fish, cucumber, and tomato on two slices of bread. Finish with top slice and cut. Serve with crunchy cucumber slices.

PER SERVING: Fat: 18 g **Protein:** 39 g **Carbohydrates:** 29 g **Sugar:** 2 g

Fresh Fish and Seafood Sandwiches

Because items like swordfish, tuna, shrimp, and other seafood cook so quickly, they are ideal for a fast sandwich. During the summer, cook your shrimp the night before and refrigerate it, or you can buy precooked and shelled shrimp, trading flavor for convenience.

GRILLED VEGETABLE AND THREE CHEESE PANINI

CALORIES: 459
SERVES 2

- 2 BABY EGGPLANTS, THINLY SLICED
- ½ YELLOW SUMMER SQUASH, CUT IN ¼" COINS
- ¼ CUP ITALIAN DRESSING
- 1 SWEET RED PEPPER, CORED AND SEEDED
- 2 TEASPOONS PARMESAN CHEESE, GRATED
- 4 SLICES TUSCAN BREAD (TRY TO GET WHOLE WHEAT OR SOURDOUGH)
- 2 SLICES MUENSTER CHEESE, THINLY SLICED
- 2 TEASPOONS GORGONZOLA CHEESE, CRUMBLED
- OIL FOR PANINI PRESS OR FRYING PAN

1. Brush eggplant and squash with Italian dressing and grill. Grill red pepper, skin side to flame until it chars. Place red pepper, while still hot, in a plastic bag. The skin will come right off! Sprinkle veggies with Parmesan cheese and set aside.

2. Spread both sides of 4 pieces of bread with Italian dressing. Load with vegetables and Muenster and Gorgonzola cheeses.

3. Place panini on lightly oiled fry pan or panini press. If using a fry pan, cover it with a second pan or foil-covered brick. Toast the sandwich on medium heat until very brown. Turn if using a frying pan.

4. Cut sandwiches and serve piping hot!

PER SERVING: Fat: 24 g **Protein:** 23 g **Carbohydrates:** 48 g **Sugar:** 2 g

SHRIMP AND CUCUMBER TEA SANDWICH

CALORIES: 164
SERVES 2

- ¼ POUND SHRIMP, COOKED
- 2 TABLESPOONS LOW-FAT CREAM CHEESE, AT ROOM TEMPERATURE
- 2 TABLESPOONS SWEET ONION, CHOPPED
- ½ TEASPOON DILL, DRIED, OR 1 TABLESPOON FRESH DILL
- 4 SLICES EXTRA-THIN WHOLE-WHEAT BREAD, CRUSTS TRIMMED
- SALT AND PEPPER TO TASTE
- 8 SLICES CUCUMBER

1. Place the shrimp, cream cheese, onion, and dill in the food processor or blender. Pulse until well mixed, but not puréed.

2. Spread the shrimp mixture on the bread. Sprinkle with salt and pepper and top with cucumber slices. Finish with final slice of bread and cut in diamonds.

PER SERVING: Fat: 5 g **Protein:** 17 g **Carbohydrates:** 16 g **Sugar:** 2 g

Tea Time
Tea sandwiches are small and dainty in order to stave off hunger until dinnertime. Traditionally, tea sandwiches are served on thinly sliced, buttered white bread lightly spread with a cream cheese or mayonnaise-based mixture and topped with fresh vegetables.

HAM AND CHEESE CHUTNEY SANDWICH

CALORIES: 290
SERVES 4

LIGHT COOKING SPRAY
¼ CUP EGG BEATERS
2 TABLESPOONS FAT-FREE MILK
1 TEASPOON DIJON MUSTARD
½ TEASPOON CINNAMON
SALT AND PEPPER TO TASTE
4 TABLESPOONS PREPARED MANGO CHUTNEY
8 SLICES WHOLE-WHEAT BREAD
8 SLICES FAT-FREE BAKED HAM
4 SLICES LOW-FAT SWISS CHEESE

1. Coat a pan or griddle with cooking spray over medium heat.

2. Combine Egg Beaters, milk, mustard, cinnamon, salt, and pepper in a medium-size bowl.

3. Spread chutney on 4 slices of bread. Top with ham and cheese slice and finish with another piece of bread.

4. Place sandwiches in egg mixture and coat on both sides. Cook each sandwich in hot pan, browning on both sides. When cheese is melted, transfer to plates.

PER SERVING: Fat: 7 g **Protein:** 22 g **Carbohydrates:** 37 g **Sugar:** 5 g

SPICY RANCH CHICKEN WRAP

CALORIES: 268
SERVES 4

2 CUPS DICED CHICKEN
1 TEASPOON MINCED GARLIC
¼ TEASPOON GROUND RED HOT PEPPER
⅛ TEASPOON GROUND CUMIN
½ CUP FLOUR
¾ CUP CHICKEN BROTH
½ CUP FAT-FREE MILK
2 TABLESPOONS LOW-FAT SOUR CREAM
SALT AND PEPPER TO TASTE
4 6-INCH CORN TORTILLAS
½ CUP LIGHT RANCH DRESSING

1. Mix chicken, garlic, hot pepper, and cumin in a saucepan over medium heat. Cook for 15 minutes until chicken is no longer pink.

2. Stir in flour, chicken broth, milk, sour cream, and salt and pepper, mixing occasionally.

3. Heat oven to 350°F. Warm tortillas in the oven.

4. Wrap chicken mixture in warmed tortillas. Drizzle ranch dressing over tortillas and serve.

PER SERVING: Fat: 11 g **Protein:** 24 g **Carbohydrates:** 17 g **Sugar:** 4 g

GINGER CHICKEN SALAD WRAP

CALORIES: 310
SERVES 4

1 CUP CHOPPED CHICKEN BREAST

¼ CUP OLIVE OIL

1 (14-OUNCE) CAN ORIENTAL MIXED VEGETABLES, DRAINED

⅔ CUP MIRACLE WHIP SALAD DRESSING

2 TABLESPOONS REDUCED-SODIUM SOY SAUCE

1 TEASPOON GROUND GINGER

4 6-INCH CORN TORTILLAS

1. Sauté chicken breast in olive oil in a large skillet over medium heat. Add vegetables and sauté until chicken is cooked. Transfer chicken and vegetables to a large bowl. Mix in the Miracle Whip, soy sauce, and ginger.

2. Heat the broiler, and warm the tortillas.

3. Spoon chicken mixture into tortillas. Roll up and serve.

PER SERVING: Fat: 16 g **Protein:** 16 g **Carbohydrates:** 24 g **Sugar:** 4 g

Rolling Tortillas

Lay the tortilla on a flat surface and place the ingredients on one half of the tortilla so that you can fold it over and roll without ingredients spilling out.

CONWAY WELSH RAREBIT MELT

CALORIES: 430
SERVES 4

¼ CUP UNSALTED BUTTER

¼ CUP FLOUR

½ CUP LIGHT BEER

½ POUND LOW-FAT EXTRA SHARP CHEDDAR CHEESE, GRATED

½ TEASPOON WORCESTERSHIRE SAUCE

2–3 DROPS TABASCO SAUCE

8 HALVES WHOLE-WHEAT ENGLISH MUFFINS, TOASTED

1. Melt butter in a saucepan over low heat. Add flour; whisk mixture until smooth.

2. Pour in beer and boil for 3 minutes, continuing to whisk.

3. Reduce heat; add Cheddar cheese, Worcestershire sauce, and Tabasco sauce. Continue to cook until all ingredients are combined. Pour mixture over toasted muffins and serve.

PER SERVING: Fat: 22 g **Protein:** 24 g **Carbohydrates:** 34 g **Sugar:** 3 g

Welsh Rarebit

This sandwich's origins come directly from Conwy, Wales. It's an eighteenth-century dish, served in taverns throughout England, and usually garnished with tomato and parsley.

MAMA'S EGG SALAD SANDWICH

CALORIES: 283
SERVES 4

6 HARD-BOILED EGGS

½ CUP FAT-FREE MIRACLE WHIP SALAD DRESSING

¼ CUP FINELY CHOPPED CELERY

2 TABLESPOONS FINELY CHOPPED FLAT-LEAF PARSLEY

SALT AND PEPPER TO TASTE

8 SLICES BREAD

1. Separate the hard-boiled egg whites from the yolks. Finely chop egg whites.

2. Press egg yolks through a sieve and add to chopped egg whites in small bowl. Add salad dressing, celery, and parsley and blend well. Season with salt and pepper to taste.

3. Chill mixture for one hour. Spread on your favorite bread.

PER SERVING: Fat: 11 g **Protein:** 15 g **Carbohydrates:** 32 g **Sugar:** 2 g

SIMPLE TUNA SALAD SANDWICH

CALORIES: 330
SERVES 1

4 OUNCES CHUNK LIGHT TUNA, CANNED IN WATER

1 TEASPOON LIGHT MAYO

½ TEASPOON DIJON MUSTARD

2 TABLESPOONS CELERY, CHOPPED

2 SLICES WHOLE-WHEAT BREAD

3 LEAVES ROMAINE LETTUCE

2 SLICES TOMATO

1. Combine tuna, mayo, mustard, and celery in a small bowl.

2. Lightly toast bread. Top bread with tuna salad, lettuce, and tomato to make sandwich.

PER SERVING: Fat: 8 g **Protein:** 37 g **Carbohydrates:** 28 g **Sugar:** 2 g

GREEK CHICKEN PITA

CALORIES: 480
SERVES 1

3 OUNCES CHICKEN BREAST, THINLY SLICED

SALT AND PEPPER TO TASTE

1 TABLESPOON OLIVE OIL

JUICE OF 1 LEMON

½ TEASPOON OREGANO

1 WHOLE-WHEAT PITA

2 TABLESPOONS FETA CHEESE, CRUMBLED

¼ CUP CUCUMBER, THINLY SLICED

¼ CUP TOMATO, CHOPPED

¼ CUP ROMAINE LETTUCE, CHOPPED

1. Season chicken with salt and pepper as desired. Add olive oil to a small pan and sauté chicken slices over medium heat. While cooking, add lemon juice and oregano to chicken. Cook until completely cooked, about 8 minutes.

2. Toast pita bread. Stuff pita bread with chicken, feta cheese, cucumber, tomato, and romaine lettuce.

PER SERVING: Fat: 22 g **Protein:** 30 g **Carbohydrates:** 43 g **Sugar:** 2 g

---

GRILLED HAM AND CHEESE

CALORIES: 360
SERVES 1

1 TEASPOON BUTTER

2 SLICES WHOLE-WHEAT BREAD

3 OUNCES PROSCIUTTO OR DELI HAM

1 SLICE GRUYÈRE CHEESE

1 TEASPOON DIJON MUSTARD

1. Heat pan and melt butter, spreading melted butter to coat pan.

2. Make sandwich with bread, ham, cheese, and mustard and place into buttered pan.

3. Cook sandwich over medium heat for 2–3 minutes on each side or until cheese melts and the bread is golden brown.

PER SERVING: Fat: 17 g **Protein:** 27 g **Carbohydrates:** 25 g **Sugar:** 2 g

GRILLED CHICKEN SANDWICH

CALORIES: 420
SERVES 1

JUICE OF 1 ORANGE
JUICE OF 1 LEMON
1 TEASPOON OLIVE OIL
½ TEASPOON LEMON PEPPER
SALT TO TASTE
1 BONELESS, SKINLESS CHICKEN BREAST
1 TEASPOON BUTTER
1 MULTIGRAIN ROLL
1 SLICE OF LOW-FAT SWISS CHEESE
3 LEAVES OF ROMAINE LETTUCE
2 SLICES TOMATO

1. Blend orange juice, lemon juice, oil, lemon pepper, and salt in a small dish. Marinate chicken breast in citrus blend, covered and refrigerated, for 4–6 hours or overnight.

2. Grill chicken breast for 10 minutes or until juices run clear and chicken is completely cooked. Meanwhile butter each side of roll and place on the grill, buttered side facing down, to lightly toast.

3. Place grilled chicken breast, cheese, lettuce, and tomato on bun and serve.

PER SERVING: Fat: 13 g **Protein:** 39 g **Carbohydrates:** 38 g **Sugar:** 2 g

THANKSGIVING WRAPS

CALORIES: 89
SERVES 12

2 CUPS COOKED TURKEY, DICED
1 STALK CELERY, MINCED
½ CUP RED SEEDLESS GRAPES, HALVED
2 TABLESPOONS RED ONION, MINCED
¼ CUP DRIED CRANBERRIES
6 TABLESPOONS LOW-FAT MAYONNAISE
1 TEASPOON DRIED THYME
SALT AND PEPPER TO TASTE
12 LARGE ROMAINE LETTUCE LEAVES

1. Toss all but the lettuce together in a large bowl.

2. Lay out the lettuce leaves, add turkey filling, and roll them up.

PER SERVING: Fat: 3 g **Protein:** 11 g **Carbohydrates:** 3 g **Sugar:** 5 g

Cranberry Additions
Dried cranberries make a tasty addition to many everyday foods. Add them to cereal, trail mix, oatmeal cookies, chocolate chip cookies, and salads for a sweet and tart surprise.

MELTED GORGONZOLA AND ASPARAGUS IN CORN TORTILLAS

CALORIES: 154
SERVES 2

1 TEASPOON OLIVE OIL

1 TABLESPOON SWEET ONION, MINCED

½ OF ONE 10-OUNCE BOX FROZEN ASPARAGUS SPEARS, THAWED AND CHOPPED

1 OUNCE GORGONZOLA CHEESE

BLACK PEPPER TO TASTE

NONSTICK SPRAY

2 CORN TORTILLAS

1. Heat the olive oil over medium setting. Add onion and asparagus and cook, stirring for 10 minutes. Remove from the heat and add the cheese and pepper.

2. Using a grill or griddle that you've prepared with nonstick spray, toast the tortillas on one side. Turn and spread with the asparagus and cheese mixture. Fold in half and brown lightly on both sides.

PER SERVING: Fat: 7 g **Protein:** 9 g **Carbohydrates:** 18 g **Sugar:** 1 g

GRILLED PORK AND MANGO SALSA SANDWICH

CALORIES: 371
SERVES 4

1 PACKAGE CORN MUFFIN MIX

1 POUND PORK TENDERLOIN, TRIMMED

2 TABLESPOONS SOY SAUCE

SALT AND PEPPER TO TASTE

2 TABLESPOONS PEANUT OIL

½ CUP MANGO SALSA

1. Using the corn muffin mix, follow the directions for corn bread. Bake; cut into 8 squares (2" × 2").

2. Sprinkle the pork tenderloin with soy sauce, salt, and pepper.

3. Heat a heavy frying pan and add the peanut oil. Sauté the pork for 8 minutes per side or until medium, turning frequently. When done, let the pork rest for 8 to 10 minutes. Slice thinly on a diagonal.

4. Place 2 pieces of corn bread on serving plates. Stack slices of pork on each. Top with mango salsa.

PER SERVING: Fat: 17 g **Protein:** 39 g **Carbohydrates:** 16 g **Sugar:** 5 g

BUFFALO MOZZARELLA WITH GREEK OLIVES AND ROASTED RED PEPPERS

CALORIES: 58
SERVES 12

- ½ CUP GREEK OLIVES, PITTED AND CHOPPED
- ½ CUP JARRED RED ROASTED PEPPERS PACKED IN OLIVE OIL, CHOPPED
- 2 TABLESPOONS RED-WINE VINEGAR
- 4 OUNCES BUFFALO MOZZARELLA CHEESE, THINLY SLICED
- 3 LARGE WHOLE-WHEAT PITAS

1. Mix the chopped olives and red peppers with the vinegar. Push the mozzarella and vegetables into the pita pockets.

2. Place on a baking sheet. Bake at 350°F until golden brown, about 15 minutes.

3. When browned and hot, cut sandwiches in quarters and serve.

PER SERVING: Fat: 1 g **Protein:** 4 g **Carbohydrates:** 11 g **Sugar:** 3 g

Buffalo Mozzarella

Unlike most available mozzarella cheese, which is made from cow's milk, buffalo mozzarella is made from the milk of water buffalo. Since buffalo milk contains far more butterfat than cow's milk, the result is a much creamier cheese that is still slightly elastic and mild like other fresh mozzarella cheese.

VEGGIE BURRITO

CALORIES: 405
SERVES 1

- 1 RED BELL PEPPER, SLICED INTO THIN STRIPS
- ½ SMALL ONION, SLICED INTO THIN STRIPS
- ½ CUP MUSHROOMS, SLICED
- 1 SMALL WHOLE-WHEAT TORTILLA
- ½ CUP BLACK BEANS, COOKED
- 2 TABLESPOONS MONTEREY JACK CHEESE, SHREDDED
- ¼ CUP TOMATO, CHOPPED
- ½ TABLESPOON FRESH CILANTRO, CHOPPED

1. In a medium nonstick pan, sauté bell pepper, onion, and mushroom slices over medium heat.

2. Put tortilla on a large plate. Top tortilla with sautéed vegetables, cooked black beans, cheese, tomato, and cilantro. Roll up tortilla to make a burrito.

PER SERVING: Fat: 11 g **Protein:** 22 g **Carbohydrates:** 59 g **Sugar:** 5 g

ROAST BEEF PITAS

CALORIES: 201
SERVES 6

- ½ CUP CHOPPED FRESH BASIL
- 2 TABLESPOONS PREPARED HORSERADISH
- ½ CUP PLAIN NONFAT YOGURT
- ⅛ TEASPOON PEPPER
- 1 POUND DELI-SLICED LEAN ROAST BEEF
- 1 HEAD BUTTER LETTUCE
- 2 TOMATOES, SLICED
- 3 WHOLE-WHEAT PITA BREADS, HALVED

1. In a large bowl, stir together the basil, horseradish, yogurt, and pepper. Spread the horseradish-yogurt mixture on the beef slices.

2. Separate lettuce into individual leaves and wrap each beef slice in a lettuce leaf. Put the lettuce-wrapped beef and 2 slices of tomato into each pita bread half. Serve immediately.

PER SERVING: Fat: 3 g **Protein:** 34 g **Carbohydrates:** 36 g **Sugar:** 4 g

CRUNCHY TUNA SALAD MELT ON RYE

CALORIES: 399
SERVES 4

- 1 (6-OUNCE) CAN TUNA PACKED IN WATER, DRAINED
- ¼ CUP ONION, DICED
- 2 TABLESPOONS CELERY, DICED
- ¾ CUP SHREDDED MONTEREY JACK CHEESE
- ¼ CUP MAYONNAISE
- 1 TABLESPOON CHOPPED PARSLEY
- SALT TO TASTE
- PEPPER TO TASTE
- 8 SLICES SEEDED RYE BREAD
- NONSTICK SPRAY OIL

1. Combine tuna, onion, celery, cheese, and mayonnaise in a bowl.

2. Season with parsley, salt, and pepper.

3. Make sandwiches out of the tuna salad and grill on a griddle or in a skillet coated with nonstick spray oil until golden and toasted.

PER SERVING: Fat: 21 g **Protein:** 21 g **Carbohydrates:** 32 g **Sugar:** 3 g

VEGGIE PITAS

CALORIES: 134
SERVES 4

- 1 CUCUMBER
- ¼ CUP CHOPPED SCALLIONS
- ½ CUP PLAIN YOGURT
- ¼ CUP SOUR CREAM
- ½ TEASPOON SALT
- ⅛ TEASPOON CAYENNE PEPPER
- 2 CARROTS, SHREDDED
- 1 TABLESPOON FRESH OREGANO LEAVES
- 1 CUP GRAPE TOMATOES, SLICED
- 4 LARGE WHOLE-WHEAT PITAS
- 8 LEAVES RED LETTUCE

1. Peel cucumber and cut in half. Remove seeds with spoon. Coarsely chop cucumber. Combine with remaining ingredients except pitas and lettuce in medium-size bowl. Cover and chill for 2–3 hours before serving.

2. When ready to serve, heat pitas in toaster oven until warm and pliable. Cut in half and line with lettuce; fill with cucumber mixture. Serve immediately.

PER SERVING: Fat: 4 g **Protein:** 10 g **Carbohydrates:** 21 g **Sugar:** 5 g

Storing Sandwich Spreads

Any sandwich spread made with mayonnaise, yogurt, or sour cream can be stored, covered, in the refrigerator up to 4 days. Make a couple of these spreads and keep them on hand so your family can make sandwiches or use them as a dip whenever they get hungry.

BEEF AND VEGGIE PITAS

CALORIES: 358
SERVES 4

- ½ POUND TOP ROUND STEAK
- 2 TABLESPOONS LOW-SODIUM SOY SAUCE
- ¼ CUP WATER
- 1½ TEASPOONS CORNSTARCH
- ⅛ TEASPOON PEPPER
- 1 TABLESPOON OLIVE OIL
- 1½ CUPS CHOPPED BROCCOLI FLORETS
- 4 BABY CARROTS, DICED
- ½ GREEN BELL PEPPER, CHOPPED
- 8 MUSHROOMS, SLICED
- 1 TOMATO, CHOPPED
- 4 WHOLE-WHEAT PITA BREADS, HALVED

1. Thinly slice the beef into bite-size strips and combine in medium-size bowl with soy sauce, water, cornstarch, and pepper. Let stand for 10 minutes.

2. Heat olive oil in wok or large skillet. Drain beef, reserving marinade. Stir-fry beef until browned, about 2–3 minutes. Remove from wok with slotted spoon and set aside.

3. Stir-fry broccoli, carrot, and bell pepper until crisp-tender, about 4 minutes. Add mushrooms and tomato; stir-fry for 2 minutes. Return beef to skillet along with marinade; bring to a boil. Boil until thickened, about 2–3 minutes.

4. Make sandwiches with the beef filling and the pita breads; serve immediately.

PER SERVING Fat: 10 g **Protein:** 32 g **Carbohydrates:** 36 g **Sugar:** 3 g

ROASTED VEGETABLE SANDWICH

CALORIES: 343
SERVES 1

½"-THICK SLICE EGGPLANT

2 ½"-THICK SLICES ZUCCHINI

2 ½"-THICK SLICES YELLOW SUMMER SQUASH

½"-THICK SLICE RED ONION

½"-THICK SLICE FENNEL BULB

2 TEASPOONS OLIVE OIL

½ TEASPOON SALT

¼ TEASPOON PEPPER

1 TEASPOON MAYONNAISE

1 TEASPOON BASIL PESTO

1 SQUARE FOCCACIA BREAD, SPLIT HORIZONTALLY

1 LARGE PIECE ROASTED RED BELL PEPPER

¼ CUP ALFALFA SPROUTS

CARROT STICKS

1. Preheat the oven to 375°F.

2. Brush the eggplant, zucchini, summer squash, red onion, and fennel slices with the olive oil and sprinkle them with salt and pepper.

3. Place them on a baking pan lined with nonstick foil and roast them in the oven for about 35 minutes. Let cool.

4. Mix the mayonnaise and pesto and spread the mixture onto the inside of both the top and bottom pieces of foccacia.

5. Layer the roasted vegetables, including the red bell pepper, on the bottom half of the foccacia bread, and then top them with alfalfa sprouts. Place the top half of foccacia bread on top and cut the sandwich in half diagonally. Serve with carrot sticks.

PER SERVING: Fat: 14 g **Protein:** 7 g **Carbohydrates:** 39 g **Sugar:** 2 g

Grilled Vegetables

From sandwich fillings to salads to side dishes, grilled vegetables are absolutely versatile. They are beautiful when dressed with a bit of sesame oil for an Asian flavor and served over brown rice. Add Mediterranean herbs, such as basil, oregano, and/or rosemary and toss them over an arugula salad. You'll get great flavor.

HUMMUS PITA SANDWICH

CALORIES: 452
SERVES 1

¼ CUP PLAIN YOGURT

¼ TEASPOON RANCH DRESSING SPICE MIX

1 SMALL CLOVE GARLIC, PEELED

PINCH OF SALT

¼ CUP CANNED GARBANZO BEANS

1 TABLESPOON TAHINI

1 TEASPOON LEMON JUICE

1 TEASPOON OLIVE OIL

PINCH OF GROUND CUMIN

1 WHOLE-WHEAT PITA BREAD ROUND

¼ CUP SHREDDED CARROTS

¼ CUP DICED ROMA TOMATOES

5 SLICES CUCUMBER

¼ CUP ALFALFA SPROUTS

1. Mix the yogurt and ranch dressing spices. Set aside in the refrigerator.

2. To make the hummus, purée the garlic and salt in a food processor. Add the garbanzo beans and purée to a paste. Add the tahini, lemon juice, olive oil, and cumin, and process until smooth, scraping down the sides of the bowl.

3. Spread the hummus on one side of the pita bread. Add carrots, tomatoes, cucumbers, and sprouts. Drizzle the yogurt sauce on and fold the pita in half like a taco.

PER SERVING: Fat: 14 g **Protein:** 15 g **Carbohydrates:** 58 g **Sugar:** 3 g

Wrap It Up!

It seems that every culture has a way of putting savory and sweet mixtures into delectable wrappings. You can put sweet and savory together, as in a fruity, curried shrimp mixture. You can make your fillings rich in fiber and stuff them into a good, multigrain pita or hero roll. Just be creative and experiment to build a diet high in whole grains and fiber for yourself and your family.

FISH TACO WITH PURPLE CABBAGE

CALORIES: 341
SERVES 1

2 CORN TORTILLAS

¼ POUND FIRM WHITE FISH SUCH AS HALIBUT OR SNAPPER

1 TEASPOON OLIVE OIL

PINCH OF SALT AND PEPPER

1 LEMON WEDGE

¼ CUP COOKED CORN KERNELS

1 TEASPOON DICED JALAPEÑO PEPPER (OPTIONAL)

¼ CUP SHREDDED PURPLE CABBAGE

1 TEASPOON TARTAR SAUCE

1. Wrap tortillas in a paper towel and warm in the microwave, then wrap in foil to keep warm.

2. Brush the fish with olive oil and sprinkle with salt and pepper. Grill for 4 minutes on each side. Break the cooked fish into smaller chunks.

3. Stack the two tortillas on top of each other and place the fish in the middle.

4. Squeeze the lemon wedge on the fish, then top with corn, jalapeño pepper, purple cabbage, and tartar sauce.

5. Fold the tortillas in half and eat with plenty of napkins.

PER SERVING: Fat: 10 g **Protein:** 28 g **Carbohydrates:** 35 g **Sugar:** 2 g

Stuffing Tortillas

You can stuff a tortilla with any sort of sandwich filling. Try mixing cooked black beans, corn, chopped tomatoes, and some chipotle sauce in adobo and putting it into a tortilla.

SUNFLOWER VEGGIE BURGERS

CALORIES: 268
SERVES 8

- 1½ CUPS BEEF BROTH
- ½ CUP WATER
- ¾ CUP MEDIUM BULGUR
- ⅓ CUP DRIED RED LENTILS
- 1½ CUPS CHOPPED MUSHROOMS
- 1 MINCED SHALLOT
- ½ TEASPOON CELERY SALT
- 1½ TEASPOONS CHOPPED FRESH OREGANO
- ½ TEASPOON CHOPPED FRESH THYME
- 1½ TEASPOONS CHOPPED FRESH SAGE
- ¼ TEASPOON ONION POWDER
- ¼ TEASPOON PAPRIKA
- 1 TEASPOON DIJON MUSTARD
- 1 TEASPOON KOSHER SALT
- 1 CUP SUNFLOWER SEEDS, SHELLED AND ROASTED (NO SALT)
- ½ CUP WHOLE-WHEAT FLOUR
- 2 TEASPOONS INSTANT YELLOW MISO
- 1 TABLESPOON SOY SAUCE
- 1 TABLESPOON WORCESTERSHIRE SAUCE
- 2 TABLESPOONS BREAD CRUMBS
- OLIVE OIL

1. Put broth, water, bulgur, and lentils in a saucepan. Bring to a simmer, cover, and turn to low for 30 minutes. Set aside.

2. In a large bowl, combine the mushrooms, shallot, herbs, spices, mustard, salt, sunflower seeds, and whole-wheat flour.

3. Stir the miso, soy sauce, and Worcestershire sauce into the warm bulgur mixture, then add the mixture to the mushroom mixture. Stir well, then stir in the bread crumbs.

4. Measure and mold the mixture into 7 or 8 portions on a wax paper–lined sheet pan. Press down the mounds with your hand to flatten them slightly into patties. Cover with plastic wrap and refrigerate 3 hours or overnight.

5. To cook the patties, brush both sides with olive oil and cook in a nonstick pan 2 minutes per side over medium-high heat. Serve hot on buns with condiments of your choice.

PER SERVING: Fat: 13 g **Protein:** 10 g **Carbohydrates:** 28 g **Sugar:** 1 g

FALAFEL SANDWICH

CALORIES: 449
SERVES 6

1 CUP DRIED GARBANZO BEANS
½ CUP CHOPPED RED ONION
3 CLOVES GARLIC, PEELED
1 TEASPOON SALT
1 TEASPOON PEPPER
1 TEASPOON GROUND CUMIN
PINCH OF CAYENNE PEPPER
1 TEASPOON BAKING POWDER
3 TABLESPOONS ALL-PURPOSE
FLOUR
3 TABLESPOONS WHOLE-WHEAT
FLOUR
2 CUPS VEGETABLE OIL
3 ROUNDS OF PITA BREAD
6 TABLESPOONS HUMMUS
1 CUP CHOPPED FRESH
TOMATOES
1 CUP SHREDDED LETTUCE
½ CUP CHOPPED CUCUMBERS
6 TABLESPOONS PLAIN YOGURT
2 TABLESPOONS CHOPPED FRESH
PARSLEY

1. Soak the garbanzo beans in 3 cups of water overnight.

2. Drain the garbanzo beans and put them in a food processor with the red onion, garlic, salt, pepper, cumin, and cayenne pepper. Pulse until everything is combined and the texture is fine but not a paste.

3. Sprinkle the baking powder and flours over the mixture and pulse again until well combined. Refrigerate for 3 hours.

4. Heat the oil in a deep fryer or large pot to 375°F. Shape falafel mixture into small balls and fry 4 to 5 at a time. Drain on paper towels.

5. Cut the pita rounds in half and open them to create a pocket bread out of each half. For each sandwich, spread the inside of a pita pocket with hummus, stuff a few falafel into it, and top with tomatoes, lettuce, and cucumbers. Drizzle yogurt over the top and sprinkle with parsley.

PER SERVING: Fat: 23 g **Protein:** 12 g **Carbohydrates:** 50 g
Sugar: 3 g

MEATLESS MEATLOAF SANDWICH

CALORIES: 396
SERVES 8

NONSTICK SPRAY OIL

1 CUP VEGETABLE BROTH

¾ CUP KASHA

¼ CUP OLIVE OIL

¾ CUP SHREDDED CARROTS

1 CUP DICED ONION

½ CUP DICED CELERY

¼ CUP GRATED PARMESAN CHEESE

2 TABLESPOONS CHOPPED FRESH PARSLEY

1 TABLESPOON DIJON MUSTARD

1 TABLESPOON WORCESTERSHIRE SAUCE

1 EGG, BEATEN

1 TEASPOON SALT

½ TEASPOON PEPPER

1 CUP FINELY CHOPPED PECANS, IN A FOOD PROCESSOR

2 TABLESPOONS TOMATO PASTE

1 TABLESPOON BROWN SUGAR

½ CUP SLICED RED ONIONS

1 TABLESPOON GRATED PARMESAN CHEESE PER SANDWICH

2 SLICES OF BREAD PER SANDWICH

1. Preheat oven to 350°F. Spray a loaf pan with oil.

2. Bring the broth to a boil in a saucepan and add the kasha. Cover, turn down the heat, and simmer for 15 minutes.

3. Add the olive oil to the sauté pan and sauté the carrots, onion, and celery in it for 5 minutes. Transfer them to a large bowl.

4. Add the Parmesan cheese, parsley, Dijon mustard, Worcestershire sauce, egg, salt, and pepper and mix together with a wooden spoon. Add the cooked kasha and pecans and combine thoroughly. Add a little beef broth if it seems too dry.

5. Press the mixture into the oiled loaf pan. Spread the tomato paste on top of the loaf, sprinkle the brown sugar over the tomato paste, scatter the red onions across, and bake 30 minutes. Remove the meatless loaf from the loaf pan and cut into slices.

6. Per sandwich: Sprinkle 1 tablespoon Parmesan cheese on each meatless loaf slice and brown in a skillet, then sandwich it between 2 slices of bread. Add lettuce, mayonnaise, ketchup, or any other sandwich ingredients you like.

PER SERVING: Fat: 23 g **Protein:** 13 g **Carbohydrates:** 40 g **Sugar:** 3 g

SAUTÉED CRAB CAKE AND AVOCADO WRAPS

CALORIES: 245
SERVES 4

1 (10-OUNCE) PACKAGE IMITATION CRABMEAT

4 TABLESPOONS LOW-FAT MAYONNAISE

1 TEASPOON DIJON-STYLE MUSTARD

1 EGG

SALT AND PEPPER TO TASTE

⅛" CANOLA OIL IN FRYING PAN

4 LARGE CABBAGE LEAVES

1 AVOCADO, PEELED AND SLICED AROUND PIT

4 SLICES FRESH LEMON, PAPER-THIN

EXTRA LEMON WEDGES AND PARSLEY SPRIGS FOR GARNISH

1. Lightly mix the crabmeat, mayonnaise, mustard, egg, salt, and pepper. Set a heavy pan over medium heat and coat the bottom with canola oil. Form cakes and sauté until well browned on both sides.

2. Blanch cabbage leaves in boiling water and then shock in cold water to stop cooking.

3. Lay out the cabbage leaves. Use a fork to mash the avocado and dab on the cakes. Roll cabbage leaves to make wraps. Decorate with lemon and place a crab cake on each. Garnish with extra lemon wedges and parsley sprigs.

PER SERVING: Fat: 17 g **Protein:** 18 g **Carbohydrates:** 7 g **Sugar:** 0 g

Lettuce-Style Wraps

Green or red cabbage leaves are very sturdy and work well for wraps. You can also try using Boston or butter lettuce, which has large thick leaves that hold up when used for wraps.

ASIAN SESAME LETTUCE WRAPS

CALORIES: 249
SERVES 4

- 2 GREEN ONIONS, CHOPPED
- 2 TABLESPOONS FRESH GINGER ROOT, GRATED
- 2 CLOVES GARLIC, MINCED
- 1 TABLESPOON VEGETABLE OIL
- 1 POUND GROUND CHICKEN
- ½ CUP LOW-SODIUM SOY SAUCE
- 1 CAN WATER CHESTNUTS, CHOPPED
- 1 TEASPOON RED PEPPER FLAKES
- ½ CUP FRESH CILANTRO, CHOPPED
- 1 LARGE HEAD OF BOSTON OR BUTTER LETTUCE
- 1 TABLESPOON SESAME SEEDS

1. Chop green onion and set aside. Peel ginger root, then grate, and mince garlic cloves. Heat the oil in a large pan; add garlic, green onion, and ginger and sauté about 3 minutes.

2. Add ground chicken to the pan and additional oil if needed. Then, add soy sauce, water chestnuts, and red pepper flakes. Cook until the chicken is brown and crumbling apart, about 5 minutes.

3. While chicken cooks, clean and chop fresh cilantro. Separate and wash lettuce leaves.

4. When chicken is cooked, add chopped cilantro and sesame seeds immediately. Serve chicken mixture and lettuce leaves in separate bowls.

PER SERVING: Fat: 14 g **Protein:** 22 g **Carbohydrates:** 10 g **Sugar:** 0 g

Vegan Option

For a vegan-friendly lettuce wrap, use tofu instead of ground chicken. The tofu will take on the flavor of the soy sauce and ginger. Firm or extra-firm tofu will hold up better in this recipe than soft tofu.

GRILLED TARRAGON CHICKEN SANDWICH

CALORIES: 378
SERVES 6

- 2 TABLESPOONS RED-WINE VINEGAR
- 1 TABLESPOON DRIED TARRAGON LEAVES
- 2 TABLESPOONS BUTTER
- 1 SHALLOT, MINCED
- ¾ CUP LOW-FAT MAYONNAISE
- ¼ TEASPOON WHITE PEPPER
- 6 BONELESS, SKINLESS CHICKEN BREASTS
- ½ TEASPOON SALT
- ⅛ TEASPOON PEPPER
- 6 HOAGIE SANDWICH BUNS, SPLIT AND TOASTED
- 6 LETTUCE LEAVES
- 2 TOMATOES, SLICED

1. Prepare and preheat grill. Meanwhile, in a small saucepan, combine the vinegar and tarragon, and bring to a boil. Cook until reduced by half and set aside.

2. In a small skillet, melt butter over medium heat. Add shallots and sauté for 5 minutes, or until tender. Transfer to a small bowl and add the mayonnaise, vinegar reduction, and white pepper. Mix well and refrigerate.

3. Pound the chicken breasts lightly with meat mallet or rolling pin. Season with salt and pepper.

4. Place the chicken on the grill on medium fire and cook, turning once and basting each side with 1 tablespoon of the mayonnaise mixture, for about 7 minutes on each side, or until done. Just before the chicken is ready, place the buns, cut-sides down, on the grill rack to warm.

5. Spread the cut sides of the buns generously with the flavored mayonnaise. Place 1 chicken piece on the bottom of each bun. Top with lettuce and tomato and then the bun top. Serve immediately.

PER SERVING: Fat: 12 g **Protein:** 32 g **Carbohydrates:** 35 g **Sugar:** 3 g

A YEAR IN PROVENCE SANDWICHES

CALORIES: 369
SERVES 4

- 1 TABLESPOON OLIVE OIL
- 1 ONION, SLICED
- 1 TEASPOON DRIED OREGANO LEAVES
- 1 TEASPOON DRIED BASIL LEAVES
- 1 TABLESPOON WATER
- ¼ CUP SLICED BLACK OLIVES
- ¼ CUP GRATED PARMESAN CHEESE
- 12–18 BABY SPINACH LEAVES
- 4 FRENCH BREAD ROLLS, SPLIT AND TOASTED
- 4 (1-OUNCE) SLICES PART-SKIM MOZZARELLA CHEESE
- 4 PLUM TOMATOES, SLICED
- 3 TABLESPOONS DIJON MUSTARD

1. Heat oil in large skillet over medium heat. Add onion; cook and stir until crisp-tender, about 5 minutes. Add oregano and basil along with water. Bring to a simmer; cook for 5 minutes until liquid evaporates. Remove from heat and stir in olives and cheese.

2. Arrange half of the spinach leaves on bottom half of each roll. Top with warm onion mixture, then cheese slices and plum tomatoes. Spread mustard on top half of each roll; place mustard-side down on tomatoes to make sandwiches. Serve immediately.

PER SERVING: Fat: 8 g **Protein:** 5 g **Carbohydrates:** 35 g **Sugar:** 3 g

Taming Onions

Onion tastes very sharp and can overwhelm a recipe. By simmering an onion in water with a bit of sugar, the sulfur compounds escape into the air, and the onion tastes very mild, almost sweet. You can do this with any onion, but it works especially well with sliced onions used in sandwiches.

Chicken à la King
(Page 198)

Pesto for Angel Hair Pasta
(Page 298)

Easy Chicken Lo Mein
(Page 217)

Black Bean Soup
(Page 149)

Beef and Broccoli Stir-Fry
(Page 237)

Grilled Mahi Mahi with Pineapple Salsa
(Page 266)

Eggs Benedict
(Page 16)

Baked Chicken Legs
(Page 206)

Penne Primavera
(Page 309)

Blueberry Muffins
(Page 15)

Sunday Morning French Toast
(Page 7)

Almond Macaroons
(Page 340)

Strawberry-Banana Smoothie,
Blueberry-Lemon Smoothie,
& Raspberry-Almond Milk Frappe
(Pages 3 and 5)

Deviled Eggs with Capers
(Page 35)

MONTE CRISTO SANDWICH

CALORIES: 373
SERVES 6

4 SLICES BACON

2 BONELESS, SKINLESS CHICKEN BREASTS

¼ CUP RASPBERRY JAM

8 SLICES WHITE BREAD

8 THIN SLICES GOUDA CHEESE

4 (1-OUNCE) SLICES HAM

¼ CUP BUTTER, SOFTENED

1. In medium skillet, cook bacon until crisp. Remove from pan and drain on paper towels; crumble and set aside. Pour drippings from skillet and discard; do not wipe skillet. Add chicken; cook over medium heat, turning once, until browned and cooked, about 8 minutes. Remove chicken from pan and let stand.

2. Spread jam on one side of each slice of bread. Layer half of slices with cheese, then ham. Thinly slice chicken breasts and place over ham. Cover with remaining cheese slices, sprinkle with bacon, and top sandwiches with remaining bread slices.

3. Spread outsides of sandwiches with softened butter. Prepare and preheat griddle, indoor dual-contact grill, or panini maker. Grill sandwiches on medium for 4–6 minutes for dual-contact grill or panini maker, or 6–8 minutes, turning once, for griddle, until bread is golden brown and cheese is melted. Cut in half and serve immediately.

PER SERVING: Fat: 19 **Protein:** 22 g **Carbohydrates:** 27 g **Sugar:** 7 g

Sliced Ham

You have several choices when buying sliced ham for sandwiches. You can purchase the super-thin slices packaged in plastic bags, boiled ham in ⅛" slices, or deli ham that you can have sliced to order. Just be sure that the amount of ham you use weighs about 1 ounce per serving to keep the nutrition information constant.

CRANBERRY TURKEY SALAD SANDWICH

CALORIES: 455
SERVES 1

½ CUP DICED SMOKED TURKEY

2 TABLESPOONS MAYONNAISE

1 TABLESPOON DICED CELERY

2 TABLESPOONS DRIED CRANBERRIES

SALT AND PEPPER TO TASTE

1 WHOLE-WHEAT CROISSANT

LEAF LETTUCE

1. Combine the smoked turkey, mayonnaise, celery, and cranberries.

2. Mix well and season with salt and pepper.

3. Cut the croissant in half horizontally, lay the lettuce on the bottom, and top it with the turkey salad. Put the top of the croissant on the sandwich and cut it in half.

PER SERVING: Fat: 22 g **Protein:** 22 g **Carbohydrates:** 38 g
Sugar: 4 g

OPEN-FACE HAM SALAD SANDWICH

CALORIES: 332
SERVES 4

4 SLICES BAKED HAM, DICED

2 OUNCES WHITE CHEDDAR CHEESE, SHREDDED

2 TEASPOONS MINCED ONION

¼ CUP DICED CELERY

1 TABLESPOON CHOPPED FRESH PARSLEY

PINCH OF CELERY SEED

1 TABLESPOON WHOLE-GRAIN MUSTARD

3 TABLESPOONS OLIVE OIL

1 EGG

4 WHOLE-WHEAT ENGLISH MUFFINS, SPLIT

1. Preheat the broiler. Put the ham in a food processor with the cheese, onion, celery, parsley, celery seed, mustard, olive oil, and egg. Pulse to combine into a spreadable consistency.

2. Spread the mixture onto the muffin halves and set them on a broiler pan lined with nonstick foil.

3. Broil until brown and bubbly. Serve hot.

PER SERVING: Fat: 18 g **Protein:** 16 g **Carbohydrates:** 30 g
Sugar: 2 g

SAUSAGE AND PEPPERS WITH MELTED MOZZARELLA CHEESE

CALORIES: 295
SERVES 2

¼ **POUND ITALIAN SAUSAGE LINK, CUT IN 8 PIECES**

½ **CUP SWEET WHITE ONIONS, THINLY SLICED**

4 **THIN SLICES WHOLE-WHEAT OR SOURDOUGH BREAD**

4 **SLICES RED ROASTED PEPPERS (FROM A JAR IS FINE)**

4 **THIN SLICES MOZZARELLA CHEESE**

½ **CUP SHREDDED NAPA CABBAGE OR ROMAINE LETTUCE**

IN THIS RECIPE YOU CAN SUBSTITUTE VEGETARIAN SAUSAGE FOR REGULAR SAUSAGE AND USE LOW-FAT CHEESE.

1. Fry sausage slices in a nonstick pan over low heat. When brown, drain on paper towels.

2. Add the onions and sizzle over low heat until wilted; reserve.

3. Toast the bread. Place the sausage slices on two pieces of toast. Arrange the onions, peppers, and cheese.

4. Run under a hot broiler until the cheese melts. Pile with shredded cabbage or lettuce for crunch.

PER SERVING: Fat: 8 g **Protein:** 25 g **Carbohydrates:** 36 g **Sugar:** 2 g

---

BABY EGGPLANT WITH TOMATO

CALORIES: 200
SERVES 2

2 **BABY EGGPLANTS, THE SIZE OF JUMBO EGGS, STEM ENDS TRIMMED, CUT CROSSWISE IN ¼" SLICES**

2 **TABLESPOONS ITALIAN DRESSING**

2 **TEASPOONS PARMESAN CHEESE**

1 **TOMATO, SLICED**

1 **TEASPOON BASIL, DRIED**

1 **TEASPOON OREGANO, DRIED**

SALT AND PEPPER TO TASTE

4 **SLICES WHOLE-WHEAT BREAD, TOASTED**

1. Preheat the broiler to 400°F. Place the cut pieces of eggplant in a bowl. Coat with Italian dressing. Place on a baking sheet, sprinkle with Parmesan cheese, and run under the broiler until golden on both sides.

2. Sprinkle tomato slices with basil, oregano, salt, and pepper.

3. Stack the eggplant and tomato on toast, top with another piece of toast, and enjoy!

PER SERVING: Fat: 7 g **Protein:** 10 g **Carbohydrates:** 33 g **Sugar:** 2 g

PEPPED-UP PORK SANDWICHES

CALORIES: 320
SERVES 4

- 1 LARGE WHITE OR YELLOW ONION, CHOPPED
- 1 LARGE RED BELL PEPPER, SEEDED AND CHOPPED
- 1 LARGE GREEN BELL PEPPER, SEEDED AND CHOPPED
- 1 CLOVE GARLIC, MINCED
- 3 TABLESPOONS PORK BROTH
- 1 TABLESPOON GARLIC STEAK SAUCE
- ½ POUND COOKED PORK, SHREDDED
- 8 SLICES, THINLY SLICED LOW-SALT BREAD

1. In a medium-size microwave-safe bowl, combine onion, peppers, garlic, and broth. Microwave on high for 5 minutes or until the onion is transparent and the peppers are soft. Add steak sauce and pork; stir to combine. Cover and microwave at 70 percent power for 2 minutes or until the mixture is heated through. Taste and add more steak sauce, if desired. Serve immediately, as sandwiches on plain or toasted bread.

PER SERVING: Fat: 16 g **Protein:** 17 g **Carbohydrates:** 25 g **Sugar:** 3 g

---

PORK BARBECUE SANDWICHES

CALORIES: 415
SERVES 4

- SPRAY COOKING OIL
- 2 TEASPOONS CANOLA OIL
- 1 SMALL GRANNY SMITH OR GOLDEN DELICIOUS APPLE, PEELED, CORED, AND GRATED
- 1 SMALL SWEET ONION, FINELY MINCED
- 2 TABLESPOONS HONEY MUSTARD SAUCE
- 2 TABLESPOONS HONEY BARBECUE SAUCE
- ⅛ TEASPOON FRESHLY GROUND BLACK PEPPER
- ½ POUND SLOW-COOKED PORK
- 8 SLICES WHOLE-WHEAT BREAD

1. Bring a nonstick sauté pan treated with spray oil to temperature over medium heat. Add the oil, apple, and onion; sauté until the onion is transparent. Add the sauces and pepper; mix well. Add the pork and simmer with the sauces, stirring until heated through. Evenly divide the pork mixture over 4 slices of the bread; top with the remaining 4 slices. Serve immediately.

PER SERVING: Fat: 19 g **Protein:** 18 g **Carbohydrates:** 43 g **Sugar:** 7 g

BACON, LETTUCE, AND TOMATO SANDWICH

CALORIES: 245
SERVES 4

6 SLICES EXTRA LEAN BACON

4 TEASPOONS FAT-FREE MIRACLE WHIP SALAD DRESSING

8 SLICES WHOLE-WHEAT BREAD, TOASTED

2 LARGE TOMATOES, THINLY SLICED

1 HEAD OF LETTUCE

1. Broil the bacon. Spread a thin layer of Miracle Whip on pieces of toasted bread. Arrange bacon and tomato slices on toast with crisp lettuce.

PER SERVING: Fat: 8 g **Protein:** 12 g **Carbohydrates:** 35 g **Sugar:** 2 g

The BLT

It is not known who coined the term *BLT*, but the term appears in cookbooks dating back to the 1930s, when it was typically made with cheese.

CRABMEAT, TOMATO, AND EGG SALAD SANDWICH

CALORIES: 493
SERVES 4

1½ CUPS COOKED CRABMEAT

4 TABLESPOONS FAT-FREE MIRACLE WHIP SALAD DRESSING

12 SLICES WHOLE-WHEAT BREAD

2 LARGE TOMATOES, THINLY SLICED

SALT AND PEPPER TO TASTE

MAMA'S EGG SALAD (SEE CHAPTER 4)

½ CUP COARSELY CHOPPED WATERCRESS

1. Smooth crabmeat moistened with a little Miracle Whip on a slice of bread. Top with tomato slices and a dash of salt and pepper to taste. Place another piece of bread over the tomato. Smooth egg salad over the second slice of bread. Top with watercress and finish with the final slice of bread.

PER SERVING: Fat: 14 g **Protein:** 40 g **Carbohydrates:** 55 g **Sugar:** 3 g

PEACH PITA SANDWICHES

CALORIES: 450
SERVES 4

- 4 PITA BREADS, HALVED
- 8 CURLY LETTUCE LEAVES
- 2 CUPS 1% LOW-SODIUM COTTAGE CHEESE
- 8 TOMATO SLICES
- 6 EXTRA-LEAN HAM SLICES, CHOPPED
- 1 (16-OUNCE) CAN SLICED CLING PEACHES, DRAINED

1. Cut pita breads in half, forming 8 pockets. Line with the lettuce leaves. Add cottage cheese, tomato slices, ham, and drained peaches. Serve immediately.

PER SERVING: Fat: 6 g **Protein:** 28 g **Carbohydrates:** 45 g **Sugar:** 8 g

Pita Breads

You can find pita breads in most bakeries and large grocery stores. Cut the breads in half to make two half moons. You may need to slightly cut between the layers to form the pocket. These breads are baked at a very high temperature so the gas inside expands quickly, forming the pocket as the structure sets.

STEAK SUBS

CALORIES: 439
SERVES 6

- 1 POUND BONELESS SIRLOIN STEAK
- ½ TEASPOON SALT
- ⅛ TEASPOON PEPPER
- 1 LOAF OAT BRAN FRENCH BREAD
- 1 CUP SHREDDED LOW-FAT EXTRA-SHARP CHEDDAR CHEESE
- 1 (7-OUNCE) JAR ROASTED RED PEPPERS, DRAINED
- SHREDDED LETTUCE
- 3 TABLESPOONS DIJON MUSTARD

1. Prepare and preheat grill. Trim excess fat from steaks and sprinkle with salt and pepper. Grill steak on both sides, turning once, until desired doneness, about 8–15 minutes. Remove from grill, cover, and let stand.

2. Cut French bread in half lengthwise. Place, cut-side down, on grill to toast for 1–2 minutes until brown. Remove from grill, set cut-side up, and sprinkle cheese on one of the halves.

3. Cut steak into thin slices against the grain. Layer on the cheese; top with red peppers and lettuce. Spread top half of bread with mustard; place mustard-side down on lettuce to make sandwich. Slice into 6 sections and serve immediately.

PER SERVING: Fat: 8 g **Protein:** 42 g **Carbohydrates:** 30 g **Sugar:** 2 g

EGGPLANT AND PORTOBELLO MUSHROOM MELT

CALORIES: 483
SERVES 4

- 1 LARGE EGGPLANT, SLICED LENGTHWISE IN ½" SLICES
- 1 SMALL VIDALIA ONION, SLICED
- 4 LARGE PORTOBELLO MUSHROOM CAPS
- ½ CUP CANOLA OIL
- SALT AND PEPPER TO TASTE
- ⅓ CUP CHOPPED FLAT-LEAF PARSLEY
- 2 TABLESPOONS FRESH THYME
- ½ CUP FAT-FREE MIRACLE WHIP SALAD DRESSING
- 8 SLICES WHOLE-WHEAT BREAD
- 4 LEAVES LETTUCE

1. Brush the slices of eggplant, onion, and mushroom with the oil. Season with salt and pepper to taste.

2. Grill mushrooms, onion, and eggplant slices on both sides until tender.

3. Mix parsley leaves and thyme with Miracle Whip.

4. Toast or grill individual slices of bread. Thinly spread Miracle Whip mix on grilled side of bread. Arrange slices of vegetables on one side of bread. Top with leaf of lettuce and another slice of grilled bread.

PER SERVING: Fat: 32 g **Protein:** 9 g **Carbohydrates:** 45 g **Sugar:** 4 g

CHAPTER 8

Poultry

SAUTÉED CHICKEN WITH ROASTED GARLIC SAUCE

CALORIES: 267
SERVES 4

- 1 HEAD ROASTED GARLIC
- ⅓ CUP LOW-SODIUM CHICKEN BROTH
- ½ TEASPOON DRIED OREGANO LEAVES
- ¼ CUP FLOUR
- ⅛ TEASPOON SALT
- ⅛ TEASPOON PEPPER
- ¼ TEASPOON PAPRIKA
- 4 (4-OUNCE) BONELESS, SKINLESS CHICKEN BREASTS
- 2 TABLESPOONS OLIVE OIL

1. Squeeze garlic cloves from the skins and combine in small saucepan with chicken broth and oregano leaves.

2. On shallow plate, combine flour, salt, pepper, and paprika. Dip chicken into this mixture to coat.

3. In large skillet, heat 2 tablespoons olive oil. At the same time, place the saucepan with the garlic mixture over medium heat. Add the chicken to the hot olive oil; cook for 5 minutes without moving. Then carefully turn chicken and cook for 4–7 minutes longer until chicken is thoroughly cooked.

4. Stir garlic sauce with wire whisk until blended. Serve with the chicken.

PER SERVING: Fat: 7 g **Protein:** 35 g **Carbohydrates:** 7 g **Sugar:** 0 g

---

CHICKEN À LA KING

CALORIES: 335
SERVES 4

- 1 CAN CONDENSED CREAM OF CHICKEN SOUP
- ¼ CUP SKIM MILK
- ½ TEASPOON WORCESTERSHIRE SAUCE
- 1 TABLESPOON MAYONNAISE
- ¼ TEASPOON GROUND BLACK PEPPER
- 2 CUPS FROZEN MIX OF PEAS AND PEARL ONIONS, THAWED
- 1 CUP SLICED MUSHROOMS, STEMMED
- ½ POUND COOKED, CHOPPED CHICKEN
- 4 SLICES WHOLE-WHEAT BREAD, TOASTED

1. Combine the soup, milk, Worcestershire, mayonnaise, and pepper in a saucepan and bring to a boil.

1. Reduce heat and add the peas and pearl onions, mushrooms, and chicken. Simmer until the vegetables and chicken are heated through.

2. Serve over toast.

PER SERVING: Fat: 9 g **Protein:** 25 g **Carbohydrates:** 37 g **Sugar:** 7 g

CHICKEN BREASTS WITH ORANGE GLAZE AND ORANGES

CALORIES: 225
SERVES 2

- 2 TABLESPOONS MARMALADE
- 2 TABLESPOONS ORANGE JUICE
- 1 TABLESPOON SOY SAUCE
- 1 TEASPOON HOT PEPPER SAUCE
- 1 TEASPOON THYME LEAVES, DRIED
- 1 TEASPOON CARDAMOM, GROUND
- 1 TABLESPOON SESAME OIL
- ½ POUND CHICKEN BREAST, HALVED, BONE IN, SKIN REMOVED
- 1 ORANGE, SLICED THINLY, SKIN ON
- 1½ CUPS COOKED BROWN RICE

1. Mix the first seven ingredients. Paint on the chicken.

2. Roast the chicken in a 350°F oven, surrounded by orange slices, for 35 minutes. Serve over rice.

PER SERVING (EXCLUDING RICE): Fat: 6 g **Protein:** 22 g
Carbohydrates: 26 g **Sugar:** 13 g

ROAST TURKEY

CALORIES: 190
SERVES 6–8

- 1 (8- TO 10-POUND) TURKEY
- 10 CLOVES GARLIC, CRUSHED
- 1 BUNCH FRESH TARRAGON, CHOPPED
- ⅓ CUP OLIVE OIL
- SALT AND FRESHLY GROUND BLACK PEPPER TO TASTE

1. Heat oven to 450°F. Place turkey breast–side down on a large cutting board and remove the backbone. Turn it over and place it breast-side up in a large roasting pan.

2. Arrange the garlic and tarragon under the turkey and in the crevices of the wings and legs. Drizzle the turkey with olive oil and season with salt and pepper.

3. Roast for 20 minutes, remove from oven, baste turkey with juices, and return to a 400°F oven.

4. Cook until the internal temperature of the turkey is 165 to 170°F on a meat thermometer. Let the turkey rest before carving.

PER SERVING: Fat: 10 g **Protein:** 24 g **Carbohydrates:** 1 g
Sugar: 0 g

INDIAN TANDOORI-STYLE CHICKEN

CALORIES: 169
SERVES 4

4 CHICKEN BREAST HALVES, BONELESS AND SKINLESS, POUNDED THIN
1 TABLESPOON GARAM MASALA
2 CLOVES GARLIC, MASHED
1 CUP LOW-FAT YOGURT

1. In a large glass pan, marinate the chicken breasts overnight in a mixture of garam masala, garlic, and yogurt.

2. Preheat the oven or grill to 400°F. Broil or grill the chicken for 4 minutes per side. The hot oven recreates the clay oven, or *tandoori*, used in India to bake meats.

PER SERVING: Fat: 6 g **Protein:** 28 g **Carbohydrates:** 4 g **Sugar:** 1 g

Asian Markets

Don't be afraid to ask the manager or owner of an Asian market about things that are unfamiliar to you. In this way, you open yourself to discovering such goodies as premade garam masala, tamarind pulp, lemongrass, and other delicious additions to your cooking.

HOT-AND-SPICY PEANUT THIGHS

CALORIES: 327
SERVES 4

NONSTICK COOKING SPRAY
4 (4-OUNCE) CHICKEN THIGHS
½ CUP LOW-SODIUM BARBECUE SAUCE
2 TEASPOONS CHILI POWDER
½ CUP CHOPPED UNSALTED PEANUTS

1. Preheat oven to 350°F. Spray a roasting pan with nonstick cooking spray and set aside. Pound chicken slightly, to ⅓" thickness.

2. In a shallow bowl, combine barbecue sauce and chili powder and mix well. Dip chicken into sauce, then dip one side into peanuts. Place, peanut-side up, in prepared pan.

3. Bake for 30–40 minutes, or until chicken is thoroughly cooked and nuts are browned. Serve immediately.

PER SERVING: Fat: 19 g **Protein:** 28 g **Carbohydrates:** 8 g **Sugar:** 3 g

ASIAN CHICKEN STIR-FRY

CALORIES: 252
SERVES 4

- **2 (5-OUNCE) BONELESS, SKINLESS CHICKEN BREASTS**
- **½ CUP LOW-SODIUM CHICKEN BROTH**
- **1 TABLESPOON LOW-SODIUM SOY SAUCE**
- **1 TABLESPOON CORNSTARCH**
- **1 TABLESPOON SHERRY**
- **2 TABLESPOONS PEANUT OIL**
- **1 ONION, SLICED**
- **3 CLOVES GARLIC, MINCED**
- **1 TABLESPOON GRATED GINGER ROOT**
- **1 CUP SNOW PEAS**
- **½ CUP CANNED SLICED WATER CHESTNUTS, DRAINED**
- **1 YELLOW SUMMER SQUASH, SLICED**
- **¼ CUP CHOPPED UNSALTED PEANUTS**

1. Cut chicken into strips and set aside. In small bowl, combine chicken broth, soy sauce, cornstarch, and sherry and set aside.

2. In large skillet or wok, heat peanut oil over medium-high heat. Add chicken; stir-fry until almost cooked, about 3–4 minutes. Remove to plate. Add onion, garlic, and ginger root to skillet; stir-fry for 4 minutes longer. Then add snow peas, water chestnuts, and squash; stir-fry for 2 minutes longer.

3. Stir chicken broth mixture and add to skillet along with chicken. Stir-fry for 3–4 minutes longer or until chicken is thoroughly cooked and sauce is thickened and bubbly. Sprinkle with peanuts and serve immediately.

PER SERVING: Fat: 12 g **Protein:** 30 g **Carbohydrates:** 15 g **Sugar:** 3 g

STEWED CHICKEN WITH VEGETABLES

CALORIES: 421
SERVES 4

1 FRYING CHICKEN, CUT UP

1 CUP CHICKEN STOCK

16 PEARL ONIONS, PEELED

2 LARGE CARROTS, PEELED AND CUT IN 1" PIECES

2 CELERY STALKS, CUT IN CHUNKS

2 CLOVES GARLIC, PEELED, SMASHED WITH THE SIDE OF A KNIFE

1 FENNEL BULB, TRIMMED, CUT IN CHUNKS

4 SMALL BLUENOSE TURNIPS, PEELED AND CUT IN CHUNKS

1 TEASPOON THYME, DRIED, OR 3 TEASPOONS FRESH

1 TEASPOON DRIED ROSEMARY

2 BAY LEAVES

1 CUP DRY WHITE WINE

2 CUPS CHICKEN BROTH

SALT AND PEPPER TO TASTE

WHEAT GRAIN NOODLES, COOKED

1. In a large stew pot, mix all ingredients. Bring to a boil. Reduce heat to a simmer; cover and cook on very low for 50 minutes. Serve with wheat grain noodles.

PER SERVING: Fat: 18 g **Protein:** 39 g **Carbohydrates:** 16 g **Sugar:** 3 g

A Crown of Laurel

Bay leaves, also known as laurel, are originally from the Mediterranean area of the world. They have a strong, woody, and somewhat spicy flavor and are usually sold dried in jars in the spice rack section of the grocery store.

POACHED CHICKEN WITH PEARS AND HERBS

CALORIES: 307
SERVES 2

- 1 RIPE PEAR, PEELED, CORED, AND CUT IN CHUNKS
- 2 SHALLOTS, MINCED
- ½ CUP DRY WHITE WINE
- 1 TEASPOON ROSEMARY, DRIED, OR 1 TABLESPOON FRESH
- 1 TEASPOON THYME, DRIED, OR 1 TABLESPOON FRESH
- SALT AND PEPPER TO TASTE
- 2 (½-POUND) CHICKEN BREASTS, BONELESS AND SKINLESS

1. Prepare the poaching liquid by mixing the first 5 ingredients and bringing to a boil in a saucepan. Salt and pepper the chicken and add to the pan. Simmer slowly for 10 minutes. Serve with pears on top of each piece.

PER SERVING: Fat: 9 g **Protein:** 41 g **Carbohydrates:** 15 g **Sugar:** 6 g

GRILLED SAN FRANCISCO-STYLE CHICKEN

CALORIES: 95
SERVES 4

- 1 TABLESPOON OLIVE OIL
- 1 TABLESPOON DIJON-STYLE MUSTARD
- 2 TABLESPOONS RASPBERRY WHITE WINE VINEGAR
- CELERY SALT AND PEPPER TO TASTE
- 1 SMALL CHICKEN, ABOUT 2½ TO 3 POUNDS, CUT IN QUARTERS

1. Heat grill to 400°F. In a small bowl, mix the olive oil, mustard, and vinegar. Sprinkle the chicken with celery salt and pepper.

2. Paint the skin side of the chicken with the mustard mixture. Spray a few drops of olive oil on the bone side.

3. Grill the chicken, bone-side to flame, for 15 minutes. Reduce heat to 325°F; cover and cook for 15 minutes.

PER SERVING: Fat: 10 g **Protein:** 40 g **Carbohydrates:** 7 g **Sugar:** 0 g

BRAISED CHICKEN WITH CITRUS

CALORIES: 274
SERVES 2

- ¼ **CUP ORANGE JUICE**
- ¼ **CUP GRAPEFRUIT JUICE, FRESH OR UNSWEETENED**
- 1 **TABLESPOON ORANGE CURAÇAO, OR OTHER LIQUEUR**
- 1 **TEASPOON SAVORY HERB, DRIED**
- ½ **TEASPOON LEMON ZEST**
- 1 **TEASPOON EXTRA-VIRGIN OLIVE OIL**
- **SALT AND PEPPER TO TASTE**
- ½ **POUND CHICKEN BREASTS, BONELESS AND SKINLESS, CUT IN CHUNKS**
- **COOKED RICE (OPTIONAL)**

1. Make poaching liquid with the first 6 ingredients. Sprinkle the chicken with salt and pepper. Poach for 10 minutes and serve over rice or chilled in a salad.

PER SERVING: Fat: 10 g **Protein:** 40 g **Carbohydrates:** 7 g **Sugar:** 1 g

---

LEMON CHICKEN

CALORIES: 254
SERVES 4–6

- ⅓ **CUP LEMON JUICE**
- 2 **TABLESPOONS LEMON ZEST**
- 3 **CLOVES GARLIC, MINCED**
- 2 **TABLESPOONS FRESH THYME, CHOPPED**
- 2 **TABLESPOONS FRESH ROSEMARY, CHOPPED**
- 2 **TABLESPOONS OLIVE OIL**
- 1 **TEASPOON SALT**
- 1 **TEASPOON FRESH GROUND BLACK PEPPER**
- 3 **POUNDS BONE-IN CHICKEN THIGHS**

1. To make the marinade, combine lemon juice, lemon zest, garlic, thyme, rosemary, olive oil, salt, and pepper in a small bowl. Place chicken in a large bowl and pour over with marinade. Let marinate in the refrigerator for 2 hours.

2. Heat oven to 425°F. Place marinated chicken in one layer in a large baking dish. Spoon leftover marinade over top of chicken.

3. Bake until chicken is completely cooked through, about 50 minutes. The internal temperature should be 175°F.

PER SERVING: Fat: 19 g **Protein:** 16 g **Carbohydrates:** 4 g **Sugar:** 0 g

BRAISED CHICKEN WITH WHITE BEANS AND KALE

CALORIES: 367
SERVES 4

1 POUND BONELESS, SKINLESS CHICKEN BREASTS

SALT AND PEPPER TO TASTE

2 TABLESPOONS OLIVE OIL

½ ONION, CHOPPED

2 CLOVES GARLIC, MINCED

1 LARGE BUNCH KALE, CHOPPED

1 TEASPOON CRUSHED RED PEPPER

1 TABLESPOON FRESH ROSEMARY, CHOPPED

1 (15-OUNCE) CAN CANNELLINI BEANS

1 (15-OUNCE) CAN DICED TOMATOES

1 CAN LOW-SODIUM CHICKEN BROTH

1. Slice chicken breasts into small pieces. Season chicken with salt and pepper.

2. Heat 2 tablespoons oil in a large pan and sauté onion and garlic for 3–4 minutes. Add chicken and cook an additional 4 minutes.

3. Add kale to the pan with the chicken in batches and cook until wilted. Season with crushed red pepper and rosemary.

4. Add beans, tomatoes, broth, salt, and pepper as desired to the pan, stir, and simmer for 10–15 minutes.

PER SERVING: Fat: 9 g **Protein:** 38 g **Carbohydrates:** 35 g **Sugar:** 5 g

Emerald Kale

Kale, a member of the cabbage family, provides a ton of nutritional value for very little calories. Kale is an excellent source of vitamin A, K, and C and is known for its health-promoting phytonutrients.

FRIED CHICKEN WITH CORNMEAL CRUST

CALORIES: 265
SERVES 4

4 (4-OUNCE) HALF BREASTS CHICKEN, BONELESS AND SKINLESS

½ CUP BUTTERMILK

½ CUP COARSE CORNMEAL

1 TEASPOON BAKING POWDER

½ TEASPOON SALT

FRESHLY GROUND PEPPER TO TASTE

½" CANOLA OR OTHER OIL IN A DEEP PAN FOR FRYING

1. Soak the chicken in buttermilk for 15 minutes. On a piece of waxed paper, mix the cornmeal, baking powder, salt, and pepper. Coat the chicken with the cornmeal mixture.

2. In a large frying pan, heat the oil to 350°F. Fry for 8 to 10 minutes per side. Drain on paper towels.

PER SERVING: Fat: 9 g **Protein:** 42 g **Carbohydrates:** 9 g **Sugar:** 1 g

TURKEY MEATBALLS

CALORIES: 476
SERVES 4

2 SLICES WHOLE GRAIN BREAD
½ CUP 2% MILK
2 EGGS
½ CUP CHILI SAUCE
½ CUP YELLOW ONION, CHOPPED
2 CLOVES GARLIC, MINCED
1 TEASPOON OREGANO, DRIED
½ TEASPOON RED PEPPER FLAKES
¼ CUP PARMESAN CHEESE, FINELY GRATED
1 POUND GROUND TURKEY MEAT
1 CUP FINE, DRY BREAD CRUMBS
TOMATO-BASED SAUCE (OPTIONAL)

IN THIS RECIPE YOU CAN SUBSTITUTE NONFAT MILK FOR 2% MILK.

1. Mix all but the bread crumbs in the food processor or blender, adding ingredients one by one.

2. Form into balls and roll in bread crumbs. Bake for 35 minutes at 325°F; turn once.

3. Serve with a tomato-based sauce, if desired.

PER SERVING (4 meatballs): Fat: 20 g **Protein:** 35 g
Carbohydrates: 45 g **Sugar:** 4 g

BAKED CHICKEN LEGS

CALORIES: 355
SERVES 4–6

6 CHICKEN LEGS AND THIGHS
2 TABLESPOONS OLIVE OIL
2 TABLESPOONS PAPRIKA
1½ TABLESPOONS ONION POWDER
1 TEASPOON SALT

1. Preheat oven to 400°F. Rinse and pat dry chicken. Coat the bottom of a large roasting pan with 1 tablespoon olive oil.

2. Coat chicken pieces lightly with remaining olive oil. Cover chicken evenly with paprika, onion powder, and salt. Place chicken pieces skin-side up inside the pan.

3. Bake chicken at 400°F for 30 minutes, then lower the temperature to 350°F and cook for 10–15 minutes. The internal temperature of the chicken thighs should be 185°F.

PER SERVING: Fat: 25 g **Protein:** 28 g **Carbohydrates:** 1 g
Sugar: 0 g

CHICKEN CACCIATORE

CALORIES: 464
SERVES 4–6

- 3 TABLESPOONS OLIVE OIL
- 1 WHOLE CHICKEN, CUT UP
- 1 CUP ONION, CHOPPED
- 1 CUP RED BELL PEPPER, CHOPPED
- 3 CLOVES GARLIC, MINCED
- 2 (15-OUNCE) CANS STEWED TOMATOES
- ¾ CUP DRY WHITE WINE
- 1 TABLESPOON ITALIAN SEASONING
- SALT AND PEPPER TO TASTE
- 1 BAY LEAF
- 3 TABLESPOONS CAPERS

1. Heat olive oil in a medium pan. Brown chicken thoroughly, about 10 minutes. Remove chicken from pan. Add onion, red bell pepper, and garlic to the hot pan; sauté until onion is tender.

2. Stir in tomatoes, wine, Italian seasoning, salt, pepper, and bay leaf. Add chicken back into the pan with sauce and bring to a boil.

3. Reduce heat to low, cover, and simmer for 40–45 minutes. Stir in capers. Remove bay leaf from the sauce.

PER SERVING: Fat: 32 g **Protein:** 25 g **Carbohydrates:** 14 g **Sugar:** 2 g

Time-Saving Tip
A recipe like this that contains a good amount of liquid and a longer cooking time at a lower temperature turns out well when made in a Crock-Pot. The slow cooker technique requires very little active cooking time.

CHICKEN SPICY THAI STYLE

CALORIES: 300
SERVES 4

2 TABLESPOONS LIME JUICE

1 TABLESPOON LOW-SODIUM SOY SAUCE

½ CUP LOW-SODIUM CHICKEN BROTH

¼ CUP DRY WHITE WINE

¼ CUP NATURAL PEANUT BUTTER

2 TABLESPOONS PEANUT OIL

1 ONION, CHOPPED

4 CLOVES GARLIC, MINCED

3 (4-OUNCE) BONELESS, SKINLESS CHICKEN BREASTS, SLICED

4 CUPS SHREDDED NAPA CABBAGE

1 CUP SHREDDED CARROTS

1. In a small bowl, combine lime juice, soy sauce, chicken broth, wine, and peanut butter and mix with wire whisk until blended. Set aside.

2. In a wok or large skillet, heat peanut oil over medium-high heat. Add onion and garlic; stir-fry until crisp-tender, about 4 minutes. Add chicken; stir-fry until almost cooked, about 3 minutes. Add cabbage and carrots; stir-fry until cabbage begins to wilt, about 3–4 minutes longer.

3. Remove food from wok and return wok to heat. Add peanut butter mixture and bring to a simmer. Return chicken and vegetables to wok; stir-fry until sauce bubbles and thickens and chicken is thoroughly cooked, about 3–4 minutes. Serve immediately.

PER SERVING: Fat: 16 g **Protein:** 34 g **Carbohydrates:** 12 g **Sugar:** 3 g

Natural Peanut Butter

Whenever possible, use natural peanut butter, not the regular kind found on store shelves. Read labels carefully. You'll notice that most regular peanut butter contains hydrogenated vegetable oil, which is a source of trans fat. The oil will separate out of the natural peanut butter as it stands; just stir it back in before using.

CHICKEN BREASTS WITH NEW POTATOES

CALORIES: 395
SERVES 6

- **12 SMALL NEW RED POTATOES**
- **2 TABLESPOONS OLIVE OIL**
- **⅛ TEASPOON WHITE PEPPER**
- **4 CLOVES GARLIC, MINCED**
- **1 TEASPOON DRIED OREGANO LEAVES**
- **2 TABLESPOONS DIJON MUSTARD**
- **4 (4-OUNCE) BONELESS, SKINLESS CHICKEN BREASTS**
- **1 CUP CHERRY TOMATOES**

1. Preheat oven to 400°F. Line a roasting pan with parchment paper and set aside. Scrub potatoes and cut each in half. Place in prepared pan.

2. In a small bowl, combine oil, pepper, garlic, oregano, and mustard and mix well. Drizzle half of this mixture over the potatoes and toss to coat. Roast for 20 minutes.

3. Cut chicken breasts into quarters. Remove pan from oven and add chicken to potato mixture. Using a spatula, mix potatoes and chicken together. Drizzle with remaining oil mixture. Return to oven and roast for 15 minutes longer.

4. Add tomatoes to pan. Roast for 5–10 minutes longer, or until potatoes are tender and browned and chicken is thoroughly cooked.

PER SERVING: Fat: 9 g **Protein:** 33 g **Carbohydrates:** 50 g **Sugar:** 4 g

HAZELNUT-CRUSTED CHICKEN BREASTS

CALORIES: 276
SERVES 2

2 (4-OUNCE) BONELESS, SKINLESS CHICKEN BREASTS
PINCH OF SALT
PINCH OF PEPPER
1 TABLESPOON DIJON MUSTARD
1 EGG WHITE
⅓ CUP CHOPPED HAZELNUTS
1 TABLESPOON OLIVE OIL

1. Place chicken between two sheets of waxed paper. Pound, starting at center of chicken, until ¼" thick. Sprinkle chicken with salt and pepper. Spread each side of chicken with some of the mustard.

2. In small bowl, beat egg white until foamy. Dip chicken into egg white, then into hazelnuts, pressing to coat both sides.

3. In skillet, heat olive oil over medium heat. Add chicken; cook for 3 minutes without moving. Then carefully turn and cook for 1–3 minutes on second side until chicken is thoroughly cooked and nuts are toasted. Serve immediately.

PER SERVING: Fat: 16 g **Protein:** 31 g **Carbohydrates:** 6 g **Sugar:** 1 g

Dijon Mustard

Dijon mustard is not the same as the yellow mustard you put on hot dogs. Only mustard made from the recipe created in Dijon, France, using brown or black mustard seeds earns the "Dijon" moniker. The flavor is much stronger than yellow mustard. It is high in potassium, calcium, and niacin and has little or no fat or cholesterol.

SESAME-CRUSTED CHICKEN

CALORIES: 363
SERVES 4

2 TABLESPOONS LOW-SODIUM SOY SAUCE

2 CLOVES GARLIC, MINCED

1 TABLESPOON GRATED GINGER ROOT

1 TABLESPOON BROWN SUGAR

1 TEASPOON SESAME OIL

4 (4-OUNCE) BONELESS, SKINLESS CHICKEN BREASTS

½ CUP SESAME SEEDS

3 TABLESPOONS OLIVE OIL

1 TABLESPOON BUTTER

1. In a large, heavy-duty food-storage plastic bag, combine soy sauce, garlic, ginger root, brown sugar, and sesame oil and mix well. Add chicken; seal bag, and squish to coat chicken with marinade. Place in a bowl and refrigerate for 8 hours.

2. When ready to eat, remove chicken from marinade; discard marinade. Dip chicken in sesame seeds to coat on all sides.

3. Heat olive oil and butter in large skillet over medium heat. Add chicken and cook for 5 minutes. Carefully turn chicken and cook for 3–6 minutes on second side or until chicken is thoroughly cooked and sesame seeds are toasted. Serve immediately.

PER SERVING: Fat: 20 g **Protein:** 28 g **Carbohydrates:** 9 g **Sugar:** 2 g

Sesame Seeds

Sesame seeds are high in an antioxidant called lignan, which can lower cholesterol and reduce blood pressure. These tiny, nutty seeds are also high in monounsaturated fats, which can raise HDL cholesterol levels. Because they are high in fat, they can go rancid easily; store them, tightly covered, in the refrigerator.

TURKEY BREAST WITH DRIED FRUIT

CALORIES: 293
SERVES 6

- 1½ POUNDS BONE-IN TURKEY BREAST
- ⅛ TEASPOON SALT
- ⅛ TEASPOON PEPPER
- 1 TABLESPOON FLOUR
- 1 TABLESPOON OLIVE OIL
- 1 TABLESPOON BUTTER OR PLANT STEROL MARGARINE
- ½ CUP CHOPPED PRUNES
- ½ CUP CHOPPED DRIED APRICOTS
- 2 GRANNY SMITH APPLES, PEELED AND CHOPPED
- 1 CUP LOW-SODIUM CHICKEN BROTH
- ¼ CUP MADEIRA WINE

1. Sprinkle turkey with salt, pepper, and flour. In large saucepan, heat olive oil and butter over medium heat. Add turkey and cook until browned, about 5 minutes. Turn turkey.

2. Add all fruit to saucepan along with broth and wine. Cover and bring to a simmer. Reduce heat to medium-low and simmer for 55–65 minutes or until turkey is thoroughly cooked. Serve turkey with fruit and sauce.

PER SERVING: Fat: 6 g **Protein:** 22 g **Carbohydrates:** 45 g **Sugar:** 15 g

Keep the Skin

Keeping the skin on chicken and turkey while it's baking ensures that the flesh remains moist and doesn't transfer much fat to the flesh. Just remove the skin and discard after cooking. The poultry will be much more flavorful and tender, and it will have fat content virtually the same as skinless.

TEXAS BBQ CHICKEN THIGHS

CALORIES: 236
SERVES 6

2 TABLESPOONS OLIVE OIL

1 ONION, CHOPPED

4 CLOVES GARLIC, MINCED

1 JALAPEÑO PEPPER, MINCED

¼ CUP ORANGE JUICE

1 TABLESPOON LOW-SODIUM SOY SAUCE

2 TABLESPOONS APPLE-CIDER VINEGAR

2 TABLESPOONS BROWN SUGAR

2 TABLESPOONS DIJON MUSTARD

1 (14-OUNCE) CAN CRUSHED TOMATOES, UNDRAINED

½ TEASPOON CUMIN

1 TABLESPOON CHILI POWDER

¼ TEASPOON PEPPER

6 (4-OUNCE) BONELESS, SKINLESS CHICKEN THIGHS

3 TABLESPOONS CORNSTARCH

¼ CUP WATER

1. In a small skillet, heat olive oil over medium heat. Add onion and garlic; cook and stir until crisp-tender, about 4 minutes. Place in a 3–4 quart slow cooker and add jalapeño, orange juice, soy sauce, vinegar, brown sugar, mustard, tomatoes, cumin, chili powder, and pepper.

2. Add chicken to the sauce, pushing chicken into the sauce to completely cover. Cover and cook on low for 8–10 hours or until chicken is thoroughly cooked.

3. In a small bowl, combine cornstarch and water; stir until smooth. Add to slow cooker and stir. Cook on high for 15–20 minutes longer until sauce is thickened.

PER SERVING: Fat: 9 g **Protein:** 28 g **Carbohydrates:** 10 g **Sugar:** 3 g

Chicken Thighs

Many people may consider chicken thighs too fatty. Though chicken thighs do contain more fat than skinless chicken breasts, they still have only **11** grams of fat per 4-ounce serving. That is less fat than one would find in the same-size serving of beef, lamb, or pork.

TURKEY CUTLETS PARMESAN

CALORIES: 275
SERVES 6

NONSTICK COOKING SPRAY
1 EGG WHITE
¼ CUP DRY BREAD CRUMBS
⅛ TEASPOON PEPPER
4 TABLESPOONS GRATED PARMESAN CHEESE, DIVIDED
6 (4-OUNCE) TURKEY CUTLETS
2 TABLESPOONS OLIVE OIL
1 (15-OUNCE) CAN NO-SALT TOMATO SAUCE
1 TEASPOON DRIED ITALIAN SEASONING
½ CUP FINELY SHREDDED PART-SKIM MOZZARELLA CHEESE

1. Preheat oven to 350°F. Spray a 2-quart baking dish with non-stick cooking spray and set aside.

2. In a shallow bowl, beat egg white until foamy. On a plate, combine bread crumbs, pepper, and 2 tablespoons Parmesan. Dip the turkey cutlets into the egg white, then into the bread crumb mixture, turning to coat.

3. In a large saucepan, heat olive oil over medium heat. Add turkey cutlets; brown on both sides, about 2–3 minutes per side. Place in prepared baking dish. Add tomato sauce and Italian seasoning to a saucepan; bring to a boil.

4. Pour sauce over cutlets in baking pan and top with mozzarella cheese and remaining 2 tablespoons Parmesan. Bake for 25–35 minutes or until sauce bubbles and cheese melts and begins to brown. Serve with pasta, if desired.

PER SERVING: Fat: 10 g **Protein:** 32 g **Carbohydrates:** 10 g **Sugar:** 3 g

TURKEY CURRY WITH FRUIT

CALORIES: 371
SERVES 6

NONSTICK COOKING SPRAY

6 (4-OUNCE) TURKEY CUTLETS

1 TABLESPOON FLOUR

1 TABLESPOON PLUS 1
TEASPOON CURRY POWDER,
DIVIDED

1 TABLESPOON OLIVE OIL

2 PEARS, CHOPPED

1 APPLE, CHOPPED

½ CUP RAISINS

1 TABLESPOON SUGAR

⅛ TEASPOON SALT

⅓ CUP APRICOT JAM

1. Preheat oven to 350°F. Spray a cookie sheet with sides with nonstick cooking spray. Arrange cutlets on prepared cookie sheet. In small bowl, combine flour, 1 tablespoon curry powder, and olive oil and mix well. Spread evenly over cutlets.

2. In medium-size bowl, combine pears, apple, raisins, sugar, salt, 1 teaspoon curry powder, and apricot jam, and mix well. Divide this mixture over the turkey cutlets.

3. Bake for 35–45 minutes or until turkey is thoroughly cooked and fruit is hot and caramelized. Serve immediately.

PER SERVING: Fat: 11 g **Protein:** 26 g **Carbohydrates:** 32 g **Sugar:** 15 g

Raisins

The sweet and chewy fruit children love can assist the fight against cholesterol. Studies have shown that consuming raisins on a daily basis can help lower cholesterol levels. Eating just 3 ounces of raisins a day caused statistically significant reductions in total cholesterol and LDL cholesterol.

CHICKEN PESTO

- **1 CUP PACKED FRESH BASIL LEAVES**
- **¼ CUP TOASTED CHOPPED HAZELNUTS**
- **2 CLOVES GARLIC, CHOPPED**
- **2 TABLESPOONS OLIVE OIL**
- **1 TABLESPOON WATER**
- **¼ CUP GRATED PARMESAN CHEESE**
- **½ CUP LOW-SODIUM CHICKEN BROTH**
- **12 OUNCES BONELESS, SKINLESS CHICKEN BREASTS**
- **1 (12-OUNCE) PACKAGE ANGEL HAIR PASTA**

1. Bring a large pot of salted water to a boil. In a blender or food processor, combine basil, hazelnuts, and garlic. Blend or process until very finely chopped. Add olive oil and water; blend until a paste forms. Then blend in Parmesan cheese; set aside.

2. In a large skillet, bring chicken broth to a simmer over medium heat. Cut chicken into strips and add to broth. Cook for 4 minutes, then add the pasta to the boiling water.

3. Cook pasta for 3–4 minutes according to package directions, until al dente. Drain and add to chicken mixture; cook and stir for 1 minute until chicken is thoroughly cooked. Add basil mixture, remove from heat, and stir until a sauce forms. Serve immediately.

PER SERVING: Fat: 9 g **Protein:** 20 g **Carbohydrates:** 42 g **Sugar:** 2 g

Herbs

Fresh herbs should be part of a healthy diet, simply because their wonderful tastes and aromas will let you reduce salt and fat without feeling deprived. Fresh herbs like basil, thyme, and oregano are also easy to grow in a pot on your windowsill. You can substitute dried herbs for fresh in a 1:3 ratio. For every tablespoon of fresh, use a teaspoon of dried.

EASY CHICKEN LO MEIN

CALORIES: 406
SERVES 4

- ⅛ TEASPOON LOW-SODIUM CHICKEN BASE
- ½ CUP PLUS 1 TABLESPOON WATER
- 2 (10-OUNCE) PACKAGES ORGANIC FROZEN CHINESE STIR-FRY VEGETABLES
- 1 TABLESPOON FREEZE-DRIED SHALLOTS
- 1 POUND COOKED DARK AND LIGHT MEAT CHICKEN
- ⅛ CUP OR TO TASTE GINGER STIR-FRY SAUCE
- 1 POUND NO-SALT-ADDED OAT BRAN PASTA
- 1 TEASPOON LEMON JUICE
- ⅛ TEASPOON MUSTARD POWDER
- 1 TEASPOON CORNSTARCH
- ¼ TEASPOON TOASTED SESAME OIL
- 4 THINLY SLICED SCALLIONS (OPTIONAL)
- LOW-SODIUM SOY SAUCE (OPTIONAL)

1. Add the chicken base and ½ cup water to a large microwave-safe bowl; microwave on high for 30 seconds. Stir to dissolve the base into the water. Add the vegetables and freeze-dried shallots; microwave on high for 3 to 5 minutes, depending on how you prefer your vegetables cooked. (Keep in mind that the vegetables will continue to steam for a minute or so while the cover remains on the dish.) Drain some of the broth into a small nonstick sauté pan and set aside. Add the chicken and stir-fry sauce to the vegetables; stir well. Cover and set aside.

2. Consult the package for the pasta. In a large pot, bring the noted amount of water to a boil, but omit the salt. Add the pasta, lemon juice, and mustard powder.

3. While the pasta cooks, in a small cup or bowl, add a tablespoon of water to the cornstarch and whisk to make a slurry. Bring the reserved broth in the sauté pan to a boil over medium-high heat. Whisk in the slurry; cook for at least 1 minute (to remove the raw cornstarch taste), stirring constantly.

4. Once the mixture thickens, remove from heat; add the toasted sesame oil to the broth mixture, then whisk again. Pour the thickened broth mixture over the vegetables and chicken; toss to mix. Cover and microwave the chicken-vegetable mixture at 70 percent power for 2 minutes or until the chicken is heated through.

5. Drain the pasta; add it to the chicken-vegetable mixture and stir to combine. Divide among 4 plates. Garnish with chopped scallion and serve with the low-sodium soy sauce at the table, if desired.

PER SERVING: Fat: 5 g **Protein:** 44 g **Carbohydrates:** 44 g **Sugar:** 2 g

APRICOT AND PISTACHIO COUSCOUS CHICKEN ROULADES

CALORIES: 474
SERVES 4

2 CUPS COOKED COUSCOUS
¼ CUP CHOPPED DRIED APRICOTS
¼ CUP CHOPPED PISTACHIOS
4 BONELESS, SKINLESS CHICKEN BREAST FILETS, POUNDED THIN
SALT AND PEPPER TO TASTE
½ CUP APRICOT PRESERVES
¼ CUP BUTTER

1. Preheat oven to 350°F. Combine the couscous with the dried apricots and pistachios. Lay chicken breasts out on plastic wrap and sprinkle them with salt and pepper.

2. Lay a row of couscous mixture on each breast in the middle, then roll each breast into a roll.

3. Place the rolls seam-side down in a buttered baking dish.

4. Melt the apricot jam with the butter and pour it over the chicken rolls.

5. Bake chicken rolls uncovered for 45 minutes.

PER SERVING: Fat: 16 g **Protein:** 31 g **Carbohydrates:** 51 g **Sugar:** 19 g

Couscous

A Moroccan specialty, couscous is used in salads, soups, stews, and appetizers and mixed with everything and anything available. Couscous can be sweetened with dried fruit, such as apricots. It's a wonderful dessert mixed with honey and fresh figs.

GRILLED CHICKEN WITH MANGO SALSA

CALORIES: 462
SERVES 6

1 CUP DICED MANGO
½ CUP DICED RED ONION
1 JALAPEÑO PEPPER
¼ BUNCH CILANTRO
1 TABLESPOON LIME JUICE
3 TABLESPOONS OLIVE OIL, DIVIDED
SALT TO TASTE
3 POUNDS CHICKEN BREASTS

1. Combine the mango and red onion in a large bowl. Cut the jalapeño pepper in half, remove the seeds, and dice the flesh. Add to the bowl.

2. Chop the cilantro and add it to the bowl.

3. Add the lime juice, 1 tablespoon olive oil, and a pinch of salt. Stir well, taste, and add more salt if needed.

4. Prepare grill. Coat chicken breasts with 2 tablespoons olive oil and place on grill. Cook for 5 to 6 minutes per side or until chicken is cooked through. Serve with mango salsa.

PER SERVING: Fat: 26 g **Protein:** 47 g **Carbohydrates:** 7 g **Sugar:** 2 g

Salsa Is Here to Stay!

It's food, music, and dancing! Starting with basic tomato salsa, the darling of the nacho tray, salsa has expanded to cover most fruit. The one requirement of salsa is that it be hot and spicy. Salsa can be fairly mild with just a bit of a bite or it can set your mouth on fire. If you use the seeds and interior veins of a chili, you increase the heat exponentially.

YOGURT "GRAVY" CHICKEN THIGHS

CALORIES: 355
SERVES 4

- 1 (16-OUNCE) PACKAGE HASH BROWNS
- 1 (10-OUNCE) PACKAGE FROZEN VEGETABLES
- 1 LARGE SWEET ONION, SLICED
- NONSTICK COOKING SPRAY
- 4 (4-OUNCE) BONELESS, SKINLESS CHICKEN THIGHS
- ¼ TEASPOON FRESHLY GROUND BLACK PEPPER
- 1 TEASPOON GARLIC POWDER
- 1 TABLESPOON CORNSTARCH
- 1 TEASPOON DRIED PARSLEY
- 2 CUPS PLAIN NONFAT YOGURT
- 1 TEASPOON ZA'ATAR OR HERB SEASONING BLEND

1. Preheat oven to 350°F.

2. Place the hash browns, frozen vegetables, and onions in an oven- and microwave-safe casserole dish treated with nonstick spray. Cover with plastic wrap and microwave on high for 3 minutes. Turn the dish and microwave on high for an additional 2–3 minutes, until the vegetables are thawed and the onion is tender.

3. Remove and discard the plastic wrap. Season the chicken with the pepper and garlic powder. Arrange the thighs over the top of the vegetable mixture.

4. Stir the cornstarch and parsley into the yogurt. Pour the mixture over the chicken and vegetable mixture, spreading the yogurt so that it covers everything in an equal layer.

5. Bake for 45 minutes or until the yogurt is bubbling and thickened and the chicken thighs are done. Sprinkle the thighs with the za'atar. Serve immediately.

PER SERVING: Fat: 4 g **Protein:** 32 g **Carbohydrates:** 45 g
Sugar: 7 g

QUICK SKILLET CHICKEN CASSEROLE

CALORIES: 307
SERVES 4

½ CUP SKIM MILK

2 TABLESPOONS MAYONNAISE

1 CUP WATER

½ TEASPOON LOW-SODIUM CHICKEN BASE

¼ CUP UNSEASONED, NO-FAT-ADDED INSTANT MASHED POTATO FLAKES

½ TEASPOON ONION POWDER

¼ TEASPOON GARLIC POWDER

¼ TEASPOON DRIED CELERY FLAKES

⅛ TEASPOON FRESHLY GROUND BLACK PEPPER

1 LARGE EGG, BEATEN

1 TEASPOON WORCESTERSHIRE SAUCE

1 TABLESPOON LEMON JUICE

1 (10-OUNCE) PACKAGE FROZEN VEGETABLES, THAWED

1 CUP SLICED BUTTON MUSHROOMS

½ POUND COOKED CHICKEN, CHOPPED

1⅓ CUPS COOKED BROWN LONG-GRAIN RICE

1. Add the milk, mayonnaise, water, chicken base, potato flakes, onion powder, garlic powder, celery flakes, pepper, egg, Worcestershire sauce, and lemon juice to a blender or the bowl of a food processor; pulse until well mixed.

2. Pour the mixture into large, deep nonstick sauté pan; bring to a boil. Reduce heat and simmer, stirring until the mixture begins to thicken.

3. Add the frozen vegetables, mushrooms, and chicken; stir to combine. Cover and simmer for 5 minutes or until the mushrooms are cooked. Serve over the rice.

PER SERVING: Fat: 8 g **Protein:** 23 g **Carbohydrates:** 35 g **Sugar:** 4 g

CHICKEN AND GREEN BEAN STOVETOP CASSEROLE

CALORIES: 305
SERVES 4

- 1 CAN CONDENSED CREAM OF CHICKEN SOUP
- ¼ CUP SKIM MILK
- 2 TEASPOONS WORCESTERSHIRE SAUCE
- 1 TEASPOON MAYONNAISE
- ½ TEASPOON ONION POWDER
- ¼ TEASPOON GARLIC POWDER
- ¼ TEASPOON GROUND BLACK PEPPER
- 4-OUNCE CAN SLICED WATER CHESTNUTS, DRAINED
- 2½ CUPS FROZEN GREEN BEANS, THAWED
- 1 CUP SLICED MUSHROOMS, STEAMED
- ½ POUND COOKED, CHOPPED CHICKEN
- 1⅓ CUPS COOKED BROWN LONG-GRAIN RICE

1. Combine the soup, milk, Worcestershire sauce, mayonnaise, onion powder, garlic powder, and pepper in a saucepan and bring to a boil.

2. Reduce heat and add the water chestnuts, green beans, mushrooms, and chicken.

3. Simmer until vegetables and chicken are heated through.

4. Serve over rice.

PER SERVING: Fat: 8 g **Protein:** 22 g **Carbohydrates:** 35 g **Sugar:** 3 g

Veggie Filler

Steamed mushrooms are a low-calorie way to add flavor to a dish and stretch the meat. If you don't like mushrooms, you can substitute an equal amount of other steamed vegetables like red and green peppers.

CHICKEN SCALLOPS STUFFED WITH SPINACH AND CHEESE

CALORIES: 324
SERVES 2

2 (¼-POUND) CHICKEN BREASTS, SKINLESS AND BONELESS, POUNDED THIN

2 TABLESPOONS FLOUR

SALT AND PEPPER TO TASTE

¼ CUP SPINACH SOUFFLÉ (FROZEN)

¼ CUP RICOTTA CHEESE

⅛ TEASPOON NUTMEG

¼ CUP OLIVE OIL

JUICE OF 1 LEMON

½ CUP CHICKEN BROTH

1. Sprinkle the pounded chicken breasts with flour, salt, and pepper on both sides.

2. Mix the spinach, cheese, nutmeg, and additional salt and pepper to make the filling. Spread on the chicken breasts. Roll them and secure with a toothpick.

3. Sauté the chicken in olive oil until lightly browned. Add the lemon juice and chicken broth. Cover and simmer for 15 to 20 minutes.

PER SERVING: Fat: 12 g **Protein:** 47 g **Carbohydrates:** 12 g **Sugar:** 2 g

Making Scallops

To make chicken or veal scallops, use a rubber-headed hammer, a tool designed for pounding meat, a 5-pound weight, or the side of a heavy metal pan. Place the meat between two doubled sheets of waxed paper, pounding from the inner to outer edges. Pounding thins and tenderizes meat.

CHICKEN WITH EGGPLANT

CALORIES: 368
SERVES 4

- 4 SKINLESS, BONELESS CHICKEN BREASTS
- 1 POUND EGGPLANT
- 2 TABLESPOONS OLIVE OIL
- 1 MEDIUM RED BELL PEPPER, FINELY CHOPPED
- 2 CLOVES GARLIC, MINCED
- ½ CUP WATER
- ¼ CUP SOY SAUCE
- ¼ CUP RED-WINE VINEGAR
- 2 TABLESPOONS AGAVE NECTAR
- 2 TABLESPOONS SESAME OIL
- ¼ TEASPOON CRUSHED RED PEPPER

1. Cut chicken breasts lengthwise into ½" wide strips. Cut eggplant lengthwise into 1" wide strips.

2. Heat olive oil in a large pan and cook chicken until well done. Transfer to a bowl and set aside.

3. Return pan to high heat and add eggplant, bell pepper, garlic, and water. Bring to a boil, then reduce heat to medium-low, cover pan, and cook until eggplant is very soft and liquid has evaporated, stirring occasionally.

4. In a small bowl, mix soy sauce, vinegar, agave nectar, and sesame oil. Add cooked chicken, soy sauce mixture, and crushed red pepper to pan with cooked eggplant and bring to boil. Reduce heat to medium and cook, occasionally stirring, for about 5 minutes.

PER SERVING: Fat: 16 g **Protein:** 43 g **Carbohydrates:** 11 g **Sugar:** 6 g

---

CHICKEN AND VEGETABLE FRITTATA

CALORIES: 286
SERVES 4

- 3 SHALLOTS, SLICED
- 2 CLOVES GARLIC, MINCED
- 1 TEASPOON BUTTER
- SALT AND PEPPER
- 8 OUNCES CHICKEN BREAST, DICED
- 1 CUP BROCCOLI FLORETS
- 1 CUP ZUCCHINI, SLICED
- 1 CUP YELLOW SQUASH
- 12 ASPARAGUS SPEARS, CHOPPED INTO 1" PIECES
- ½ CUP LOW-FAT MILK
- 8 EGGS
- ¼ CUP PARMESAN CHEESE, GRATED

1. Preheat oven to 350°F. Sauté shallots, garlic, and butter in small pan over medium heat until soft, about 3 minutes. Be careful to not burn garlic.

2. Salt and pepper diced chicken breast as desired. Add chicken to pan with shallots and garlic and sauté until chicken is cooked.

3. Grease a round casserole dish. Place all vegetables and chicken with shallots into the greased dish.

4. Whisk together milk, eggs, and Parmesan cheese and pour over contents in the dish.

5. Bake at 350°F for 20–25 minutes, until eggs are set, but not brown.

PER SERVING: Fat: 14 g **Protein:** 32 g **Carbohydrates:** 9 g **Sugar:** 1 g

POACHED MEDITERRANEAN CHICKEN WITH OLIVES, TOMATOES, AND HERBS

CALORIES: 330
SERVES 2

- 1 CUP LOW-SALT CHICKEN BROTH
- 1 LARGE FRESH TOMATO, CORED AND CHOPPED
- 4 OUNCES PEARL ONIONS, FRESH OR FROZEN
- 4 TO 6 CLOVES ROASTED GARLIC
- 10 SPICY BLACK OLIVES, SUCH AS KALAMATA OR SICILIAN
- 10 GREEN OLIVES, PITTED (NO PIMIENTOS)
- ½ TEASPOON OREGANO LEAVES, DRIED, CRUMBLED
- 1 TEASPOON MINT LEAVES, DRIED, CRUMBLED
- 4 FRESH BASIL LEAVES, TORN
- 2 (4-OUNCE) CHICKEN BREASTS, BONELESS AND SKINLESS
- SALT AND PEPPER TO TASTE
- ½ TEASPOON LEMON ZEST
- 4 SPRIGS PARSLEY

1. Make the poaching liquid by placing all of the ingredients except for the chicken, salt and pepper, lemon zest, and parsley in a large saucepan. Bring to a boil; reduce heat and simmer for 5 minutes.

2. Add the chicken, salt, and pepper. Simmer for another 8 minutes and add lemon zest. Sprinkle with parsley and serve.

PER SERVING: Fat: 12 g **Protein:** 43 g **Carbohydrates:** 11 g **Sugar:** 1 g

Choosing Tomatoes

In season, use vine-ripe tomatoes. Off-season, use quality canned rather than greenhouse tomatoes. Tomatoes should be aromatic; tomatoes with no aroma will have no taste. Avoid tomatoes with leathery, dark patches—this is a sign of blossom-end rot.

DUCK BREASTS SAUTÉED WITH RUM-RAISIN SAUCE

CALORIES: 215
SERVES 4

- 2 DUCK BREASTS, ABOUT ½ POUND EACH, SKINLESS AND BONELESS
- SALT AND PEPPER TO TASTE
- 2 TABLESPOONS FLOUR
- ¼ TEASPOON GROUND NUTMEG
- ¼ TEASPOON GROUND CLOVES
- 1 TABLESPOON EXTRA-VIRGIN OLIVE OIL
- ½ CUP CHICKEN BROTH
- 2 TABLESPOONS GOLDEN RUM
- ½ CUP GOLDEN RAISINS (SULTANA)
- EXTRA SALT AND PEPPER, TO TASTE
- 1 TEASPOON QUICK-BLENDING FLOUR
- ¼ CUP LIGHT CREAM

1. Roll the duck breasts in a mixture of salt, pepper, flour, nutmeg, and cloves. Sauté in olive oil over medium heat until brown on both sides. Set aside, covered with aluminum foil on a warm platter.

2. To the pan in which the duck was cooked, add chicken broth and rum. Bring to a boil. Add raisins, salt, pepper, and flour. Turn the heat down and simmer for 5 minutes. Add cream and pour over duck breasts.

PER SERVING: Fat: 8 g **Protein:** 14 g **Carbohydrates:** 18 g **Sugar:** 6 g

Duck? Delicious!

While most people believe duck meat to be extremely fattening, it is the skin that is the culprit and not the meat of the duck. Duck meat is actually very lean when prepared without the skin and contains large amounts of protein and iron.

JERK CHICKEN

CALORIES: 177
SERVES 8

2 POUNDS CHICKEN PIECES

1 SMALL ONION, CHOPPED

2 GREEN ONIONS, CHOPPED INTO LARGE PIECES

1 JALAPEÑO PEPPER, SEEDS AND MEMBRANES REMOVED

3 CLOVES GARLIC

1 TEASPOON BLACK PEPPER

¾ TEASPOON SALT

½ TEASPOON DRIED THYME

¼ TEASPOON CAYENNE PEPPER

1 TABLESPOON SOY SAUCE

¼ CUP LIME JUICE

3 TABLESPOONS COOKING OIL

1. Wash and pat dry chicken. Place in a large glass baking dish.

2. In a food processor or blender, combine onion, green onions, jalapeño, and garlic and chop. Add black pepper, salt, thyme, cayenne pepper, soy sauce, lime juice, and oil and process until smooth.

3. Pour mixture over chicken and stir well to coat evenly. Cover with plastic wrap and refrigerate for 12 hours or overnight.

4. Preheat oven to 425°F. Place chicken in one layer in a greased roasting pan. Bake for approximately 50 minutes.

PER SERVING: Fat: 7 g **Protein:** 26 g **Carbohydrates:** 2 g **Sugar:** 0 g

Turn Up the Heat!

If you can handle more heat, crank up the spiciness by substituting the jalapeño pepper with two chopped habañero peppers with their seeds.

SKEWERED CHICKEN SATE WITH BABY EGGPLANT

CALORIES: 438
SERVES 4

- 12 BAMBOO SKEWERS, SOAKED FOR 1 HOUR IN WATER
- 1 POUND SKINLESS, BONELESS CHICKEN BREAST, CUT IN BITE-SIZE CHUNKS
- 2 BABY EGGPLANTS, CUT IN HALVES LENGTHWISE, UNPEELED
- ¼ CUP LEMON JUICE
- ¼ CUP SOY SAUCE
- SALT AND PEPPER TO TASTE
- ½ CUP CREAMY PEANUT BUTTER
- ¼ CUP SOY SAUCE
- 1 TABLESPOON PINEAPPLE JUICE
- 1 TEASPOON CHILI SAUCE (SUCH AS TABASCO)
- 1 HEAD ROMAINE LETTUCE LEAVES (SAVE SMALL WHITE HEARTS FOR SALAD)

1. Skewer the chicken and eggplants on separate skewers. Mix the lemon juice, soy sauce, salt, and pepper. Brush the lemon-soy mixture on the eggplant halves and the chicken.

2. Set grill on medium or use the broiler on high.

3. Make the peanut dipping sauce by mixing the peanut butter, soy sauce, pineapple juice, and chili sauce. If too thick, add more pineapple juice.

4. Grill the chicken and eggplants for 4–5 minutes per side, turning frequently.

5. Dip skewered chicken and eggplant in peanut dipping sauce and enjoy! Use the lettuce leaves as wraps to prevent burning your hands or getting sticky.

PER SERVING: Fat: 24 g **Protein:** 51 g **Carbohydrates:** 11 g **Sugar:** 2 g

APPLE-SPICED TURKEY TENDERLOINS

CALORIES: 197
SERVES 4

- 2 (8-OUNCE) TURKEY TENDERLOINS, CUT IN HALF
- 1 SMALL GRANNY SMITH APPLE, PEELED, CORED, AND SLICED
- ½ CUP APPLE CIDER OR APPLE JUICE
- 1 TABLESPOON, PLUS 2 TEASPOONS CORNSTARCH
- 2 TEASPOONS BROWN SUGAR
- ¼ TEASPOON CINNAMON
- ⅛ TEASPOON GROUND GINGER
- PINCH OF GROUND CLOVES
- PINCH OF GROUND ALLSPICE
- PINCH OF GROUND NUTMEG
- ½ TEASPOON DIJON MUSTARD
- ¼ TEASPOON MUSTARD POWDER

1. Place the turkey tenderloins between waxed paper or plastic wrap. Use a wooden mallet or rolling pin to pound to ½" thickness. Place in 1 layer in a 10" round Pyrex pie plate. Arrange the apple slices in a circle in the center of the pie plate.

2. In a small bowl, mix together all the remaining ingredients. Pour the mixture over the tenderloins and apple slices. Cover the pie pan tightly with heavy-duty, microwave-safe plastic wrap.

3. Microwave on high for 5 minutes. Turn the plate a half turn. Microwave on high for 4 minutes. Carefully pierce the plastic with a fork to release the steam. Let stand for several minutes and then remove the plastic and serve.

PER SERVING: Fat: 2 g **Protein:** 26 g **Carbohydrates:** 16 g **Sugar:** 6 g

Herb Hints

Rosemary can easily overpower a dish. When left whole in herb-roasted dishes, the flavor isn't as intense (and diners can easily push the rosemary leaves to the side, if they wish). Grinding rosemary in with other spices releases the essential oils and intensifies its flavor. In most cases if you intend to grind it, you'll use about half the amount of dried rosemary called for in a recipe.

HERBED CHICKEN AND BROCCOLI CASSEROLE

CALORIES: 356
SERVES 4

- 2 CUPS BROCCOLI
- ½ POUND COOKED CHICKEN, CHOPPED
- ½ CUP SKIM MILK
- 2 TABLESPOONS MAYONNAISE
- 1 CUP PLAIN NONFAT YOGURT
- ½ TEASPOON LOW-SODIUM CHICKEN BASE
- ¼ CUP UNSEASONED, NO-FAT-ADDED INSTANT MASHED POTATO FLAKES OR POTATO FLOUR
- ⅛ TEASPOON DRIED OREGANO
- ¼ TEASPOON DRIED PARSLEY
- ¼ TEASPOON GARLIC POWDER
- ¼ TEASPOON ONION POWDER
- ⅛ TEASPOON CELERY SEED
- ⅛ TEASPOON FRESHLY GROUND BLACK PEPPER
- 1 LARGE EGG, BEATEN
- 1 TABLESPOON LEMON JUICE
- ½ CUP GRATED CHEDDAR CHEESE
- ½ CUP COMMERCIAL BREAD CRUMBS
- BUTTER-FLAVORED COOKING SPRAY

1. Preheat oven to 350°. Treat an 11" × 7" casserole dish with nonstick spray.

2. Steam the broccoli until tender; drain. Spread out the chicken on the bottom of the prepared dish and cover it with the broccoli.

3. Put the milk, mayonnaise, yogurt, chicken base, potato granules, oregano, parsley, garlic powder, onion powder, celery seed, pepper, egg, and lemon juice in a blender or the bowl of a food processor and pulse until well mixed; pour over the broccoli. Mix together the cheese and bread crumbs; spread the mixture over the top of the casserole. Lightly spray the top of the crumbs with the butter-flavored spray. Bake for 30 minutes.

PER SERVING: Fat: 15 g **Protein:** 30 g **Carbohydrates:** 23 g
Sugar: 7 g

CHAPTER 9

Beef, Pork, Lamb, and Veal

VEAL ROAST WITH AGRO DOLCE

CALORIES: 308
SERVES 10

1 (5-POUND) ROLLED BONELESS VEAL SHOULDER ROAST

3 TABLESPOONS SUGAR

¼ CUP VINEGAR

3 SHALLOTS, MINCED

½ CUP GOLDEN RAISINS

2 TEASPOONS CAPERS

½ CUP WHITE WINE

1 TABLESPOON CANNED BEEF CONSOMMÉ

SALT AND PEPPER TO TASTE

1. Preheat the oven to 325°F. Place the meat in a roasting pan and set in the oven. Roast the meat for 3 hours or until meat thermometer registers 170°F. Transfer the meat to a serving platter. Remove string and let stand 15 minutes before serving.

2. While roast cools, make agro dolce sauce. Mix the sugar and vinegar together in a saucepan and cook over low heat, stirring constantly, until sugar has caramelized.

3. Add the shallots, raisins, capers, wine, and consommé. Simmer, stirring occasionally, until everything is melded together, about 5 minutes.

4. Season to taste with salt and pepper if necessary.

5. Serve warm with sliced roast veal.

PER SERVING: Fat: 9 g **Protein:** 41 g **Carbohydrates:** 10 g **Sugar:** 8 g

FILET MIGNON AND ROASTED RED PEPPER WRAPS

CALORIES: 415
SERVES 2

4 LARGE, OUTSIDE LEAVES OF ROMAINE LETTUCE

1 TABLESPOON OLIVE OIL

1 SWEET ONION, SUCH AS VIDALIA, CHOPPED FINE

1 CLOVE GARLIC, MINCED

SALT AND PEPPER TO TASTE

1 (8-OUNCE) FILET MIGNON, SLICED THINLY

4 SLICES WHITE AMERICAN CHEESE

1 TEASPOON WORCESTERSHIRE SAUCE

½ TEASPOON TABASCO SAUCE, OR TO TASTE

2 OUNCES ROASTED RED PEPPER, CHOPPED (FROM A JAR IS FINE)

OMIT THE CHEESE IN THIS RECIPE TO CUT BACK ON CALORIES.

1. Lay the lettuce out on paper towels. Skim the olive oil in the bottom of a medium-size frying pan; set on medium heat. Sauté the onion and garlic for 1–2 minutes.

2. Sprinkle salt and pepper on the filet mignon and sauté quickly.

3. Place a piece of cheese on each lettuce leaf; pile on onions, garlic, and filet mignon. Sprinkle with Worcestershire sauce and Tabasco sauce. Add roasted red peppers. Wrap and serve.

PER SERVING: Fat: 31 g **Protein:** 44 g **Carbohydrates:** 7 g **Sugar:** 2 g

STUFFED MEAT LOAF

CALORIES: 362
SERVES 8

NONSTICK COOKING SPRAY

1 TABLESPOON BUTTER

1 ONION, CHOPPED

1 (8-OUNCE) PACKAGE SLICED MUSHROOMS

½ (10-OUNCE) PACKAGE FROZEN SPINACH, THAWED AND DRAINED

2 TABLESPOONS CHOPPED FRESH PARSLEY

1 RECIPE WHOLE-GRAIN MEAT LOAF (SEE CHAPTER 9), UNCOOKED

2 TABLESPOONS KETCHUP

2 TABLESPOONS MUSTARD

1. Preheat oven to 350°F. Spray a 9" × 5" loaf pan with non-stick cooking spray and set aside. In medium saucepan, melt butter over medium heat. Add onion and mushrooms; cook and stir for 3 minutes. Then add spinach; cook until the vegetables are tender and the liquid evaporates.

2. Remove from heat and stir in parsley. Press half of the meat loaf mixture into prepared pan. Top with mushroom mixture, keeping mixture away from sides of pan. Top with remaining meat loaf mixture.

3. In small bowl, combine ketchup and mustard and mix well. Spoon over meat loaf. Bake for 55–65 minutes or until internal temperature registers 165°F. Let stand for 10 minutes, then cut into slices.

PER SERVING: Fat: 17 g **Protein:** 28 g **Carbohydrates:** 18 g **Sugar:** 3 g

---

SIRLOIN STEAK AND TOMATO SALAD ON SCANDINAVIAN FLAT BREAD

CALORIES: 469
SERVES 2

2 TABLESPOONS PLUS 2 TEASPOONS FRENCH DRESSING (SEE CHAPTER 3)

SALT AND PEPPER TO TASTE

NONSTICK SPRAY OR 1 TEASPOON OLIVE OIL

4 FLAT BREADS

4 SLICES RIPE TOMATO, HALVED

½ POUND LEAN, BONELESS SIRLOIN STEAK, SLICED THINLY

1. Marinate the steak in French dressing for 20 minutes. Sprinkle with salt and pepper. Heat a frying pan to medium high and use nonstick spray or oil.

2. Quickly sear the slices of steak on both sides and pile on the flat bread. Add tomato slices and a bit more French dressing. Serve and crunch away!

PER SERVING: Fat: 24 g **Protein:** 41 g **Carbohydrates:** 31 g **Sugar:** 4 g

CORNED BEEF HASH

CALORIES: 283
SERVES 6

2 TABLESPOONS OLIVE OIL

2 ONIONS, CHOPPED

4 CLOVES GARLIC, MINCED

8 FINGERLING POTATOES, CHOPPED

4 CARROTS, CHOPPED

¼ CUP WATER

½ POUND DELI CORNED BEEF, DICED

⅛ TEASPOON GROUND CLOVES

⅛ TEASPOON WHITE PEPPER

3 TABLESPOONS LOW-SODIUM CHILI SAUCE

1. Place olive oil in a large saucepan; heat over medium heat. Add onion and garlic; cook and stir for 3 minutes. Add potatoes and carrots; cook and stir until potatoes are partially cooked, about 5 minutes.

2. Add water, corned beef, cloves, pepper, and chili sauce. Stir well, then cover, reduce heat to low, and simmer for 10–15 minutes or until blended and potatoes are cooked. Serve immediately.

PER SERVING: Fat: 11 g **Protein:** 24 g **Carbohydrates:** 15 g **Sugar:** 3 g

Corned Beef

Corned beef is a very high-sodium food, made of brisket that has been pickled or "corned" in a mixture of water, vinegar, sugars, and salt. When you use it, use a small amount (about an ounce per person), mainly for flavor. Adding lots of vegetables helps makes this treat healthier.

GREEK MEATBALLS

CALORIES: 210
SERVES 10

2 POUNDS LEAN GROUND BEEF

1 CUP BUCKWHEAT, COOKED

1 ONION, MINCED

4 CLOVES OF GARLIC, MINCED

2 TABLESPOONS ITALIAN SEASONING

1 BUNCH FRESH MINT LEAVES, CHOPPED

2 TEASPOONS WHITE VINEGAR

2 EGGS, BEATEN

SALT AND GROUND PEPPER TO TASTE

½ CUP OLIVE OIL

1. Mix beef, buckwheat, onion, garlic, Italian seasoning, mint, vinegar, eggs, salt, and pepper in a bowl. Using your fingers, roll the mixture into meatballs.

2. Heat the oil in a medium pan over medium-high heat. Fry the meatballs in the oil in batches. Use a slotted spoon to move the balls in the oil to brown all sides.

3. Place cooked meatballs on a paper towel to drain.

4. If meatballs remain raw in the center, place on a baking sheet and into a 325°F oven for 15–20 minutes.

PER SERVING: Fat: 11 g **Protein:** 21 g **Carbohydrates:** 6 g **Sugar:** 0 g

BEEF WITH BELL PEPPERS

CALORIES: 358
SERVES 4

1 POUND LEAN BEEF

4 BELL PEPPERS, MEMBRANES AND SEEDS REMOVED, CHOPPED

3 CLOVES OF GARLIC, MINCED

JUICE OF 2 LEMONS

1 CAN OF CHICKPEAS, DRAINED

4 STALKS CELERY, CHOPPED

3 LARGE SHALLOTS, SLICED

SALT AND PEPPER TO TASTE

1. Preheat oven to 350°F.

2. Cut beef into cubes. Place all ingredients in a casserole dish and bake for 30 minutes.

PER SERVING: Fat: 13 g **Protein:** 31 g **Carbohydrates:** 31 g **Sugar:** 8 g

GRILLED LAMB CHOPS WITH GARLIC, ROSEMARY, AND THYME

CALORIES: 287
SERVES 2

2 CLOVES GARLIC

½ TEASPOON SALT

1 TEASPOON LEMON ZEST, MINCED

1 TEASPOON FRESH ROSEMARY, CHOPPED

1 TEASPOON FRESH THYME, CHOPPED

1 TABLESPOON OLIVE OIL

PEPPER TO TASTE

4 1¼"-THICK LAMB CHOPS

1. Take garlic cloves and mash into a paste. Add ½ teaspoon of salt.

2. In a bowl, stir together lemon zest, garlic paste, rosemary, thyme, oil, and add pepper to taste. Rub the herb-garlic paste onto the lamb chops and set them aside to marinate for 15 minutes.

3. Grill lamb chops for 4–5 minutes on each side for medium-rare doneness.

PER SERVING: Fat: 15 g **Protein:** 35 g **Carbohydrates:** 1 g **Sugar:** 0 g

STEAK AND MUSHROOM KABOBS

CALORIES: 321
SERVES 3

1 POUND OF SIRLOIN STEAK

3 TABLESPOONS OLIVE OIL

¼ CUP BALSAMIC VINEGAR

1 TABLESPOON WORCESTERSHIRE SAUCE

½ TEASPOON SALT

2 CLOVES GARLIC, MINCED

FRESH GROUND PEPPER TO TASTE

½ POUND OF LARGE WHITE MUSHROOMS

1. Cut steak into 1½" cubes.

2. Combine oil, vinegar, Worcestershire Sauce, salt, garlic, and pepper to make marinade.

3. Wash mushrooms and cut in half. Place steak and mushrooms in shallow bowl with marinade and place in refrigerator for 1–2 hours.

4. Place mushrooms and steak cubes on wooden or metal skewers. Grill 4 minutes per side for medium-rare steak. Try placing mushrooms and steak on separate skewers to allow for additional cooking time for mushrooms.

PER SERVING: Fat: 17 g **Protein:** 25 g **Carbohydrates:** 16 g **Sugar:** 3 g

---

BEEF AND BROCCOLI STIR-FRY

CALORIES: 290
SERVES 4

¾ POUND SIRLOIN BEEF, SLICED INTO ½" THICK PIECES

SALT AND PEPPER TO TASTE

1½ TABLESPOONS CORNSTARCH

3 TABLESPOONS PEANUT OIL

1 TEASPOON FRESH GINGER, MINCED

½ POUND BROCCOLI FLORETS

3 CLOVES GARLIC

¼ CUP SOY SAUCE

JUICE OF 1 LARGE ORANGE

½ TEASPOON CRUSHED RED PEPPER

1. Season beef with salt and pepper. Coat beef with cornstarch.

2. Heat 2 tablespoons of oil in a wok over medium-high heat, then stir-fry beef and ginger for 1–2 minutes. Transfer beef to a bowl, cover, and set aside.

3. Add remaining oil to the hot wok. Add broccoli and garlic and stir-fry for 3–4 minutes, until broccoli is tender. Take care not to burn garlic.

4. Pour soy sauce, orange juice, water, and red pepper into the wok with the broccoli and bring to a boil. Return the cooked beef to the wok. Stir until sauce thickens, about 2–3 minutes.

PER SERVING: Fat: 18 g **Protein:** 21 g **Carbohydrates:** 12 g **Sugar:** 5.5 g

BOEUF BOURGUIGNON

CALORIES: 383
SERVES 6–8

2 POUNDS STEWING BEEF, CUBED
SALT AND PEPPER TO TASTE
1 TABLESPOON OLIVE OIL
3 CLOVES GARLIC, MINCED
3 ONIONS, QUARTERED
2 CUPS RED COOKING WINE
¾ POUND CARROTS, SLICED
¾ POUND WHITE MUSHROOMS, SLICED
1 BUNCH OF FRESH ROSEMARY, LEAVES CHOPPED
1 BUNCH OF FRESH THYME, CHOPPED

1. Cut beef into ½" cubes, season with salt and pepper.

2. Place 1 tablespoon olive oil in a large pan over medium heat. Place beef in the pan to brown on the outside. Add garlic and onions to the pan and cook until tender. Add red wine, bring to a boil, and then simmer.

3. Add carrots, mushrooms, and herbs to the pan. Add a few cups of water to increase volume of liquid. Let cook for 3 hours, occasionally stirring.

PER SERVING: Fat: 25 g **Protein:** 21 g **Carbohydrates:** 14 g
Sugar: 3 g

FILET MIGNON

CALORIES: 266
SERVES 2

1 (8-OUNCE) FILET MIGNON
SALT AND PEPPER TO TASTE
NONSTICK SPRAY
½ CUP WHITE BUTTON MUSHROOMS, CHOPPED
2 OUNCES DRY RED WINE
2 OUNCES BEEF BROTH
2 TEASPOONS AIOLI (OPTIONAL)

1. Sprinkle the filet mignon with salt and pepper. Heat a heavy fry pan prepared with nonstick spray over medium-high flame.

2. Sear the filet mignon quickly on both sides. Stir in the mushrooms. Remove beef when at desired level of doneness. Add the liquids and bring to a boil. Pour the sauce over the beef. Serve hot with optional aioli.

PER SERVING: Fat: 11 g **Protein:** 33 g **Carbohydrates:** 3 g
Sugar: 0 g

BEEF TENDERLOIN WITH CHIMICHURRI

CALORIES: 435
SERVES 2

- 1 CUP PARSLEY
- 3 CLOVES OF GARLIC
- ¼ CUP CAPERS, DRAINED
- 2 TABLESPOONS RED-WINE VINEGAR
- 1 TEASPOON DIJON MUSTARD
- 2 TABLESPOONS OLIVE OIL
- 2 (5-OUNCE) BEEF TENDERLOINS
- SALT AND PEPPER TO TASTE

1. Blend together parsley, garlic, capers, vinegar, mustard, and oil. Season with salt and pepper as desired.

2. Grill steaks to medium-rare. Serve with chimichurri.

PER SERVING: Fat: 30 g **Protein:** 37 g **Carbohydrates:** 4 g **Sugar:** 0 g

GRILLED PEPPER STEAK

CALORIES: 284
SERVES 2

- 2 CUBED STEAKS (ALSO CALLED SANDWICH STEAKS)
- SALT AND PEPPER TO TASTE
- 1 TEASPOON STEAK SAUCE, SUCH AS A1 OR LEA & PERRIN'S
- 4 FRYING PEPPERS, CORED, SEEDED, AND HALVED (THE THIN-SKINNED, LIGHT-GREEN VARIETY)
- 2 RED ONIONS, SLICED THICK
- 1 LARGE PORTOBELLO MUSHROOM
- ¼ CUP ITALIAN DRESSING (SEE CHAPTER 3)
- 2 CUPS LETTUCE

1. Set the grill on high. Sprinkle the steaks with salt and pepper and spread with steak sauce.

2. Brush the peppers, onion slices, and mushroom with Italian dressing. Grill steaks for about 4 minutes per side for medium and grill the vegetables until they are slightly charred.

3. Place the steaks on beds of lettuce and pile the veggies on top. Slice the mushroom and arrange with the steaks, peppers, and onions.

PER SERVING: Fat: 15 g **Protein:** 28 g **Carbohydrates:** 9 g **Sugar:** 2 g

STUFFED BELL PEPPERS

CALORIES: 327
SERVES 6

2 LARGE GREEN BELL PEPPERS
2 LARGE RED BELL PEPPERS
2 LARGE YELLOW BELL PEPPERS
1 POUND GROUND BEEF
¼ POUND GROUND PORK
¼ CUP GRAPE NUTS CEREAL
½ CUP COOKED BROWN RICE
½ CUP DICED ONION
¼ CUP DICED CARROTS
¼ CUP DICED CELERY
2 CUPS TOMATO SAUCE
SALT AND PEPPER

1. Preheat oven to 350°F.

2. Cut peppers in half through the stem and discard seeds, stem, and membrane. Lay pepper cups in a casserole dish.

3. Mix together the meat, cereal, rice, onion, carrots, celery, and ½ cup tomato sauce. Season mixture with salt and pepper.

4. Stuff each pepper half with a ball of meat mixture, mounding it on top.

5. Pour tomato sauce over tops of stuffed peppers, cover with foil, and bake 45–60 minutes.

PER SERVING: Fat: 17 g **Protein:** 20 g **Carbohydrates:** 22 g **Sugar:** 5 g

---

CORNED BEEF AND CABBAGE

CALORIES: 300
SERVES 10

3 POUNDS CORNED BEEF BRISKET
3 CARROTS, CUT INTO 3" PIECES
3 ONIONS, QUARTERED
1 CUP WATER
½ SMALL HEAD OF CABBAGE, CUT INTO WEDGES

1. Place beef, carrots, onions, and water in a slow cooker. Cover and cook on low for 8–10 hours.

2. Add cabbage to the slow cooker; be sure to submerge the cabbage in liquid. Turn the heat up to high, cover, and cook for up to 3 hours.

PER SERVING: Fat: 20 g **Protein:** 21 g **Carbohydrates:** 7 g **Sugar:** 1 g

FILET MIGNON WITH VEGETABLES

CALORIES: 442
SERVES 8–10

1 (16-OUNCE) PACKAGE BABY CARROTS, HALVED LENGTHWISE
1 (8-OUNCE) PACKAGE FROZEN PEARL ONIONS
16 NEW POTATOES, HALVED
2 TABLESPOONS OLIVE OIL
2 POUNDS FILET MIGNON
⅛ TEASPOON SALT
⅛ TEASPOON WHITE PEPPER
½ CUP DRY RED WINE

1. Preheat oven to 425°F. Place carrots, onions, and potatoes in a large roasting pan and drizzle with olive oil; toss to coat. Spread in an even layer. Roast for 15 minutes, then remove from oven.

2. Top with filet mignon; sprinkle the meat with salt and pepper. Pour wine over meat and vegetables.

3. Return to oven; roast for 20–30 minutes longer until beef registers 150°F for medium. Remove from oven, tent with foil, and let stand for 5 minutes, then carve to serve.

PER SERVING: Fat: 11 g **Protein:** 54 g **Carbohydrates:** 10 g **Sugar:** 2 g

---

BEEF WITH MUSHROOM KABOBS

CALORIES: 215
SERVES 4

¼ CUP DRY RED WINE
1 TABLESPOON OLIVE OIL
⅛ TEASPOON SALT
⅛ TEASPOON CAYENNE PEPPER
1 TABLESPOON DRIED BASIL LEAVES
2 CLOVES GARLIC, MINCED
1 POUND BEEF SIRLOIN STEAK
½ POUND BUTTON MUSHROOMS
½ POUND CREMINI MUSHROOMS
1 TABLESPOON LEMON JUICE

1. In a medium-size glass bowl, combine wine, olive oil, salt, pepper, basil leaves, and garlic, and mix well. Cut steak into 1½" cubes and add to wine mixture. Stir to coat, cover, and refrigerate for 1 hour.

2. When ready to cook, prepare and preheat grill. Drain steak, reserving marinade. Trim mushroom stems and discard; brush mushrooms with lemon juice. Thread steak and mushrooms onto metal skewers.

3. Grill for 7–10 minutes, turning once and brushing with marinade, until beef is deep golden brown and mushrooms are tender. Discard remaining marinade.

PER SERVING: Fat: 7 g **Protein:** 39 g **Carbohydrates:** 10 g **Sugar:** 1 g

PORK TENDERLOIN WITH CARAWAY SAUERKRAUT

CALORIES: 309
SERVES 2

- 1 TEASPOON OLIVE OIL
- 8 OUNCES PORK TENDERLOIN
- SALT AND PEPPER TO TASTE
- 1 TEASPOON FLOUR
- 2 MEDIUM RED ONIONS, CHOPPED
- ¼ CUP LOW-SALT CHICKEN BROTH
- 8 OUNCES SAUERKRAUT, DRAINED
- 1 TEASPOON CARAWAY SEEDS

1. Heat the oil in a frying pan over medium heat. Sprinkle the pork tenderloin with salt, pepper, and flour. Sauté the pork over medium heat for 4 minutes; turn the pork and add onions.

2. Continue to sauté until the pork is lightly browned on both sides and the onions have softened slightly.

3. Add the chicken broth, sauerkraut, and caraway seeds. Cover and simmer for 25 minutes. Pork should be pink.

PER SERVING: Fat: 15 g **Protein:** 36 g **Carbohydrates:** 4 g
Sugar: 0 g

PAN-FRIED PORK CHOPS WITH APPLE

CALORIES: 273
SERVES 4

- 4 BONELESS PORK LOIN CHOPS
- 2 TEASPOONS OLIVE OIL
- 2 TABLESPOONS FRESH ROSEMARY, CHOPPED
- ¼ TEASPOON SALT
- ½ TEASPOON FRESH GROUND PEPPER
- 1 MEDIUM GRANNY SMITH APPLE, CORED AND QUARTERED
- ¼ CUP GOLDEN RAISINS
- ¾ CUP RED WINE
- NONSTICK COOKING SPRAY

1. Rub pork chops lightly with 1 teaspoon of olive oil. Combine rosemary, salt, and pepper and rub evenly on both sides of pork chops.

2. In a hot skillet, add remaining oil and cook apple and raisins over medium heat, stirring, for 4 minutes.

3. Add half of the wine, continuously stirring, until liquid evaporates. Add remaining wine and cook on medium-low heat for 15 minutes.

4. In a pan covered with cooking spray over medium heat, cook pork chops for 6 minutes on each side. Serve chops with apple mixture.

PER SERVING: Fat: 6 g **Protein:** 35 g **Carbohydrates:** 15 g
Sugar: 7 g

LONDON BROIL WITH GRILLED VEGETABLES

CALORIES: 354
SERVES 2

- 2 TABLESPOONS OLIVE OIL
- 1 TEASPOON RED-WINE VINEGAR
- 1 TABLESPOON STEAK SAUCE
- 1 TEASPOON SALT, OR TO TASTE
- 1 TEASPOON RED PEPPER FLAKES, OR TO TASTE
- 1 ZUCCHINI, CUT IN 1" CHUNKS
- 1 ORANGE OR YELLOW PEPPER, SEEDED AND CORED, CUT IN QUARTERS
- 2 SWEET ONIONS, CUT IN THICK CHUNKS
- 4 CHERRY TOMATOES
- ½ POUND LONDON BROIL, CUT IN CHUNKS
- 4 WOODEN SKEWERS, PRESOAKED FOR 30 MINUTES

1. In a small bowl, mix the olive oil, vinegar, steak sauce, and seasonings and set aside. Skewer the vegetables.

2. Brush the vegetables with the dressing. Toss the London broil in the rest of the dressing to coat and skewer.

3. Heat grill to 350°F and roast the vegetables and meat to the desired level of doneness.

PER SERVING: Fat: 12 g **Protein:** 39 g **Carbohydrates:** 26 g **Sugar:** 2 g

Keep Your Eye on the Beef

Beef is high-quality protein, but beware—when you eat too much of it or have it with rich sauces, the caloric count skyrockets.

SWEET AND SPICY KIELBASA

CALORIES: 283
SERVES 6

- 1 TEASPOON BOURBON
- PINCH OF DRIED RED PEPPER FLAKES
- 1 POUND PORK SHOULDER
- ½ POUND BEEF CHUCK
- 1 TEASPOON FRESHLY GROUND BLACK PEPPER
- ½ TEASPOON GROUND ALLSPICE
- 1 TEASPOON GARLIC POWDER
- ⅛ TEASPOON GROUND MUSTARD
- 1 TEASPOON BROWN SUGAR

1. Preheat indoor grill or bring a large, deep nonstick sauté pan or grill pan to temperature over medium-high heat.

2. Put the bourbon in a microwave-safe bowl and add the pepper flakes; microwave on high for 15 seconds or until the mixture is hot. In a large bowl, combine the seasoned bourbon with all the remaining ingredients *except* ¼ teaspoon of the black pepper; mix well. Shape into 6 patties. Place the patties on the grill, sprinkling the tops of the patties with the remaining pepper, and close the lid. Grill for 3–4 minutes or until the juices run clear.

PER SERVING: Fat: 15 g **Protein:** 31 g **Carbohydrates:** 1 g **Sugar:** 1 g

WASABI-ROASTED FILET MIGNON

CALORIES: 330
SERVES 12

- 1 (3-POUND) FILET MIGNON ROAST
- ¼ TEASPOON PEPPER
- 1 TEASPOON POWDERED WASABI
- 2 TABLESPOONS SESAME OIL
- 2 TABLESPOONS SOY SAUCE

1. Preheat oven to 400°F. If the roast has a thin end and a thick end, fold the thin end under so the roast is about the same thickness. Place on a roasting pan.

2. In a small bowl, combine pepper, wasabi, oil, and soy sauce, and mix well. Brush half over roast. Roast the beef for 30 minutes, then remove and brush with remaining wasabi mixture. Return to oven for 5–10 minutes longer or until meat thermometer registers at least 145°F for medium rare.

3. Remove from oven, cover, and let stand for 15 minutes before slicing to serve.

PER SERVING: Fat: 24 g **Protein:** 26 g **Carbohydrates:** 2 g **Sugar:** 0 g

LAMB SHANKS WITH WHITE BEANS AND CARROTS

CALORIES: 417
SERVES 4

- 4 LAMB SHANKS, WELL TRIMMED
- SALT AND PEPPER TO TASTE
- 1 TABLESPOON OLIVE OIL
- 1 LARGE YELLOW ONION, CHOPPED
- 4 GARLIC CLOVES, MINCED
- 1 CARROT, PEELED AND CUT IN CHUNKS
- 2 TABLESPOONS TOMATO PASTE
- 1 CUP DRY RED WINE
- 1 CUP CHICKEN BROTH
- 2 BAY LEAVES
- ¼ CUP PARSLEY, CHOPPED
- 2 (13-OUNCE) CANS WHITE BEANS, DRAINED

1. Sprinkle the lamb shanks with salt and pepper; brown in the olive oil, adding onion, garlic, and carrot. Cook for 5 minutes. Stir in tomato paste, red wine, chicken broth, bay leaves, and parsley.

2. Cover the pot and simmer for 1 hour. Add white beans and simmer for another 30 minutes.

PER SERVING: Fat: 12 g **Protein:** 31 g **Carbohydrates:** 44 g **Sugar:** 7 g

Not Crazy About Lamb?
When people don't like lamb, it's usually the fat, not the lamb, they dislike. When you prepare roast lamb, stew, or shanks, be sure to remove all of the fat.

CURRIED LAMB

CALORIES: 420
SERVES 4

- 2 TABLESPOONS CANOLA OIL
- 2 POUNDS SHOULDER LAMB CHOPS, BONE IN, TRIMMED OF FAT
- 4 WHITE ONIONS, CHOPPED
- 4 CLOVES GARLIC, CHOPPED
- 2 SERRANO OR SCOTCH BONNET CHILIES, CORED, SEEDED, AND CHOPPED
- 1" GINGER ROOT, PEELED AND MINCED
- 2 CARROTS, PEELED AND CHOPPED
- 1 STALK CELERY WITH LEAVES, CHOPPED
- 2 FRESH TOMATOES, CHOPPED
- 1 RED ROASTED PEPPER, CHOPPED
- 1 CUP CHICKEN BROTH
- 2 TABLESPOONS CURRY POWDER
- ½ CUP DRY WHITE WINE
- SALT AND PEPPER TO TASTE

1. Heat the canola oil over medium flame in a large pot. Brown the lamb and then add the rest of the vegetables.

2. Stir in the chicken broth. Mix the curry powder with the white wine to dissolve it and stir into the pot.

3. Cover the pot and reduce heat to a simmer. Cook over very low heat for 3 hours. Cool and remove the bones and any fat that has come to the top of the stew.

4. Reheat just before serving. Salt and pepper to taste.

PER SERVING: Fat: 19 g **Protein:** 37 g **Carbohydrates:** 22 g **Sugar:** 2 g

SIRLOIN MEATBALLS IN SAUCE

CALORIES: 367
SERVES 6

- 1 TABLESPOON OLIVE OIL
- 3 CLOVES GARLIC, MINCED
- ½ CUP MINCED ONION
- 2 EGG WHITES
- ½ CUP DRY BREAD CRUMBS
- ¼ CUP GRATED PARMESAN CHEESE
- ½ TEASPOON CRUSHED FENNEL SEEDS
- ½ TEASPOON DRIED OREGANO LEAVES
- 2 TEASPOONS WORCESTERSHIRE SAUCE
- ⅛ TEASPOON PEPPER
- ⅛ TEASPOON CRUSHED RED PEPPER FLAKES
- 1 POUND 95 PERCENT LEAN GROUND SIRLOIN
- SPAGHETTI SAUCE

1. In a small saucepan, heat olive oil over medium heat. Add garlic and onion; cook and stir until tender, about 5 minutes. Remove from heat and place in a large mixing bowl.

2. Add egg whites, bread crumbs, Parmesan, fennel, oregano, Worcestershire sauce, pepper, and red pepper flakes and mix well. Add sirloin; mix gently but thoroughly until combined. Form into 12 meatballs.

3. In large nonstick saucepan, place spaghetti sauce and bring to a simmer. Carefully add meatballs to sauce. Return to a simmer, partially cover, and simmer for 15–25 minutes or until meatballs are thoroughly cooked.

PER SERVING: Fat: 13 g **Protein:** 48 g **Carbohydrates:** 14 g **Sugar:** 2 g

Baking Meatballs

You can also bake these meatballs and freeze them plain to use in other recipes like Meatball Pizza (see this chapter). Place meatballs on a cookie sheet. Bake at 375°F for 15–25 minutes or until meatballs are browned and cooked through. Cool for 30 minutes, then chill until cold. Freeze individually in freezer bags. To thaw, let stand in refrigerator overnight.

STEAK WITH MUSHROOM SAUCE

CALORIES: 264
SERVES 6

1–1¼ POUNDS FLANK STEAK
2 TABLESPOONS RED WINE
1 TABLESPOON OLIVE OIL
1 TABLESPOON BUTTER
1 ONION, MINCED
1 (8-OUNCE) PACKAGE SLICED MUSHROOMS
2 TABLESPOONS FLOUR
1½ CUPS LOW-SODIUM BEEF BROTH
¼ TEASPOON GROUND CORIANDER
2 TEASPOONS WORCESTERSHIRE SAUCE
⅛ TEASPOON PEPPER

1. In a glass dish, combine flank steak, red wine, and olive oil. Cover and marinate for at least 8 hours.

2. When ready to eat, prepare and preheat grill. Drain steak, reserving marinade.

3. In a large skillet, melt butter over medium heat. Add onion and mushrooms; cook and stir until liquid evaporates, about 8–9 minutes. Stir in flour; cook and stir for 2 minutes. Add beef broth and marinade from beef and bring to a boil. Stir in coriander, Worcestershire sauce, and pepper; reduce heat to low and simmer while cooking steak.

4. Cook steak 6" from medium coals for 7–10 minutes, turning once, until steak reaches desired doneness. Remove from heat, cover, and let stand for 10 minutes. Slice thinly against the grain and serve with mushroom sauce.

PER SERVING: Fat: 12 g **Protein:** 36 g **Carbohydrates:** 3 g **Sugar:** 1.5 g

ASIAN BEEF KABOBS

CALORIES: 254
SERVES 4

- 2 TABLESPOONS OLIVE OIL
- 1 TEASPOON WASABI POWDER
- 1 TABLESPOON LOW-SODIUM SOY SAUCE
- 1 TABLESPOON LEMON JUICE
- 2 RED BELL PEPPERS, SLICED
- 1 (8-OUNCE) PACKAGE CREMINI MUSHROOMS
- 1 ZUCCHINI, SLICED ½" THICK
- 1 POUND BEEF SIRLOIN STEAK, CUBED

1. In a small bowl, combine olive oil and wasabi powder; mix well. Add soy sauce and lemon juice and mix well.

2. Thread peppers, mushrooms, zucchini, and steak on metal skewers. Brush with the marinade and let stand for 10 minutes.

3. Prepare and preheat grill. Grill skewers 6" from medium coals for 7–10 minutes, turning once and brushing with wasabi mixture several times, until beef reaches desired doneness and vegetables are crisp-tender. Serve immediately. Discard any remaining marinade.

PER SERVING: Fat: 9 g **Protein:** 39 g **Carbohydrates:** 10 g **Sugar:** 1 g

Cremini Mushrooms

Cremini mushrooms are baby portobellos. These light-brown fungi have more flavor than button mushrooms. Because mushrooms don't synthesize sugars, they are very low in carbohydrates. They are a good source of fiber and niacin. They are fat-free and cholesterol-free and have a nice amount of fiber per serving.

STEAK-AND-PEPPER KABOBS

CALORIES: 205
SERVES 4

- 2 TABLESPOONS BROWN SUGAR
- ½ TEASPOON GARLIC POWDER
- ⅛ TEASPOON CAYENNE PEPPER
- ¼ TEASPOON ONION SALT
- ½ TEASPOON CHILI POWDER
- ⅛ TEASPOON GROUND CLOVES
- 1 (1-POUND) SIRLOIN STEAK, CUT IN 1" CUBES
- 2 RED BELL PEPPERS, CUT IN STRIPS
- 2 GREEN BELL PEPPERS, CUT IN STRIPS

1. In a small bowl, combine brown sugar, garlic powder, cayenne pepper, onion salt, chili powder, and cloves, and mix well. Toss sirloin steak with brown sugar mixture. Place in a glass dish and cover; refrigerate for 2 hours.

2. When ready to cook, prepare and preheat grill. Thread steak cubes and pepper strips on metal skewers. Grill 6" from medium coals for 5–8 minutes, turning once, until steak reaches desired doneness and peppers are crisp-tender. Serve immediately.

PER SERVING: Fat: 6 g **Protein:** 38 g **Carbohydrates:** 10 g **Sugar:** 4 g

Dry Rubs

A dry rub adds flavor and moistness to meat and also makes it easier for the meat to caramelize on the grill because there is less moisture to dilute the sugars. You can create rubs with any types of flavoring or seasoning you'd like. Make a large batch and store in a tightly covered jar in a cool place for up to 3 months.

WHOLE-GRAIN MEAT LOAF

CALORIES: 325
SERVES 8

NONSTICK COOKING SPRAY
1 TABLESPOON OLIVE OIL
1 ONION, FINELY CHOPPED
3 CLOVES GARLIC, MINCED
1 CUP MINCED MUSHROOMS
⅛ TEASPOON PEPPER
1 TEASPOON DRIED MARJORAM LEAVES
1 EGG
1 EGG WHITE
½ CUP CHILI SAUCE
¼ CUP MILK
1 TABLESPOON WORCESTERSHIRE SAUCE
4 SLICES WHOLE-GRAIN OATMEAL BREAD
8 OUNCES 85 PERCENT LEAN GROUND BEEF
8 OUNCES GROUND TURKEY
8 OUNCES GROUND PORK
3 TABLESPOONS KETCHUP

1. Preheat oven to 325°F. Spray a 9" × 5" loaf pan with non-stick cooking spray and set aside. In a large saucepan, heat olive oil over medium heat. Add onion, garlic, and mushrooms; cook and stir until tender, about 6 minutes. Place in large mixing bowl, sprinkle with pepper and marjoram, and let stand for 15 minutes.

2. Add egg, egg white, chili sauce, milk, and Worcestershire sauce, and mix well. Make crumbs from the oatmeal bread and add to onion mixture.

3. Add all of the meat and work gently with your hands just until combined. Press into prepared loaf pan. Top with ketchup. Bake for 60–75 minutes, or until internal temperature registers 165°F. Remove from oven, cover with foil, and let stand for 10 minutes before slicing.

PER SERVING: Fat: 15 g **Protein:** 27 g **Carbohydrates:** 23 g **Sugar:** 2 g

Meat Loaf Secrets

There are a few tricks to making the best meat loaf. First, combine all the other ingredients and mix well, then add the meat last. The less the meat is handled, the more tender the meat loaf will be. Then, when it's done baking, remove from the oven, cover with foil, and let sit for 10 minutes to let the juices redistribute.

MEATBALL PIZZA

CALORIES: 437
SERVES 6

1 TABLESPOON OLIVE OIL

1 ONION, CHOPPED

1 GREEN BELL PEPPER, CHOPPED

½ CUP SHREDDED CARROTS

1 (6-OUNCE) CAN NO-SALT TOMATO PASTE

2 TABLESPOONS MUSTARD

¼ CUP WATER

1 WHOLE-GRAIN PIZZA CRUST, PREBAKED

12 PLAIN SIRLOIN MEATBALLS (SEE CHAPTER 9), BAKED

1 CUP SHREDDED EXTRA-SHARP CHEDDAR CHEESE

½ CUP SHREDDED PART-SKIM MOZZARELLA CHEESE

1. Preheat oven to 400°F. In a medium saucepan, heat olive oil over medium heat. Add onion, bell pepper, and carrots; cook and stir until crisp-tender, about 5 minutes. Add tomato paste, mustard, and water and bring to a simmer. Simmer, stirring frequently, for 5 minutes.

2. Spread the sauce over the pizza crust. Cut the meatballs in half and arrange on the pizza. Sprinkle with Cheddar and mozzarella cheeses.

3. Bake for 20–30 minutes or until crust is golden brown, pizza is hot, and cheese is melted and bubbling. Let stand for 5 minutes, then serve.

PER SERVING: **Fat:** 15 g **Protein:** 24 g **Carbohydrates:** 40 g **Sugar:** 7 g

Pizza Variations

Once you have the basic recipe down, it's very easy to make your own pizzas. Use lots of vegetables for added flavor and nutrition, and to reduce the amount of meat you need. You can use deli-sliced roast beef, cooked chicken, Canadian bacon, or ham to top your pizza, or just use vegetables and cheese.

WHOLE-WHEAT SPAGHETTI AND MEATBALLS

CALORIES: 386
SERVES 6–8

- **1 RECIPE SIRLOIN MEATBALLS IN SAUCE (SEE THIS CHAPTER)**
- **1 (8-OUNCE) CAN NO-SALT TOMATO SAUCE**
- **½ CUP GRATED CARROTS**
- **1 (16-OUNCE) PACKAGE WHOLE-WHEAT SPAGHETTI**
- **½ CUP GRATED PARMESAN CHEESE, DIVIDED**

1. Bring a large pot of water to a boil. Prepare the Sirloin Meatballs in Sauce, adding tomato sauce and grated carrots to the sauce. Simmer until meatballs are cooked.

2. Cook spaghetti in water according to package directions or until almost al dente. Drain spaghetti, reserving ¼ cup cooking water. Add spaghetti to meatballs in sauce along with ¼ cup of the cheese. Simmer, stirring gently, for 5–6 minutes or until pasta is al dente, adding reserved cooking water if necessary for desired sauce consistency. Sprinkle with the remaining ¼ cup Parmesan cheese and serve immediately.

PER SERVING: Fat: 12 g **Protein:** 29 g **Carbohydrates:** 45 g **Sugar:** 3 g

Whole-Wheat Spaghetti

Whole-wheat spaghetti has a much stronger taste than regular pasta. Serve it with strongly flavored sauces until your family is used to the taste. You can also gradually switch to whole-wheat pastas by starting out using just a third whole-wheat pasta (and the other two-thirds plain) and increasing the proportion of whole wheat each time you serve it.

BEEF RISOTTO

CALORIES: 365
SERVES 6

2 CUPS WATER

2 CUPS LOW-SODIUM BEEF BROTH

2 TABLESPOONS OLIVE OIL

½ POUND SIRLOIN STEAK, CHOPPED

1 ONION, MINCED

2 CLOVES GARLIC, MINCED

1½ CUPS ARBORIO RICE

2 TABLESPOONS STEAK SAUCE

¼ TEASPOON PEPPER

1 POUND ASPARAGUS, CUT INTO 2" PIECES

¼ CUP GRATED PARMESAN CHEESE

1 TABLESPOON BUTTER

1. In a medium saucepan, combine water and broth; heat over low heat until warm; keep on heat.

2. In a large saucepan, heat olive oil over medium heat. Add beef; cook and stir until browned. Remove from pan with slotted spoon and set aside. Add onion and garlic to pan; cook and stir until crisp-tender, about 4 minutes.

3. Add rice; cook and stir for 2 minutes. Add the broth mixture, a cup at a time, stirring until the liquid is absorbed, about 15 minutes. When there is 1 cup broth remaining, return the beef to the pot and add the steak sauce, pepper, and asparagus. Cook and stir until rice is tender, beef is cooked, and asparagus is tender, about 5 minutes. Stir in Parmesan and butter and serve immediately.

PER SERVING: Fat: 11 g **Protein:** 47 g **Carbohydrates:** 30 g
Sugar: 5 g

BEEF ROLL UPS WITH PESTO

CALORIES: 290
SERVES 6

½ CUP PACKED BASIL LEAVES

½ CUP PACKED BABY SPINACH LEAVES

3 CLOVES GARLIC, MINCED

⅓ CUP TOASTED CHOPPED HAZELNUTS

⅛ TEASPOON WHITE PEPPER

2 TABLESPOONS GRATED PARMESAN CHEESE

2 TABLESPOONS OLIVE OIL

2 TABLESPOONS WATER

3 TABLESPOONS FLOUR

½ TEASPOON PAPRIKA

6 (4-OUNCE) TOP ROUND STEAKS, ¼" THICK

2 OIL-PACKED SUN-DRIED TOMATOES, MINCED

1 TABLESPOON CANOLA OIL

1 CUP LOW-SODIUM BEEF BROTH

1. In a blender or food processor, combine basil, spinach, garlic, hazelnuts, and white pepper, and blend or process until finely chopped. Add Parmesan and blend again. Add olive oil and blend until a paste forms, then add water and blend.

2. On a shallow plate, combine flour and paprika and mix well. Place beef between sheets of waxed paper and pound until ⅛" thick. Spread pesto on one side of the pounded beef and sprinkle with tomatoes. Roll up, fastening closed with toothpicks.

3. Dredge roll ups in flour mixture. Heat canola oil in large saucepan and brown roll ups on all sides, about 5 minutes total. Pour beef broth into pan and bring to a simmer. Cover, reduce heat to low, and simmer for 40–50 minutes or until beef is tender.

PER SERVING: Fat: 18 g **Protein:** 29 g **Carbohydrates:** 15 g **Sugar:** 4 g

PORK TENDERLOIN WITH BLACKBERRY GASTRIQUE

CALORIES: 384
SERVES 4

- 1 TABLESPOON OLIVE OIL
- 1 TABLESPOON COARSE GRAIN MUSTARD
- 1 (1½-POUND) PORK TENDERLOIN
- 1 TABLESPOON KOSHER SALT
- 1 TEASPOON GROUND BLACK PEPPER
- 1 SHALLOT, MINCED
- ½ CUP BLACKBERRIES, FRESH OR FROZEN
- 1 TABLESPOON BALSAMIC VINEGAR
- ½ CUP BLACKBERRY PRESERVES

1. Preheat a grill or grill-pan over high heat.

2. Rub 1 teaspoon olive oil and coarse grain mustard on the tenderloin, then sprinkle the kosher salt and black pepper on it.

3. Grill the tenderloin on all sides, for a total of about 10 minutes. Set the tenderloin aside, cover it with foil, and let it rest at least 10 minutes before slicing.

4. Sauté the shallots until tender in remaining olive oil. Remove from heat and stir in the blackberries, balsamic vinegar, and blackberry preserves.

5. Cut the tenderloin in ½"-thick slices, arrange the slices on a platter, and spoon the blackberry sauce over them.

PER SERVING: Fat: 12 g **Protein:** 35 g **Carbohydrates:** 30 g **Sugar:** 16 g

Temperature Tip

The internal temperature of the tenderloin will go up about 5 degrees after it has been removed from the heat. It should be 155°F when done. The roast should be allowed to stand, prior to cutting, covered with a kitchen towel. This practice keeps the juices in the meat and makes it more succulent. Cutting the meat instantly makes the juices run out, leaving the meat dry.

LONDON BROIL WITH ONIONS AND SWEET POTATO STICKS

CALORIES: 384
SERVES 2

- 1 TABLESPOON OLIVE OIL
- ½ POUND LONDON BROIL, DICED
- SALT AND PEPPER
- STEAK SEASONING
- ½ CUP SWEET ONION, CHOPPED
- HOT RED PEPPER FLAKES TO TASTE
- 1 TEASPOON WORCESTERSHIRE SAUCE
- 2 TABLESPOONS SALSA
- 2 LARGE SWEET RED BELL PEPPERS, CUT LENGTHWISE, CORED AND SEEDED
- BAKED SWEET POTATO STICKS (SEE RECIPE BELOW)

1. Heat olive oil over medium flame in a frying pan. Season the steak with salt, pepper, and steak seasoning. Add steak and onions to the pan and sauté until the steak reaches the desired level of doneness.

2. Sprinkle steak with hot pepper flakes and Worcestershire sauce. Mix in salsa and stuff the red peppers with the mixture.

3. Serve with the baked sweet potato sticks on the side.

PER SERVING: (with baked sweet potato sticks) **Fat:** 15 g **Protein:** 38 g **Carbohydrates:** 26 g **Sugar:** 5 g

What Is London Broil?

Surprisingly, London broil is not actually a cut of beef but is, in fact, a cooking method. Although many grocery stores and butchers may have a very lean piece of meat labeled as a London broil, it is likely to be a top round roast or top round steak.

BAKED SWEET POTATO STICKS

SERVES 2

- 1 LARGE SWEET POTATO, PEELED, CUT LIKE FRENCH FRIES
- 1 TABLESPOON OLIVE OIL
- SALT AND PEPPER TO TASTE
- 1 TEASPOON THYME LEAVES, DRIED
- 1 TEASPOON SAGE LEAVES, DRIED

1. Blanch the peeled potato slices in boiling water for 4 to 5 minutes. Dry on paper towels.

2. Sprinkle with olive oil, salt, pepper, and herbs. Bake in an aluminum pan at 350°F until crisp, about 10 minutes.

BLACK BEAN CHILI WITH BEEF AND CORN

CALORIES: 429
SERVES 4

- 2 TABLESPOONS OLIVE OR OTHER COOKING OIL
- ½ POUND GROUND BEEF
- 1 LARGE RED ONION, CHOPPED
- 2 CLOVES GARLIC, MINCED
- 1 LARGE SWEET RED BELL PEPPER, CORED, SEEDED, AND CHOPPED
- 1 SMALL HOT PEPPER, CORED, SEEDED, AND MINCED
- 1 TEASPOON GROUND CUMIN
- 1 TEASPOON DRIED CILANTRO OR PARSLEY (FRESH IS BETTER)
- 8 OUNCES FROZEN CORN NIBLETS
- 2 (13-OUNCE) CANS BLACK BEANS, DRAINED
- 1 CUP CRUSHED TOMATOES (CANNED IS FINE)
- SALT AND PEPPER TO TASTE
- JUICE OF ½ LIME
- 2 OUNCES MONTEREY JACK CHEESE, SHREDDED
- CORN BREAD OR TORTILLA (OPTIONAL)

1. In a large, ovenproof casserole, heat the oil over medium flame. Brown the beef. Move to one side of the casserole dish and sauté the vegetables for 5 minutes. Stir in the cumin and herbs and mix well.

2. Preheat oven to 340°F. Stir in the corn, black beans, tomatoes, salt, and pepper. Sprinkle with lime juice. Stir to mix.

3. Spread the top with cheese and bake for 30 minutes, or until hot and bubbling. Serve with corn bread or tortillas.

PER SERVING: Fat: 13 g **Protein:** 23 g **Carbohydrates:** 69 g **Sugar:** 10 g

Legumes

Beans are legumes, as are other foods such as lentils, peas, soybeans, and peanuts. Not only are legumes good for farmers to produce because their roots produce nitrogen, which fertilizes land, but they are delicious and full of healthy protein for you!

GINGER BEEF AND NAPA CABBAGE

CALORIES: 446
SERVES 4

- 3 TABLESPOONS SOY SAUCE
- 2 CLOVES OF GARLIC, MINCED
- 1 TABLESPOON FRESH GINGER, MINCED
- 1 TEASPOON AGAVE NECTAR
- ½ TEASPOON CRUSHED RED PEPPER FLAKES
- 1 POUND BEEF TENDERLOIN OR SIRLOIN STEAK
- 1 CUP BEEF BROTH
- 2 TEASPOONS CORNSTARCH
- 2 TABLESPOONS PEANUT OIL
- 1 LARGE ONION, SLICED THIN
- ½ HEAD NAPA CABBAGE, SHREDDED
- 3 GREEN ONIONS, SLICED

1. Combine soy sauce, garlic, ginger, agave nectar, and red pepper in a small bowl. Slice beef into ¼" thick strips. Toss beef in soy-ginger sauce. Cover, and place in refrigerator for at least 30 minutes to marinate.

2. Mix broth and cornstarch and set aside.

3. Heat half the oil in a large pan over medium heat. Add onion to the pan and cook for 5 minutes until tender and slightly brown. Remove from heat.

4. Heat remaining oil over medium-high heat. Add beef and cabbage to the pan and stir-fry for 5 minutes or until beef is only slightly pink in the center and cabbage is tender. Add cooked onion and the broth to the pan. Cook for about 2 minutes, until sauce boils. Reduce heat to low and allow sauce to thicken.

5. Garnish with green onion before serving.

PER SERVING: Fat: 32 g **Protein:** 25 g **Carbohydrates:** 15 g **Sugar:** 2 g

SCALLOPED POTATO AND SAUSAGE CASSEROLE WITH GREENS

CALORIES: 277
SERVES 4

- 1 TEASPOON VEGETABLE OIL
- 8 OUNCES LEAN PORK BREAKFAST SAUSAGE, CRUMBLED
- 1 YELLOW ONION, SLICED
- 1 SMALL ZUCCHINI, ENDS REMOVED, DICED
- 1 (10-OUNCE) PACKAGE CHOPPED FROZEN SPINACH, THAWED AND SQUEEZED OF MOISTURE
- ¼ TEASPOON NUTMEG
- SALT AND PEPPER TO TASTE
- NONSTICK COOKING SPRAY
- 2 IDAHO OR OTHER RUSSET POTATOES, PEELED AND SLICED THINLY
- ¼ CUP PARMESAN CHEESE, GRATED
- ⅓ CUP 2% MILK
- ½ CUP BREAD CRUMBS

IN THIS RECIPE YOU CAN SUBSTITUTE NONFAT MILK FOR 2% MILK AND REPLACE SAUSAGE WITH VEGETARIAN SAUSAGE.

1. Heat the oil in a large frying pan and sauté the sausage, onion, and zucchini. Stir to break up the sausage and mix well.

2. Stir in the spinach, nutmeg, salt, and pepper. Set aside.

3. Prepare a 9" pie plate with nonstick spray. Cover the bottom with half of the sliced potatoes, add the sausage filling, and cover the top with the rest of the potatoes. Sprinkle with cheese and add milk.

4. Cover the top with bread crumbs; press down to moisten with milk. Bake for 50 minutes at 325°F, or until the potatoes are soft.

PER SERVING: Fat: 5 g **Protein:** 13 g **Carbohydrates:** 50 g
Sugar: 4 g

COUNTRY-STYLE PORK RIBS

CALORIES: 186
SERVES 4

- **SALT AND PEPPER TO TASTE**
- **GARLIC POWDER TO TASTE**
- **CAYENNE PEPPER TO TASTE**
- **1 CUP WATER**
- **1 TEASPOON LIQUID SMOKE**
- **2 TABLESPOONS WORCESTERSHIRE SAUCE**
- **1 CUP ANY GOOD BARBECUE SAUCE**

1. Sprinkle the ribs with salt and pepper, garlic powder, and cayenne pepper. Rub the spices into the meat and bone on both sides. Place them in a turkey roasting pan with the water and liquid smoke on the bottom. Sprinkle with Worcestershire sauce.

2. Set the oven at 225°F. Cover the ribs tightly with aluminum foil. Roast them for 4–5 hours. They should be "falling off the bone" tender.

3. Remove foil and brush the ribs with barbeque sauce. Bake for another 15–20 minutes or until dark brown.

PER SERVING: Fat: 7 g **Protein:** 5 g **Carbohydrates:** 25 g **Sugar:** 6 g

Liquid Smoke

Liquid smoke is a flavoring for food used to give a smoky, barbequed flavor without the wood chips! It is most often made out of hickory wood, which producers burn to capture and condense the smoke. They filter out impurities in the liquid and bottle the rest.

ROAST LEG OF VEAL

CALORIES: 174
SERVES 8

1 (5-POUND) VEAL LEG ROAST, SHANK HALF OF THE LEG, BONE IN

1 TABLESPOON PREPARED MUSTARD, DIJON-STYLE

2 TABLESPOONS ALL-PURPOSE FLOUR

1 TABLESPOON BUTTER, ROOM TEMPERATURE

1 TEASPOON DRIED SAGE, CRUMBLED

2 TEASPOONS DRIED ROSEMARY, CRUMBLED

SALT AND FRESHLY GROUND BLACK PEPPER TO TASTE

1 CUP CHICKEN BROTH

½ CUP DRY WHITE WINE

IN THIS RECIPE YOU CAN SUBSTITUTE THE BUTTER WITH OLIVE OIL OR HEART-HEALTHY MARGARINE.

1. Make sure the veal is well trimmed and has no skin on it. Set oven at 400°F. Make a paste of the mustard, flour, butter, herbs, salt, and pepper. Coat the veal with the mustard mixture.

2. Place veal in a roasting pan and place in the hot, preheated oven. Roast for 15 minutes. Turn down heat and baste with ¼ cup chicken broth and in 15 minutes with ¼ cup wine.

3. Reduce heat to 325°F. Continue to roast and baste the meat for another 45 minutes, or until the internal temperature reaches 150°F.

4. Let the meat rest on a platter for 15 minutes before carving. Serve with pan juices; if dry, add ½ cup boiling water to pan and whisk.

PER SERVING: Fat: 7 g **Protein:** 22 g **Carbohydrates:** 1 g **Sugar:** 0 g

VEAL AND SPINACH IN LEMON SAUCE

CALORIES: 194
SERVES 6

- 3 TABLESPOONS OLIVE OR CANOLA OIL
- 1½ POUNDS LEAN VEAL, CUT INTO CUBES
- 1 LARGE WHITE ONION, CHOPPED
- ¼ CUP WATER
- 1 TABLESPOON LEMON JUICE
- ¼ TEASPOON FRESHLY GROUND BLACK PEPPER
- ¼ TEASPOON FENNEL SEEDS, CRUSHED
- ¼ TEASPOON GARLIC POWDER
- ⅛ TEASPOON SALT-FREE CHILI POWDER
- 3 GREEN ONIONS, WHITE AND GREEN PART CHOPPED
- 2 (10-OUNCE) PACKAGES FROZEN SPINACH
- 1 LEMON, CUT INTO 6 WEDGES (OPTIONAL)

1. Bring oil to temperature over medium-high heat in a large, deep nonstick sauté pan; brown the veal. Add the onion and sauté until transparent. Add the water, lemon juice, pepper, fennel seeds, garlic powder, and chili powder. Bring to a boil, then reduce heat; cover and simmer for 1 hour or until the veal is tender, stirring occasionally and adding more water, if necessary.

2. Add the green onions and spinach. Cover and simmer for 10 minutes. Serve immediately. Garnish with lemon wedges, if desired.

PER SERVING: Fat: 11 g **Protein:** 20 g **Carbohydrates:** 5 g **Sugar:** 0 g

CHAPTER 10

Seafood

SESAME-CRUSTED MAHI MAHI

CALORIES: 282
SERVES 4

- 2 TABLESPOONS DIJON MUSTARD
- 1 TABLESPOON LOW-FAT SOUR CREAM
- ½ CUP SESAME SEEDS
- 2 TABLESPOONS OLIVE OIL
- 1 LEMON, CUT INTO WEDGES
- 4 (4-OUNCE) MAHI MAHI OR SOLE FILETS

1. Rinse filets and pat dry. In a small bowl, combine mustard and sour cream and mix well. Spread this mixture on all sides of fish. Roll in sesame seeds to coat.

2. Heat olive oil in large skillet over medium heat. Pan-fry fish, turning once, for 5–8 minutes or until fish flakes when tested with fork and sesame seeds are toasted. Serve immediately with lemon wedges.

PER SERVING: Fat: 17 g **Protein:** 18 g **Carbohydrates:** 5 g **Sugar:** 1 g

---

BROILED SWORDFISH

CALORIES: 210
SERVES 4

- 1 TABLESPOON OLIVE OIL
- 2 TABLESPOONS DRY WHITE WINE
- 1 TEASPOON LEMON ZEST
- ¼ TEASPOON SALT
- ⅛ TEASPOON WHITE PEPPER
- 1 TEASPOON DRIED DILL WEED
- 1¼ POUNDS SWORDFISH STEAKS
- 4½"-THICK TOMATO SLICES

1. Preheat broiler. In small bowl, combine oil, wine, zest, salt, pepper, and dill weed and whisk to blend.

2. Place steaks on a broiler pan. Brush steaks with oil mixture. Broil 6" from heat for 4 minutes. Turn fish over and brush with remaining oil mixture. Top with tomatoes. Return to broiler and broil for 4–6 minutes or until fish flakes when tested with a fork.

PER SERVING: Fat: 9 g **Protein:** 21 g **Carbohydrates:** 2 g **Sugar:** 0 g

Cooking Fish

The general rule for broiling, grilling, or sautéing fish is to cook it for 10 minutes per inch of thickness. Properly cooked fish is opaque and flakes easily when a fork is inserted into the flesh and twisted. In other words, the fish should break apart into thin layers, or flakes.

CAJUN-RUBBED FISH

CALORIES: 233
SERVES 4

½ TEASPOON BLACK PEPPER
¼ TEASPOON CAYENNE PEPPER
½ TEASPOON LEMON ZEST
½ TEASPOON DRIED DILL WEED
⅛ TEASPOON SALT
1 TABLESPOON BROWN SUGAR
4 5-OUNCE SWORDFISH STEAKS
OLIVE OR VEGETABLE OIL, AS
   NEEDED

1. Prepare and preheat grill. In a small bowl, combine pepper, cayenne pepper, lemon zest, dill weed, salt, and brown sugar and mix well. Sprinkle onto both sides of the swordfish steaks and rub in. Set aside for 30 minutes.

2. Brush grill with oil. Add swordfish; cook without moving for 4 minutes. Carefully turn steaks and cook for 2–4 minutes on second side until fish just flakes when tested with fork. Serve immediately.

PER SERVING: Fat: 7 g **Protein:** 24 g **Carbohydrates:** 10 g
Sugar: 2 g

BAKED LEMON SOLE WITH HERBED CRUMBS

CALORIES: 294
SERVES 4

2 SLICES WHOLE-GRAIN BREAD,
   CRUMBLED
2 TABLESPOONS MINCED PARSLEY
2 CLOVES GARLIC, MINCED
1 TEASPOON DRIED DILL WEED
2 TABLESPOONS OLIVE OIL
NONSTICK COOKING SPRAY
4 (6-OUNCE) SOLE FILETS
2 TABLESPOONS LEMON JUICE
PINCH OF SALT
⅛ TEASPOON WHITE PEPPER

1. Preheat oven to 350°F. In a small bowl, combine bread crumbs, parsley, garlic, and dill weed, and mix well. Drizzle with olive oil and toss to coat.

2. Spray a 9" baking dish with nonstick cooking spray and arrange filets in dish. Sprinkle with lemon juice, salt, and pepper. Divide crumb mixture on top of filets.

3. Bake for 12–17 minutes or until fish flakes when tested with a fork and crumb topping is browned. Serve immediately.

PER SERVING: Fat: 9 g **Protein:** 35 g **Carbohydrates:** 10 g
Sugar: 1 g

GRILLED MAHI MAHI WITH PINEAPPLE SALSA

CALORIES: 142
SERVES 8

1 CUP DICED PINEAPPLE
½ CUP DICED RED ONION
¼ CUP MINCED GREEN BELL PEPPER
¼ CUP MINCED RED BELL PEPPER
¼ BUNCH CILANTRO
1 TABLESPOON WHITE WINE VINEGAR
¼ TEASPOON HOT PEPPER SAUCE
SALT TO TASTE
2 POUNDS MAHI MAHI OR OTHER FIRM-FLESHED FISH
2 TABLESPOONS OLIVE OIL
PEPPER TO TASTE

1. Combine the pineapple, red onion, green bell pepper, and red bell pepper in a large bowl.

2. Chop the cilantro and add it to the bowl.

3. Add the vinegar, hot sauce, and a pinch of salt. Stir well, taste, and add more salt if needed.

4. Prepare your grill. Coat the fish with olive oil and season with pepper. Place on hot grill. Let cook for 3–4 minutes per side or until fish is opaque. Top with pineapple salsa and serve.

PER SERVING: Fat: 4 g **Protein:** 21 g **Carbohydrates:** 8 g **Sugar:** 4 g

MAHI MAHI TACOS WITH AVOCADO AND FRESH CABBAGE

CALORIES: 251
SERVES 4

1 POUND MAHI MAHI
SALT AND PEPPER TO TASTE
1 TEASPOON OLIVE OIL
1 AVOCADO
4 CORN TORTILLAS
2 CUPS OF CABBAGE, SHREDDED
2 LIMES, QUARTERED

1. Season fish with salt and pepper. Heat oil in a large pan over medium heat. Once the oil is hot, sauté fish for about 3–4 minutes on each side. Slice or flake fish into 1 ounce pieces.

2. Slice avocado in half. Remove seed and, using a spoon, remove the flesh from the skin. Slice the avocado halves into ½" thick slices.

3. In a small pan, warm corn tortillas; cook for about 1 minute on each side.

4. Place one-fourth of mahi mahi of each tortilla, top with avocado and cabbage. Serve with lime wedges.

PER SERVING: Fat: 9 g **Protein:** 25 g **Carbohydrates:** 21 g **Sugar:** 2 g

ZESTY CRUMB-COATED COD

CALORIES: 153
SERVES 3

JUICE FROM 1 LEMON
1 SLICE WHOLE-WHEAT BREAD
1 POUND COD FILET
SALT AND PEPPER TO TASTE

1. Preheat the broiler.

2. Squeeze 2 tablespoons of lemon juice into a food processor. Place bread in the food processor and pulse until crumbs form.

3. Place cod in a baking pan and squeeze lemon over to your liking. Sprinkle cod with salt and pepper. Pat cod filet with the bread crumbs, turning filet so you get both sides.

4. Broil for about 8 minutes or until crumbs turn golden.

PER SERVING: Fat: 1 g **Protein:** 28 g **Carbohydrates:** 6 g **Sugar:** 2 g

TUNA CASSEROLE

CALORIES: 278
SERVES 4

1 (10-OUNCE) CAN LOW-SODIUM CREAM OF CHICKEN SOUP
½ CUP FAT-FREE MILK
2 CUPS COOKED WHOLE-WHEAT MACARONI NOODLES
10 OUNCES FROZEN CUT GREEN BEANS
1 (6-OUNCE) CAN TUNA, DRAINED
½ TEASPOON FRESHLY GROUND BLACK PEPPER
LIGHT COOKING SPRAY
5 TABLESPOONS BREAD CRUMBS

1. Preheat oven to 400°F.

2. Mix the soup and milk together in a small bowl.

3. In a medium-size bowl, mix the noodles, green beans, tuna, and pepper, then add the soup/milk mixture and gently fold.

4. Pour mixture into a baking dish coated with light cooking spray and cover with foil.

5. Bake until the casserole starts to bubble, about 25 minutes. Uncover and sprinkle bread crumbs on top. Bake uncovered until crumbs are browned.

PER SERVING: Fat: 7 g **Protein:** 19 g **Carbohydrates:** 37 g **Sugar:** 4 g

HALIBUT WITH BANANA SALSA

CALORIES: 237
SERVES 6

- 1 CUP DICED BANANAS
- ¼ CUP MINCED SWEET ONION
- ¼ CUP MINCED GREEN BELL PEPPER
- 2 TABLESPOONS LEMON JUICE
- 2 TABLESPOONS CHOPPED CILANTRO
- 2 POUNDS HALIBUT FILETS
- 2 TABLESPOONS OLIVE OIL

1. Combine the bananas, sweet onion, and green bell pepper in a large bowl.

2. Add the lemon juice and cilantro and toss to coat.

3. Prepare grill. Coat halibut with olive oil. Place fish on grill for 3–4 minutes per side or until fish is opaque.

PER SERVING: Fat: 7 g **Protein:** 31 g **Carbohydrates:** 8 g **Sugar:** 4 g

Salsas and Salads

Transform a chicken or shrimp salad with pineapple or mango salsa. Spoon tomato salsa over ham salad. Make a fresh-flavored coleslaw with shredded napa cabbage and absolutely any salsa for great taste and lots more fiber. Add even more protein and fiber by sprinkling toasted pepitas over the tops of these salads and the coleslaw.

SHRIMP AND VEGETABLES OVER NAPA CABBAGE

CALORIES: 213
SERVES 2

- 1 CLOVE GARLIC, MINCED
- 1 TEASPOON SESAME SEEDS
- 1 TABLESPOON PEANUT OIL
- 1 CARROT, SHREDDED
- ½ LARGE ZUCCHINI, SHREDDED
- ½ CUP JICAMA, PEELED AND CHOPPED FINE
- ¼ CUP DRY WHITE WINE
- 1 TABLESPOON LEMON JUICE
- 1 OUNCE DRY SHERRY
- ½ POUND RAW SHRIMP, PEELED AND DEVEINED
- ½ HEAD NAPA CABBAGE, SHREDDED
- FRESH ORANGE SECTIONS TO GARNISH (OPTIONAL)

1. In a large frying pan, sauté the garlic and sesame seeds in peanut oil, stirring for 5 minutes. Add the vegetables and mix. Pour in the wine and lemon juice. Simmer to burn off alcohol; cover.

2. When the vegetables are crisp-tender, add the sherry and shrimp. Stir and cook until the shrimp turn pink. Serve over napa cabbage.

PER SERVING: Fat: 11 g **Protein:** 5 g **Carbohydrates:** 15 g **Sugar:** 2 g

GRILLED TUNA STEAK WITH VEGETABLES AND PINE NUTS

CALORIES: 277
SERVES 2

1 CUP NAPA CABBAGE, SHREDDED

½ CUP PEA PODS, CHOPPED COARSELY

½ CUP CARROTS, SHREDDED

3 TABLESPOONS TOMATO SAUCE

¼ CUP PINE NUTS, TOASTED

2 (¼ POUND) TUNA STEAKS

1 TEASPOON SESAME OIL

1 TEASPOON LIME JUICE

SALT AND PEPPER TO TASTE

1. Poach the vegetables in the tomato sauce for 8 minutes or until crisp-tender. Add the pine nuts and set aside.

2. Set grill on medium-high. Spread the tuna with sesame oil, lime juice, salt, and pepper. Grill for 4 minutes per side for medium.

3. Serve with tomato-poached vegetables.

PER SERVING: Fat: 13 g **Protein:** 18 g **Carbohydrates:** 25 g **Sugar:** 3 g

ROAST STUFFED STRIPED BASS

CALORIES: 395
SERVES 2

2 SLICES WHOLE-GRAIN BREAD, TOASTED

1 STALK CELERY, CHOPPED FINELY

¼ CUP PARSLEY, CHOPPED

2 TABLESPOONS UNSALTED BUTTER, MELTED

½ CUP CANNED WATER CHESTNUTS

1 TABLESPOON LEMON JUICE

SALT AND PEPPER TO TASTE

¾ POUND FILET OF STRIPED BASS, SKIN ON

IN THIS RECIPE YOU CAN SUBSTITUTE OLIVE OIL FOR BUTTER.

1. Place everything but the striped bass in the food processor or blender. Pulse until well crumbled.

2. Set oven on 350°F. Place striped bass on a baking sheet. Spread stuffing on fish.

3. Bake the fish for 12–15 minutes, or until the stuffing is well browned.

PER SERVING: Fat: 19 g **Protein:** 36 g **Carbohydrates:** 22 g **Sugar:** 2 g

Stripers

Striped bass are native to a large portion of the East Coast and range as far south as northern Florida. The fish has lean, white meat and a mild flavor and is especially tasty when stuffed with vegetables and bread crumbs or grilled.

PISTACHIO-CRUSTED RED SNAPPER

CALORIES: 283
SERVES 4

- 1 TABLESPOON LEMON JUICE
- 1 TEASPOON GRATED ORANGE ZEST
- 1 TEASPOON GRATED LEMON ZEST
- 2 TABLESPOONS OLIVE OIL
- ⅓ CUP CHOPPED PISTACHIOS
- 1 SLICE LIGHT WHOLE-GRAIN BREAD, CRUMBLED
- NONSTICK COOKING SPRAY
- 1 POUND RED SNAPPER FILETS
- PINCH OF SALT
- ⅛ TEASPOON PEPPER

1. Preheat oven to 375°F. In a small bowl, combine lemon juice, orange zest, lemon zest, and olive oil. In another small bowl, combine chopped pistachios and crumbled bread. Drizzle lemon mixture over bread mixture and toss to coat.

2. Spray a 9"-square glass baking dish with nonstick cooking spray. Arrange fish in dish and sprinkle with salt and pepper. Top evenly with the crumb mixture, patting into place.

3. Bake for 15–25 minutes, or until fish is opaque and flakes when tested with fork and crumb mixture is browned. Serve immediately.

PER SERVING: Fat: 15 g **Protein:** 18 g **Carbohydrates:** 4 g **Sugar:** 1 g

---

SEAFOOD RISOTTO

CALORIES: 397
SERVES 6

- 2 CUPS WATER
- 2½ CUPS LOW-SODIUM CHICKEN BROTH
- 2 TABLESPOONS OLIVE OIL
- 1 ONION, MINCED
- 3 CLOVES GARLIC, MINCED
- 1½ CUPS ARBORIO RICE
- 1 CUP CHOPPED CELERY
- 1 TABLESPOON FRESH DILL WEED
- ¼ CUP DRY WHITE WINE
- ½ POUND SOLE FILETS
- ¼ POUND SMALL RAW SHRIMP
- ½ POUND BAY SCALLOPS
- ¼ CUP GRATED PARMESAN CHEESE
- 1 TABLESPOON BUTTER

1. In a medium saucepan, combine water and broth and heat over low heat. Keep mixture on heat.

2. In a large saucepan, heat olive oil over medium heat. Add onion and garlic; cook and stir until crisp-tender, about 3 minutes. Add rice; cook and stir for 3 minutes.

3. Start adding broth mixture, a cup at a time, stirring frequently, adding more liquid when the previous addition is absorbed. When only 1 cup of broth remains to be added, stir in celery, dill, wine, sole filets, shrimp, and scallops to rice mixture. Add last cup of broth.

4. Cook, stirring constantly, for 5–7 minutes or until fish is cooked and rice is tender and creamy. Add Parmesan and butter, stir, and serve.

PER SERVING: Fat: 11 g **Protein:** 28 g **Carbohydrates:** 35 g **Sugar:** 2 g

COD AND POTATOES

CALORIES: 362
SERVES 4

NONSTICK COOKING SPRAY
3 YUKON GOLD POTATOES
¼ CUP OLIVE OIL
⅛ TEASPOON WHITE PEPPER
1½ TEASPOONS DRIED HERBS DE PROVENCE, DIVIDED
4 (4-OUNCE) COD STEAKS
1 TABLESPOON BUTTER OR MARGARINE
2 TABLESPOONS LEMON JUICE

1. Preheat oven to 350°F. Spray a 9" glass baking dish with nonstick cooking spray. Thinly slice the potatoes. Layer in the baking dish, drizzling each layer with a tablespoon of olive oil, a sprinkle of pepper, and some of the herbs de Provence.

2. Bake for 35–45 minutes or until potatoes are browned on top and tender when pierced with a fork. Arrange cod steaks on top of potatoes. Dot with butter and sprinkle with lemon juice and remaining herbs de Provence.

3. Bake for 15–25 minutes longer or until fish flakes when tested with fork.

PER SERVING: Fat: 17 g **Protein:** 18 g **Carbohydrates:** 36 g **Sugar:** 4 g

SALMON VEGETABLE STIR-FRY

CALORIES: 371
SERVES 4

2 TABLESPOONS RICE VINEGAR
1 TABLESPOON SUGAR
1 TABLESPOON GRATED GINGER ROOT
1 TABLESPOON CORNSTARCH
2 TABLESPOONS HOISIN SAUCE
⅛ TEASPOON WHITE PEPPER
2 TABLESPOONS PEANUT OIL
1 ONION, SLICED
½ POUND SUGAR-SNAP PEAS
3 CARROTS, SLICED
1 RED BELL PEPPER, SLICED
¾ POUND SALMON FILET

1. In small bowl, combine rice vinegar, sugar, ginger root, cornstarch, hoisin sauce, and pepper. Mix well and set aside.

2. In large skillet or wok, heat peanut oil over high heat. Add onion, peas, and carrots. Stir-fry for 3–4 minutes or until vegetables begin to soften. Add red bell pepper.

3. Immediately place salmon filet on top of vegetables. Reduce heat to medium, cover skillet or wok and cook for 4–5 minutes or until salmon flakes when tested with fork.

4. Stir the vinegar mixture and add to skillet or wok. Turn heat to medium-high and stir-fry to break up the salmon for 2–3 minutes until the sauce bubbles and thickens. Serve immediately over hot cooked rice.

PER SERVING: Fat: 11 g **Protein:** 30 g **Carbohydrates:** 11 g **Sugar:** 1.5 g

SEARED SCALLOPS WITH FRUIT

CALORIES: 207
SERVES 3–4

1 POUND SEA SCALLOPS
PINCH OF SALT
⅛ TEASPOON WHITE PEPPER
1 TABLESPOON OLIVE OIL
1 TABLESPOON BUTTER OR
   MARGARINE
2 PEACHES, SLICED
¼ CUP DRY WHITE WINE
1 CUP BLUEBERRIES
1 TABLESPOON LIME JUICE

1. Rinse scallops and pat dry. Sprinkle with salt and pepper and set aside.

2. In large skillet, heat olive oil and butter over medium-high heat. Add the scallops and don't move them for 3 minutes. Carefully check to see if the scallops are deep golden brown. If they are, turn and cook for 1–2 minutes on the second side.

3. Remove scallops to serving plate. Add peaches to skillet and brown quickly on one side, about 2 minutes. Turn peaches and add wine to skillet; bring to a boil. Remove from heat and add blueberries. Pour over scallops, sprinkle with lime juice, and serve immediately.

PER SERVING: Fat: 7 g **Protein:** 26 g **Carbohydrates:** 35 g
Sugar: 8 g

Scallops

Scallops are shellfish that are very low in fat. Sea scallops are the largest, followed by bay scallops and calico scallops. They should smell very fresh and slightly briny, like the sea. If they smell fishy, do not buy them. There may be a small muscle attached to the side of each scallop; pull that off and discard it because it can be tough.

SCALLOPS ON SKEWERS WITH TOMATOES

CALORIES: 202
SERVES 4

- **1 POUND SEA SCALLOPS**
- **12 CHERRY TOMATOES**
- **4 GREEN ONIONS, CUT IN HALF CROSSWISE**
- **½ CUP CHOPPED PARSLEY**
- **1 TABLESPOON FRESH OREGANO LEAVES**
- **3 TABLESPOONS OLIVE OIL**
- **2 TABLESPOONS LEMON JUICE**
- **2 CLOVES GARLIC**
- **⅛ TEASPOON SALT**
- **⅛ TEASPOON PEPPER**

1. Prepare and preheat broiler. Rinse scallops and pat dry. Thread on skewers along with cherry tomatoes and green onions.

2. In a blender or food processor, combine remaining ingredients. Blend or process until smooth. Reserve ¼ cup of this sauce.

3. Brush remaining sauce onto the food on the skewers. Place on broiler pan. Broil 6" from heat for 3–4 minutes per side, turning once during cooking time. Serve with remaining sauce.

PER SERVING: Fat: 11 g **Protein:** 26 g **Carbohydrates:** 5 g **Sugar:** 1 g

Uncooked Sauces

You can store uncooked sauces like chimichurri sauce and pesto in the refrigerator up to 3 days. For longer storage, freeze them. Pour about 2 tablespoons into ice cube trays and freeze until solid. Pop the frozen cubes into a heavy-duty freezer bag, label, and freeze up to 6 months. To defrost, let stand in refrigerator overnight.

SESAME-PEPPER SALMON KABOBS

CALORIES: 319
SERVES 4

1 POUND SALMON STEAK

2 TABLESPOONS OLIVE OIL, DIVIDED

¼ CUP SESAME SEEDS

1 TEASPOON PEPPER

1 RED BELL PEPPER

1 YELLOW BELL PEPPER

1 RED ONION

8 CREMINI MUSHROOMS

⅛ TEASPOON SALT

1. Prepare and preheat grill. Cut salmon steak into 1" pieces, discarding skin and bones. Brush salmon with half of the olive oil.

2. In a small bowl, combine sesame seeds and pepper and mix. Press all sides of salmon cubes into the sesame seed mixture.

3. Slice bell peppers into 1" slices and cut red onion into 8 wedges; trim mushroom stems and leave caps whole. Skewer coated salmon pieces, peppers, onion, and mushrooms on metal skewers. Brush vegetables with remaining olive oil and sprinkle with salt.

4. Grill 6" from medium coals, turning once during cooking time, until the sesame seeds are very brown and toasted and fish is just done, about 6–8 minutes. Serve immediately.

PER SERVING: Fat: 20 g **Protein:** 30 g **Carbohydrates:** 7 g **Sugar:** 2 g

ALMOND SNAPPER WITH SHRIMP SAUCE

CALORIES: 272
SERVES 6

1 EGG WHITE
¼ CUP DRY BREAD CRUMBS
⅓ CUP GROUND ALMONDS
⅛ TEASPOON SALT
⅛ TEASPOON WHITE PEPPER
6 (4-OUNCE) RED SNAPPER FILETS
3 TABLESPOONS OLIVE OIL
1 ONION, CHOPPED
4 CLOVES GARLIC, MINCED
1 RED BELL PEPPER, CHOPPED
¼ POUND SMALL RAW SHRIMP, DESHELLED AND DEVEINED
1 TABLESPOON LEMON JUICE
½ CUP LOW-FAT SOUR CREAM
½ TEASPOON DRIED DILL WEED

1. Place egg white in a shallow bowl; beat until foamy. On a shallow plate, combine bread crumbs, almonds, salt, and pepper and mix well. Dip fish into egg white, then into crumb mixture, pressing to coat. Let stand on a wire rack for 10 minutes.

2. In a small saucepan, heat 1 tablespoon olive oil over medium heat. Add onion, garlic, and bell pepper; cook and stir until tender, about 5 minutes. Add shrimp; cook and stir just until shrimp curl and turn pink, about 1–2 minutes. Remove from heat and add lemon juice; set aside.

3. In a large saucepan, heat remaining 2 tablespoons olive oil over medium heat. Add coated fish filets. Cook for 4 minutes on one side, then carefully turn and cook for 2–5 minutes on second side until coating is browned and fish flakes when tested with a fork.

4. While fish is cooking, return saucepan with shrimp to medium heat. Add sour cream and dill weed. Heat, stirring, until mixture is hot.

5. Remove fish from skillet and place on serving plate. Top each with a spoonful of shrimp sauce and serve immediately.

PER SERVING: Fat: 13 g **Protein:** 31 g **Carbohydrates:** 27 g **Sugar:** 1 g

SCALLOPS ON SKEWERS WITH LEMON

CALORIES: 173
SERVES 4

2 TABLESPOONS LEMON JUICE

1 TEASPOON GRATED LEMON ZEST

2 TEASPOONS SESAME OIL

2 TABLESPOONS CHILI SAUCE

⅛ TEASPOON CAYENNE PEPPER

1 POUND SEA SCALLOPS

4 STRIPS LOW-SODIUM BACON

1. Prepare and preheat grill or broiler. In a medium-size bowl, combine lemon juice, zest, sesame oil, chili sauce, and cayenne pepper and mix well. Add scallops and toss to coat. Let stand for 15 minutes.

2. Make skewers with the scallops and bacon. Thread a skewer through one end of a bacon slice, then add a scallop. Curve the bacon around the scallop and thread onto the skewer so it surrounds the scallop halfway. Repeat with 3–4 more scallops and the bacon slices.

3. Repeat with remaining scallops and bacon slices. Grill or broil 6 inches from heat source for 3–5 minutes per side, until bacon is crisp and scallops are cooked and opaque. Serve immediately.

PER SERVING: Fat: 6 g **Protein:** 32 g **Carbohydrates:** 2 g **Sugar:** 0 g

Bacon

If you read labels and choose carefully, you can have bacon as an occasional treat. Many companies now make low-sodium bacon. In health-food stores you can often find organic bacon that has better nutrition. Also consider Canadian bacon. More like ham, this meat has less sodium, fat, and chemicals like nitrates than regular bacon.

SEA BASS WRAPPED IN SAVOY CABBAGE

CALORIES: 354
SERVES 4

4 LARGE LEAVES SAVOY CABBAGE

4 TABLESPOONS UNSALTED BUTTER, SOFTENED

1 TABLESPOON GRATED FRESH GINGER ROOT

1 TEASPOON GRATED ORANGE ZEST

1 MINCED SHALLOT

4 (1"-THICK) SEA BASS FILETS

SALT AND PEPPER TO TASTE

½ CUP COCONUT MILK

¼ CUP FRESH LEMON JUICE

3" PIECE LEMONGRASS, THINLY CHOPPED

½ CUP HEAVY CREAM

1 TABLESPOON GRATED LEMON ZEST

1. Preheat oven to 375°F.

2. Blanch the savoy cabbage leaves in boiling water to soften and make them flexible, then plunge them into ice water to cool. Lay them out on paper towels to drain.

3. Combine the soft butter, grated ginger root, orange zest, and shallot to make a compound butter.

4. Divide the compound butter among the blanched cabbage leaves. Season the sea bass filets with salt and pepper and place one on each cabbage leaf. Wrap the cabbage leaves around the fish filets to make packages.

5. Place packages seam-side down in a baking dish. Pour the coconut milk and lemon juice over the packages. Top with lemongrass.

6. Cover and bake for 20 minutes. Remove the packages from the baking dish, place on a serving platter, and cover with foil. Strain the baking liquid into a saucepan and bring to a boil. Add the heavy cream and simmer to reduce into a slightly thickened sauce. Pour sauce over the packages on the platter. Sprinkle with lemon zest and serve hot.

PER SERVING: Fat: 25 g **Protein:** 25 g **Carbohydrates:** 6 g **Sugar:** 1 g

Wrapping Food Before Cooking

Sea bass wrapped in savoy cabbage produces the same moist results as wrapping it in pastry or a paper bag! However, the cabbage retains its nutritional and fiber value. The paper bag wrapping for food must be discarded and the puff pastry will get soggy and retain its fattening properties. Try wrapping chicken or duck breasts in cabbage and enjoy a healthy, super-succulent dinner.

SEAFOOD IN THAI-CURRY BEAN SAUCE

CALORIES: 234
SERVES 4

- 2 TEASPOONS SESAME OR CANOLA OIL
- 1 TEASPOON CURRY POWDER
- ¼ TEASPOON FRESHLY GROUND BLACK PEPPER
- ⅛ TEASPOON GROUND CUMIN
- ⅛ TEASPOON GROUND CORIANDER
- PINCH OF DRIED RED PEPPER FLAKES
- PINCH OF GROUND FENNEL SEEDS
- PINCH OF GROUND CLOVES
- PINCH OF GROUND MACE
- 1 TABLESPOON PLUS ¼ CUP WATER
- 1 SMALL SWEET ONION, FINELY CHOPPED
- 2 CLOVES GARLIC, MINCED
- 1 TABLESPOON NO-SALT-ADDED, UNSWEETENED APPLESAUCE
- ¼ CUP DRY WHITE WINE
- ¼ TEASPOON LOW-SODIUM CHICKEN BOUILLON
- ⅛ TEASPOON DRIED LIME JUICE GRANULES, CRUSHED
- ⅛ TEASPOON DRIED GROUND LEMONGRASS
- ¼ PACKED CUP FRESH PARSLEY LEAVES
- ¼ PACKED CUP FRESH BASIL LEAVES
- 1 TABLESPOON FREEZE-DRIED SHALLOTS
- 1⅓ CUPS CANNED NO-SALT-ADDED CANNELLINI BEANS, DRAINED AND RINSED
- ½ POUND SHELLED AND DEVEINED SHRIMP
- ½ POUND SCALLOPS

1. Bring the oil to temperature in a large, deep, nonstick sauté pan over medium heat. Add the curry powder, pepper, cumin, coriander, red pepper flakes, fennel seeds, cloves, and mace; sauté for 1 minute. Remove 1 teaspoon of the seasoned oil from the pan and set aside. Add the 1 tablespoon water and bring it to temperature, stirring to mix it with the seasoned oil remaining in the pan. Add the onion and sauté over moderately low heat until the onion is soft. Add the garlic and sauté for 1 minute, being careful not to burn the garlic.

2. Add the applesauce and wine and simmer the mixture until the wine is reduced by half. Add the chicken base and stir to dissolve it and mix it into the onion mixture. Add the ¼ cup water and bring to a boil. Add the lime juice granules, lemon-grass, parsley, basil, shallots, and ⅓ cup of the beans. Reduce heat and simmer, stirring, for 1 minute.

3. Transfer the wine-bean mixture to a blender or food processor container; pulse to purée. Pour the wine-bean purée back into the saucepan and add the remaining beans. Simmer to bring the entire mixture to temperature, then keep warm.

4. Wash the shrimp and scallops under cold water. Blot dry between paper towels. Bring a nonstick skillet or sauté pan to temperature over moderately high heat. Add the seasoned oil. When the oil is hot (but not smoking), add the shrimp and sauté for 2 minutes on each side or until cooked through. Using a slotted spoon, transfer the shrimp to a plate and keep warm.

5. Add the scallops to the skillet and sauté for 1 minute on each side or until cooked through. Divide the bean sauce among 4 shallow bowls and arrange the shellfish on top.

PER SERVING: Fat: 4 g **Protein:** 26 g **Carbohydrates:** 19 g **Sugar:** 3 g

BAKED OYSTERS WITH SHRIMP STUFFING

CALORIES: 222
SERVES 2

1 TEASPOON BUTTER

2 SHALLOTS, CHOPPED

2 SLICES BACON, FRIED AND CRUMBLED

1 TABLESPOON LEMON JUICE

2 SLICES STALE WHITE BREAD, CRUMBLED

8 RAW OYSTERS, ON THE HALF SHELL, LIQUOR RESERVED

4 MEDIUM SHRIMP, RAW, PEELED, DEVEINED, AND CHOPPED

PLENTY OF FRESHLY GROUND PEPPER

SALT, IF NECESSARY

IN THIS RECIPE YOU CAN SUBSTITUTE VEGETARIAN BACON FOR REGULAR BACON AND REPLACE BUTTER WITH OLIVE OIL.

1. Set oven at 425°F. Melt the butter; add shallots and sauté for 5 minutes on medium heat. Add the crumbled bacon and lemon juice.

2. Stir in the bread crumbs and mix in the oyster liquor. Taste for saltiness, add shrimp, and grind on pepper.

3. Divide the bread and shrimp mixture among the oysters. Bake for 12–15 minutes, or until the oysters are bubbling and the topping is well browned.

PER SERVING: Fat: 10 g **Protein:** 16 g **Carbohydrates:** 20 g **Sugar:** 2 g

Regional Oysters

Depending on where they come from, oysters can have different flavors. Some oysters are extremely sweet and light in flavor. Some Pacific Coast oysters taste metallic, and oysters from certain estuaries have a distinctly swampy flavor. Oysters from Long Island Sound are exported to Japan and France and are very sweet tasting.

SALMON AND BROCCOLI STIR-FRY

CALORIES: 273
SERVES 2

½ **POUND BROCCOLI FLORETS**

½ **POUND SALMON FILET, SKIN REMOVED**

1 **TABLESPOON CANOLA OIL**

1 **TEASPOON ASIAN SESAME OIL**

1 **TEASPOON GINGER ROOT, MINCED**

2 **SLICES PICKLED GINGER, CHOPPED**

1 **CLOVE GARLIC, MINCED**

1 **TEASPOON HOISIN SAUCE**

1 **CUP BROWN RICE, COOKED**

5 **SCALLIONS, CHOPPED, FOR GARNISH**

1. Blanch the broccoli in boiling water for 5 minutes; drain.

2. Toss the broccoli and salmon over medium-high heat with the canola oil and sesame oil. Cook, stirring for 3–4 minutes.

3. Add the ginger root, pickled ginger, garlic, and hoisin sauce and serve over rice, garnished with scallions.

PER SERVING: Fat: 6 g **Protein:** 25 g **Carbohydrates:** 7 g **Sugar:** 1.5 g

Food Safety

When preparing a dish that lists fish, seafood, or poultry as one of the ingredients, be sure to keep the fish, seafood, or chicken ice cold during preparation to ensure food safety. If you will be doing a lot of handling or if the food will be on the counter for a long time, keep a bowl with ice nearby to place the ingredients in while you are tending to other steps of the recipe.

BAKED FILET OF SOLE WITH SHRIMP SAUCE AND ARTICHOKES

CALORIES: 368
SERVES 2

5 MEDIUM SHRIMP, COOKED

1 SHALLOT, CHOPPED

¼ CUP LOW-FAT MAYONNAISE

¼ TEASPOON DILL, DRIED

2 TABLESPOONS ORANGE JUICE

1 (9-OUNCE) PACKAGE FROZEN ARTICHOKE HEARTS

2 (6-OUNCE) SOLE FILETS

NONSTICK COOKING SPRAY

SALT AND PEPPER TO TASTE

4 TABLESPOONS FINE DRY BREAD CRUMBS

1. Preheat oven to 375°F. Pulse the shrimp, shallot, mayonnaise, dill, and orange juice in the blender. Set the sauce aside.

2. Cook the frozen artichokes to package directions. Place sole on a baking sheet prepared with nonstick spray. Sprinkle the filets with salt and pepper. Arrange the artichokes around the sole. Spoon sauce over all. Sprinkle with bread crumbs.

3. Bake for 15 minutes, or until the sole is hot and bubbling and the artichokes crisply browned on top.

PER SERVING: Fat: 13 g **Protein:** 43 g **Carbohydrates:** 20 g
Sugar: 2 g

Artichokes

Artichokes are the flowers of a large plant and are available November through May. There are two varieties—those with thorns ("unarmed"), which are known as "Roman," and the prickly type, which have little thorns at the triangular tip of each leaf. The soft heart, or center, of the artichoke can be eaten raw or cooked sprinkled with olive oil, salt, and pepper.

CORN-CRUSTED SALMON WITH PARSLEY AND RADISH TOPPING

CALORIES: 371
SERVES 2

4 RADISHES, THINLY SLICED

½ CUP PARSLEY, ITALIAN FLAT-LEAF, MINCED

1 TABLESPOON OLIVE OIL

2 TABLESPOONS RED-WINE VINEGAR

½ TEASPOON CELERY SALT

2 (6-OUNCE) SALMON FILETS

1 TABLESPOON LEMON JUICE

¼ CUP CORNMEAL

¼ CUP 2% MILK

½ TEASPOON DILL, DRIED

3 TABLESPOONS OLIVE OIL

RED PEPPER FLAKES TO TASTE

NONSTICK SPRAY

IN THIS RECIPE YOU CAN SUBSTITUTE NONFAT MILK FOR 2% MILK IN THE TOPPING FOR THE SALMON

1. Mix the radishes, parsley, olive oil, vinegar, and celery salt. Set aside.

2. Make sure the salmon has no pin bones; sprinkle with lemon juice. Mix together the cornmeal, milk, dill, olive oil, and red pepper flakes. Spread on the salmon and rest it in the refrigerator for 30 minutes.

3. Set oven at 350°F. Prepare a baking dish or metal sheet with nonstick spray. Place salmon on the baking dish or sheet.

4. Bake the salmon for 20 minutes, or until the topping is brown and the salmon flakes. Serve with radish-parsley topping.

PER SERVING: Fat: 21 g **Protein:** 36 g **Carbohydrates:** 10 g **Sugar:** 2 g

PISTACHIO-CRUSTED HALIBUT

CALORIES: 484
SERVES 2

2 (6-OUNCE) SKINLESS HALIBUT
FILETS
½ CUP LOW-FAT MILK
¼ CUP SHELLED PISTACHIOS
1½ TABLESPOONS CORNMEAL
1 TEASPOON GARLIC POWDER
⅛ TEASPOON CAYENNE PEPPER
¼ TEASPOON SALT
FRESH GROUND WHITE PEPPER
2 TABLESPOONS OLIVE OIL

1. Place filets in a glass baking dish and pour milk over top, cover, and chill for 30 minutes.

2. Toast pistachios lightly and chop finely with a chef's knife. Mix together pistachios, cornmeal, garlic powder, and cayenne pepper in a bowl.

3. Remove fish from the milk, season with salt and white pepper, then dredge in pistachio mixture. Place filets on a clean plate.

4. Heat oil in a large pan over medium-high heat. Once oil is hot, sauté filets 3–4 minutes per side, until lightly browned on the outside and cooked through in the center.

PER SERVING: Fat: 26 g **Protein:** 49 g **Carbohydrates:** 13 g **Sugar:** 3 g

Fun Facts

Did you know that during harvesting season pistachio trees are shaken to remove the nuts from the branches? Pistachios must be shelled before eaten one by one and therefore the body is fooled into thinking more nuts have been consumed. This concept of tricking the mind into telling the body to eat less in sometimes called the "Pistachio Principle."

LEMON-GARLIC SHRIMP AND VEGETABLES

CALORIES: 190
SERVES 2

2 TABLESPOONS LOW-SODIUM SOY SAUCE

1 TEASPOON LEMON ZEST

1½ TABLESPOONS LEMON JUICE

½ TEASPOON AGAVE NECTAR

½ CUP WATER

BLACK PEPPER TO TASTE

NONSTICK COOKING SPRAY

1 CELERY STALK

1 CUP RED CABBAGE, SHREDDED

½ RED BELL PEPPER, THINLY SLICED

3 CLOVES GARLIC, CHOPPED

½ CUP BEAN SPROUTS

1 TEASPOON SESAME OIL

½ POUND RAW SHRIMP, PEELED AND DEVEINED

1. Mix soy sauce, lemon zest, lemon juice, agave nectar, water, and pepper in a small bowl, set aside.

2. Spray a large pan with nonstick cooking spray. Place pan over medium heat.

3. Add celery and cabbage to the pan, sauté for 1 minute. Add bell pepper, garlic, and bean sprouts and sauté until all vegetables are crisp-tender. Transfer vegetables to a plate and cover.

4. Add oil to the pan, and once oil is hot, place shrimp in the hot pan and cook until opaque. Return vegetables to the pan with the cooked shrimp.

5. Pour soy sauce mixture over the shrimp and vegetables and cook for 3–4 minutes, until sauce has reduced.

PER SERVING: Fat: 4 g **Protein:** 26 g **Carbohydrates:** 11 g **Sugar:** 2 g

PLANKED SALMON WITH DILL SAUCE

CALORIES: 388
SERVES 10

1 CEDAR PLANK (AVAILABLE AT SPECIALTY COOKING STORES)

GRAPESEED OIL

3½ POUNDS SALMON FILET, CHECKED FOR PIN BONES

JUICE OF 1 LEMON

8 JUNIPER BERRIES

SALT AND PEPPER TO TASTE

1 LEMON, THINLY SLICED

1 CUP MAYONNAISE

¼ CUP FRESH DILL WEED, CHOPPED

1 TEASPOON HORSERADISH

SALT AND PEPPER TO TASTE

IN THIS RECIPE, YOU CAN SUBSTITUTE LOW-FAT MAYONNAISE FOR REGULAR MAYONNAISE.

1. Soak the plank in water. When thoroughly soaked, lightly oil the side on which the salmon will lie. Set the salmon on the plank. Sprinkle with lemon juice and press the juniper berries into the flesh at intervals. Add salt, pepper, and lemon slices.

2. Place the plank over indirect heat on a hot grill and close lid. Roast for about 15–20 minutes or until the salmon begins to flake.

3. Mix the rest of the ingredients together in a small bowl and serve with the fish.

PER SERVING: Fat: 28 g **Protein:** 32 g **Carbohydrates:** 2 g
Sugar: 1 g

Fish Bones

The larger the fish, the more likely you will find bones in a filet. Before cooking, hold a pair of pliers and run the finger of your other hand down the filet, against the grain. Whenever you feel a bone, press down close to it. It will pop up, and you can then pull it out with the pliers.

SMOKED SALMON, EGGS, AND CHEESE PUFFED CASSEROLE

CALORIES: 478
SERVES 2

4 EGGS, SEPARATED

2 SLICES WHOLE-GRAIN BREAD

4 OUNCES CREAM CHEESE, AT ROOM TEMPERATURE

½ CUP WHITE ONION, CHOPPED

PEPPER TO TASTE

¼ CUP 2% MILK

NONSTICK SPRAY

⅛ POUND SMOKED SALMON

IN THIS RECIPE YOU CAN SUBSTITUTE NONFAT MILK FOR 2% MILK AND REPLACE SOUR CREAM WITH LOW-FAT SOUR CREAM.

1. Preheat the oven to 400°F. Beat the egg whites until stiff and set aside. Cut bread into quarters.

2. Place the egg yolks, cream cheese, onion, pepper, bread, and milk in the food processor or blender and purée until smooth and creamy.

3. Prepare a 1-quart soufflé dish with nonstick spray; place bread in the bottom of the dish. In a bowl, fold the beaten egg whites into the cheese mixture and gently mix in the salmon. Pour into the dish.

4. Bake for 30 minutes or until puffed and golden.

PER SERVING: Fat: 33 g **Protein:** 27 g **Carbohydrates:** 20 g **Sugar:** 3 g

Omega-3 Fatty Acids

Salmon is an excellent source of omega-3 fatty acids, which can improve heart function and lower blood pressure. You can get omega-3 fatty acids from most cold-water fish, such as albacore tuna, salmon, and trout, which tend to have more of these good fats than other fish.

ASIAN SESAME-CRUSTED SCALLOPS

1 LARGE RIPE TOMATO, SLICED

2 OUNCES SOY SAUCE

1 OUNCE SESAME OIL

JUICE OF ½ LIME

1" FRESH GINGER ROOT, PEELED AND MINCED

½ POUND DIVER SCALLOPS, EACH WEIGHING 1+ OUNCE (3–4 PER PERSON)

1 EGG, BEATEN

½ CUP SESAME SEEDS

2 TABLESPOONS PEANUT OIL

SALT AND PEPPER TO TASTE

1. Make beds on 2 serving plates with the cabbage and the tomatoes. In a small bowl, mix together the soy sauce, sesame oil, lime juice, and minced ginger to create sauce.

2. Rinse the scallops and pat them dry on paper towels. Dip scallops in beaten egg. Then cover them with sesame seeds that you have spread out on waxed paper.

3. Heat the peanut oil in a nonstick frying pan. Sear the scallops over medium heat until browned on both sides and hot through. Do not overcook, or they will get tough. Arrange the scallops over the greens and tomatoes; add salt and pepper. Drizzle with the sauce.

PER SERVING: Fat: 14 g **Protein:** 27 g **Carbohydrates:** 12 g **Sugar:** 4 g

CLASSIC PARISIAN MUSSELS

CALORIES: 436
SERVES 4

- 2 TABLESPOONS BUTTER
- ½ WHITE ONION, MINCED
- 3 CLOVES GARLIC, MINCED
- 4 POUNDS MUSSELS, CLEANED
- 3 TABLESPOONS FLAT-LEAF PARSLEY, CHOPPED
- 1 BAY LEAF
- 5 WHOLE BLACK PEPPERCORNS
- 2 CUPS DRY WHITE WINE

1. Place a large stockpot over medium heat. Melt butter, sauté onion and garlic until translucent.

2. Turn heat to high and add all additional ingredients to the pot. Bring contents to a boil, cover pot with lid, and cook until the mussels open, about 5 minutes.

3. Remove the pot from the heat. Transfer mussels to serving dish using a slotted spoon.

4. Using a ladle, spoon the broth from the pot over the mussels before serving. Be careful to leave any sand or sediment from the mussels behind in the bottom of the pot.

PER SERVING: Fat: 13 g **Protein:** 33 g **Carbohydrates:** 18 g **Sugar:** 1 g

How to Clean Mussels

Soak the mussels in water for 20 minutes, discard dirty water. To remove the beard, grab the beard and sharply pull it toward the hinge side of the mussel. Before cooking, scrub with a brush under cold water. Throw away any mussels that are cracked or open.

SALMON LOAF

SERVES 8

2 TABLESPOONS OLIVE OIL
½ CUP CHOPPED SHALLOTS
½ CUP LIGHT RITZ CRACKERS, CRUSHED
½ CUP FAT-FREE MILK
1 EGG, BEATEN
4 TEASPOONS LEMON JUICE
1 (14-OUNCE) CAN SALMON
LIGHT COOKING SPRAY

1. Preheat oven to 350°F

2. Heat the olive oil in a skillet over medium heat. Sauté the shallots until tender.

3. In a large bowl, mix the shallots, cracker crumbs, milk, egg, and lemon juice. Beat well. Add salmon to the bowl and mix well.

4. Lightly spray a baking pan. Place salmon mixture in the baking pan and bake for about 1 hour or until brown.

PER SERVING: Fat: 11 g **Protein:** 12 g **Carbohydrates:** 11 g **Sugar:** 2 g

Canned Salmon

The skin and bones you'll find in a can of salmon are edible. You can eat them (and get lots of calcium) or discard them; it's your choice! Canned salmon comes in two varieties: pink, which is less expensive, and red sockeye, which is more expensive but very flavorful. You can also find salmon in a pouch, which has less liquid.

HERB AND LEMON BAKED HALIBUT

CALORIES: 168
SERVES 4

2 LEMONS, SLICED
1 POUND FRESH HALIBUT
1 TABLESPOON OLIVE OIL
1 TEASPOON SALT
PEPPER TO TASTE
½ CUP CHOPPED PARSLEY
2 TABLESPOONS CHOPPED BASIL
2 TABLESPOONS THYME

1. Preheat oven to 375°F.

2. Place the lemon slices in a baking pan.

3. Rub the fish on both sides with olive oil, salt, pepper, parsley, basil, and thyme.

4. Place the halibut over the lemons and bake for about 20 minutes or until the fish flakes and cooks through.

PER SERVING: Fat: 6 g **Protein:** 24 g **Carbohydrates:** 4 g **Sugar:** 0 g

Cooking with Herbs

You can add any herbs or seasonings you want to a recipe to give it your own personal signature. Halibut live in northern waters; most dishes that feature halibut also showcase herbs common to northern areas, and this recipe is no exception. Play around with different flavors from more temperate climates, and try adding some spice.

CUBAN-STYLE BRAISED FISH

CALORIES: 243
SERVES 4

2 TEASPOONS OLIVE OIL

1 ONION, CHOPPED

2 CLOVES GARLIC, DICED

4 TOMATOES, DICED

3 JALAPEÑOS, DICED

¾ CUP LOW-SODIUM CHICKEN BROTH

½ CUP OLIVES, THINLY SLICED

1 POUND HALIBUT

1. Heat the olive oil in a large deep skillet over medium heat.

2. Add the onion and garlic and sauté for 5 minutes.

3. Add the tomatoes, jalepeños, chicken broth, and olives. Let simmer.

4. Add halibut and cook until fish flakes, about 10 minutes.

PER SERVING: Fat: 10 g **Protein:** 27 g **Carbohydrates:** 13 g **Sugar:** 1 g

Cuban Cuisine

Cuban cuisine has been influenced over centuries by Spanish, French, African, Arabic, Chinese, and Portuguese cultures. Most Cuban food is sautéed or slow-cooked over a low flame. Sofrito is a traditional seasoning; it consists of onion, green pepper, garlic, oregano, and ground pepper quick-fried in olive oil. Tomato-based sauces are also traditional in Cuban cooking.

LIME-SEARED SCALLOPS

CALORIES: 238
SERVES 4

4 TEASPOONS OLIVE OIL, DIVIDED
1½ POUNDS SCALLOPS
2 TEASPOONS MINCED GARLIC
2 SMALL SHALLOTS, CHOPPED
JUICE FROM 2 LIMES

1. In a deep skillet, heat 2 teaspoons olive oil for 4 minutes.

2. Drain juices from scallops and pat dry with a paper towel.

3. Add the scallops and sear them on each side for about 3 minutes, until scallops have a golden brown texture.

4. Remove scallops from skillet and set aside in a bowl.

5. Mix 2 teaspoons olive oil, garlic, shallots, and lime juice in a small bowl.

6. Pour lime marinade over scallops, mixing lightly with a wooden spoon.

7. Place scallops in the fridge for about 1 hour to marinate. Serve cold or heat up in microwave.

PER SERVING: Fat: 6 g **Protein:** 31 g **Carbohydrates:** 19 g **Sugar:** 1 g

Shopping for the Perfect Scallop

When purchasing scallops, note that "dry-packed" scallops are additive-free, while "wet-packed" scallops contain sodium tri-polyphosphate (STP), a salt-based preservative that causes the scallops to absorb water. This means they are bloated and the seller gets a better price per pound.

ZESTY FISH FRITTERS

CALORIES: 151
SERVES 4

- **2 TABLESPOONS LEMON JUICE, DIVIDED**
- **1 TEASPOON GARLIC POWDER**
- **½ TEASPOON DRIED GROUND GINGER**
- **½ TEASPOON AJOWAN SEEDS, POUNDED OR GROUND WITH A MORTAR AND PESTLE**
- **½ TEASPOON GROUND TURMERIC**
- **½ TEASPOON SALT-FREE RED CHILI POWDER**
- **½ TEASPOON GROUND CORIANDER**
- **¼ TEASPOON GARAM MASALA SPICE BLEND**
- **1 LARGE EGG**
- **1 TEASPOON CANOLA OIL**
- **¼ CUP UNBLEACHED ALL-PURPOSE FLOUR**
- **NONSTICK COOKING SPRAY**

1. Preheat oven to 400°.

2. Rinse the fish in cold water and pat dry. Cut into 1" pieces. Rub the fish with 1 tablespoon of the lemon juice and set aside.

3. In a small bowl, mix the remaining lemon juice with the garlic, ginger, ajowan, turmeric, chili powder, coriander, and garam masala to form a paste. Smear the fish pieces with spice paste.

4. In a small bowl, beat the egg with the canola oil. Put the flour in another small bowl. Treat a nonstick baking sheet with the nonstick spray. Dip each piece of seasoned fish in the egg mixture, then quickly dip it in the flour so there is just a light dusting of flour on each piece.

5. Arrange the floured fish pieces on the baking tray, leaving some space between them. Spray the tops of the pieces with a light layer of the spray oil. Bake for 10–15 minutes, until lightly browned.

PER SERVING: Fat: 3 g **Protein**: 22 g **Carbohydrates:** 6 g **Sugar:** 1 g

Seasonings Primer

Ajowan seed is also called sometimes called ajwain, carom, and lovage. It's a popular spice in Indian cooking, with a flavor similar to thyme. It's often used in bread and bean dishes too.

BAKED RED SNAPPER ALMANDINE

CALORIES: 177
SERVES 4

- **1 POUND RED SNAPPER FILETS**
- **4 TEASPOONS UNBLEACHED ALL-PURPOSE FLOUR**
- **¼ TEASPOON FRESHLY GROUND WHITE OR BLACK PEPPER**
- **¼ TEASPOON SALT-FREE CHILI POWDER**
- **⅛ TEASPOON DRIED PARSLEY**
- **⅛ TEASPOON DRIED LEMON GRANULES, CRUSHED**
- **⅛ TEASPOON GARLIC POWDER**
- **⅛ TEASPOON ONION POWDER**
- **PINCH OF GROUND CORIANDER**
- **2 TEASPOONS OLIVE OIL**
- **2 TABLESPOONS GROUND RAW ALMONDS**
- **2 TEASPOONS UNSALTED BUTTER**
- **1 TABLESPOON LEMON JUICE**

1. Preheat oven to 375°F.

2. Rinse the red snapper filets and pat dry between layers of paper towels. Add the flour, white (or black) pepper, chili powder, parsley, lemon granules, garlic powder, onion powder, and coriander to a small bowl; mix to combine. Sprinkle the filets with the seasoned flour, front and back.

3. In an ovenproof nonstick skillet over medium heat, sauté the filets in the olive oil until they are nicely browned on both sides. Combine the ground almonds and butter in a microwave-safe dish and microwave on high for 30 seconds or until the butter is melted; stir to combine. Pour the almond-butter mixture and lemon juice over the filets. Bake for 3–5 minutes or until the almonds are nicely browned.

PER SERVING: Fat: 7 g **Protein:** 24 g **Carbohydrates:** 3 g **Sugar:** 1 g

Fish Facts

Baking times given for fish dishes assume the filet is about 1" thick at the thickest part. Fold "tails" or thinner sections under the fish to create an even thickness throughout to help ensure even baking times. That way you'll avoid ending up with some of the fish dry and overdone.

SHRIMP WITH CHIVE BUTTER SAUCE

CALORIES: 158
SERVES 4

½ **CUP WATER**

¼ **TEASPOON LOW-SODIUM CHICKEN BASE**

1 **TEASPOON CORNSTARCH**

1–2 **TABLESPOONS COLD WATER**

1 **TABLESPOON LEMON JUICE**

¼ **CUP CHOPPED FRESH CHIVES**

¼ **TEASPOON FRESHLY GROUND WHITE PEPPER**

4 **TEASPOONS COLD UNSALTED BUTTER**

1 **POUND COOKED SHRIMP**

1 **DROP LEMON OIL OR ⅛ TEASPOON DRIED LEMON GRANULES (OPTIONAL)**

1. Bring the water to a boil in a saucepan. Add the chicken base and stir to mix. Combine the cornstarch and cold water to make a slurry, whisking to remove any lumps. Whisk the slurry into the broth. Bring the mixture to a boil again, then reduce the heat. Simmer, whisking constantly until the mixture thickens.

2. Remove from heat. Add the lemon juice and whisk to combine. Stir in the chives and pepper. (If you prefer a more intense lemon flavor, add the optional lemon oil or lemon granules at this time.) Add the cold butter, 1 teaspoon at a time, whisking to combine with the sauce. Serve immediately with the cooked shrimp.

PER SERVING: Fat: 5 g **Protein:** 23 g **Carbohydrates:** 2 g **Sugar:** 0 g

Lemon-Seasoned Bread Crumbs

Mildly flavored fish, such as catfish, cod, halibut, orange roughy, rockfish, and snapper, benefit from the distinctive flavor of lemon. Lemon also reduces the need for salt. Adding slices of lemon to the top of the fish infuses the filets with the citrus flavor. Grated lemon or lime zest is a great way to enhance that flavor or give a flavor boost to a crunchy bread crumb topping for fish.

CHAPTER 11

Pasta and Vegetarian Entrées

PESTO FOR ANGEL HAIR PASTA

CALORIES: 466
SERVES 4

½ CUP PINE NUTS (PIGNOLES)
(CAN SUBSTITUTE WALNUTS)

4 CLOVES GARLIC

½ CUP OLIVE OIL

2 CUPS BASIL LEAVES, STEMMED
AND PACKED INTO MEASURING
CUP

SALT AND PEPPER TO TASTE

½ CUP PARMESAN CHEESE,
GRATED

1 POUND COOKED ANGEL HAIR
PASTA OR POLENTA

1. Spread the pine nuts on a baking sheet and lightly toast under the broiler.

2. Place the garlic and olive oil in blender and blend until chopped. Add basil leaves, salt, pepper, and Parmesan cheese a bit at a time until you have the consistency of coarse cornmeal. Serve over hot angel hair pasta or polenta.

PER SERVING (INCLUDING PASTA): Fat: 50 g **Protein:** 8 g
Carbohydrates: 5 g **Sugar:** 1 g

ASIAN NOODLES WITH TOFU AND EDAMAME

CALORIES: 340
SERVES 2

2 CUPS SOBA NOODLES, COOKED

1 CARROT, SLICED

½ CUP EDAMAME, SHELLED

½ CUP SNOW PEAS

½ PACKAGE FIRM TOFU, CUBED

½ CUP BEAN SPROUTS

1 GREEN ONION, CHOPPED

2 TABLESPOONS LOW-SODIUM
SOY SAUCE

1 TEASPOON SESAME SEEDS

BLACK PEPPER TO TASTE

1. Bring 1½ quarts of water to boil and cook soba noodles until done.

2. Drain noodles, rinse with cold water, and set aside.

3. In a second pot, steam carrots, edamame, snow peas, and tofu for 3 minutes. Drain excess water.

4. Mix together noodles with vegetables and tofu. Add bean sprouts, green onion, and soy sauce. Sprinkle with sesame seeds and pepper as desired.

PER SERVING: Fat: 21 g **Protein:** 18 g **Carbohydrates:** 23 g
Sugar: 3 g

EGGPLANT SOUFFLÉ

CALORIES: 126
SERVES 4

- **1 LARGE OR 2 MEDIUM EGGPLANTS**
- **1 TABLESPOON PEANUT OIL**
- **2 CLOVES GARLIC, MINCED**
- **1 SMALL WHITE ONION, MINCED**
- **4 EGGS, SEPARATED**
- **SALT AND PEPPER TO TASTE**
- **1 TEASPOON CURRY POWDER, OR TO TASTE**
- **NONSTICK SPRAY**

1. Wrap the eggplant in aluminum foil packages with 1 teaspoon water added to each. Roast the eggplant at 400°F for 1 hour, or until very soft when pricked with a fork. Cool, cut in half, scoop out flesh, and discard skin.

2. Heat peanut oil and sauté garlic and onion over medium heat until softened, about 8–10 minutes. Mix with eggplant and purée in the food processor or blender until very smooth. Mix in egg yolks and pulse, adding salt, pepper, and curry powder. Place in a 1-quart soufflé dish, prepared with nonstick spray.

3. Preheat oven to 400°F. Beat the egg whites until stiff. Fold into the eggplant mixture. Bake until puffed and golden, about 45 minutes.

PER SERVING: Fat: 9 g **Protein:** 9 g **Carbohydrates:** 13 g **Sugar:** 1 g

---

OKRA STUFFED WITH GREEN PEPPERCORNS

CALORIES: 30
SERVES 2

- **6 OKRA, STEMMED**
- **½ CUP VEGETABLE BROTH**
- **3 TEASPOONS GREEN PEPPERCORNS, PACKED IN BRINE**
- **1 TEASPOON BUTTER**
- **1 TEASPOON CUMIN**
- **SALT AND MORE PEPPER, TO TASTE**

IN THIS RECIPE YOU CAN REPLACE BUTTER WITH OLIVE OIL OR HEART-HEALTHY MARGARINE.

1. Poach the okra in the vegetable broth until slightly softened, about 4 minutes. Remove from the broth and place on a work surface, reserving broth in the saucepan.

2. Rinse the peppercorns and poke them into and down the center of the okra. Return to broth; add butter and cumin. Add salt and pepper to taste. Serve as is or with rice.

PER SERVING: Fat: 2 g **Protein:** 1 g **Carbohydrates:** 4 g **Sugar:** 1 g

PASTA CARBONARA

CALORIES: 428
SERVES 6

- **1 POUND SPAGHETTI**
- **½ CUP EGG BEATERS**
- **¼ CUP GRATED PARMIGIANO-REGGIANO CHEESE**
- **¼ CUP GRATED PECORINO-ROMANO CHEESE**
- **LIGHT SALT AND CRACKED PEPPER TO TASTE**
- **½ CUP DICED PANCETTA**

1. Cook spaghetti according to package directions.

2. In a mixing bowl, whisk the Egg Beaters, Parmigiano, Pecorino, salt, and pepper until it is thick and creamy.

3. Mix the egg mixture and pasta together carefully.

4. Add the pancetta.

PER SERVING: Fat: 11 g **Protein:** 21 g **Carbohydrates:** 57 g **Sugar:** 1 g

Egg Beaters with Pasta

It is important to make sure the pasta is very hot when added to the egg mixture because it blends better with the pasta to make a creamy coating. If the egg mixture is not hot enough, the sauce will appear chunky.

VEGETABLE PASTA

CALORIES: 313
SERVES 6

- **1 POUND WHOLE-WHEAT SPAGHETTI**
- **10 OUNCES MIXED FROZEN VEGETABLES, THAWED**
- **1 TEASPOON FRESHLY GRATED ROSEMARY**
- **2 TEASPOONS MINCED ONION**
- **2 TEASPOONS MINCED GARLIC**
- **SALT AND PEPPER TO TASTE**
- **¼ CUP PARMESAN CHEESE**
- **SALT AND PEPPER TO TASTE**

1. Cook spaghetti according to directions.

2. In a skillet over medium heat, toss the mixed vegetables to warm them.

3. Mix rosemary, onion, garlic, salt, and pepper with the vegetables.

4. Pour vegetables over spaghetti and serve, sprinkling with Parmesan cheese.

PER SERVING: Fat: 2 g **Protein:** 14 g **Carbohydrates:** 64 g **Sugar:** 3 g

MEDITERRANEAN CHICKPEA BAKE

CALORIES: 352
SERVES 4

5 TABLESPOONS OLIVE OIL

1 LARGE ONION, FINELY CHOPPED

4 CLOVES GARLIC, MINCED

1 LARGE TOMATO, CHOPPED

2 TEASPOONS GROUND CUMIN

1 TEASPOON PAPRIKA

2 LARGE BUNCHES FRESH SPINACH, WASHED

2 CUPS CHICKPEAS, COOKED

SALT AND PEPPER TO TASTE

1. Heat olive oil in a pan over medium heat.

2. Fry onion and garlic for 2–3 minutes, until the onion starts to become translucent, then add tomato, cumin, and paprika. Continue cooking for 5 minutes.

3. Add spinach and chickpeas to the pan.

4. Reduce the heat and cover with a lid. Cook, stirring frequently, until the spinach is wilted and the chickpeas are tender. Add salt and pepper to taste.

PER SERVING: Fat: 20 g **Protein:** 13 g **Carbohydrates:** 35 g **Sugar:** 3 g

---

SPAGHETTI WITH CREAMY TOMATO SAUCE

CALORIES: 354
SERVES 6–8

1 RECIPE SPAGHETTI SAUCE

½ CUP FAT-FREE HALF-AND-HALF

1 (16-OUNCE) PACKAGE WHOLE-GRAIN PASTA

½ CUP GRATED PARMESAN CHEESE

1. Bring large pot of water to a boil. Prepare spaghetti sauce as directed. During last 5 minutes of cooking time, add half-and-half to sauce and stir to blend.

2. Cook pasta in boiling water according to package directions until al dente. Drain and add to spaghetti sauce; cook and stir for 1 minute to let the pasta absorb some of the sauce. Sprinkle with Parmesan and serve immediately.

PER SERVING: Fat: 6 g **Protein:** 10 g **Carbohydrates:** 36 g **Sugar:** 2 g

Tomatoes

Tomatoes are an excellent heart-healthy food, high in vitamins C and A and with no fat or cholesterol. They are usually sold unripe in the supermarket. Let them stand at room temperature for 1–2 days until they give to slight pressure. Don't store tomatoes in the refrigerator; their texture will become mealy.

MINI VEGGIE BURGERS

CALORIES: 251
SERVES 4

1 (13-OUNCE) CAN RED KIDNEY BEANS, DRAINED

½ CUP DRIED BREAD CRUMBS (MORE IF BEANS ARE VERY WET)

½ CUP RED ONION, CHOPPED

2 TABLESPOONS WORCESTERSHIRE SAUCE

2 TABLESPOONS BARBECUE SAUCE

1 EGG

1 TEASPOON OREGANO, ROSEMARY, THYME, BASIL, OR SAGE

SALT AND PEPPER TO TASTE

½ CUP BROWN RICE, COOKED

2 TABLESPOONS CANOLA OIL

HAMBURGER ROLLS (OPTIONAL)

1. Pulse all but the rice, canola oil, and rolls in the food processor or blender. Turn into a bowl.

2. Add brown rice to bean mixture.

3. Form into mini burgers. Heat oil to 300°F and fry burgers until very hot. Serve on rolls or plain.

PER SERVING: Fat: 10 g **Protein:** 11 g **Carbohydrates:** 34 g **Sugar:** 8 g

The Praises of Brown Rice

Unlike white rice, which is rice with its outer layers removed, brown rice has lost only the hard outer hull of the grain when it gets to the store. As a result, brown rice contains many more nutrients than its more processed relative. Also, the fiber in brown rice decreases your risk for colon cancer and helps lower cholesterol!

CITRUS SCALLOPS PASTA

CALORIES: 331
SERVES 5

1 (16-OUNCE) PACKAGE OF WHOLE-WHEAT SPAGHETTI

3 TABLESPOONS BUTTER

2 TABLESPOONS OLIVE OIL

1 TEASPOON LEMON ZEST

1¼ POUNDS SEA OR BAY SCALLOPS

BLACK PEPPER TO TASTE

1 HEAD RADICCHIO, SHREDDED

2 CUPS BABY SPINACH

JUICE OF 1 LEMON

BLACK PEPPER TO TASTE

1. Cook spaghetti per package instructions.

2. Melt butter and oil in a medium pan. Add lemon zest, scallops, and pepper to the pan. Cook scallops for 1–2 minutes per side.

3. Mix spaghetti, radicchio, spinach, and lemon juice in a large bowl. Transfer spaghetti to dinner plates and top with scallops and lemon butter.

PER SERVING: Fat: 12 g **Protein:** 28 g **Carbohydrates:** 29 g **Sugar:** 1 g

STUFFED PEPPERS WITH RICE AND SPICE

CALORIES: 329
SERVES 2

- 1 OUNCE OLIVE OIL
- ¼ CUP RED ONION, CHOPPED FINE
- 1 CLOVE GARLIC, MINCED
- 2 SPRIGS FRESH PARSLEY, MINCED
- 1 TEASPOON CORIANDER SEEDS, CRACKED
- TABASCO SAUCE TO TASTE
- 1 TEASPOON DRIED THYME
- SALT AND PEPPER TO TASTE
- 1 CUP BASMATI RICE, COOKED
- 2 EXTRA-LARGE SWEET RED OR GREEN BELL PEPPERS
- NONSTICK COOKING SPRAY
- 2 CUPS PLUM TOMATOES, DRAINED AND PURÉED
- 2 TABLESPOONS PARMESAN CHEESE, GRATED

1. Heat olive oil over medium-low flame. Stir in onions and garlic and sauté for 4 minutes. Add the parsley, coriander, Tabasco, thyme, salt, and pepper. When well mixed, spoon in the rice, stirring to coat with oil, herbs, and spices.

2. Preheat the oven to 350°F. Split the peppers lengthwise and lay them in a baking pan prepared with nonstick spray. Fill the peppers with the rice mixture.

3. Pour the puréed tomatoes over the top. Sprinkle with Parmesan cheese. Bake for 35 minutes.

PER SERVING: Fat: 16 g **Protein:** 9 g **Carbohydrates:** 41 g **Sugar:** 1 g

RATATOUILLE WITH WHITE BEANS

CALORIES: 409
SERVES 2

- ¼ CUP OLIVE OIL
- 2 BABY EGGPLANTS, CHOPPED
- 1 ONION, SLICED
- 2 CLOVES GARLIC, MINCED
- 1 SMALL ZUCCHINI, CHOPPED
- 2 MEDIUM TOMATOES, CHOPPED
- 1 TEASPOON EACH OF DRIED PARSLEY, THYME, AND ROSEMARY; IF FRESH, 1 TABLESPOON OF EACH
- SALT AND PEPPER TO TASTE
- 1 (13-OUNCE) CAN WHITE BEANS

1. Heat the olive oil. Sauté the eggplant, onion, garlic, and zucchini for 5 minutes.

2. Add tomatoes, herbs, salt, and pepper. Cover and simmer for 10 minutes. Warm the beans and serve by pouring vegetables over the beans.

PER SERVING: Fat: 16 g **Protein:** 24 g **Carbohydrates:** 59 g **Sugar:** 3 g

A Provençal Delight

Ratatouille is a versatile vegetable stew that can be served hot (either alone or as a side dish), at room temperature, or even cold as an appetizer on toast or crackers. As an appetizer, it is similar to the Italian tomato, onion, and basil salad called bruschetta.

PIZZA WITH GOAT CHEESE AND VEGETABLES

CALORIES: 178
SERVES 8

1 POUND PIZZA DOUGH

1 CUP TOMATO SAUCE FROM A JAR OR YOUR OWN

1 MEDIUM ZUCCHINI, SLICED THINLY

1 SMALL ONION, CUT THINLY

20 GREEK OR ITALIAN OLIVES, PITTED AND SLICED

2 TEASPOONS OLIVE OIL

8 OUNCES GOAT CHEESE

1. Preheat oven to 475°F. Roll out the pizza dough to fit a 12" pan or pizza stone. Spread with sauce. Arrange the zucchini over the sauce.

2. Sprinkle with onion and olives and spray with olive oil. Dot the top with cheese and bake for 15 minutes, or until the crust is brown, the cheese melts, and the topping bubbles.

PER SERVING: Fat: 13 g **Protein:** 6 g **Carbohydrates:** 9 g
Sugar: 2 g

SQUASH BLOSSOM POLENTA

CALORIES: 162
SERVES 4

4 CUPS WATER

1 TEASPOON SALT

1 CUP COARSE-GROUND YELLOW CORNMEAL

2 TABLESPOONS BUTTER

1 CUP CHOPPED ZUCCHINI SQUASH BLOSSOMS

1. Put water and salt in a saucepan and bring to a boil. Reduce heat to medium low. Gradually add cornmeal and stir constantly until it has thickened, about 15 minutes.

2. Stir in butter, then add the chopped squash blossoms.

3. Serve immediately for soft polenta, or pour into a greased 9" × 13" baking dish and let cool. When cool, it can be cut into squares or triangles and grilled, sautéed, or baked.

PER SERVING: Fat: 6 g **Protein:** 2 g **Carbohydrates:** 23 g
Sugar: 0 g

Know Your Edible Flowers
Bean blossoms have a sweet, beanie flavor. Nasturtiums have a wonderfully peppery flavor similar to watercress. Violets, roses, and lavender lend a sweet flavor to salads or desserts. Bright yellow calendulas are an economic alternative to expensive saffron, though not quite as pungent. Other flowers may have a spicy or peppermint flavor.

WHOLE-WHEAT PASTA IN BLEU CHEESE SAUCE

CALORIES: 309
SERVES 4

- 4 TEASPOONS OLIVE OIL
- 2 CLOVES GARLIC, MINCED
- ½ CUP NONFAT COTTAGE CHEESE
- 2 OUNCES CRUMBLED BLEU CHEESE
- SKIM MILK, AS NEEDED (OPTIONAL)
- 4 CUPS COOKED WHOLE-WHEAT PASTA
- ¼ CUP FRESHLY GRATED PARMESAN CHEESE
- FRESHLY GROUND BLACK PEPPER
- DRY-TOASTED CHOPPED WALNUTS (OPTIONAL)

1. Heat the olive oil in a large nonstick skillet. Add the garlic and sauté for 1 minute. Lower the heat, stir in the cottage cheese, and bring it to temperature. Add the bleu cheese and stir to combine; thin the sauce with a little skim milk, if necessary.

2. Toss with the pasta and divide into 4 equal servings. Top each serving with 1 tablespoon of the Parmesan cheese, freshly ground black pepper to taste, and toasted walnuts.

PER SERVING: Fat: 11 g **Protein:** 16 g **Carbohydrates:** 38 g **Sugar:** 2 g

BAKED BARLEY CASSEROLE

CALORIES: 394
SERVES 4

- 1 CUP BARLEY
- 3 TABLESPOONS OLIVE OIL
- 1½ CUPS DICED ONION
- 2 TABLESPOONS BUTTER
- ½ TEASPOON SALT
- ¼ TEASPOON PEPPER
- 6 CUPS BEEF BROTH
- ½ CUP CHOPPED ITALIAN FLAT-LEAF PARSLEY FOR GARNISH

1. Preheat oven to 350°F.

2. Sauté the barley in the olive oil until the barley starts to brown. Transfer the barley to a 3-quart casserole dish.

3. Sauté the onion in butter until it starts to brown and add to the casserole dish. Season with salt and pepper and add 3 cups beef broth.

4. Cover the casserole and bake for 60 minutes.

5. Add the remaining beef broth, cover, and bake until the liquid is absorbed, about 40 minutes. Add parsley for garnish.

PER SERVING: Fat: 20 g **Protein:** 16 g **Carbohydrates:** 38 g **Sugar:** 0 g

ZUCCHINI ONION CASSEROLE

CALORIES: 188
SERVES 8

- 2½ CUPS THINLY SLICED SWEET ONION
- 2½ CUPS SLICED ZUCCHINI
- 2 MEDIUM-LARGE SLICED RIPE RED TOMATOES
- 10 LEAVES FRESH BASIL
- 1 TABLESPOON DRIED ROSEMARY
- SALT AND PEPPER TO TASTE
- 2 CUPS SEASONED CROUTONS
- 2 CUPS SHREDDED CHEDDAR CHEESE

1. Preheat oven to 350°F.

2. In a 3-quart baking dish, layer half of each of the sweet onion, zucchini, and tomatoes. Season the vegetables with herbs, salt, and pepper.

3. Scatter half of the croutons over the seasoned vegetables and half of the cheese over the croutons.

4. Repeat the layering with the remaining vegetables, season with salt and pepper, and sprinkle the remaining croutons and cheese on top.

5. Cover with lid or aluminum foil and bake for 60 minutes. Serve hot.

PER SERVING: Fat: 11 g **Protein:** 9 g **Carbohydrates:** 12 g **Sugar:** 1 g

---

PUMPKIN-FILLED RAVIOLI

CALORIES: 130
SERVES 4

- 10 OUNCES CANNED PUMPKIN
- 1 EGG
- ¼ CUP PARMESAN CHEESE, GRATED
- SALT AND PEPPER TO TASTE
- 1 TEASPOON SAVORY LEAVES, DRIED
- ½ TEASPOON SAGE
- 2 TEASPOONS BUTTER, MELTED
- 24 WONTON WRAPPERS
- *IN THIS RECIPE YOU CAN SUBSTITUTE OLIVE OIL FOR BUTTER.*

1. Using the electric mixer, beat together the first 7 ingredients. Lay out the wonton wrappers. Spoon filling on one side of each.

2. Dipping your finger in cold water, moisten the edges of the wonton wrappers and press together, making sure edges are tightly sealed.

3. Prepare a 4-quart pot of boiling, salted water. Cook the ravioli until they rise to the surface; serve hot with butter, sauce, or gravy.

PER SERVING: Fat: 5 g **Protein:** 11 g **Carbohydrates:** 36 g **Sugar:** 3 g

PASTA SALAD WITH CRUNCHY VEGETABLES

CALORIES: 362
SERVES 8

½ CUP LOW-FAT MAYONNAISE

⅓ CUP OLIVE OIL

¼ CUP WHITE WINE VINEGAR

2 CLOVES GARLIC, MINCED

1 TEASPOON CHOPPED FRESH OREGANO

¼ CUP CHOPPED FLAT-LEAF PARSLEY

⅛ TEASPOON PEPPER

2 RED BELL PEPPERS, CHOPPED

4 STALKS CELERY, CHOPPED

1 YELLOW SUMMER SQUASH, CHOPPED

1 PINT GRAPE TOMATOES

1 (16-OUNCE) PACKAGE WHOLE-GRAIN ROTINI PASTA

1. Bring a large pot of water to a boil. In a large bowl, combine mayonnaise, olive oil, vinegar, garlic, oregano, parsley, and pepper and mix well with wire whisk to blend.

2. Stir in bell peppers, celery, squash, and tomatoes, and mix well. Cook pasta according to package directions until al dente. Drain and immediately add to salad in bowl. Stir gently to coat pasta with dressing. Cover and refrigerate for 4 hours before serving.

PER SERVING: Fat: 15 g **Protein:** 12 g **Carbohydrates:** 46 g **Sugar:** 3 g

Whole-Grain Pasta

If you're avoiding simple carbohydrates, whole-grain pastas are a wonderful way to start eating pasta again. These pastas are readily available in the local grocery store. They have a stronger flavor than plain pastas, so you may want to mix the two kinds half-and-half at first to introduce whole-grain pasta to your family.

PENNE PRIMAVERA

CALORIES: 401
SERVES 4

½ CUP DICED ONION
½ CUP DICED CARROT
¼ CUP DICED RED BELL PEPPER
2 TABLESPOONS OLIVE OIL
½ CUP CHICKEN BROTH
1 CUP ASPARAGUS TIPS
1 CUP BROCCOLI FLORETS
½ CUP CREAM
½ CUP PEAS
½ CUP GRATED PARMESAN CHEESE
SALT AND PEPPER TO TASTE
4 CUPS COOKED PENNE PASTA

1. Sauté onions, carrots, and red bell pepper in oil until tender.

2. Add chicken broth, asparagus, and broccoli and simmer for 5 minutes.

3. Add cream and peas and simmer for 5 minutes.

4. Stir in Parmesan cheese and remove from heat.

5. Season with salt and pepper and serve sauce over cooked penne pasta.

PER SERVING: Fat: 19 g **Protein:** 15 g **Carbohydrates:** 40 g **Sugar:** 5 g

Primavera

In Italian, *primavera* means "spring." Thus, it's appropriate to use young baby vegetables in this dish. You can use frozen baby peas, but sugar snaps are excellent and a fine source of fresh great-tasting fiber too. Some primavera recipes also call for bits of chicken or chopped shrimp—all delicious.

HOMEMADE MACARONI AND CHEESE

CALORIES: 336
SERVES 5

2 CUPS WHOLE-WHEAT ELBOW MACARONI OR PENNE
2 CUPS BROCCOLI FLORETS
NONSTICK COOKING SPRAY
1 CUP LOW-FAT COTTAGE CHEESE
1 TABLESPOON DIJON MUSTARD
¼ TEASPOON TABASCO SAUCE
SALT AND PEPPER TO TASTE
4 OUNCES SHARP CHEDDAR CHEESE, SHREDDED
4 OUNCES PART SKIM MOZZARELLA CHEESE, SHREDDED

1. Boil noodles in a large pot for 6 minutes. Add broccoli and cook for 2 more minutes or until the noodles are al dente. Drain, and reserve ½ cup of cooking liquid. Return noodles and broccoli to the pot.

2. Preheat oven to 400°F. Grease medium soufflé dish using cooking spray and set aside.

3. Mix cottage cheese, reserved cooking liquid, mustard, and Tabasco until smooth.

4. Stir cottage cheese mixture into noodles and broccoli, season with salt and pepper. Mix in Cheddar and mozzarella cheeses.

5. Transfer to the greased dish. Bake for 20 minutes or until cheese is melted and top is golden brown.

PER SERVING: Fat: 13 g **Protein:** 23 g **Carbohydrates:** 35 g **Sugar:** 4 g

TOP HAT PIZZA

CALORIES: 397
SERVES 8

2 (1-POUND) PACKAGES OF PIZZA DOUGH

2 CUPS SHREDDED PART-SKIM MOZZARELLA CHEESE

1 RED BELL PEPPER, THINLY SLICED

1 GREEN BELL PEPPER, THINLY SLICED

1 (4-OUNCE) CAN CHOPPED GREEN CHILIES, DRAINED

½ CUP SLICED BLACK OLIVES

2 GREEN ONIONS, SLICED

1 AVOCADO, SLICED

1 TABLESPOON LEMON JUICE

½ TEASPOON SEASONED SALT

⅛ TEASPOON PEPPER

12 PLUM TOMATOES, SLICED

⅛ TEASPOON HOT PEPPER SAUCE

1. Preheat oven to 425°F. Prebake pizza dough for 5 minutes; remove from oven. Let cool for 10 minutes.

2. Sprinkle cooled crust with mozzarella cheese, red and green bell peppers, chilies, olives, and green onions. Bake until toppings are hot and cheese is melted, 15 to 20 minutes.

3. Meanwhile, prepare avocados, sprinkling with lemon juice. In a small bowl, combine salt, pepper, plum tomatoes, and hot pepper sauce; toss to coat. When pizza comes out of oven, top with avocados and tomato mixture; serve immediately.

PER SERVING: Fat: 11 g **Protein:** 16 g **Carbohydrates:** 30 g **Sugar:** 5 g

LASAGNA FLORENTINE

CALORIES: 473
SERVES 8

NONSTICK COOKING OIL

5 CUPS TOMATO SAUCE

1 (1-POUND) BOX WHOLE-WHEAT LASAGNA NOODLES, COOKED

3 EGGS

16 OUNCES RICOTTA CHEESE

2 CUPS MOZZARELLA CHEESE, SHREDDED

2 CUPS CHOPPED COOKED SPINACH

½ CUP CHOPPED FRESH PARSLEY

SALT AND PEPPER TO TASTE

½ CUP GRATED PARMESAN CHEESE

1. Preheat oven to 350°F. Spray a baking dish with nonstick cooking oil and spread 1 cup tomato sauce on the bottom. Cover the sauce with a layer of cooked noodles.

2. In a bowl combine the eggs, ricotta, and 1 cup mozzarella cheese until well blended. Stir in the spinach, parsley, salt, and pepper.

3. Spread half of the ricotta mixture over the noodles in the pan, then top the ricotta with a layer of noodles. Ladle 2 cups of the tomato sauce over the noodles and top with another layer of noodles.

4. Spread the remaining ricotta mixture over the noodles. Top with another layer of noodles. Ladle the remaining tomato sauce over the noodles.

5. Scatter the remaining mozzarella cheese over the sauce, then sprinkle the Parmesan cheese over it. Bake for 75 minutes.

PER SERVING: Fat: 18 grams **Protein:** 25 g **Carbohydrates:** 52 g **Sugar:** 3 g

Spinach and Florentine

The cheeses and spinach are a high-protein and high-fiber combination. Fresh baby spinach is delicious and easy to deal with in the kitchen. You can also substitute arugula for spinach. If you want to get very aromatic, try adding some chopped watercress to the spinach.

PASTA FAGIOLI

1 (16-OUNCE) PACKAGE ZITI PASTA

2 TABLESPOONS OLIVE OIL

2 CLOVES GARLIC, MINCED

1½ CUPS SUGAR SNAP PEAS

1½ CUPS DICED COOKED EXTRA-LEAN HAM

1 CUP COOKED NAVY BEANS

¼ CUP SUN-DRIED TOMATOES PACKED IN OIL, DRAINED AND CHOPPED

1½ CUPS LOW-FAT, REDUCED-SODIUM CHICKEN BROTH

½ TEASPOON KOSHER OR SEA SALT

¼ TEASPOON CRACKED BLACK PEPPER

¼ CUP GRATED PARMESAN CHEESE

1. Cook the pasta according to package directions.

2. Meanwhile, heat a large skillet over medium heat and add the olive oil. Sauté the garlic for 2 minutes, being careful not to burn it. Add the peas and stir-fry for about 3 minutes. Stir in the ham, beans, tomatoes, broth, salt, and pepper and simmer for 5 minutes.

3. Toss the stir-fried bean mixture with the pasta and Parmesan cheese.

PER SERVING: Fat: 7 g **Protein:** 20 g **Carbohydrates:** 57 g
Sugar: 8 g

Little Bits

Don't waste the unused tomato paste left in the can. Spoon out tablespoon-size portions and place them on plastic wrap or in sandwich baggies. Seal the packages and store in the freezer. When you need tomato paste in a recipe, add the frozen paste directly to the sauce; there is no need to defrost it.

VEGETABLE LASAGNA WITH BUFFALO MOZZARELLA

CALORIES: 414
SERVES 10

- 1 PACKAGE LASAGNA
- ¼ CUP OLIVE OIL
- 1 FRESH ZUCCHINI, CUT IN THIN COINS
- 1 CUP BROCCOLI FLORETS, CUT IN SMALL PIECES
- 1 YELLOW PEPPER, CORED, SEEDED, AND DICED
- ½ PINT GRAPE TOMATOES, CUT IN HALVES
- 6 SCALLIONS, CHOPPED
- 10 FRESH BASIL LEAVES, TORN
- ¼ CUP FRESH PARSLEY, CHOPPED
- SALT AND PEPPER TO TASTE
- 2 PINTS RICOTTA CHEESE
- ½ CUP PARMESAN CHEESE, GRATED
- 2 EGGS, BEATEN
- NONSTICK COOKING SPRAY
- 2 CUPS OF YOUR FAVORITE PASTA SAUCE
- 5 OUNCES BUFFALO MOZZARELLA CHEESE

1. While cooking the lasagna noodles (undercook a bit to avoid soggy lasagna), heat the oil in a large sauce pan or frying pan over medium flame. Sauté the vegetables for 10 minutes, adding the herbs, salt, and pepper at the end.

2. Preheat oven to 325°F. In a large bowl, mix the ricotta, Parmesan cheese, and eggs. Mix in the vegetables. Prepare a 9" × 13" lasagna pan with nonstick cooking spray.

3. Cover the bottom with sauce and then with strips of cooked lasagna. Spoon the ricotta and vegetable mixture over the pasta. Cover with a second layer of lasagna and repeat until you get to the top of the pan.

4. Spread the final layer of lasagna with sauce. Bake for 35 minutes. Five minutes before serving, dot the top with mozzarella cheese. When it melts, serve.

PER SERVING: Fat: 18 g **Protein:** 22 g **Carbohydrates:** 44 g **Sugar:** 2 g

SPAGHETTI WITH CRAB AND CORN

CALORIES: 485
SERVES 6

- 1 POUND WHOLE-WHEAT SPAGHETTI
- 2 TABLESPOONS VEGETABLE OIL
- 5 SLICES BACON
- 2 SMALL ONIONS
- 2 STALKS CELERY, FINELY CHOPPED
- ½ SMALL RED BELL PEPPER, CHOPPED
- 3 GARLIC CLOVES, CRUSHED
- 1 CUP NONFAT MILK
- 1 CUP LOW-SODIUM CHICKEN STOCK
- 2 TABLESPOONS FLOUR
- 10 OUNCES FRESH CRABMEAT
- 10 OUNCES FROZEN CORN, THAWED
- 1 TEASPOON CAYENNE PEPPER
- ½ CUP LOW-FAT SHREDDED CHEDDAR CHEESE

1. Cook the pasta according to package directions.

2. Heat the vegetable oil in a skillet on medium heat, then add the bacon and cook it until crisp.

3. Remove bacon from skillet and pat with paper towels to remove fat and oils.

4. Sauté onions, celery, bell pepper, and garlic in the leftover oil.

5. Whisk in milk and chicken stock until bubbling, then add the flour and turn the heat down to low.

6. Stir in crab, corn, and cayenne pepper according to taste. Mix well on low heat for about 5 minutes.

7. Add the cheese.

8. Toss entire mixture with drained pasta and serve.

PER SERVING: Fat: 11 g **Protein:** 30 g **Carbohydrates:** 74 g **Sugar:** 8 g

FRESH TOMATO WITH ANGEL HAIR PASTA

CALORIES: 277
SERVES 4–6

½ CUP PINE NUTS

4 RIPE BEEFSTEAK TOMATOES

¼ CUP EXTRA-VIRGIN OLIVE OIL

1 TABLESPOON LEMON JUICE

¼ CUP PACKED FRESH BASIL LEAVES

½ TEASPOON SALT

⅛ TEASPOON WHITE PEPPER

1 POUND ANGEL HAIR PASTA

1. Bring a large pot of water to a boil for the pasta. Place small skillet over medium heat for 3 minutes. Add pine nuts; cook and stir for 3–5 minutes or until nuts begin to brown and are fragrant. Remove from heat and pour nuts into a serving bowl.

2. Chop tomatoes into ½" pieces and add to pine nuts along with olive oil, lemon juice, basil, salt, and pepper. Add pasta to the boiling water; cook and stir until al dente, according to package directions. Drain and add to tomato mixture in bowl. Toss gently and serve immediately.

PER SERVING: Fat: 18 g **Protein:** 19 g **Carbohydrates:** 25 g **Sugar:** 2 g

Fresh Basil

If you have a garden—or even just a sunny windowsill—by all means grow basil; it's easy to grow and requires very little maintenance. There are lots of kits available on the market or the Internet. Just be sure to use the basil before the plant starts to flower. You can also find fresh basil in the produce aisle of your supermarket.

LASAGNA

1 POUND DRY LASAGNA NOODLES

1 MEDIUM ZUCCHINI, SLICED

1 CUP LOW-FAT COTTAGE CHEESE

1 EGG WHITE

½ CUP SKIM MILK SHREDDED MOZZARELLA CHEESE

¼ POUND EXTRA-LEAN GROUND BEEF

1 JAR REDUCED-SODIUM CHUNKY VEGETABLE SPAGHETTI SAUCE

½ TEASPOON GROUND FENNEL

NONSTICK COOKING SPRAY

1. Cook lasagna noodles according to package directions.

2. Cook zucchini in boiling water for 2 minutes. Drain.

3. Mix cottage cheese, egg white, and mozzarella cheese in a medium-size bowl. Set aside.

4. Brown beef in a deep skillet and drain.

5. Stir in the spaghetti sauce and fennel. Simmer for 5 minutes.

6. Spray your cooking pan lightly with nonstick cooking spray and preheat oven to 350°F.

7. Spread a small amount of the sauce on bottom of cooking pan.

8. Layer the noodles, zucchini, cottage cheese mixture, and sauce in that order.

9. Top with remaining mozzarella.

10. Bake at 350°F for 30 minutes or until lasagna is bubbly and golden brown.

PER SERVING: Fat: 6 g **Protein:** 24 g **Carbohydrates:** 70 g **Sugar:** 5 g

BROCCOLI AND NOODLE CASSEROLE

CALORIES: 473
SERVES 4

10 OUNCES FROZEN BROCCOLI

4 TABLESPOONS MARGARINE

4 TABLESPOONS FLOUR

2 CUPS FAT-FREE MILK

SALT AND PEPPER TO TASTE

4 CUPS OF WATER

2 CUPS WHOLE-WHEAT
MACARONI NOODLES

4 HARD-BOILED EGGS, SLICED

¼ CUP GRATED LOW-FAT SWISS
CHEESE

1 CUP BREAD CRUMBS

1. Preheat oven to 350°F.

2. Cook broccoli in boiling water until tender.

3. Drain broccoli, cool, and cut into 1" pieces.

4. Melt the margarine in a deep skillet on medium heat.

5. Add the flour, milk, salt, and pepper and mix until creamy. Remove from heat and set aside.

6. Boil water on and cook the noodles about 15 minutes or until soft, then drain and set aside.

7. In a casserole dish, arrange alternate layers of noodles, broccoli, sliced cooked eggs, cream sauce, and cheese.

8. Sprinkle evenly with bread crumbs.

9. Bake for 30 minutes or until bubbling.

PER SERVING: Fat: 19 g **Protein:** 23 g **Carbohydrates:** 54 g
Sugar: 3 g

Versatile Vegetables

You can use nearly any vegetable for this casserole. Asparagus and cauliflower are good alternatives—and there's no rule saying you can only use one vegetable at a time! You can also play around with different cheeses and pastas to find a combination that suits your palate.

WILD RICE AND ONION PASTA

CALORIES: 320
SERVES 4

½ CUP WILD RICE
1 CUP WATER
½ POUND LINGUINE
1 TABLESPOON OLIVE OIL
2 TABLESPOONS BUTTER
2 ONIONS, CHOPPED
3 CLOVES GARLIC, MINCED
½ CUP GRATED PARMESAN
   CHEESE
¼ CUP CHOPPED PARSLEY
¼ CUP CHOPPED FRESH BASIL

1. In a small saucepan, combine wild rice and water. Bring to a boil over high heat, cover, reduce heat, and simmer for 35–40 minutes or until wild rice is tender. Meanwhile, bring a large pot of water to a boil. Add linguine and cook.

2. In heavy saucepan, combine olive oil and butter over medium heat. Add onions and garlic; cook and stir until onions begin to caramelize, about 10–15 minutes.

3. When pasta is done, drain in a colander, reserving about ⅓ cup of the pasta water. Add pasta and reserved water to skillet with onions and reduce heat to low. Add wild rice to skillet; cook and stir for 2 minutes. Sprinkle with cheese, parsley, and basil. Stir and serve immediately.

PER SERVING: Fat: 14 g Protein: 16 g Carbohydrates: 39 g Sugar: 1 g

Wild Rice

Wild rice is actually not a rice but the seed of a grass plant. It grows wild in northern Minnesota; the highest quality rice is harvested by Native Americans who glide through lakes in canoes. Always use long-grain wild rice. Rice with broken grains will cook up mushy and tasteless.

VEGETABLE POTPIE

CALORIES: 480
SERVES 6

- ½ **MEDIUM ONION, DICED**
- 2 **CARROTS, PEELED AND DICED**
- 2 **CELERY STALKS, DICED**
- ½ **CUP SLICED LEEKS**
- 2 **TABLESPOONS BUTTER**
- ¼ **CUP FLOUR**
- 3 **CUPS CHICKEN BROTH**
- 1 **POTATO, PEELED AND CUBED**
- ½ **CUP CUT GREEN BEANS**
- 1 **BAY LEAF**
- ½ **CUP FROZEN PEAS**
- ½ **CUP CREAM**
- **SALT AND PEPPER TO TASTE**
- ¼ **CUP CHOPPED CHIVES**
- 8 **WHOLE-WHEAT BISCUITS, UNBAKED**

1. Sauté onion, carrots, celery, and leeks in butter until tender. Dust with flour, stir, and cook a few minutes. Add chicken broth, potato, and green beans. Bring to a boil, add bay leaf, and simmer for 40 minutes until vegetables are cooked and liquid is thickened.

2. Stir in peas and cream and remove from heat. Remove bay leaf, season with salt and pepper, and stir in chopped chives. Pour filling into a 9" × 13" baking dish and place on a baking sheet with sides.

3. Preheat oven to 400°F.

4. Place the unbaked biscuits on top of the filling and bake for 45 minutes or until the biscuit top is baked.

5. Scoop out individual portions and serve hot.

PER SERVING: Fat: 19 g **Protein:** 14 g **Carbohydrates:** 65 g **Sugar:** 6 g

Other Ways to Pot a Pie

You can make a country-style pie in an earthenware casserole. Try cornmeal batter on top, as opposed to whole-wheat piecrust. Biscuits are wonderful because they absorb some of the gravy or liquids in the pie as they bubble up, turning a pie into a cobbler. Try topping a pie with a nutty crust made with ground walnuts, butter, whole-wheat flour, and orange zest.

ACORN SQUASH, CRANBERRIES, AND WILD RICE

CALORIES: 295
SERVES 4

2 ACORN SQUASH, WHOLE

1 CUP COOKED WILD RICE

1 TABLESPOON BALSAMIC VINEGAR

½ CUP TOASTED PECANS, CHOPPED

½ CUP DRIED CRANBERRIES

4 TEASPOONS MAPLE SYRUP

1. Pierce the squash all over with a fork. Place squash on a paper towel in the microwave oven. Cook on high for 5 minutes, turn over, and cook for 10 more minutes. Let stand 5 to 10 minutes.

2. Meanwhile, combine the cooked wild rice, balsamic vinegar, pecans, and dried cranberries. Set aside.

3. Cut the squash in half, remove the seeds, and place cut-side up in a casserole dish.

4. Spoon the wild rice mixture into the hollowed-out squash. Cover and cook on high in the microwave for several minutes to heat through.

5. Drizzle maple syrup on top before serving.

PER SERVING: Fat: 11 g **Protein:** 4 g **Carbohydrates:** 48 g **Sugar:** 8 g

All-American
The combination of wild rice and cranberries is as American as a dish can be! Both of these ingredients were originally cultivated by Native Americans, who introduced them to the colonists. The sweet yet tart flavor of the cranberries pairs well with the nutty flavor of the rice and gives you all the fiber you need.

BEAN BURRITO TORTE

CALORIES: 389
SERVES 6

- 1 CUP REFRIED BEANS
- 1 CUP SOUR CREAM
- 1 TABLESPOON TACO SEASONING
- 9 (8") WHOLE-WHEAT TORTILLAS
- ½ CUP ENCHILADA SAUCE
- 1 CUP SHREDDED CHEDDAR CHEESE
- 1 AVOCADO, PEELED, PITTED, AND SLICED
- ¼ CUP BLACK OLIVES
- ½ CUP DICED TOMATOES
- ¼ CUP CHOPPED GREEN ONIONS
- 1 CUP SHREDDED ICEBERG LETTUCE

1. Preheat oven to 350°F. Oil a 9" cake pan.

2. Mix the refried beans, ½ cup of sour cream, and taco seasoning together.

3. Place 3 tortillas on the bottom of the cake pan. Spread half of the refried bean mixture over the tortillas. Spoon half of the enchilada sauce over the beans. Sprinkle half of the Cheddar cheese over the enchilada sauce.

4. Place 3 tortillas on top of the cheese. Repeat the layering with the remaining bean mixture, enchilada sauce, and cheese.

5. Top with the last 3 tortillas, cover tightly with foil, and bake for 30 minutes. Remove from oven, remove the foil, cut into six wedges, and invert the pan onto a plate.

6. Remove the pan and garnish the top of the torte with the remaining sour cream, avocado, black olives, diced tomatoes, and green onions. Place the shredded lettuce around the torte on the plate and serve.

PER SERVING: Fat: 20 g **Protein:** 13 g **Carbohydrates:** 45 g **Sugar:** 4 g

Southwest Flavors

You can do hundreds of variations on any southwestern recipe. By adding avocados to the Bean Burrito Torte, you add another dimension. A spritz of fresh lime served on the side acts like a sparkler. A layer of cooked corn also adds a dimension. A sprinkling of fresh cilantro or parsley also adds savor. Just keep building!

STUFFED ARTICHOKES

CALORIES: 238
SERVES 4

4 LARGE ARTICHOKES

JUICE AND RIND OF ½ LEMON

1 TEASPOON CORIANDER SEEDS

2 TABLESPOONS BUTTER OR OLIVE OIL

1 CELERY STALK, CHOPPED

¼ CUP VIDALIA ONION, CHOPPED

2 CLOVES GARLIC, CHOPPED

1 CUP CORN BREAD CRUMBS OR COMMERCIAL CORN BREAD STUFFING

1 TEASPOON OREGANO

SALT AND PEPPER TO TASTE

⅓ CUP VEGETABLE BROTH TO MOISTEN CRUMBS

4 TABLESPOONS PARMESAN CHEESE (4 TEASPOONS RESERVED FOR TOPPING)

4 TEASPOONS BUTTER OR OLIVE OIL FOR TOPPING

NONSTICK SPRAY

1. Using scissors, remove the sharp leaf points of the artichokes and cut off the ends of the stems. Pull off the large outside leaves. Bring 2 quarts of water to a boil with the lemon and coriander over high heat. Add the artichokes and return to a boil. Reduce to a simmer and cook artichokes for 15 minutes. Drain and let cool.

2. Heat the butter or olive oil and add the celery, onion, and garlic. Sauté over medium heat for 10 minutes, or until softened. Add the corn bread crumbs, oregano, salt and pepper, broth, and part of the cheese.

3. Cut the artichokes in halves and remove the "chokes." Arrange in a baking dish prepared with nonstick spray. Spoon the stuffing into the areas left by the chokes.

4. Sprinkle with cheese and dot with extra butter or drizzle with olive oil. At this point, the stuffed artichokes can be covered and refrigerated. When ready to bake, remove wrapping and bake for 30 minutes at 350°F.

PER SERVING: Fat: 13 g **Protein:** 5 g **Carbohydrates:** 29 g **Sugar:** 2 g

Time-Saving Tip

If you are short on time or unable to find nice artichokes at your local grocery store, substitute fresh artichokes with jarred or canned artichokes. Be sure to choose plain chokes that are not marinated, which will work best for this recipe.

PUMPKIN RISOTTO

CALORIES: 116
SERVES 4

- 1 SMALL PUMPKIN (ABOUT 3 POUNDS)
- 1 TABLESPOON BUTTER OR MARGARINE
- 1 CUP BASMATI RICE
- 4 CUPS VEGETABLE BROTH
- 1/8 TEASPOON CLOVES, GROUND
- 1 TEASPOON SAGE, DRIED, OR 4 FRESH SAGE LEAVES, TORN
- SALT AND PEPPER TO TASTE

1. Peel pumpkin and remove the seeds. Dice pumpkin to make 2 cups. Melt the butter or margarine in a large flameproof casserole dish over medium heat. Add the rice and stir to coat. Mix in the pumpkin.

2. Stirring constantly, slowly pour ½ cup of the broth into the rice mixture. Stirring, add the cloves, sage, salt, and pepper.

3. When the rice has absorbed the broth, the pot will hiss. Continue to add broth a little at a time until the rice has absorbed all of it. If still dry, add water, as with the broth, a little at a time.

4. Serve hot or at room temperature.

PER SERVING: Fat: 3 g **Protein:** 2 g **Carbohydrates:** 24 g **Sugar:** 2 g

Rice Texture

The rice you use in risotto should give the dish a creamy texture, but be careful not to overcook—there should also be a firmness to the inside part of the grain of rice.

LENTILS WITH STEWED VEGETABLES

CALORIES: 361
SERVES 4

¼ CUP OLIVE OIL

1 ONION, CHOPPED

1 SMALL PIECE OF GINGER, PEELED AND COARSELY CHOPPED

5 GARLIC CLOVES, CHOPPED

5 CUPS WATER

1½ TEASPOONS CURRY POWDER

½ TEASPOON GROUND TURMERIC

½ TEASPOON GROUND CUMIN

1 CUP LENTILS

2 CARROTS, QUARTERED LENGTHWISE, THEN SLICED CROSSWISE

¼ TEASPOON CRUSHED RED PEPPER FLAKES

1 TEASPOON SALT

1 CUP GREEN PEAS

4 CUPS FRESH SPINACH

1. Place olive oil in large pot over medium heat. Cook onion, stirring occasionally, until golden brown.

2. In a blender, purée ginger, garlic, and ⅓ cup water in a blender. Add purée to cooked onion and continue cooking and stirring until all water is evaporated, about 5 minutes.

3. Turn heat down to low and add curry powder, turmeric, and cumin. Stir in lentils and remaining water and simmer, covered, occasionally stirring, for about 30 minutes.

4. Add carrots, red pepper flakes, and salt and simmer, covered, stirring occasionally, until carrots are tender, about 15 minutes.

5. Stir in peas and spinach and simmer, uncovered, about 20 minutes.

PER SERVING: Fat: 14 g **Protein:** 16 g **Carbohydrates:** 43 g **Sugar:** 6 g

BLACK BEANS AND SWEET BELL PEPPERS

CALORIES: 420
SERVES 2

- 2 LARGE BELL PEPPERS
- 2 TABLESPOONS OLIVE OIL
- ¼ RED ONION, MINCED
- 2 CLOVES GARLIC, MINCED
- 1½ CUPS BLACK BEANS, DRAINED AND WELL RINSED
- 1 SMALL TOMATO
- 1 BUNCH CILANTRO, CHOPPED
- SALT AND PEPPER TO TASTE
- ¼ CUP MONTEREY JACK CHEESE, SHREDDED

1. Slice peppers in half vertically and clean membranes and seeds from insides. Place peppers in a baking dish.

2. Heat oil in a medium pan and sauté onion for 2–3 minutes, until soft and translucent. Add garlic and sauté for 1 minute.

3. Transfer onion and garlic mixture to a large bowl. Add beans, tomato, and cilantro and mix well. Add salt and pepper to season.

4. Stuff each pepper half with the bean mixture. Cover the dish with foil and bake at 400°F for 35 minutes.

5. Carefully, take dish from the oven and remove foil. Sprinkle cheese on each pepper and return dish to the oven, uncovered. Cook until cheese in completely melted.

PER SERVING: Fat: 20 g **Protein:** 18 g **Carbohydrates:** 45 g
Sugar: 6 g

TOFU AND VEGGIE STIR-FRY

CALORIES: 491
SERVES 2

1 CUP QUINOA, UNCOOKED
½ BLOCK TOFU
SALT AND PEPPER TO TASTE
1 TABLESPOON OLIVE OIL
1 CUP RED CABBAGE, SHREDDED
1 CARROT, SLICED
1 CUP BROCCOLI FLORETS
5 WHITE MUSHROOMS, SLICED
JUICE OF ½ ORANGE
3 TABLESPOONS SOY SAUCE

1. Add quinoa to a small saucepan and pour 2 cups of water over it. Bring the pan to a boil, cover, and turn down the heat to a low simmer. Let it cook for about 15 minutes, then remove from heat.

2. Cut tofu into 1" cubes; season with salt and pepper. Pour olive oil into skillet on medium-high heat. Add tofu and cook for about 5 minutes.

3. Add red cabbage, carrot, broccoli, and mushrooms to the tofu. Stir, and allow to cook for 5 minutes.

4. Add orange juice and soy sauce and stir, allowing excess liquid to evaporate.

5. Put the cooked quinoa in the skillet with the tofu and vegetables. Mix together and add salt and pepper, as needed.

PER SERVING: Fat: 14 g **Protein:** 24 g **Carbohydrates:** 70 g
Sugar: 3 g

BAKED RICOTTA CHEESE CASSEROLE WITH HOT PEPPERS AND VEGETABLES

CALORIES: 125
SERVES 4

- 1 TABLESPOON OLIVE OIL
- ½ CUP SWEET RED ONION, CHOPPED
- 1 MEDIUM ZUCCHINI, CHOPPED
- 1 MEDIUM CARROT, PEELED AND GRATED
- 2 JALAPEÑO PEPPERS, SEEDED AND MINCED
- 2 BEATEN EGGS
- 1 POUND RICOTTA CHEESE
- 2 TABLESPOONS PARMESAN CHEESE, GRATED
- 1 TEASPOON DRIED OREGANO
- ½ CUP FRESH BASIL
- SALT AND PEPPER TO TASTE
- NONSTICK COOKING SPRAY
- 1 CUP TOMATO SAUCE
- 1 TABLESPOON CAPERS OR GREEN PEPPERCORNS TO GARNISH (OPTIONAL)

1. Heat the olive oil in a nonstick pan. Sauté the vegetables in olive oil for 5 minutes. Preheat the oven to 350°F.

2. Mix the beaten eggs with the cheeses, herbs, salt, and pepper. Stir in the vegetables. Prepare a gratin pan with nonstick spray. Add the cheese and vegetables mixture. Spread top with tomato sauce and bake for 30 minutes. Serve hot, topped with your garnish of choice.

PER SERVING: Fat: 11 g **Protein:** 5 g **Carbohydrates:** 4 g **Sugar:** 14 g

Cutting Down on Salt
Ricotta cheese has a naturally high salt content so you may want to keep that in mind when adding additional salt for flavoring.

BARLEY RISOTTO WITH MUSHROOMS AND THYME

CALORIES: 262
SERVES 4

3 (12-OUNCE) CANS OF LOW-SODIUM VEGETABLE BROTH

4 TEASPOONS OLIVE OIL

1 CUP OF ONION, FINELY CHOPPED

1 CUP PEARLED BARLEY

1 TABLESPOON FRESH THYME, CHOPPED

½ POUND PORTOBELLO MUSHROOMS, SLICED

2 CLOVES GARLIC, MINCED

1 TEASPOON ITALIAN SEASONING

SALT AND PEPPER TO TASTE

1. Boil vegetable broth in a large saucepan. Remove from heat and cover.

2. Place 2 teaspoons olive oil in a large skillet over low heat. Sauté onion in heated oil until soft and translucent.

3. Add barley, thyme, and 2 cups of heated broth to pan with onion; bring to a boil. Immediately, reduce heat to simmer until the broth has mostly absorbed, continuously stirring, about 5 minutes.

4. Add remaining heated broth to barley mixture ½ cup at a time, allowing broth to absorb before adding additional ½ cups. Continuously stir risotto until done, about 45 minutes.

5. Heat remaining oil in a second large skillet over high heat. Add mushrooms and sauté until slightly browned. Add in garlic and Italian seasoning, reduce heat to medium, cover, and cook until mushrooms are soft.

6. Add risotto to mushrooms, stir to combine, and season with salt and pepper.

PER SERVING: Fat: 5 g **Protein:** 7 g **Carbohydrates:** 49 g **Sugar:** 3 g

Time for Thyme

Thyme is included in a French culinary combination of herbs called bouquet garni that includes parsley, thyme, and bay leaves. Bouquet garni is often used to season soups and stews. Research shows that thyme has antibacterial properties. Thyme acts as a natural food preservative.

WINTER ROOT VEGETABLE SOUFFLÉ

CALORIES: 200
SERVES 4

- ½ LARGE VIDALIA ONION, CUT IN BIG CHUNKS
- 2 CARROTS, PEELED AND CHOPPED
- 2 PARSNIPS, PEELED AND CHOPPED
- 2 BABY TURNIPS, PEELED AND CUT IN PIECES
- 1 TEASPOON SALT, IN WATER FOR BOILING VEGETABLES
- 4 EGGS, SEPARATED, WHITES RESERVED
- 1 TEASPOON DRIED SAGE
- 2 TABLESPOONS PARSLEY, CHOPPED, FRESH ONLY
- 1 TABLESPOON FLOUR
- ½ TEASPOON TABASCO SAUCE, OR TO TASTE
- ½ CUP 2% MILK
- NONSTICK COOKING SPRAY

IN THIS RECIPE YOU CAN SUBSTITUTE NONFAT MILK FOR 2% MILK.

1. Set oven on 400°F. Place the cleaned vegetables in a pot of cold, salted water to cover. Bring to a boil; reduce heat and simmer until the veggies are very tender when pierced with a fork.

2. Drain the vegetables and cool slightly. Place in the blender and purée. With the blender running on medium speed, add the egg yolks, one at a time. Then add the sage, parsley, flour, Tabasco sauce, and milk. Pour into a bowl.

3. Prepare a 2-quart soufflé dish with nonstick spray. Beat the egg whites until stiff. Fold the egg whites into the purée. Pour into the soufflé dish.

4. Bake the soufflé for 20 minutes at 400°F. Reduce heat to 350°F and bake for 20 minutes more. Don't worry if your soufflé flops just before serving; it will still be light and delicious.

PER SERVING: Fat: 6 g **Protein:** 11 g **Carbohydrates:** 28 g **Sugar:** 5 g

Soufflé Tip
It's okay to have a soufflé flop, especially in the case of cheese and vegetable soufflés. A dessert soufflé should never fall. If, as directed, you start the soufflé with the oven on 400°F and then reduce the temperature, you are more likely to produce a high soufflé!

FRENCH BREAD PIZZA

CALORIES: 402
SERVES 8

- 1 LOAF OAT BRAN FRENCH BREAD
- 3 TABLESPOONS OLIVE OIL, DIVIDED
- 1 ONION, CHOPPED
- 1 GREEN BELL PEPPER, CHOPPED
- 1 RED BELL PEPPER, CHOPPED
- 3 GARLIC CLOVES, MINCED
- 2 TEASPOONS DRIED BASIL LEAVES
- 1 TEASPOON DRIED OREGANO LEAVES
- 2 CUPS PIZZA SAUCE
- 3 TOMATOES, SLICED
- ½ CUP SLICED BLACK OLIVES
- 2 CUPS SHREDDED CARROTS
- 1 CUP SHREDDED PART-SKIM MOZZARELLA CHEESE
- ½ CUP GRATED PARMESAN CHEESE

1. Preheat oven to 450°F. Slice the bread in half lengthwise. Drizzle cut sides of both halves with 2 tablespoons oil and place on a baking sheet.

2. In a large skillet, heat the remaining 1 tablespoon oil over medium heat. Add onion, bell peppers, garlic, basil, and oregano and cook for 5 minutes, or until tender. Remove from heat.

3. Spoon 1 cup spaghetti sauce on each piece of bread. Top evenly with the onion-pepper mixture, tomatoes, and black olives. Then sprinkle evenly with the carrots, mozzarella cheese, and Parmesan cheese.

4. Bake for 14 to 18 minutes or until cheese is melted and bubbly and the bread is lightly browned. Cut each loaf into 4 pieces to serve.

PER SERVING: Fat: 12 g **Protein:** 12 g **Carbohydrates:** 28 g **Sugar:** 5 g

Shredded Carrots

Shredded carrots are a surprise ingredient on this pizza, and they also sneak their way into many recipes for spaghetti sauce. Not only is it a good way to get your kids to eat vegetables, but it helps thicken the sauce and adds a slight sweetness. If you want them to melt into the sauce, it's best to shred the carrots yourself; preshredded carrots can be dry.

CHAPTER 12

Desserts

TEA-POACHED PRUNES

CALORIES: 289
SERVES 4

½ CUP SUGAR
2 CUPS WATER
3 BLACK CURRANT TEA BAGS
3 CUPS PITTED PRUNES

1. In a saucepan, combine the sugar and water and heat over low to dissolve the sugar. Add the tea bags and simmer for 5 minutes.

2. Add the prunes to the simmering liquid and place a piece of parchment paper over the surface of the liquid. Poke a few slits in the paper to let steam escape.

3. Simmer the prunes for 15 minutes.

4. Remove from heat and let prunes cool in poaching liquid. Refrigerate in liquid until ready to serve.

PER SERVING: Fat: 1 g **Protein:** 2 g **Carbohydrates:** 62 g **Sugar:** 46 g

FRESH FIG AND RASPBERRY COMPOTE

CALORIES: 242
SERVES 4

½ CUP HONEY
¼ CUP WATER
12 RIPE MISSION FIGS
1 CUP RIPE RED RASPBERRIES
1 TABLESPOON CHOPPED FRESH MINT LEAVES

1. Mix honey and water together in a glass bowl and microwave on high for 20 seconds. Remove, stir, and let chill in the refrigerator.

2. Cut the figs into quarters and add them to the chilled honey syrup.

3. Add the raspberries and mint to the chilled syrup and let sit for 15 minutes in the refrigerator.

4. To serve, scoop the figs and raspberries onto four dessert plates.

PER SERVING: Fat: 1 g **Protein:** 2 g **Carbohydrates:** 62 g **Sugar:** 57 g

BLACKBERRY COBBLER

CALORIES: 367
SERVES 8

8 WHOLE-WHEAT BISCUITS, UNBAKED
8 CUPS BLACKBERRIES
¼ CUP FLOUR
¾ CUP SUGAR
¼ CUP CREAM

1. Preheat oven to 350°F.

2. Prepare biscuit dough recipe, cut biscuit circles out, and set them aside.

3. Toss the blackberries, flour, and sugar together, then put the mixture into a 9" × 11" baking dish.

4. Bake the blackberries for 25 minutes, remove from oven, and place the unbaked biscuits on top of the hot berries.

5. Brush the biscuit tops with cream and return the cobbler to the oven to bake for another 25 minutes. Serve warm.

PER SERVING: Fat: 8 g **Protein:** 7 g **Carbohydrates:** 58 g **Sugar:** 26 g

---

MANGO SORBET

CALORIES: 60
SERVES 12

½ CUP SUGAR
¼ CUP WATER
3 CUPS MANGO PURÉE
¼ CUP LEMON JUICE

1. Combine sugar and water in a saucepan and heat just until sugar dissolves. Remove from heat and chill.

2. Combine chilled sugar syrup, mango purée, and lemon juice.

3. Freeze in an ice-cream freezer according to manufacturer's instructions.

PER SERVING: Fat: 0 g **Protein:** 0 g **Carbohydrates:** 15 g **Sugar:** 11 g

BLUEBERRY SORBET

CALORIES: 53
SERVES 12

½ CUP SUGAR
¼ CUP WATER
3 CUPS BLUEBERRY PURÉE
¼ CUP LEMON JUICE

1. Combine sugar and water in a saucepan and heat just until sugar dissolves. Remove from heat and chill.

2. Combine chilled sugar syrup, blueberry purée, and lemon juice.

3. Freeze in an ice-cream freezer according to manufacturer's instructions.

PER SERVING: Fat: 0 g **Protein:** 0 g **Carbohydrates:** 14 g **Sugar:** 9 g

PEAR SORBET

CALORIES: 64
SERVES 12

½ CUP SUGAR
¼ CUP WATER
3 CUPS POACHED PEAR PURÉE
¼ CUP LEMON JUICE

1. Combine sugar and water in a saucepan and heat just until sugar dissolves. Remove from heat and chill.

2. Combine chilled sugar syrup, pear purée, and lemon juice.

3. Freeze in an ice-cream freezer according to manufacturer's instructions.

PER SERVING: Fat: 0 g **Protein:** 0 g **Carbohydrates:** 16 g **Sugar:** 12 g

Sorbet Ice Cubes

Before putting the purée in the ice-cream maker, spoon them into an ice-cube tray and freeze solid. You can add them to iced tea, lemonade, or fruit punch for a delicious extra flavor. Plus you will get vitamins, antioxidants, and fiber from the puréed fruit. At the very least, squeeze some fresh lemon into your ice-cube trays to give your water some flavor.

APPLE PIE

CALORIES: 489
SERVES 6

- **2 ROLLED-OUT CIRCLES OF WHOLE-WHEAT PIE DOUGH**
- **5 CUPS PEELED, SLICED APPLES**
- **4 TABLESPOONS CORNSTARCH**
- **½ CUP SUGAR**
- **1 TABLESPOON APPLE PIE SPICE**
- **4 TABLESPOONS APPLE BUTTER**
- **2 TABLESPOONS SUGAR, FOR SPRINKLING ON TOP CRUST**

1. Preheat oven to 350°F.

2. Line pie pan with one of the pie-dough circles. Cut slits in the other pie-dough circle and set aside.

3. Mix apples in a bowl with cornstarch, sugar, and spice.

4. Pile the apples into the dough-lined pie pan, then dot them with the apple butter. Cover apples with the pie-dough circle with slits to form the top crust. Crimp edges together to seal the crust.

5. Brush the crust with water and sprinkle with sugar. Bake for 60 minutes.

PER SERVING: Fat: 18 g **Protein:** 3 g **Carbohydrates:** 77 g **Sugar:** 45 g

---

CANTALOUPE SORBET

CALORIES: 51
SERVES 12

- **½ CUP SUGAR**
- **¼ CUP WATER**
- **3 CUPS CANTALOUPE PURÉE**
- **¼ CUP LEMON JUICE**

1. Combine sugar and water in a saucepan and heat just until sugar dissolves. Remove from heat and chill.

2. Combine chilled sugar syrup, cantaloupe purée, and lemon juice.

3. Freeze in an ice-cream freezer according to manufacturer's instructions. If you don't have one, you can freeze the mixture in a 9" × 13" pan until frozen. Break it into chunks, process in a food processor, and return to the freezer in the pan. Repeat the processing after the mixture has frozen again to make a smooth, scoopable sorbet.

PER SERVING: Fat: 0 g **Protein:** 1 g **Carbohydrates:** 13 g **Sugar:** 9 g

OVEN-ROASTED PEARS

CALORIES: 217
SERVES 4

4 RIPE BOSC PEARS
1½ CUPS MARSALA WINE

1. Preheat oven to 450°F.

2. Place pears upright in a baking dish and pour the marsala wine over them. Bake the pears for 20 minutes. Add water or more marsala if the dish starts to get dry.

3. Baste the pears with the liquid in the dish and bake 20 minutes more.

4. Baste the pears again and bake longer until a knife inserted in a pear goes in easily.

5. Remove the pears from the oven and baste them several times as they cool. Serve at room temperature with a knife and fork.

PER SERVING: Fat: 0.5 g **Protein:** 1 g **Carbohydrates:** 31 g
Sugar: 22 g

CARAMEL CORN–CHOCOLATE TRUFFLES

CALORIES: 91
SERVES 18

2–3 CUPS CARAMEL CORN
1⅔ CUP CREAM
1 CUP CHOCOLATE CHIPS

1. Mince the caramel corn in a food processor by pulsing several times. Set aside in an airtight container.

2. Bring the cream to a boil in a saucepan and immediately remove from heat.

3. Add the chocolate chips, cover, and let sit for 3 minutes. Stir the chocolate and cream together until smooth. Refrigerate for 45–60 minutes.

4. Scoop heaping teaspoons of the chocolate mixture onto foil-lined cookie sheets and refrigerate until firm.

5. Roll the firm truffle balls in the minced caramel corn and serve within a few hours.

PER SERVING: Fat: 6 g **Protein:** 1 g **Carbohydrates:** 10 g
Sugar: 8 g

HAWAIIAN-STYLE SNOW CONES

CALORIES: 259
SERVES 4

- 4 TABLESPOONS RED BEAN PASTE
- 4 SMALL SCOOPS VANILLA ICE CREAM
- 4 CUPS SHAVED ICE
- ½ CUP FLAVORED SYRUP FOR SNOW CONES

1. Place a tablespoon of sweet red bean paste in the bottom of four insulated paper cones or cups.

2. Top the sweet red bean paste with a scoop of vanilla ice cream in each cone or cup.

3. Put a cup of shaved ice on top of the vanilla ice cream in each cone or cup.

4. Drizzle 2 tablespoons of flavored syrup over each shaved ice mound. Serve immediately.

PER SERVING: Fat: 7 g **Protein:** 3 g **Carbohydrates:** 48 g **Sugar:** 37 g

---

STRAWBERRY SORBET

CALORIES: 50
SERVES 12

- ½ CUP SUGAR
- ¼ CUP WATER
- 3 CUPS STRAWBERRY PURÉE
- ¼ CUP LEMON JUICE

1. Combine sugar and water in a saucepan and heat just until sugar dissolves. Remove from heat and chill.

2. Combine chilled sugar syrup, strawberry purée, and lemon juice.

3. Freeze in an ice-cream freezer according to manufacturer's instructions.

PER SERVING: Fat: 0 g **Protein:** 0 g **Carbohydrates:** 12 g **Sugar:** 8 g

Sorbet or Sherbet?

Sherbet (not "sherbert," as it's often mispronounced) includes milk. It's like a watery ice cream. Sorbets, Italian ices, and granites are all related, giving you a great fruity chill-down on a hot day or after an evening meal. If they are puréed, they will have less fiber, but you can always serve them with berries, cut-up peaches, or whatever is in season.

STUFFED APRICOTS

CALORIES: 255
SERVES 4

1 TABLESPOON BUTTER
4 RIPE APRICOTS
1/3 CUP SUGAR
1/4 CUP SOFT BUTTER
1 EGG WHITE
1/4 CUP GROUND ALMONDS
1/8 CUP BREAD CRUMBS
1/2 CUP WHITE WINE

1. Preheat oven to 350°F. Butter a baking dish large enough to fit 8 apricot halves snugly in one layer.

2. Cut the apricots in half and remove the stones. Place apricot halves cut-side up in the prepared baking dish. Set aside.

3. In a bowl, cream the sugar and butter together until fluffy. Beat in the egg white, then stir in the almonds and bread crumbs.

4. Place a scoop of the almond filling on top of each apricot. Pour the white wine around the apricots on the bottom of the baking dish.

5. Bake apricots uncovered for 45 minutes, basting with the liquid at the bottom of the pan.

PER SERVING: Fat: 14 g **Protein:** 4 g **Carbohydrates:** 24 g
Sugar: 18 g

ALMOND MACAROONS

CALORIES: 156
SERVES 12

2 EGG WHITES
1/4 CUP SUGAR
1/4 CUP APPLESAUCE
1 1/4 CUPS SHREDDED COCONUT
1/4 CUP CHOPPED CANDIED
   ORANGE PEEL
3/4 CUP GROUND ALMONDS
2 TABLESPOONS FLOUR

1. Preheat oven to 350°F. Line baking sheet pan with parchment paper.

2. Whip the egg whites with the sugar until frothy. Stir in the remaining ingredients.

3. Form mixture into walnut-size balls and place them on the prepared cookie sheet.

4. Bake for 20 minutes.

5. Cool, then peel cookies off the parchment paper.

PER SERVING: Fat: 9 g **Protein:** 3 g **Carbohydrates:** 15 g
Sugar: 7 g

APPLE TART TATIN

CALORIES: 414
SERVES 6

- **4 TABLESPOONS BUTTER**
- **½ CUP BROWN SUGAR**
- **6 APPLES, PEELED, CORED, AND QUARTERED**
- **1 SHEET FROZEN PUFF PASTRY, THAWED IN THE REFRIGERATOR**

1. Preheat oven to 375°F.

2. Sauté the butter and brown sugar in a cast-iron skillet until the foam subsides and it caramelizes. Remove from heat.

3. Place the apple quarters on the bottom of the pan, lining them up around the edge and ending in the center.

4. Cut the corners off the puff pastry to make a rough round and place it on the apples. Cut a small slit in the center to let steam escape.

5. Bake the skillet in the oven for 45 minutes. Remove, invert onto a plate, and carefully lift, leaving the tart on the plate. Cut into wedges and serve hot.

PER SERVING: Fat: 23 g **Protein:** 3 g **Carbohydrates:** 49 g **Sugar:** 32 g

---

BAKED APPLES

CALORIES: 346
SERVES 4

- **4 APPLES, CORED**
- **⅓ CUP BROWN SUGAR**
- **¼ CUP CHOPPED PECANS**
- **1 TEASPOON GRATED LEMON ZEST**
- **1 TEASPOON GROUND CINNAMON**
- **¼ CUP GOLDEN RAISINS**
- **¼ CUP BUTTER, MELTED**
- **⅔ CUP APPLE JUICE**

1. Preheat oven to 350°F.

2. Place the apples close together in a baking dish.

3. In a bowl, combine the brown sugar, pecans, lemon zest, cinnamon, and golden raisins. Sprinkle this mixture into the holes in the apples where the cores used to be. Drizzle the melted butter over the filling.

4. Pour juice into the baking dish around the bottom of the apples. Cover with foil and bake the apples for 30 minutes.

5. Uncover and baste the apples with the liquid at the bottom of the dish and return them to the oven for 10 minutes. Remove baked apples from the oven and serve warm with the basting liquid drizzled over them.

PER SERVING: Fat: 17 g **Protein:** 2 g **Carbohydrates:** 50 g **Sugar:** 45 g

CARROT CAKE

CALORIES: 488
SERVES 12

- 2 CUPS ALL-PURPOSE FLOUR
- 2 TEASPOONS BAKING POWDER
- 2 TEASPOONS BAKING SODA
- 1 TEASPOON SALT
- 1¾ CUPS SUGAR
- 1¼ CUPS VEGETABLE OIL
- 4 EGGS
- 3 CUPS SHREDDED CARROTS
- ½ CUP CHOPPED WALNUTS
- 2 TABLESPOONS SHREDDED COCONUT
- ¾ CUP CRUSHED PINEAPPLE

1. Preheat oven to 300°F. Grease and flour a 9" × 13" × 2" rectangular pan. Set aside.

2. Combine the flour, baking powder, baking soda, and salt in a bowl and set aside.

3. Combine the sugar and oil in a mixing bowl. Add the eggs one at a time, beating after each addition. Add the flour mixture and mix well. Add the carrots, walnuts, coconut, and pineapple and mix well.

4. Scrape the batter into the prepared pan and bake for 45 minutes or until a toothpick inserted in the middle comes out clean.

5. Let cool to room temperature before cutting and serving.

PER SERVING: Fat: 30 g **Protein:** 5.5 g **Carbohydrates:** 51 g **Sugar:** 32 g

Cream Cheese Frosting

To make frosting for the carrot cake, cream ½ cup softened cream cheese, ¼ cup softened butter, and 1 teaspoon vanilla using an electric mixer on low. Slowly add 1½ cups powdered sugar. When frosting is fluffy, spread on the cake. Garnish with orange or lemon zest for added tang.

PINEAPPLE UPSIDE-DOWN CUPCAKES

CALORIES: 353
SERVES 10

NONSTICK COOKING SPRAY
¼ CUP UNSALTED BUTTER
¾ CUP BROWN SUGAR
1 CUP DICED PINEAPPLE
¼ CUP DRIED CHERRIES
2 EGG WHITES, ROOM TEMPERATURE
½ CUP SALTED BUTTER
1 CUP SUGAR
2 EGG YOLKS
1 TEASPOON VANILLA
1½ CUPS FLOUR
2 TEASPOONS BAKING POWDER
½ CUP MILK

1. Preheat oven to 350°F. Prepare the cups or tins with nonstick spray.

2. Melt unsalted butter and brown sugar in a saucepan over low heat until the mixture starts to foam and the sugar starts to caramelize. Remove from heat and pour into the muffin tin, dividing evenly among 10 cups.

3. Divide the pineapple and cherries among the muffin tin cups on top of the caramelized sugar mixture and set aside. Whip the egg whites to stiff peaks and set aside.

4. Cream the salted butter with the sugar with an electric mixer until fluffy. Beat in the egg yolks and vanilla. In a separate bowl combine the flour and baking powder. Add it to the butter-egg mixture in two parts, alternating with the milk. Fold the whipped egg whites into the cake batter and pour the batter over the fruit in the muffin tin.

5. Bake for 25 minutes. Remove the cupcakes from the oven, then invert the tin onto a cookie sheet with sides. Leave the muffin tin on top for 5 minutes, then remove it and let the cupcakes cool.

PER SERVING: Fat: 15 g **Protein:** 4 g **Carbohydrates:** 50 g
Sugar: 38 g

BLUEBERRY CLAFOUTI

CALORIES: 253
SERVES 6

½ TABLESPOON SOFT BUTTER
3 EGGS
¼ CUP CREAM
1 CUP WHOLE MILK
¼ CUP SUGAR
PINCH OF SALT
1 TABLESPOON VANILLA
⅔ CUP FLOUR
4 CUPS BLUEBERRIES
¼ CUP POWDERED SUGAR

1. Preheat oven to 350°F. Butter a 10" round baking dish.

2. Mix the eggs, cream, milk, sugar, salt, vanilla, and flour with an electric mixer on medium speed for about 5 minutes until frothy.

3. Pour ¼ of the batter into the prepared baking dish and bake for 5 minutes. Remove from the oven.

4. Sprinkle the blueberries evenly over the baked batter in the dish and then pour the rest of the batter over them.

5. Bake 35 minutes longer. Remove from the oven and let cool. Sprinkle powdered sugar over it and serve at room temperature.

PER SERVING: Fat: 7 g **Protein:** 6 g **Carbohydrates:** 40 g **Sugar:** 20 g

French Country Desserts

French rustic tarts are a marvel of simplicity and ingenuity. A simple batter is transformed into a fruity delight. Fresh fruits straight from the orchard or garden are put to good use. Add nuts for extra fiber and spices to spike the flavors.

POACHED PEARS

CALORIES: 197
SERVES 4

2 TABLESPOONS LEMON JUICE

4 RIPE PEARS, PEELED, HALVED, AND CORED

½ CUP SUGAR

2 CUPS WATER

1 STRIP LEMON PEEL

1 VANILLA BEAN, SPLIT LENGTHWISE

1. Rub the lemon juice on the pears.

2. In a saucepan, combine the sugar and water and heat over low to dissolve the sugar. Add the lemon peel and vanilla bean and simmer for 5 minutes.

3. Add the pear halves to the simmering liquid and place a piece of parchment paper over the surface of the liquid. Poke a few slits in the paper to let steam escape.

4. Simmer the pears until tender for 20–25 minutes. Poke them with a paring knife to test for tenderness.

5. Remove from heat and let pears cool in poaching liquid. Refrigerate in liquid until ready to serve.

PER SERVING: Fat: 1 g **Protein:** 1 g **Carbohydrates:** 50 g **Sugar:** 28 g

Poached Fruit

Fruit can be poached in juice, wine, or water. The wonderful thing about poaching fruit is that it will keep for days if you refrigerate it; it'll keep for weeks if you freeze it. For fruits that tend to discolor—think apples and pears—use a bit of lemon juice in the poaching liquid to acidulate it and prevent browning.

POACHED QUINCE

CALORIES: 125
SERVES 4

2 TABLESPOONS LEMON JUICE
2 QUINCES, PEELED, CORED, AND SLICED
½ CUP SUGAR
2 CUPS WATER
1 STRIP LEMON PEEL
1 VANILLA BEAN, SPLIT LENGTHWISE

1. Rub the lemon juice on the quinces.

2. In a saucepan, combine the sugar and water and heat over low to dissolve the sugar. Add the lemon peel and vanilla bean and simmer for 5 minutes.

3. Add the quince slices to the simmering liquid and place a piece of parchment paper over the surface of the liquid. Poke a few slits in the paper to let steam escape.

4. Simmer the quinces until tender, 20–25 minutes. Poke them with a paring knife to test for tenderness.

5. Remove from heat and let quinces cool in poaching liquid. Refrigerate in liquid until ready to serve.

PER SERVING: Fat: 0 g **Protein:** 0 g **Carbohydrates:** 32 g **Sugar:** 29 g

The Allure of the Quince

Quinces were known by the ancient Greeks as "love apples." They grow on beautiful flowering trees, and the fruit looks a bit gnarled. They make excellent jams and jellies because they have a great deal of pectin, the stiffening agent in jams and jellies. Their distinctive flavor is very good in combination with other fruits in compotes.

RUM-RAISIN RICE PUDDING

CALORIES: 390
SERVES 6

½ CUP RAISINS

½ CUP DARK RUM

3 CUPS MILK

1 CUP UNCOOKED BROWN BASMATI RICE

½ CUP SUGAR

1 TEASPOON VANILLA

1 TABLESPOON GRATED ORANGE ZEST

1 MASHED BANANA

½ CUP CREAM

1. Preheat the oven to 325°F.

2. Combine the raisins and rum and set aside.

3. Mix the milk and brown rice in a saucepan and bring to a boil, stirring occasionally. Cover, reduce heat to low, and simmer for 15 minutes. Remove from heat.

4. Stir in the raisins, rum, sugar, vanilla, orange zest, banana, and cream. Spoon the rice pudding into a baking dish, cover with foil, and place it in a larger roasting pan. Pour hot water around the sides of the pudding dish into the roasting pan to make a water bath and bake for 30 minutes. Take off the foil and bake another 15 minutes.

5. Remove from the oven and serve warm or let cool, cover, and chill in the refrigerator.

PER SERVING: Fat: 10 g **Protein:** 7 g **Carbohydrates:** 58 g **Sugar:** 32 g

Fruit Puddings

Puddings come with many bases, including bread, tapioca, rice, and cornstarch. Most puddings include milk, cream, and lots of sugar. However, when you have too much coming from your orchard, garden, or bushes, you can use a lot more as it will cook down. Also, many puddings are extremely delicious and healthy, such as rice and tapioca.

SQUASH PUMPKIN PIE

CALORIES: 437
SERVES 6

- 1 CUP COOKED PUMPKIN PURÉE
- 1 CUP COOKED BUTTERNUT SQUASH PURÉE
- 1 CUP BROWN SUGAR
- 1 TABLESPOON FLOUR
- ½ TEASPOON SALT
- 1 TABLESPOON PUMPKIN PIE SPICE
- ¼ TEASPOON GROUND CORIANDER
- 1⅓ CUPS CREAM
- 2 EGGS
- 1 TEASPOON VANILLA
- 1 ROLLED-OUT CIRCLE OF WHOLE-WHEAT PIE DOUGH

1. Preheat oven to 400°F.

2. In a bowl, combine all the ingredients except the pie dough with a whisk.

3. Line a pie pan with the pie dough, flute the edges, and pour filling into it.

4. Bake 15 minutes. Turn the oven down to 350°F and bake another 45 minutes. Cover crust edge with foil if it starts to get too dark during baking.

5. Cool completely before cutting.

PER SERVING: Fat: 24 g **Protein:** 6 g **Carbohydrates:** 51 g **Sugar:** 14 g

Pumpkin Pie Spice

Although you can buy prepared pumpkin pie spice mixes, you can adapt it to your own tastes by making it yourself. Mix 1½ teaspoons ground cinnamon, ½ teaspoon freshly grated nutmeg, ½ teaspoon ground ginger, ¼ teaspoon allspice, ¼ teaspoon ground cloves. If you are going to use the spices immediately, mince some fresh ginger into the mixture and omit the dried ginger.

POLENTA PEAR TART

CALORIES: 345
SERVES 6

2 ROLLED-OUT CIRCLES OF
CORNMEAL DOUGH
¼ CUP GROUND ALMONDS
2 TABLESPOONS SUGAR
6–8 POACHED PEAR HALVES
1 EGG, BEATEN
2 TABLESPOONS COARSE SUGAR

1. Preheat oven to 375°F.

2. Line a 9" fluted tart pan with a removable bottom with one of the dough circles.

3. Sprinkle the dough in the tart pan with the ground almonds and sugar. Arrange the pear halves on the almond-sugar mixture, cut-sides down and points facing in.

4. Place the second dough circle on top of the pears and press down around the rim to cut off extra dough, if any. Brush with egg and sprinkle with coarse sugar.

5. Bake 40 minutes, let cool to room temperature, slice, and serve.

PER SERVING: Fat: 4 g **Protein:** 8 g **Carbohydrates:** 68 g **Sugar:** 39 g

Polenta Is Versatile

Puddings, piecrust, muffins, and other lovely creations from polenta are healthful and so good for you. Polenta was commonly used by peasants in the past, but you can benefit from its nutrients today. Avoid white-flour piecrusts, cornstarch puddings, and muffins made with white flour.

SUNFLOWER SEED SHORTBREAD

CALORIES: 163
SERVES 12

½ CUP BUTTER, SOFTENED
¼ CUP SUGAR
½ TEASPOON VANILLA
1 CUP ALL-PURPOSE FLOUR
¼ CUP WHOLE-WHEAT FLOUR
½ TEASPOON SALT
1 EGG WHITE
½ CUP TOASTED SUNFLOWER SEEDS, SHELLED

1. Preheat oven to 325° F.

2. Combine butter and sugar in a bowl and mix with a wooden spoon or electric mixer until slightly fluffy but not whipped.

3. Add vanilla and mix well.

4. Add flours and salt and mix to form a smooth dough.

5. Press dough into a 9" pie plate, and brush the dough with the egg white. Sprinkle the sunflower seeds on top of the dough, press in, and bake for 20 minutes. Remove from oven and cut into 12 wedges immediately. Let cool.

PER SERVING: Fat: 10 g **Protein:** 3 g **Carbohydrates:** 15 g
Sugar: 5 g

OATMEAL RAISIN COOKIES

CALORIES: 327
SERVES 24

- 1½ **CUPS BUTTER, SOFTENED**
- 1½ **CUPS BROWN SUGAR**
- 1 **CUP SUGAR**
- 2 **EGGS**
- ½ **CUP WATER**
- 2 **TEASPOONS VANILLA**
- 6 **CUPS ROLLED OATS, QUICK-COOK**
- 2 **CUPS FLOUR**
- 2 **TEASPOONS SALT**
- 1 **TEASPOON BAKING SODA**
- 3 **CUPS RAISINS**

1. Preheat oven to 350°F.

2. Cream the butter, brown sugar, and sugar with an electric mixer until fluffy.

3. Add eggs, water, and vanilla and combine well, scraping the sides of the bowl frequently.

4. Mix the oats, flour, salt, and baking soda together in a bowl. Add it to the butter mixture, stirring well to combine into a smooth dough. Stir in the raisins.

5. Drop dough in mounds onto a cookie sheet. Press down with a wet palm to flatten them slightly. Bake cookies 12 minutes. Cool on a rack.

PER SERVING: Fat: 11 g **Protein:** 5 g **Carbohydrates:** 53 g **Sugar:** 16 g

Oatmeal

Sneak oatmeal into brownies, bars, and other rich cookies to scrub the fat, cholesterol, and trans fat out of your arteries and intestines. Cook up some Irish oatmeal for breakfast and then add it to other foods, including cookies.

WHOLE-WHEAT PEANUT BUTTER COOKIES

CALORIES: 283
SERVES 18

6 OUNCES SOFT BUTTER

1 CUP PEANUT BUTTER

1 CUP BROWN SUGAR

½ CUP SUGAR

2 EGGS

2 TEASPOONS VANILLA

1½ CUPS ALL-PURPOSE FLOUR

1 CUP WHOLE-WHEAT FLOUR

¼ TEASPOON SALT

1¼ TEASPOONS BAKING POWDER

½ TEASPOON BAKING SODA

½ CUP SUGAR IN A BOWL

1. Preheat oven to 350°F.

2. Cream together the butter, peanut butter, brown sugar, and sugar with an electric mixer until fluffy.

3. Add eggs and vanilla and combine well. Scrape the sides of the bowl.

4. Mix the flours, salt, baking powder, and baking soda together in a bowl. Add it to the butter mixture, stirring well to combine into a smooth dough.

5. Form dough into 1" balls and place them on a cookie sheet. Dip a dinner fork into the bowl of sugar and press a crosshatch mark into each cookie. Dip fork frequently into the sugar to prevent sticking. Bake cookies 10 minutes. Cool on a rack.

PER SERVING: Fat: 15 g **Protein:** 6 g **Carbohydrates:** 32 g
Sugar: 26 g

SESAME SEED COOKIES

CALORIES: 65
SERVES 15

4½ TEASPOONS HONEY
1½ TABLESPOONS BUTTER
½ CUP POWDERED SUGAR
1 TABLESPOON WATER
½ CUP SESAME SEEDS
PINCH OF SALT
2 TABLESPOONS FLOUR

1. Stir the honey, butter, powdered sugar, and water together in a saucepan. Turn the heat to medium and bring to a boil. Boil for 1 minute and remove from heat.

2. Stir in the sesame seeds, salt, and flour. Let cool to room temperature.

3. Preheat oven to 350°F. Line baking sheets with parchment paper or silicone mats.

4. Roll the cookie dough into balls, and place them 4" apart from each other on the prepared baking sheets.

5. Bake for 8 minutes, then let cool on racks. Peel off the cooled cookies and store in an airtight container.

PER SERVING: Fat: 3 g **Protein:** 2 g **Carbohydrates:** 6 g
Sugar: 5 g

Learning About Seeds

Seeds are delicious, high in both fiber and in protein. However, people with diverticulitis or diverticulosis cannot eat them. They get caught in the little intestinal pockets that these diseases produce. There they go bad and cause pain, gas, and attendant swelling. Children and adults without these diseases will benefit from a good daily dose of seeds in the diet. Eating nuts and seeds while you're healthy will help prevent intestinal problems.

DANDY CANDY

2 CUPS SUGAR

2 TABLESPOONS COCOA POWDER

½ CUP MILK

6 TABLESPOONS BUTTER

½ CUP PEANUT BUTTER

2 CUPS ROLLED OATS

½ TEASPOON VANILLA

1. Mix the sugar and cocoa powder together in a saucepan.

2. Add the milk and butter and bring to a boil. Cook for 2 minutes and remove from heat.

3. Stir in the peanut butter, oats, and vanilla.

4. Lay out waxed paper. Drop teaspoons of the mixture onto it and let them cool.

PER SERVING: Fat: 8 g **Protein:** 4 g **Carbohydrates:** 30 g **Sugar:** 26 g

Unbaked Sweets

There are many kinds of fudge-type candies that do not require baking. The more seeds, nuts, and dried fruit you can add to them, the better. Big bowls and wooden spoons will facilitate the process. Start with the Dandy Candy recipe and then invent your own variations.

PECAN PIE BARS

CALORIES: 236
SERVES 24

1¼ CUPS BUTTER, DIVIDED
1 CUP ALL-PURPOSE FLOUR
1 CUP WHOLE-WHEAT FLOUR
½ TEASPOON SALT
1½ CUPS BROWN SUGAR, DIVIDED
⅓ CUP BROWN RICE SYRUP
2 TABLESPOONS CREAM
2 CUPS CHOPPED PECANS

1. Preheat oven to 350°F. Line a 13" × 9" × 2" baking pan with nonstick foil.

2. Cut ¾ cup of the butter into small pieces and put them in a food processor with the flours, salt, and ½ cup brown sugar. Pulse until sandy in texture.

3. Press the mixture into the bottom of the prepared pan and bake for 20 minutes.

4. Meanwhile, melt the remaining ½ cup butter in a saucepan, add the remaining 1 cup brown sugar, brown rice syrup, and cream. Simmer for 1 minute. Stir, remove from heat, add the pecans, and stir to combine.

5. Pour the filling onto the crust and spread to make it even. Return to the oven to bake for 20 minutes. Cool completely before cutting.

PER SERVING: Fat: 17 g **Protein:** 3 g **Carbohydrates:** 20 g **Sugar:** 15 g

CHAPTER 12: DESSERTS   355

APRICOT–CHOCOLATE CHIP SQUARES

CALORIES: 411
SERVES 18

1 CUP UNSALTED BUTTER, SOFTENED
¾ CUP BROWN SUGAR
¾ CUP SUGAR
2 EGGS
1 TEASPOON VANILLA
2¼ CUPS ALL-PURPOSE FLOUR
½ TEASPOON SALT
1 TEASPOON BAKING SODA
1 CUP CHOCOLATE CHIPS
1 CUP CHOPPED DRIED APRICOTS
2 CUPS GRANOLA
1 CUP CHOPPED CASHEWS

1. Preheat oven to 375°F.

2. Cream the butter, brown sugar, and sugar with an electric mixer until fluffy.

3. Add eggs and vanilla and combine well. Scrape the sides of the bowl.

4. Mix the flour, salt, and baking soda together in a bowl. Add it to the butter mixture, stirring well to combine into a smooth dough. Stir in chocolate chips, dried apricots, granola, and cashews.

5. Press dough into a foil-lined 15½" × 10½" × 1" baking pan and bake for 20 minutes. Cool on a rack and cut into squares.

PER SERVING: Fat: 22 g **Protein:** 7 g **Carbohydrates:** 47 g **Sugar:** 32 g

POPCORN COOKIES

CALORIES: 50
SERVES 18

- **2–3 CUPS PLAIN POPCORN**
- **1 TABLESPOON BUTTER, MELTED**
- **2 EGG WHITES, ROOM TEMPERATURE**
- **⅔ CUP SUGAR**
- **1 TEASPOON VANILLA**
- **½ TEASPOON SALT**
- **36 BLANCHED, SKINLESS ALMONDS, TOASTED**

1. Preheat oven to 325°F. Line baking sheets with parchment paper or silicone mats.

2. Mince the popcorn in a food processor by pulsing several times. Measure 1½ cups for the recipe. (Discard any extra.) Toss the popcorn with the melted butter.

3. Whip the egg whites until frothy. Add the sugar gradually, continuing to whip the egg whites to stiff peaks.

4. Fold the egg whites and popcorn together. Stir in the vanilla and salt.

5. Drop teaspoons of the popcorn mixture onto the prepared baking sheets and top each one with an almond. Bake for 7 minutes. Let cool and store in an airtight container.

PER SERVING: Fat: 2 g **Protein:** 1 g **Carbohydrates:** 8 g **Sugar:** 7 g

Blanching and Toasting Almonds

To blanch and skin whole almonds, boil them for 1 minute. Drain and cool for a few minutes. Slip the skins off by pinching the almonds between your thumb and forefinger. The skins will slip right off and the almonds will pop out. To toast almonds, place them on a cookie sheet in a 350°F oven for 12–15 minutes.

CORNMEAL COOKIES

CALORIES: 248
SERVES 9

½ CUP SOFT BUTTER
¾ CUP SUGAR
1 EGG
1 CUP ALL-PURPOSE FLOUR
½ CUP CORNMEAL
½ TEASPOON BAKING SODA
½ TEASPOON SALT
¼ CUP DRIED CURRANTS
1 TEASPOON GRATED ORANGE ZEST

1. Preheat oven to 350°F. Line baking sheets with parchment paper or silicone mats.

2. Combine the butter, sugar, and egg with an electric mixer until smooth.

3. Add the flour, cornmeal, baking soda, and salt. Mix to combine.

4. Stir in the currants and orange zest. Put tablespoons of the dough onto the prepared baking sheets, 1" apart from each other.

5. Bake 10–12 minutes. Cool on a rack.

PER SERVING: Fat: 11 g **Protein:** 3 g **Carbohydrates:** 35 g **Sugar:** 27 g

Cornmeal in Your Cookies!

Coarsely ground cornmeal crisps up nicely when baked. Cornmeal is satisfying and loaded with fiber that takes time to digest. It leaves you feeling full for a good long time and releases energy slowly without any peaks or valleys. Experiment with white or yellow cornmeal, adding it to brownies and other super-rich treats for a healthful note.

MACADAMIA MANDELBROT

CALORIES: 265
SERVES 6

2 OUNCES UNSALTED BUTTER, SOFTENED
¼ CUP SUGAR
1 EGG
½ TEASPOON VANILLA
1 TEASPOON BAKING POWDER
PINCH OF SALT
½ CUP ALL-PURPOSE FLOUR
½ CUP WHOLE-WHEAT FLOUR
½ CUP TOASTED MACADAMIA NUTS

1. Preheat oven to 350°F. Grease a baking sheet pan.

2. Cream the butter and sugar with an electric mixer. Add egg and vanilla and beat to incorporate.

3. In a separate bowl combine the baking powder, salt, and flours. Add this dry mixture to the egg-butter mixture and combine to make a smooth dough. Stir in macadamia nuts.

4. Scrape dough out onto the prepared baking sheet pan and form it into a domed log using wet fingers. Bake for 30 minutes, remove from oven and cool for 5 minutes. Turn the oven down to 275°F.

5. Cut the log into ¾"-wide slices and place the slices back on the baking sheet, cut-sides facing up. Bake 15 minutes, turn cookies over, and bake 10 minutes more. Cool on a rack.

PER SERVING: Fat: 15 g **Protein:** 4 g **Carbohydrates:** 25 g **Sugar:** 17 g

WALNUT BISCOTTI

CALORIES: 96
SERVES 10

1 EGG
¼ CUP SUGAR
¾ TEASPOON BAKING POWDER
PINCH OF SALT
½ CUP ALL-PURPOSE FLOUR
¼ CUP WHOLE-WHEAT FLOUR
½ CUP TOASTED WALNUTS,
** CHOPPED**

1. Preheat oven to 350°F. Grease a baking sheet pan or line it with parchment.

2. Whip the egg and sugar together with an electric mixer until light yellow in color and very fluffy.

3. In a separate bowl combine the baking powder, salt, and flours. Add dry mixture to the egg mixture and combine to make a smooth dough. Stir in walnuts.

4. Scrape dough out onto the prepared baking sheet pan and form it into a broad, flat log using wet fingers. Bake for 30 minutes, remove from oven, and cool for 5 minutes. Turn the oven down to 275°F.

5. Cut the log into ½"-wide slices and place the slices back on the baking sheet, cut-sides facing up. Bake 15 minutes, turn cookies over, and bake 10 minutes more. Cool on a rack.

PER SERVING: Fat: 4 g **Protein:** 2 g **Carbohydrates:** 12 g
Sugar: 5 g

Biscotti

Biscotti means "twice baked" in Italian. It starts out like a sweet bread and then, cut into slices and rebaked, turns into a delicious cookie with endless variations. Various dried fruits, different kinds of nuts, and other flavorings spike biscotti. You can throw in seeds to add to the crunch.

CRANBERRY PISTACHIO BISCOTTI

CALORIES: 152
SERVES 10

2 OUNCES UNSALTED BUTTER, SOFTENED

¼ CUP SUGAR

1 EGG

½ TEASPOON VANILLA

¼ TEASPOON GRATED NUTMEG

1 TEASPOON BAKING POWDER

PINCH OF SALT

½ CUP ALL-PURPOSE FLOUR

½ CUP WHOLE-WHEAT FLOUR

½ CUP SHELLED PISTACHIOS

¼ CUP DRIED CRANBERRIES, CHOPPED

1. Preheat oven to 350°F. Grease a baking sheet pan.

2. Cream the butter and sugar with an electric mixer. Add egg and vanilla and beat to incorporate.

3. In a separate bowl combine the nutmeg, baking powder, salt, and flours. Add this dry mixture to the egg-butter mixture and combine to make a smooth dough. Stir in pistachios and cranberries.

4. Scrape dough out onto the prepared baking sheet pan and form it into a broad, flat log using wet fingers. Bake for 30 minutes, remove from oven, and cool for 5 minutes. Turn the oven down to 275°F.

5. Cut the log into ½"-wide slices and place the slices back on the baking sheet, cut-sides facing up. Bake 15 minutes, turn cookies over, and bake 10 minutes more. Cool on a rack.

PER SERVING: Fat: 8 g **Protein:** 3 g **Carbohydrates:** 17 g **Sugar:** 9 g

MOM'S GOLDEN SQUARES

CALORIES: 275
SERVES 12

½ **TABLESPOON SOFT BUTTER**
2 **CUPS GRAHAM CRACKER CRUMBS**
1 **CUP CHOCOLATE CHIPS**
½ **CUP CHOPPED WALNUTS**
1 **CAN SWEETENED CONDENSED MILK**

1. Preheat oven to 350°F.

2. Butter an 8"-square baking pan, line it with waxed paper, and grease the waxed paper. Set aside.

3. Combine the graham cracker crumbs, chocolate chips, and walnuts in a mixing bowl. Add the sweetened condensed milk and mix to combine.

4. Scrape the mixture into the prepared pan and bake for 40 minutes until the top is golden brown.

5. Remove from the oven and invert the pan onto a foil-lined flat surface. Remove the waxed paper and let mixture cool before cutting into squares.

PER SERVING: Fat: 12 g **Protein:** 5 g **Carbohydrates:** 38 g
Sugar: 15 g

When You Can't Go Wrong

It's hard to make a non-delicious cookie or bar when you use chocolate chips and nuts. Stick with whole-wheat flour whenever possible or cut white flour with a grain flour. All sorts of nuts work for the fiber balance. Try mixing various sorts of toasted nuts, such as sweet hazelnuts with more tart walnuts. Mix almonds with pecans for a new crunch.

PECAN LACE COOKIES

4½ TEASPOONS DARK CORN SYRUP
1½ TABLESPOONS BUTTER
½ CUP POWDERED SUGAR
1 TABLESPOON WATER
½ CUP FINELY CHOPPED PECANS
PINCH OF SALT
2 TABLESPOONS FLOUR

1. Stir the corn syrup, butter, powdered sugar, and water together in a saucepan. Turn the heat to medium and bring to a boil. Boil for 1 minute and remove from heat.

2. Stir in the pecans, salt, and flour. Let cool to room temperature.

3. Preheat oven to 350°F. Line baking sheets with parchment paper or silicone mats.

4. Roll the cookie dough into balls and place them 4" apart from each other on the prepared baking sheets.

5. Bake for 8 minutes, then let cool on racks. Peel off the cooled cookies and store in an airtight container.

PER SERVING: Fat: 4 g **Protein:** 1 g **Carbohydrates:** 7 g **Sugar:** 6 g

Tuiles

Tuiles are lace cookies that have been molded into a curved shape while they are still warm. The name is French for "tiles" and refers to curved terra-cotta roof tiles. To mold them, put a piece of parchment paper over the cookies right after they come out of the oven and roll the two parchment papers with the cookies sandwiched between them up on a rolling pin. Let cool completely, then carefully unroll the tuiles.

HAZELNUT STICKS

CALORIES: 178
SERVES 12

5 TABLESPOONS SOFT BUTTER
½ CUP SUGAR
1 EGG
1 CUP TOASTED HAZELNUTS
1 CUP ALL-PURPOSE FLOUR

1. Cream the butter and sugar with an electric mixer until smooth.

2. Add the egg, beat it in, and scrape down the sides of the bowl.

3. Add the hazelnuts and mix. Add the flour and mix to combine.

4. Wrap the dough in plastic wrap, press it down into a ½"-thick, 3"-wide rectangle and refrigerate for 4 hours.

5. Preheat oven to 350°F. Line baking sheets with parchment paper or silicone mats. Remove the dough from the freezer, unwrap, and slice into ½"-thick sticks. Bake 10 minutes, turn the cookies over, and bake 5–10 minutes longer, depending on how dark you want them to be. Cool on a rack.

PER SERVING: Fat: 11 g **Protein:** 3 g **Carbohydrates:** 18 g **Sugar:** 13 g

HIDDEN SURPRISE CAKES

CALORIES: 124
SERVES 12

NONSTICK COOKING SPRAY

1 CUP UNBLEACHED ALL-PURPOSE FLOUR

⅛ TEASPOON SALT

1 TEASPOON BAKING POWDER

3 LARGE EGGS

¾ CUP SUGAR

1 TABLESPOON LEMON JUICE

½ TEASPOON LEMON ZEST (OPTIONAL)

6 TABLESPOONS HOT SKIM MILK

1 (1.2-OUNCE) PACKAGE ORGANIC DARK-CHOCOLATE PEPPERMINT CUPS

1 TABLESPOON COCOA POWDER

1. Preheat oven to 350°. Treat a 12-section muffin pan with nonstick spray or line with foil liners.

2. In a small bowl, mix together the flour, salt, and baking powder. Add the eggs to the bowl of a food processor or a mixing bowl; pulse or beat until fluffy and lemon colored. Add the sugar, lemon juice, and the optional lemon zest, if using; pulse or beat to mix. Add the flour mixture; process or mix just enough to blend. Add the hot milk and process or mix until blended.

3. Spoon the batter halfway up the muffin sections in the prepared muffin pan. Cut each peppermint cup into 4 equal pieces. Add 1 piece to each muffin section. Spoon the remaining batter over the top of the candy.

4. Bake for 15 minutes or until the cakes are light golden brown and firm to touch. Dust the tops of the cakes with cocoa. Move to a rack to cool.

PER SERVING: Fat: 3 g **Protein:** 3 g **Carbohydrates:** 23 g
Sugar: 15 g

Sweet Savvy

Dove Dark Chocolate Promises are sodium-free, while Dove Milk Chocolate Promises have 25 milligrams of sodium per serving. Some premium chocolates are even higher in sodium content. Not all chocolates are created equal, so be sure you check the labels.

STEAMED RASPBERRY-LEMON CUSTARD

CALORIES: 121
SERVES 4

2 LARGE EGGS

¼ TEASPOON CREAM OF TARTAR

1 LEMON, ZESTED AND JUICED

¼ TEASPOON PURE LEMON EXTRACT

3 TABLESPOONS UNBLEACHED ALL-PURPOSE FLOUR

¼ CUP GRANULATED SUGAR

NONSTICK COOKING SPRAY

40 FRESH RASPBERRIES

12 ADDITIONAL FRESH RASPBERRIES (OPTIONAL)

2–4 TEASPOONS POWDERED SUGAR (OPTIONAL)

FRESH MINT LEAVES (OPTIONAL)

1. Separate the egg yolks and whites. Add the egg whites to a large bowl and set aside the yolks. Use an electric mixer or wire whisk to beat the egg whites until frothy. Add the cream of tartar; continue to whip or whisk until soft peaks form.

2. In a small bowl, mix together the lemon zest, lemon juice, lemon extract, flour, sugar, and egg yolks; gently fold into the whites with a spatula.

3. Treat 4 (6-ounce) ramekins with nonstick spray. Place 10 raspberries in the bottom of each. Spoon the batter into the ramekins and set them in a steamer with a lid; cover and steam for 15–20 minutes.

4. To remove the custards from the ramekins, run a thin knife around edges; turn upside down onto plates. Garnish with raspberries, mint, and a dusting of powdered sugar, if desired.

PER SERVING: **Fat:** 3 g **Protein:** 4 g **Carbohydrates:** 22 g **Sugar:** 13 g

Steaming Savvy

To steam custards at the same time with other dishes that might affect taste, wrap the ramekins in plastic wrap (so they won't pick up the other aromas) and put them in the top tier of the steamer.

OLD-FASHIONED APPLE AND PEACH CRISP

CALORIES: 360
SERVES 4

NONSTICK COOKING SPRAY

2 TART APPLES, PEELED, CORED, AND SLICED

4 MEDIUM PEACHES, BLANCHED, SKINS AND PITS REMOVED, SLICED

JUICE OF ½ LEMON

½ CUP FLOUR

¼ CUP DARK BROWN SUGAR

½ TEASPOON CINNAMON

½ TEASPOON CORIANDER SEED, GROUND

½ TEASPOON CARDAMOM SEED, GROUND

½ TEASPOON SALT

1 CUP OATMEAL

½ STICK BUTTER, SOFTENED

VANILLA ICE CREAM OR WHIPPED CREAM (OPTIONAL)

IN THIS RECIPE YOU CAN SUBSTITUTE LOW-FAT FROZEN YOGURT FOR ICE CREAM OR WHIPPED CREAM TO MAKE THIS A HEALTHIER DESSERT. YOU COULD ALSO REPLACE THE BUTTER WITH HEART-HEALTHY MARGARINE.

1. Preheat the oven to 350°F. Prepare a gratin dish or baking dish with nonstick spray.

2. Distribute the apple and peach slices in the dish and sprinkle with lemon juice.

3. Using your hands, thoroughly mix together the flour, brown sugar, spices, salt, oatmeal, and butter. Spread over the crisp and bake for 45 minutes, or until the fruit is bubbling and the top is brown. Serve with vanilla ice cream or whipped cream.

PER SERVING: Fat: 14 g **Protein:** 6 g **Carbohydrates:** 60 g **Sugar:** 39 g

7-Day Meal Plans to Achieve Your Weight-Loss Goals

The following meal plans are between 1,200–1,800 calories. These are perfect for incorporating into your lifestyle to achieve your weight-loss goals. The most important part of a meal plan is the composition of calories coming from protein, vegetables, fruits, and whole grains. Meals with asterisks indicate that the recipe can be found in this book.

DAY 1

BREAKFAST	SNACK	LUNCH	SNACK	DINNER
Tomato and Feta Frittata*	Apple with cinnamon and Stevia	Blood Orange Salad with Shrimp and Baby Spinach*	2 tablespoons hummus 1 cup carrots, celery, and peppers	Garlic shrimp with bok choy 1 cup green beans

DAY 2

BREAKFAST	SNACK	LUNCH	SNACK	DINNER
1 egg (poached, fried, or scrambled) 1 whole-wheat English muffin or Ezekial English Muffin (Tip: serve the egg on top) 1 slice tomato 1 apple	¼ cup almonds 1 plum	Greek Chicken Pita* 1 cup grapes	2 celery stalks 2 Laughing Cow wedges	6 ounces scallops on skewers with lemon 2 cups baby spinach 5 grilled asparagus

DAY 3

BREAKFAST	SNACK	LUNCH	SNACK
2 whole-grain waffles 1 tablespoon natural peanut butter or almond butter ½ banana sliced	1 cup cottage cheese ½ cup pineapple	Sunflower Veggie Burger* 1 cup baby carrots 1 cup arugula	¼ cup healthy nut trail mix 1 cup carrot sticks

DINNER	DESSERT
Sesame-pepper salmon kebabs 1 medium-size baked potato (Tip: top with 1 tablespoon of plain Greek yogurt)	Fruit kebab

DAY 4

BREAKFAST	SNACK	LUNCH	SNACK	DINNER
Spinach and Gorgonzola Egg White Omelet*	1 cup 0% Greek yogurt ½ teaspoon organic honey 1 teaspoon ground flax seed	Veggie Burrito*	1 serving of whole-grain crackers 1 ounce low-fat cottage cheese 1 cup cucumber slices	4 ounces grilled chicken 2 cups summer squash and zucchini (Tip: mix in with pasta) ½ cup cooked whole-grain pasta with marinara sauce

DAY 5

BREAKFAST	LUNCH	SNACK	DINNER
½ sliced banana ½ cup oatmeal ¼ cup nuts (almonds or walnuts)	Peach Pita Sandwiches* 2 cups baby spinach salad with 1 teaspoon olive oil and 2 teaspoons balsamic vinegar	1 tablespoon sunbutter 1 medium apple	6 ounces broiled haddock 1 baked potato (Tip: top with 1 tablespoon plain Greek yogurt) 1–2 cups stewed tomatoes and spinach

DAY 6

BREAKFAST	SNACK	LUNCH	SNACK	DINNER
1 egg, scrambled ¼ cup broccoli ½ link turkey sausage (al fresco) 1 cup sweet potato wedges	½ grapefruit 1 serving whole-grain crackers ½ cup low-fat cottage cheese	Mama's Egg Salad Sandwich* 1 cup grapes	1 tablespoon natural peanut butter or almond butter Celery sticks 1 tablespoon sesame seeds	6 ounces shrimp, stir-fried Sugar snap peas Water chestnuts Onions 1 cup cooked quinoa

DAY 7

BREAKFAST	SNACK	LUNCH	SNACK
Chicken Breakfast Burrito*	Blackberry-Mango Smoothie*	Fish taco 1 cup purple cabbage	¼ cup of almonds 1 cup melon

DINNER	DESSERT
4 ounces grilled swordfish 2 cups grilled eggplant 1 cup cooked bulgur	1 cup grilled pineapple topped with ½ cup vanilla Greek yogurt

Index

Kabobs, 249; Steak Subs, 194; Steak with Mushroom Sauce, 247; Stuffed Bell Peppers, 240; Stuffed Meat Loaf, 234; Sweet and Spicy Kielbasa, 243; Wasabi-Roasted Filet Mignon, 244; Whole-Grain Meat Loaf, 250; Whole-Wheat Spaghetti and Meatballs, 252

Beets: Beet and Cabbage Borscht, 151; Beets with Beet Greens, 82

Berries: about: dried cranberries, 174; Acorn Squash, Cranberries, and Wild Rice, 321; Blackberry Buckwheat Flapjacks, 6; Blackberry Cobbler, 335; Blackberry-Mango Smoothie, 2; Blueberry Clafouti, 344; Blueberry Cornmeal Pancakes, 7; Blueberry-Lemon Smoothie, 3; Blueberry Muffins, 15; Blueberry Oat Bran Muffins, 19; Blueberry Pancakes, 10; Blueberry Sorbet, 336; Cranberry Pistachio Biscotti, 361; Cranberry Turkey Salad Sandwich, 190; Exotic Fruit Salad, 112; Fresh Fig and Raspberry Compote, 334; Fruit Skewers with Dip, 55; Olallieberry Polenta Scones, 18; Raspberry-Almond Milk Frappe, 5; Scandinavian Summer Fruit Soup, 136; Steamed Raspberry-Lemon Custard, 366; Strawberry-Banana Smoothie, 3; Strawberry Sorbet, 339; Yogurt and Fruit Parfait, 11

Beverages: Banana-Kiwi Smoothie, 4; Blackberry-Mango Smoothie, 2; Blueberry-Lemon Smoothie, 3; Raspberry-Almond Milk Frappe, 5; Smoothie with Chocolate and Coffee, 4; Strawberry-Banana Smoothie, 3

Bread crumbs, 94, 295

Breads. See also Pancakes and waffles; Pizzas; Sandwiches and wraps: about: muffin batter, 23; Apple Date Bread, 21; Banana Chocolate Pecan Pancakes, 6; Banana Nut Bread, 11; Barely There Egg White Bruschetta, 15; Blueberry Muffins, 15; Blueberry Oat Bran Muffins, 19; Eggplant Crostini, 30; Grilled Vegetable Foccacia, 40; Lemon Bruschetta with Chopped Olives, 28; Oatmeal Raisin Scones, 2, 14; Olallieberry Polenta Scones, 18; Pear Tea Bread, 22; Pita Toast with Herbs and Cheese, 37; Rhubarb Muffins, 23; Sunday Morning French Toast, 7; White Bean Bruschetta, 39

Breakfast, 1–25; Apple Date Bread, 21; Baked Apple Pancakes, 13; Baked Grapefruit with Honey and Chambord, 12; Baked Scrambled Eggs, 17; Banana Chocolate Pecan Pancakes, 6; Banana-Kiwi Smoothie, 4; Banana Nut Bread, 11; Barely There Egg White Bruschetta, 15; Blackberry Buckwheat Flapjacks, 6; Blackberry-Mango Smoothie, 2; Blueberry Cornmeal Pancakes, 7; Blueberry-Lemon Smoothie, 3; Blueberry Muffins, 15; Blueberry Oat Bran Muffins, 19; Blueberry Pancakes, 10; Chicken Breakfast Burrito, 9; Cornmeal Grits, 5; Cottage Cheese Pancakes, 10; Double Corn Waffles, 8; Egg and Cheese Breakfast Pizza, 16; Eggs Benedict, 16; Eggs Florentine, 17; Herbed Omelet with Vegetables, 20; Maple Turkey Sausage, 18; Oatmeal, 9; Oatmeal Raisin Scones, 2; Olallieberry Polenta Scones, 18; Pear Tea Bread, 22; Raspberry-Almond Milk Frappe, 5; Rhubarb Muffins, 23; Sausage and Egg Casserole, 24; Sausage and Spicy Eggs, 10; Simple and Skinny Cheese Omelet, 14; Smoked Fish and Eggs with Grilled Tomatoes, 12; Smoothie with Chocolate and Coffee, 4; Spinach and Gorgonzola Egg White Omelet, 13; Strawberry-Banana Smoothie, 3; Sunday Morning French Toast, 7; Tomato and Feta Frittata, 8; Veggie Pancakes, 25; Yogurt and Fruit Parfait, 11

Broccoli: about: using stems, 139; Beef and Broccoli Stir-Fry, 237; Beef and Veggie Pitas, 178; Broccoli and Noodle Casserole, 318; Broccoli Cheddar Rice, 88; Broccoli Slaw, 107; Broccoli Soup with Cheese, 139; Chicken and Vegetable Frittata, 224; Herbed Chicken and Broccoli Casserole, 230; Homemade Macaroni and Cheese, 310; Penne Primavera, 309; Salmon and Broccoli Stir-Fry, 280; Vegetable Lasagna with Buffalo Mozzarella, 314

Broccoli rabe: Broccoli Rabe with Lemon and Cheese, 84; Polenta with Broccoli Rabe, 87

Burritos, 9, 176, 322

Cabbage: Beet and Cabbage Borscht, 151; Coleslaw, 108; Corned Beef and Cabbage, 240; Ginger Beef and Napa Cabbage, 258; Grilled Tuna Salad with Asian Vegetables and Spicy Dressing, 127; Grilled Tuna Steak with Vegetables and Pine Nuts, 269; Mahi Mahi Tacos with Avocado and Fresh Cabbage, 266; Minestrone Vegetable Soup, 153; Sea Bass Wrapped in Savoy Cabbage, 277; Shrimp and Vegetables over Napa Cabbage, 268; Sweet and Sour Red Cabbage, 81

Cantaloupe Sorbet, 337

Carrots: Baby Vegetable Salad, 130; Beef, Barley, and Vegetable Soup, 142; Beef and Veggie Pitas, 178; Carrot Cake, 342; Carrot Salad, 120; Carrots with an English Accent, 89; Filet Mignon with Vegetables, 241; Minestrone Vegetable Soup, 153; Vegetable-Barley Stew, 147; Veggie Pancakes, 25; Veggie Pitas, 178; Winter Root Vegetable Soufflé, 330

Cauliflower, in Creamy Cauliflower Soup, 137

Celery: Celery Soup, 150; Pasta Salad with Crunchy Vegetables, 308; Stuffed Celery, 34

Celery Root Salad, 122

Cheese: about: buffalo mozzarella, 176; feta, 124; Butternut Squash Cheese Muffins, 103; Cheese, Olive, and Cherry Tomato Kabobs, 41; Cheese Polenta, 78; Cheese Straws, 40; Chicken Scallops Stuffed with Spinach and Cheese, 223; Cottage Cheese Pancakes, 10; Cream Cheese Frosting, 342; Egg and Cheese Breakfast Pizza, 16; eggs with. See Eggs; Greek Quesadillas, 46; Homemade Macaroni and Cheese, 310; Honey and Cheese Stuffed Figs, 39; Parmesan Tuilles, 38; Pita Toast with Herbs and Cheese, 37; pizza with. See Pizzas; salads with. See Salads; sandwiches with. See Sandwiches and wraps; Smoked Salmon, Eggs, and Cheese Stuffed Casserole, 286; Sour Cream and Gorgonzola Dip for Crudités, 60; Stuffed Celery, 34; Stuffed Cucumbers, 36; Stuffed Jalapeño Peppers, 29; Stuffed Onions, 94; Stuffed Snow Peas, 48; Vegetable Lasagna with Buffalo Mozzarella, 314; Walnut Cheese Bites, 35; Winter Root Vegetable Soufflé, 330

Chicken: about: food safety, 280; keeping skin on, 212; making juicier, 42; making scallops, 223; slow cooker technique, 207; thighs, 213; Apricot and Pistachio Couscous Chicken Roulades, 218; Asian Chicken Stir-Fry, 201; Asian Sesame Lettuce Wraps, 186; Baked Chicken Legs, 206; Baked Chicken Wings, 32; Braised Chicken with Citrus, 204; Braised Chicken with White Beans and Kale, 205; Broiled Herb-Crusted Chicken Tenders, 37; Chicken à la King, 198; Chicken and Green Bean Stovetop Casserole, 222; Chicken and Pineapple Finger Sandwiches, 42; Chicken and Rice Soup, 157; Chicken and Vegetable Frittata, 224; Chicken Breakfast Burrito, 9; Chicken Breasts with New Potatoes, 209; Chicken Breasts with Orange Glaze and Oranges, 199; Chicken Cacciatore, 207; Chicken Pesto, 216; Chicken Salad, 117; Chicken Scallops Stuffed with Spinach and Cheese, 223; Chicken Spicy Thai Style, 208; Chicken with Eggplant, 224; Crispy Cobb Salad, 114; Easy Chicken Lo Mein, 217; Fried Chicken with Cornmeal Crust, 205; Ginger Chicken Salad Wrap, 171; Greek Chicken Pita, 173; Grilled Chicken Sandwich, 174; Grilled Chicken with Mango Salsa, 219; Grilled San Francisco-Style Chicken, 203; Grilled Tarragon Chicken Sandwich, 187; Hawaiian Chicken Skewers, 44; Hazelnut-Crusted Chicken Breasts, 210; Herbed Chicken and Broccoli Casserole, 230; Hot-and-Spicy Peanut Thighs, 200; Indian Tandoori-Style Chicken, 200; Jerk Chicken, 227; Lemon Chicken, 204; Marinated Chicken and Brown Rice Salad with Water Chestnuts, 128; Monte Cristo Sandwich, 189; Poached Chicken with Pears and Herbs, 203; Poached Mediterranean Chicken with Olives, Tomatoes, and Herbs, 225; Quick Skillet Chicken Casserole, 221; Sautéed Chicken with Roasted Garlic Sauce, 198; Sesame-Crusted Chicken, 211; Skewered Chicken Sate with Baby Eggplant, 228; Spicy Ranch Chicken Wrap, 170; Stewed Chicken with Vegetables, 202; Texas BBQ Chicken Thighs, 213; Yogurt "Gravy" Chicken Thighs, 220

Chocolate: about: buying, 365; Apricot-Chocolate Chip Squares, 356; Banana Chocolate Pecan Pancakes, 6; Caramel Corn-Chocolate Truffles, 338; Dandy Candy, 354; Hidden Surprise Cakes, 365; Mom's Golden Squares, 362; Smoothie with Chocolate and Coffee, 4

Cilantro, in Spicy Cilantro Dip, 56

Citrus: about: zests, 138; Avocado Grapefruit Salad, 118; Baked Grapefruit with Honey and Chambord, 12; Blood Orange Salad with Shrimp and Baby Spinach, 125; Braised Chicken with Citrus, 204; Ceviche–Fresh Seafood in Citrus, 42; Chicken Breasts with Orange Glaze and Oranges, 199; Citrus Scallops Pasta, 303; Exotic Fruit Salad, 112; Fruit Skewers with Dip, 55; Lemon Chicken, 204; Lemon Pepper Dressing, 66; Lemon-Seasoned Bread Crumbs, 295; Orange and Onion Salad, 106; Steamed Raspberry-Lemon Custard, 366; Veal and Spinach in Lemon Sauce, 262

Coconut: about: milk substitutes, 152; pairing, 45; Baked Coconut Shrimp, 45; Coconut Curried Ban-Apple Soup, 152

Coffee, Smoothie with Chocolate and, 4

Corn and polenta. See also Pancakes and waffles: about: cornmeal, 358; masa harina, 100; polenta, 349; stuffing tomatoes with corn, 96; Black Bean Chili with Beef and Corn, 257; Cheese Polenta, 78; Corn and Tomato Salad, 117; Cornmeal Cookies, 358; Cornmeal Grits, 5; Corn Polenta Chowder, 144; Corn Soup, 154; Crisp Polenta Sauce with Tomato Sauce, 78; Fried Chicken with Cornmeal Crust, 205; Lima Bean Succotash, 85; Polenta Pear Tart, 349; Polenta with Broccoli Rabe, 87; Popcorn Cookies, 357; Roasted Corn on the Cob, 96; Sesame Corn Wafers, 100; Southwestern Corn Salad, 113; Southwest Tortilla Soup, 156; Spaghetti with Crab and Corn, 315; Squash Blossom Polenta, 305

Couscous: about, 218; Apricot and Pistachio Couscous Chicken Roulades, 218; Couscous Tabouli, 85; Curried Couscous, 101

Cucumbers: about: English, 28; Cucumber, Dill, and Sour Cream Sauce, 68; Cucumber and Red Onion Salad, 111; Cucumber Dill Canapés, 28; Cucumber Raita, 109; Cucumber Salad with Yogurt and Dill, 109; Cucumber Soup, 139; Greek Salad, 124; Shrimp and Cucumber Tea Sandwich, 169; Stuffed Cucumbers, 36; Veggie Pitas, 178

Desserts, 333–67; about: biscotti, 360; French country desserts, 344; fruit puddings, 347; poached fruit, 345; sorbet ice cubes, 336; sorbets vs. sherbets, 339; steaming custard, 366; tuiles, 363; unbaked sweets, 354; Almond Macaroons, 340; Apple Pie, 337; Apple Tart Tatin, 341; Apricot-Chocolate Chip Squares, 356; Baked Apples, 341; Blackberry Cobbler, 335; Blueberry Clafouti, 344; Blueberry Sorbet, 336; Cantaloupe Sorbet, 337; Caramel Corn-Chocolate Truffles, 338; Carrot Cake, 342; Cornmeal Cookies, 358; Cranberry Pistachio Biscotti, 361; Cream Cheese Frosting, 342; Dandy Candy, 354; Fresh Fig and Raspberry Compote, 334; Hawaiian-Style Snow Cones, 339; Hazelnut Sticks, 364; Hidden Surprise Cakes, 365; Macadamia Mandelbrot, 359; Mango Sorbet, 335; Mom's Golden Squares, 362; Oatmeal Raisin Cookies, 351; Old-Fashioned Apple and Peach Crisp, 367; Oven-Roasted Pears, 338; Pear Sorbet, 336; Pecan Lace Cookies, 363; Pecan Pie Bars, 355; Pineapple Upside-Down Cupcakes, 343; Poached Pears, 345; Poached Quince, 346; Polenta Pear Tart, 349; Popcorn Cookies, 357; Rum-Raisin Rice Pudding, 347; Sesame Seed Cookies, 353; Squash Pumpkin Pie, 348; Steamed Raspberry-Lemon Custard, 366; Strawberry Sorbet, 339; Stuffed Apricots, 340; Sunflower Seed Shortbread, 350; Tea-Poached Prunes, 334; Walnut Biscotti, 360; Whole-Wheat Peanut Butter Cookies, 352

Dips. See Sauces, spreads, dips, and dressings

Dry rubs, 249

Duck: about: food safety, 280; meat characteristics, 226; Duck Breasts Sautéed with Rum-Raisin Sauce, 226

Edamame: about: buying shelled, 56; Asian Noodles with Tofu and Edamame, 298; Edamame (side dish), 79; Spicy Cilantro Dip, 56

Eggplant: about, 97, 148; Baby Eggplant with Tomato (sandwich), 191; Caponata Baked with Brie, 31; Chicken with Eggplant, 224; Eggplant and Portobello Mushroom Melt, 195; Eggplant Crostini, 30; Eggplant Soufflé, 299; Eggplant with Romesco Sauce, 97; Grilled Tuna Salad with Asian Vegetables and Spicy Dressing, 127; Grilled Vegetable and Three Cheese Panini, 169; Ratatouille, 148; Ratatouille with White Beans, 304; Roasted Vegetable Sandwich, 179; Skewered Chicken Sate with Baby Eggplant, 228

Eggs: about: nutritional value, 17; Aioli, 66; Baked Scrambled Eggs, 17; Barely There Egg White Bruschetta, 15; Chicken and Vegetable Frittata, 224; Crabmeat, Tomato, and Egg Salad Sandwich, 193; Deviled Eggs with Capers, 35; Egg and Cheese Breakfast Pizza, 16; Egg Drop Soup with Lemon, 141; Eggs Benedict, 16; Eggs Florentine, 17; Herbed Omelet with Vegetables, 20; Mama's Egg Salad Sandwich, 172; Onion Soup with Poached Egg Float, 141; Poached Salmon Salad with Hard-Boiled Eggs, 131; Sausage and Egg Casserole, 24; Sausage and Spicy Eggs, 10; Simple and Skinny Cheese Omelet, 14; Smoked Fish and Eggs with Grilled Tomatoes, 12; Smoked Salmon, Eggs, and Cheese Stuffed Casserole, 286; Spinach and Gorgonzola Egg White Omelet, 13; Steamed Raspberry-Lemon Custard, 366; Tomato and Feta Frittata, 8; Winter Root Vegetable Soufflé, 330

Endive, in Pear, Roquefort, and Walnuts on Endive, 30

Fats: omega-3 fatty acids, 286; puréed fruit as substitute, 22; using less, 104, 152

Fennel: Arugula and Fennel Salad with Pomegranate, 110; Baby Vegetable Salad, 130; Baked Fennel, 83; Cold Fennel Soup, 155; Shaved Fennel, Kumquat, and Frisée Salad, 121

Figs: about, 107; Fig and Parmesan Curl Salad, 107; Fresh Fig and Raspberry Compote, 334; Honey and Cheese Stuffed Figs, 39

Fish. See Seafood

Flowers, edible, 305

Food safety, 280

French toast, 7

Fruit. See also Desserts; specific fruit: about: poached, 345; puréed as fat substitute, 22; Exotic Fruit Salad, 112; Fruit Skewers with Dip, 55; Scandinavian Summer Fruit Soup, 136; Seared Scallops with Fruit, 272

Garlic: about: rubs, 86; Roasted Garlic Sauce, 198

Grains. See also Breads; Corn and polenta; Oatmeal; Pancakes and waffles; Pasta; Rice: about: barley, 147; preparing bulgur, 119; quinoa, 98; Baked Barley Casserole, 306; Barley Risotto with Mushrooms and Thyme, 329; Beef, Barley, and Vegetable Soup, 142; Quinoa Pilaf, 98; Tabouli Salad, 119; Vegetable-Barley

Stew, 147; Wheat Berry Salad, 129; Whole-Grain Meat Loaf, 250

Green beans: Baby Vegetable Salad, 130; Beef, Barley, and Vegetable Soup, 142; Chicken and Green Bean Stovetop Casserole, 222; French-Glazed Green Beans, 91; Roasted Green Beans with Pine Nuts, 99; Sesame Green Beans, 80

Grenadine, 118

Grill seasoning, 79

Herbs and spices, 94, 216, 229, 290, 293, 329

Hummus, 58, 180

Jicama, 129

Kale: Braised Chicken with White Beans and Kale, 205; Colcannon, 95

Kiwis: Banana-Kiwi Smoothie, 4; Exotic Fruit Salad, 112; Fruit Skewers with Dip, 55

Kumquats, in Shaved Fennel, Kumquat, and Frisée Salad, 121

Lamb: about: flavor of, 244; removing fat, 244; Curried Lamb, 245; Grilled Lamb Chops with Garlic, Rosemary, and Thyme, 236; Lamb Shanks with White Beans and Carrots, 244; Lollipop Lamb Chops, 32

Leek and Potato Soup (Hot or Cold), 143

Lemon. See Citrus

Lentils. See Beans and legumes

Liquid smoke, 260

Mangos: about, 61; Blackberry-Mango Smoothie, 2; Exotic Fruit Salad, 112; Grilled Chicken with Mango Salsa, 219; Mango Salsa, 61; Mango Sorbet, 335

Meal plans, 369–71

Mincemeat-Style Chutney, 71

Mint Chimichurri Sauce, 69

Mushrooms: about: types of, 126, 248; as veggie filler, 222; Baby Vegetable Salad, 130; Baked Mushroom Dip with Spinach, 65; Barley Risotto with Mushrooms and Thyme, 329; Beef and Veggie Pitas, 178; Beef with Mushroom Kabobs, 241; Chicken and Green Bean Stovetop Casserole, 222; Eggplant and Portobello Mushroom Melt, 195; Herbed Omelet with Vegetables, 20; Mushroom Spread, 57; Open-Face Wild Mushroom Wontons, 52; Oriental Tuna-Mushroom Soup, 164; Portobello Mushroom Salad with Gorgonzola, Peppers, and Bacon, 126; Steak and Mushroom Kabobs, 237; Steak with Mushroom Sauce, 247; Veggie Burrito, 176

Mustard: about: 62; Dijon, 210; Creamy Mustard Dip, 63; Mustard Cream Sauce (Hot), 67

Nuts and seeds. See also Peanuts and peanut butter: about: blanching nuts, 35, 357; buying and storing, 43; cashew butter, 161; nut nutrition, 91; pistachios, 283; seeds, 353; sesame seeds, 211; toasting, 99, 357; Almond

Chutney, 71; Mint Chimichurri Sauce, 69; Mushroom Spread, 57; Mustard Cream Sauce (Hot), 67; Pesto For Angel Hair Pasta, 298; Red-Wine Butter Sauce, 71; Roasted Garlic Sauce, 198; Sauce Maltaise, 65; Seven-Layer Mexican Dip, 54; Sour Cream and Gorgonzola Dip for Crudités, 60; Spaghetti Sauce, 76; Spicy Cilantro Dip, 56; Super Spicy Salsa, 57; Sweet and Sour Dressing, 66; Tartar Sauce, 69; White Bean Dip, 59; Yogurt Cheese Spinach Dip, 75

Seafood, 263–95; about: buying, 33, 289; canned salmon, 289; cleaning mussels, 288; cooking fish, 264, 294; cooking with herbs, 290; crab cakes, 36; fish bones, 285; food safety, 280; fresh sandwiches, 168; littleneck clams, 160; oysters, 41, 279; scallops, 272, 292; tuna, 127, 132; wrapping before cooking, 277; Almond Snapper with Shrimp Sauce, 275; Asian Sesame-Crusted Scallops, 287; Avocado and Shrimp Salad, 109; Baked Coconut Shrimp, 45; Baked Filet of Sole with Shrimp Sauce and Artichokes, 281; Baked Lemon Sole with Herbed Crumbs, 265; Baked Oysters with Shrimp Stuffing, 279; Baked Red Snapper Almandine, 294; Baked Stuffed Artichokes, 50; Baked Stuffed Clams, 33; Blood Orange Salad with Shrimp and Baby Spinach, 125; Broiled Swordfish, 264; Broiled Swordfish Club, 168; Cajun-Rubbed Fish, 265; Ceviche–Fresh Seafood in Citrus, 42; Citrus Scallops Pasta, 303; Clams Casino, 49; Classic Parisian Mussels, 288; Cod and Potatoes, 271; Corn-Crusted Salmon with Parsley and Radish Topping, 282; Crabmeat, Tomato, and Egg Salad Sandwich, 193; Crabmeat and Shrimp Salad, 114; Crabmeat Salad with Rice and Asian Spices, 116; Crunchy Tuna Salad Melt on Rye, 177; Cuban-Style Braised Fish, 291; Curried Shrimp Salad in a Papaya, 120; Fish Taco with Purple Cabbage, 181; Fresh Tuna Salad a la Niçoise, 132; Grilled Mahi Mahi with Pineapple Salsa, 266; Grilled Tuna Salad with Asian Vegetables and Spicy Dressing, 127; Grilled Tuna Steak with Vegetables and Pine Nuts, 269; Halibut with Banana Salsa, 268; Herb and Lemon Baked Halibut, 290; Herbed Clam Dip, 64; Hollywood Lobster Salad, 115; Lemon-Garlic Shrimp and Vegetables, 284; Lemon-Seasoned Bread Crumbs with, 295; Lime-Seared Scallops, 292; Mahi Mahi Tacos with Avocado and Fresh Cabbage, 266; Maryland Crab Cakes, 36; Mediterranean Seafood Soup, 160; Oriental Tuna-Mushroom Soup, 164; Pistachio-Crusted Halibut, 283; Pistachio-Crusted Red Snapper, 270; Planked Salmon with Dill Sauce, 285; Poached Salmon Salad with Hard-Boiled Eggs, 131; Raw Oysters on the Half Shell with Mignonette Sauce, 41; Roast Stuffed Striped Bass, 269; Salmon and Broccoli Stir-Fry, 280; Salmon Loaf, 289; Salmon Vegetable Stir-Fry, 271; Sautéed Crab Cake and Avocado Wraps, 185; Savory Fish Stew, 140; Scallops on Skewers with Lemon, 276; Scallops on Skewers with Tomatoes, 273; Sea Bass Wrapped in Savoy Cabbage, 277; Seafood in Thai-Curry Bean Sauce, 278; Seafood Risotto, 270; Seared Scallops with Fruit, 272; Sesame-Crusted Mahi Mahi, 264; Sesame-Pepper Salmon

Kabobs, 274; Shrimp and Cucumber Tea Sandwich, 169; Shrimp and Vegetables over Napa Cabbage, 268; Shrimp with Chive and Butter Sauce, 295; Simple Tuna Salad Sandwich, 172; Smoked Fish and Eggs with Grilled Tomatoes, 12; Smoked Salmon, Eggs, and Cheese Stuffed Casserole, 286; Spaghetti with Crab and Corn, 315; Tuna Casserole, 267; Zesty Crumb-Coated Cod, 267; Zesty Fish Fritters, 293

Seeds. See Nuts and seeds

Sides and snacks, 77–104; Bagel Chips, 86; Baked Fennel, 83; Baked Stuffed Tomatoes, 104; Baked Sweet Potatoes, 86; Beets with Beet Greens, 82; Broccoli Cheddar Rice, 88; Broccoli Rabe with Lemon and Cheese, 84; Butternut Squash Cheese Muffins, 103; Carrots with an English Accent, 89; Cheese Polenta, 78; Chili Fries, 79; Colcannon, 95; Couscous Tabouli, 85; Crisp Polenta Sauce with Tomato Sauce, 78; Curried Couscous, 101; Edamame, 79; Eggplant with Romesco Sauce, 97; French-Glazed Green Beans, 91; Golden Delicious Risotto, 102; Herb-Seasoned Roasted Red Onions, 90; Lima Bean Succotash, 85; Mini Hot-Pepper Pizzas, 93; Oven-Fried Potato Wedges, 89; Peas with Butter Lettuce, 80; Polenta with Broccoli Rabe, 87; Potato Soufflé, 92; Quinoa Pilaf, 98; Roasted Chickpeas with Parmesan, 87; Roasted Corn on the Cob, 96; Roasted Garlic Spinach, 81; Roasted Green Beans with Pine Nuts, 99; Sesame Corn Wafers, 100; Sesame Green Beans, 80; Skinny Baked Potato, 88; Spice and Honey Nuts, 91; Stuffed Onions, 94; Summer Swiss Chard, 82; Sweet and Sour Red Cabbage, 81; Sweet Potatoes Mash, 90; Wild Rice with Walnuts and Apples, 84; Yams with Coconut Milk, 83

Skewers, creating, 44

Sodium/salt, 52, 145, 328

Soups and stews, 133–65; about: compost broth, 165; creamy soups, 150; soaking beans, 149; summer soups in winter, 154; Avocado Soup, Chilled with Lime Float, 138; Baked Potato Soup, 162; Beans for Soup, 145; Beef, Barley, and Vegetable Soup, 142; Beet and Cabbage Borscht, 151; Black Bean Chili with Beef and Corn, 257; Black Bean Soup, 149; Broccoli Soup with Cheese, 139; Butternut Squash Soup, 143; Cashew Zucchini Soup, 161; Celery Soup, 150; Chicken and Rice Soup, 157; Coconut Curried Ban-Apple Soup, 152; Cold Basil and Fresh Tomato Soup, 138; Cold Fennel Soup, 155; Cold Tomato Soup with Tofu, 140; Corn Polenta Chowder, 144; Corn Soup, 154; Creamy Cauliflower Soup, 137; Creamy Tortilla Soup, 156; Cucumber Soup, 139; Egg Drop Soup with Lemon, 141; Fresh Yellow Tomato Soup, 146; Gazpacho Mary, 135; Harvest Stew, 137; Leek and Potato Soup (Hot or Cold), 143; Mediterranean Seafood Soup, 160; Minestrone Vegetable Soup, 153; Onion Soup with Poached Egg Float, 141; Oriental Tuna-Mushroom Soup, 164; Pepper Pot Soup, 163; Pumpkin Soup, 142; Quick Thick Peanut Soup, 165; Ratatouille, 148; Red Lentil Soup, 135; Savory Fish Stew, 140; Scandinavian Summer Fruit Soup, 136; Southwest Tortilla Soup, 156; Spinach

the hungry
Editor

Foodies Unite!

Bring your appetite and follow The Hungry Editor who really loves to eat. She'll be discussing (and drooling over) all things low-fat and full-fat, local and fresh, canned and frozen, highbrow and lowbrow. . .

When it comes to good eats, The Hungry Editor (and her tastebuds) do not discriminate!

It's a Feeding Frenzy—dig in!

Sign up for our newsletter at

www.adamsmedia.com/blog/cooking

and download our free **Top Ten Gourmet Meals for $7** recipes!